Revisiting The Great White N

TRANSGRESSIONS: CULTURAL STUDIES AND EDUCATION

Cultural studies provides an analytical toolbox for both making sense of educational practice and extending the insights of educational professionals into their labors. In this context *Transgressions: Cultural Studies and Education* provides a collection of books in the domain that specify this assertion. Crafted for an audience of teachers, teacher educators, scholars and students of cultural studies and others interested in cultural studies and pedagogy, the series documents both the possibilities of and the controversies surrounding the intersection of cultural studies and education. The editors and the authors of this series do not assume that the interaction of cultural studies and education devalues other types of knowledge and analytical forms. Rather the intersection of these knowledge disciplines offers a rejuvenating, optimistic, and positive perspective on education and educational institutions. Some might describe its contribution as democratic, emancipatory, and transformative. The editors and authors maintain that cultural studies helps free educators from sterile, monolithic analyses that have for too long undermined efforts to think of educational practices by providing other words, new languages, and fresh metaphors. Operating in an interdisciplinary cosmos, Transgressions: Cultural Studies and Education is dedicated to exploring the ways cultural studies enhances the study and practice of education. With this in mind the series focuses in a non-exclusive way on popular culture as well as other dimensions of cultural studies including social theory, social justice and positionality, cultural dimensions of technological innovation, new media and media literacy, new forms of oppression emerging in an electronic hyperreality, and postcolonial global concerns. With these concerns in mind cultural studies scholars often argue that the realm of popular culture is the most powerful educational force in contemporary culture. Indeed, in the twenty-first century this pedagogical dynamic is sweeping through the entire world. Educators, they believe, must understand these emerging realities in order to gain an important voice in the pedagogical conversation.

Without an understanding of cultural pedagogy's (education that takes place outside of formal schooling) role in the shaping of individual identity – youth identity in particular – the role educators play in the lives of their students will continue to fade. Why do so many of our students feel that life is incomprehensible and devoid of meaning? What does it mean, teachers wonder, when young people are unable to describe their moods, their affective affiliation to the society around them. Meanings provided young people by mainstream institutions often do little to help them deal with their affective complexity, their difficulty negotiating the rift between meaning and affect. School knowledge and educational expectations seem as anachronistic as a ditto machine, not that learning ways of rational thought and making sense of the world are unimportant.

But school knowledge and educational expectations often have little to offer students about making sense of the way they feel, the way their affective lives are shaped. In no way do we argue that analysis of the production of youth in an electronic mediated world demands some "touchy-feely" educational superficiality. What is needed in this context is a rigorous analysis of the interrelationship between pedagogy, popular culture, meaning making, and youth subjectivity. In an era marked by youth depression, violence, and suicide such insights become extremely important, even life saving. Pessimism about the future is the common sense of many contemporary youth with its concomitant feeling that no one can make a difference.

If affective production can be shaped to reflect these perspectives, then it can be reshaped to lay the groundwork for optimism, passionate commitment, and transformative educational and political activity. In these ways cultural studies adds a dimension to the work of education unfilled by any other sub-discipline. This is what Transgressions: Cultural Studies and Education seeks to produce—literature on these issues that makes a difference. It seeks to publish studies that help those who work with young people, those individuals involved in the disciplines that study children and youth, and young people themselves improve their lives in these bizarre times.

Revisiting The Great White North?

Reframing Whiteness, Privilege, and Identity in Education (Second Edition)

Edited by

Darren E. Lund
University of Calgary, Canada

and

Paul R. Carr
Université du Québec en Outaouais, Canada

SENSE PUBLISHERS
ROTTERDAM/BOSTON/TAIPEI

A C.I.P. record for this book is available from the Library of Congress.

ISBN: 978-94-6209-867-1 (paperback)
ISBN: 978-94-6209-868-8 (hardback)
ISBN: 978-94-6209-869-5 (e-book)

Published by: Sense Publishers,
P.O. Box 21858,
3001 AW Rotterdam,
The Netherlands
https://www.sensepublishers.com/

Cover image courtesy of Wim van Passel (© Wim van Passel)

Printed on acid-free paper

Reviews of the first edition of
The Great White North? Exploring Whiteness, Privilege, and Identity in Education (2007, Sense Publishers)

I found this book as interesting, provocative, and productive as its cover blurbs promise. The editors have chosen a wide range of authors, most of whom are Canadian, who are able to speak knowledgeably about particular local situations, events, and structures, but who are also able to situate these in wider discourses (e.g., in the history of Western philosophy – see chapter by Lindo). This book should serve to alert researchers and teachers to undeniable examples of how racism has been experienced in a wide range of situations (from the perspectives of the colonized, but also from the perspectives of critically aware White people), and how the Whiteness discourse legitimates historical structures of privilege. Readers who are not Canadian should find the examples resonant with events with which they are more familiar. I see it as useful for researchers, graduate students, and teacher-education students in mounting a strong argument for recognizing that Whiteness has structured many contemporary institutions and that resistance to Whiteness discourse is a responsibility of all, especially those in education.

Kelleen Toohey
Faculty of Education, Simon Fraser University
International Migration & Integration, 9, 423–424. (2008).

The Great White North? constitutes an important contribution to the field, particularly for those who struggle with how to make Whiteness and its effects visible to our White students, our colleagues, and those who develop educational policies on equity and curriculum development. In this edited volume, Carr and Lund create an opportunity to extend the work relating to the pedagogy of anti-racism education. They do this by interrogating how educators' failure to engage in critical self-reflective practice runs the risk of their being complicit in perpetuating racist structures, including the institutionalization of White privilege. It is important to note that two of the contributors are community activists. Each chapter concludes with a set of questions for reflection. These will be useful for teachers practicing in a range of contexts from the university classroom to informal, community-based environments.

Evelyn Hamdon
Faculty of Education, University of Alberta
Alberta Journal of Educational Research, 54(4), 482-488. (2008).

Carr and Lund, both White Canadian antiracist scholars, have created a space for established and emerging scholars, approaching Whiteness from varied epistemic terrains, to articulate its tensions and its societal and institutional implications. The strength of this volume lies in its exploration of the nuances of racial (and other) identities as they intersect the trump-card of White identity and how the complexities of anti-oppression theorizing and practice are taken up; specifically, Indegeneity, cultural, gender, and religious identities are explored vis-à-vis White identity, creating an effective overview of the vastness and richness of the intersections of White studies in Canada and beyond. This volume is a must read for educators and practitioners committed to anti-oppression work. Concluding each chapter are a series of critical questions, providing the reader with the opportunity to develop a heuristic for the task that Dei names as "how we can deconstruct White identity without falling into the easy slippage of acknowledging responsibility and complicity" (p. ix).

Maryam Nabavi
Faculty of Education, University of British Columbia
Multicultural Perspectives, 10(4), 236. (2008)

By challenging all of us to broaden our perceptions and to examine and question the latent whiteness permeating the very pores of our social universe, Carr and Lund and those who have contributed to their work invite us to journey and live and teach differently. A Canadian work, theirs certainly has applicability and interest for readers both within and beyond Canada. This reviewer signals a tip of the hat to them for this worthwhile and timely contribution to antiracist literature. I invite you to read and ponder Carr and Lund's message and decide for yourself if it can help bring about constructive change in you, your ways of perceiving, and what and how you teach.

Peter Heffernan
Faculty of Education, University of Lethbridge
Notos: Journal of the Second Languages and Intercultural Council of the Alberta Teachers' Association, 8(1), 30-31. (2008)

BLURB FROM THE BACK COVER:

The Great White North? provides a timely and important mode of addressing and examining the contradictions of Whiteness, and also challenging its insinuation into the very pores of the Canadian social universe. While the context of the book is distinctly Canadian, there are urgent messages here on race and anti-racism for the international community. Carr and Lund have provided educators with a vibrant contribution to the critical anti-racist literature. This is a book that needs to be put on reading-lists across the disciplines!

Peter McLaren
Professor, Graduate School of Education and Information Studies
University of California at Los Angeles

Naming Whiteness and White identity is a political project as much as an intellectual engagement, and the co-editors of this collection must be commended for creating the space for such naming to take place in public and academic discourses. Is it noteworthy to acknowledge that both Paul and Darren are White, and that they are overseeing this work on Whiteness? I believe that it is, not because others cannot write about the subject with clarity and insight, as is clearly evident in the diverse range of contributors to this book. Rather, naming their positions as White allies embracing a rigorous conceptual and analytical discourse in the social justice field is an important signal that White society must also become intertwined in the entrenched racism that infuses every aspect of our society. As Paul and Darren correctly point out, race is still a pivotal concern for everything that happens in society, and especially in schools.

Excerpt from the Foreword by George J. Sefa Dei
Professor and Chair, Department of Sociology and Equity Studies
Ontario Institute for Studies in Education at the University of Toronto

Praise for
Revisiting The Great White North?
Reframing Whiteness, Privilege, and Identity in Education
(Second Edition)
Darren E. Lund & Paul R. Carr (Eds.)

Revisiting The Great White North? Reframing Whiteness, Privilege, and Identity in Education offers terrific grist for examining the persistence of Whiteness even as it shape-shifts. Chapters are comprehensive, theoretically rich, and anchored in personal experience. Authors' reflections on the seven years since publication of the first edition of this book complexify how we understand Whiteness, while simultaneously driving home the need not only to grapple with it, but to work against it.

Christine Sleeter, Professor Emerita California State University Monterey Bay

Our understanding of racial inequities in education will be impoverished unless we look deeply at White privilege, its variation in different contexts, and resistances to change. Such is the call in this important book by Lund, Carr, and colleagues, whose analyses within Canadian contexts, framed and re-framed for this captivating revised edition, will be useful to educators and scholars around the world. Read this book today.

Kevin Kumashiro, Dean, School of Education, University of San Francisco
President, National Association for Multicultural Education
Author of *Bad Teacher!: How Blaming Teachers Distorts the Bigger Picture*

Given the evolving but continuing contentious nature of Whiteness studies, it is particularly appropriate that Darren Lund and Paul Carr have given the contributors to their original 2007 text the opportunity to revisit, rethink, reconceptualize, and reframe their earlier work. The result is an interesting, invigorating, and unsettling group of chapters that challenge readers to also revisit and rethink their own ideas about Whiteness, privilege, and power. Situated in the Canadian context, this book nevertheless has important insights and lessons for all societies with a history of White hegemony and systemic racism in their institutions, especially in education, as well as the myths, practices, and traditions that help sustain racism and privilege. Teachers, administrators, policymakers, and researchers will all benefit from this critical work.

Sonia Nieto, Professor Emerita, Language, Literacy, and Culture
College of Education, University of Massachusetts, Amherst

Lund and Carr bring together a superb collection of authors who collectively challenge readers to go beyond liberal platitudes about race. Sure we should celebrate diversity, but until educators confront the political, social and economic consequences of inequitably distributed privilege, the path towards equality and freedom will remain elusive. By immersing us in the discourse of Whiteness, the essays in this book illuminate that very path.

Joel Westheimer, University Research Chair & Professor, Faculty of Education University of Ottawa

This book reads like a complicated and impassioned conversation among spirited colleagues trying to make sense of the privilege and dominance of Whiteness in the "Great White North" of Canada. These authors excavate and expose the idea and practices of Whiteness as it is asserted, narrated, and embodied in multiple contexts. As a White scholar from what some of the authors call "our neighbor to the south," I was challenged to see here in the United States what White privilege bestows, and to consider how a raceless way of looking at the world deflects attention from social advantage. The unexamined attitude of what chapter author Lisa Comeau aptly calls White solipsism counts certain advantages as simply and predictably earned on a level playing field. This book shows that there is much more to consider about privilege and advantage in our multicultural but White dominated societies, in particular here in North America but elsewhere too. The second edition includes "reframing" chapters by the authors, as well as some new entries, that attest to the issues and challenges raised by a worldwide financial crisis and growing wealth gap in many societies to education for social justice and for critical dialogue about race, exclusion, and privilege.

AG Rud, Distinguished Professor, College of Education Washington State University

It is heartening to see *The Great White North?* going into its second edition. This is one of the most timely and important works on Whiteness, critical race education and anti-racism to have come out of Canada. While the themes in the book are distinctly Canadian the message is universal. This book is a must-read for students, teachers and scholars interested in making Canada and the world a better and just place.

M. Ayaz Naseem, Graduate Program Director & Associate Professor of Education Concordia University

The Canadian multicultural mosaic is a powerful metaphor, one that shapes how many Canadians think about their identities. But this metaphor often masks ways in which racism and colonialism operate in society. The authors of *Revisiting The Great White North? Reframing Whiteness, Privilege, and Identity in Education* challenge the benignancy of Whiteness from personal and sociological perspectives. Avoiding the pitfall of essentialism, these essays offer complex interrogations of race, oppression, identity, and racial consciousness, connected to place and co-relational relationships with others, and provoking questions on each page.

E. Wayne Ross, Professor, Faculty of Education University of British Columbia

The publication of this second edition of *The Great White North*, as tempo-analytically re-framing the original debates and propositions in the first edition, is an important event that occasions our appreciation with respect to its timeliness and immense relevance to actively re-conceptualize both our learning and pedagogical contexts for the urgently needed pragmatics of anti-racism education and its desirable attachments of onto-existential liberation. With all the original chapters realigned for this purpose, and with the addition of a new experiential perspective from an African-Quebecois academic, these critical interventions help us achieve the urgently needed deconstructions of Whiteness as extra-conceptual, extra-descriptive, extra-analytical, even extra-historical, and astonishingly, extra-cultural. To decompose such extra-logic assumptions and de-hegemonize our learning and instructional contexts, these enhanced disquisitions represent selectively liberating praxes that should be strategically deployed for our academic environments, in concerned schooling locations, and certainly across the Canadian public space.

Ali A. Abdi, Professor & Co-Director, Centre for Global Citizenship & Education Research
University of Alberta

Having taught race relations and multicultural issues for more than a decade I am extremely happy to see this important book go into its second edition. *Revisiting The Great White North? Reframing Whiteness, Privilege, and Identity in Education* discloses the true reality of race relations in Canada. The book demands a reflexive consideration from the reader to ponder upon what it means to be White in the Canadian context. This book is a must read for anyone under the misconception that race relations in Canada are any less problematic those in the U.S. or other racially charged contexts in the world.

Adeela Arshad-Ayaz, Assistant Professor, Department of Education
Concordia University

In *Revisiting The Great White North? Reframing Whiteness, Privilege, and Identity in Education*, Whiteness studies scholars write and speak in dialogue with the emergent movements of postcolonialism, critical race studies, critical pedagogy, and the Hegelian/Marxist tradition, with the understanding that White identity is always constructed relationally, and through the production of colonized minds and bodies.

The authors in this important volume are at the forefront of the critical re-thinking of Whiteness studies, across cultural settings, and with broad implications for how educators cross the borders that racism and colonialism have erected, and work to implement a genuinely democratic multicultural pedagogy.

Dennis Carlson, Professor, College of Education, Health & Society Miami University

TABLE OF CONTENTS

Foreword to the Second Edition (2014)   xix

Foreword (2007)   xxv
George J. Sefa Dei

Acknowledgements (2014)   xxxi

Acknowledgements (2007)   xxxiii

Introduction: Reframing Whiteness (2014)   1
Darren E. Lund & Paul R. Carr

Section 1: Conceptualizing Whiteness

Exploring the Authority of Whiteness in Education:
An Auto-Ethnographic Journey   13
Kathleen S. Berry

Reframing: Kathleen S. Berry (2014)   27

Before I Was White I Was Presbyterian   31
Tim McCaskell

Reframing: Tim McCaskell (2014)   41

Being White and Being Right: Critiquing Individual and Collective Privilege   43
James Frideres

Reframing: James Frideres (2014)   55

Section 2: Whiteness and Second Peoples

Going Native: A White Guy's Experience Teaching in an
Aboriginal Context   59
Herbert C. Northcott

Reframing: Herbert C. Northcott (2014)   69

On Indigenous Academia: The Hermeneutics of Indigenous
Western Institutional Participation—Eleven Theorems (2014)   71
Tracey Lindberg

"Don't Blame Me for What My Ancestors Did": Understanding
the Impact of Collective White Guilt   89
Julie Caouette & Donald M. Taylor

Reframing: Julie Caouette & Donald M. Taylor (2014)   105

Section 3: Developing and De-Constructing White Identity

Development of Anti-Racist White Identity in Canadian
Educational Counsellors   111
Christine Wihak

Reframing: Christine Wihak (2014)   123

"Radical Stuff": Starting a Conversation about Racial Identity and
White Privilege   125
Susan A. Tilley & Kelly D. Powick

Reframing: Susan A. Tilley & Kelly D. Powick (2014)   137

Who Can/Should Do This Work? The Colour of Critique   141
Carl E. James

Reframing: Carl E. James (2014)   155

Section 4: Learning, Teaching, and Whiteness

The Parents of Baywoods: Intersections between Whiteness and
Jewish Ethnicity   159
Cynthia Levine-Rasky

Reframing: Cynthia Levine-Rasky   175

Re-inscribing Whiteness through Progressive Constructions
of "the Problem" in Anti-Racist Education   179
Lisa Comeau

Reframing: Lisa Comeau (2014)   189

Discourses on Race and "White Privilege" in the Next
Generation of Teachers   193
R. Patrick Solomon and Beverly-Jean M. Daniel

Reframing: Beverly-Jean M. Daniel (2014)   205

White Female Teachers and Technology in Education: Reproducing
the Status Quo   207
Brad J. Porfilio

Reframing: Brad J. Porfilio (2014)   223

Section 5: The Institutional Merit of Whiteness

Whiteness and Philosophy: Imagining Non-White Philosophy in Schools   229
Laura Mae Lindo

Reframing: Laura Mae Lindo (2014)   239

De-Centering Normal: Negotiating Whiteness as White School
Administrators in a Diverse School Community   241
Debbie Donsky & Matt Champion

Reframing: Debbie Donsky and Matt Champion (2014)   251

"A Group That Plays Together Stays Together": Tracing a Story of
Racial Violence   253
Gulzar R. Charania

Reframing: Gulzar R. Charania (2014)   267

The Whiteness of Educational Policymaking   269
Paul R. Carr

Reframing: Paul R. Carr (2014)   281

A Chronic Identity Intoxication Syndrome: Whiteness as Seen by an
African-Canadian Francophone Woman (2014)   283
Gina Thésée

Additional Whiteness Resources (2014)   293

Biographies (2014)   295

Index   303

GEORGE J. SEFA DEI

FOREWORD TO THE SECOND EDITION (2014)

In one of my recent graduate classes at the Ontario Institute for Studies in Education of the University of Toronto (OISE/UT), the subject of the heavy might of Whiteness came up. The focus was on just how the sanctity and racial polity of Whiteness continues to weigh down heavily on contemporary society. Some of us wanted to signal equally the fragility, *emptiness*, falsity, dependency status, and the ontological nihilism of Whiteness. Understandably, there was a section of the class that wanted the gaze kept upon the heavy weight of Whiteness, its material and systemic consequences and, in fact, how Whiteness is consuming and consequential in its reach. The discussion increasingly intensified, leaving the "fact of Whiteness," as one we were called upon to revisit, in order to unearth this toll of Whiteness, and at the same time, the life forces it wakes to steal, in effect, through its amorphous definition.

The ambiguity inherent to Whiteness enters through the praxis of Others (as in those objectified) and further gains its momentum from the Others' life force. The logic follows that Whiteness works to *other* by way of race because it stems from pernicious otherness in its diffused epistemology. Thus, we must recognize the toll of Whiteness for both White dominant bodies and non-White bodies, and the produced dialectic of humanities through the colonial relationship, underpinning the colonizer and colonized. Frantz Fanon (1967) long ago made the point immeasurably clear when he named the structural and intimate violence effacing Whiteness as the imperialist colonial structure, erecting through the production of what he rightly termed "combat breathing." Combat breathing is at once the provocation and coercion of the Others' life force rising to meet the demands of Whiteness, and fight for its life. We must remember combat breathing as the colonizer's tool for the forbidding desire to establish Others in order for us to share the superfluous burden of Whiteness. In the moments of combat breathing, what is established are the means of subversion of the Others' life force, as a means for Whiteness' amorphous and, as such, irresponsible way of being. Whiteness as the dominant structure must be acknowledged as disparagingly hopeless. The evasive attempt to subdue the Others' life force, to which, in any event, materializes, but through the imaginings and distorted gaze of Whiteness, results in the consequent theft of the Other's force of life because, at once, the Other must resist and yet constitute the maddening ontological dilemma. Because Whiteness cannot labour the toll of its inability to create and, furthermore, destroy the Others' life force, for which it depends on for its ontology, way of being, and, thus, the very problematic, it harbors and yet evades it, which brings us to our inquiry: the "accountability of Whiteness." We insist the unrelenting "un-accountability of Whiteness" must be accounted for in the anti-racist and anti-colonial struggles, which is why we must speak to the ontological "nihilism of Whiteness" and its rightful origin of otherness that it at once seeks to be and be rid of, while off-putting it onto the Other, through violence, undergirding the existential irrationality of racism.

The early schools of thought on Whiteness studies, namely, Whiteness as location and a form of identification (Frankenberg, 1993, 1997a, 1997b), the call for the abolition of Whiteness (Giroux, 1997a, 1997b), and the contemporary re-articulation of Whiteness (Kincheloe, Steinberg, Rodriguez, & Chennault, 1998; Roediger, 1999) continue to inform debates on Whiteness to this day. In many ways the current re-articulations speak to ideas of seduction, and desires, of fantasizing Whiteness. We question through what and to whose material, spiritual, and intellectual expense Whiteness hails through to define itself to embody form and, more importantly, to become a subject imbued for desire amidst its relativistic and destabilizing epistemology?

I have personally struggled to rethink the possibilities of Whiteness, particularly in the supreme reign and context of neoliberalism and the sway of corporate capital. It has not been easy. But I am not just speaking of how Whiteness is commodified, nor other aspects of the political economy of Whiteness. In fact, as much as I want to hold on to the possibilities for Whiteness in terms of what it allows us to trouble, resist, and work for change, it is Whiteness as a system of dominance, privilege, and oppression that tends to be over-determining in a context of neoliberalism and corporate capital. Whiteness is being produced and consumed with huge material costs and benefits to individuals and groups. Whiteness undergirds the politics and political economy of schooling education in the ways we produce what is considered valid knowledge, how we see "excellence," how we seek accountability measures, how the school curriculum should be taught, and what students are supposed to come out of school with, i.e., the merit badges of schooling.

Notwithstanding all this, I want us to hold onto the possibilities of Whiteness to engage the role of White bodies doing anti-racist work, in order to be mindful of the limitations of such race work. How do we use our positions of power and influence to do critical race and equity work? How can people privileged by a system work against it? Can dominant groups understand their Whiteness as it is denied? What does it take to do this work? Is there a material, emotional, physical and spiritual toll on bodies? How do such bodies come to terms with their bodily engagements in such work (see also Howard, 2009)? The concern is the theoretical and methodological pitfalls and lapses. Yet can we also ask about the strengths of progressive work done by White anti-racist workers as allies? For the racially oppressed, if there is a discomfort in asking this latter question, then we must ask why? The White/dominant/colonizer does not easily divest or rid him/herself of power and privilege. Power does not concede anything unless through force and resistance. If one is granted power and privilege through history, identity, or culture, it is not easy to ask that they undo power and privilege through resistance. We could ask the privileged to take responsibility and seek accountability and ensure that they engage their power and privilege in ways that bring about social justice and productive change. But we must first recognize the default embedded in the contradiction the privilege of Whiteness occupies in relation to doing race work, without the conscientiousness of the racially oppressed and, furthermore, the divestment of White privilege.

The disembodiment of White privilege is a necessary prerequisite for allied White anti-racist scholarship and progressive contributions to the field of anti-racist and anti-colonial work. And as one student in the class noted, such work must be in connection to the deconstruction of the self in Whiteness, which must transpire from the self to the larger community, enveloped in the dominant structures of Whiteness (Delaney, 2012). Therefore, we must ensure our anti-racist scholarship is consolidated with anti-racist practice/systems/structures, so as to destabilize and finally subvert the colonial situation. There must, however, be caution for White dominant bodies and for non-White bodies in particular, suspicion for what Albert Memmi (1974) tells us is the White dominant's disposition toward myths/moral/ideology/imaginings, produced in order to escape the all-too-consuming emptiness of Whiteness, again and again. We must continually acknowledge the ongoing process of destabilizing the privilege of Whiteness, which delineates the parameters of the constituents of, and progressive scholarship done by, White anti-racist scholars.

It is in this context that it is rightly argued that our knowledge of Whiteness must be complemented with the view of those who have been oppressed by Whiteness. There is a vital symbiotic connection or what I call a "co-relational relationship" between the oppressed/oppressor; non-White disadvantage/White privilege; and dominant/subordinate. The oppressor needs the oppressed to understand their oppressive acts. This is a point Frantz Fanon long expressed. But the oppressor cannot claim to know about oppression any more than Whites/dominant can claim to know fully about Whiteness. Howard (2009) has posed the question: What does this mean for Whites doing critical anti-racist work? Why ask this question, one may wonder? As already noted, given that Whiteness is often denied through the dominant's claim of ignorance to their privilege, and/or such privilege being "invisible" to privilege, we must expect theoretical, philosophical, and methodological lapses in the dominant's ability to understand privilege, Whiteness, and oppression. You do not fully know what you claim not to possess, see, or benefit from. As Fanon (1969) prophetically foretold, we continue the colonial situation, a lie when we do not put Whiteness in its place, and as mentioned, this place is indeed distorted. We must begin with the undoing/subversion of Whiteness to speak to the mighty toll it continues to burden us with, in order to continue the necessary anti-racist struggle for colonial demise. This requires us to return the gaze that configures the "fact of Blackness" in myths of racial degeneracy back onto its imaginary emblem of Whiteness.

Again, as Albert Memmi (1974) long ago expressed, "it is not easy for the [White dominant body] to escape mentally from [the concrete] situation" of

White domination, "to refuse its ideology while continuing to live with its actual relationships" (p. 64). The situation of the Whiteness lays its might in the structures of White domination so as to create the near impossible ontological dilemma for the dominant body, in which he or she no longer recognizes the oppressed, or he or she no longer recognizes oneself again (Fanon, 1969; Memmi, 1974). The repudiation of Whiteness cannot be left intact, for space to be left only for perpetual resistance to the inevitable reorganization of the colonial encounter, and thus the damaging co-relational relationship between the colonizer and the colonized body.

As we engage in these discussions I would also stress that we must consistently eschew essentialist and reductionist orientations. I do not say this lightly, especially since, as a student in my OISE/UT graduate class on Frantz Fanon (who prefers anonymity) noted, "I feel like we are constantly dichotomizing Blackness and Whiteness, colonized and colonizer—making it impossible to bring the two together." I know others may share such a feeling. As to why some may feel this way is not a question for me to address here. Suffice to say that the concepts of colour, especially Whiteness and Blackness, warrant refinement. They warrant an optical and linguistic decolonization, by which we mean for them to be situated in their rightful history, and so as to be returned respectfully to their cultural memories, dispossessed by the prisms of racism. We must break through the compulsive and pervasive mediations of racist exchanges. Racism has always collaborated intertextually with other powerful configurations within the political economy (e.g., class, gender, sexuality, and politics). Therefore, we must re-engage Fanon's concept of the Manichean divide, in order to depose the reckless direction of the political economy in place. This economy mediates knowledge exchanges between White dominant and non-White bodies that produce the dominant meta-narrative and subversion for an ongoing colonial co-relational relation, which can make it exclusively the Others' problem to labour, while already labouring the ignorance of Whiteness, White privilege, and accountability.

At the heart of racist practices/racisms in society is a supremacist thinking that must be read not in terms of beliefs but in how particular prisms/worldviews/senses undergird every part of society. We must be bold to link and talk of Whiteness as a thought system that rationalizes racist practice to bear its brunt upon the colonized body. Unless this denial and the so-called "invisibility of Whiteness" is properly dealt with in the anti-racist work, our practices may well end up affirming/entrenching/supporting the status quo. Such work can be suspect even when well intentioned.

REFERENCES

Delaney, L. (2012, October). Unpublished class contribution to *SES 3915: Frantz Fanon and education: Pedagogical challenges*. Department of Humanities, Social Sciences and Social Justice Education, Ontario Institute for Studies in Education of the University of Toronto, Toronto, ON.

Fanon, F. (1963). *The wretched of the earth*. New York, NY: Grove Press.

Fanon, F. (1967). *Black skin, White masks*. New York, NY: Grove Press.

Fanon, F. (1969). Toward the African revolution: Political essays. New York, NY: Grove Press.

Fanon, F. (1988). *A dying colonialism*. New York, NY: Grove Press.

Frankenberg, R. (1993). *White women, race matters: The social construction of Whiteness*. Minneapolis, MN: University of Minnesota Press.

Frankenberg, R. (Ed.). (1997a). *Displacing whiteness: Essays in social and cultural criticism*. Durham, NC: Duke University Press.

Frankenberg, R. (1997b). Introduction: Local whiteness, localizing whiteness. In R. Frankenberg (Ed.), *Displacing whiteness: Essays in social and cultural criticism* (pp. 1–33). Durham, NC: Duke University Press.

Giroux, H. A. (1997a). Racial politics and the pedagogy of whiteness. In M. Hill (Ed.), *Whiteness: A critical reader* (pp. 294–315). New York, NY: New York University Press.

Giroux, H. A. (1997b). Rewriting the discourse of racial identity: Towards a pedagogy and politics of whiteness. *Harvard Educational Review, 67*(2), 285–320.

Howard, P. S. (2008). Colliding positions on what counts as racially progressive: A critical race Africology of the film, Crash. In P. Howard & G. J. S. Dei (Eds.), *Crash politics and antiracism: Interrogations of liberal race discourse* (pp. 25–48). New York, NY: Peter Lang.

Howard, P. (2009). *The double-edged sword: A critical Africology of collaboration between Blacks and Whites in racial equity work* (Unpublished PhD dissertation). Department of Sociology and Equity Studies, Ontario Institute for Studies in Education of the University of Toronto, Toronto, ON.

Kincheloe, J. L., Steinberg, S., Rodriguez, N., & Chennault, R. (Eds.). (1998). *White reign: Deploying whiteness in America*. New York, NY: St. Martin's Press.

Memmi, A. (1974). *The colonizer and the colonized*. Boston, MA: Beacon Press.

Roediger, D. R. (1999). *The wages of whiteness: Race and the making of the American working class*. London, UK: Verso.

GEORGE J. SEFA DEI

FOREWORD (2007)

It is a pleasure to write the foreword for this book—which addresses in a direct and explicit way particular topics in anti-racism that have been hidden from view or seen to be secondary by most people—for a number of reasons. I have known Paul Carr since the beginning of his doctoral studies at OISE in the early 1990s, and am pleased that he has continued to interrogate "race" from a problematized vantage point, and also to bring forward a critical analysis of policymaking based on his own experience. I first came to know Darren Lund as an anti-racism scholar in the mid-1990s, when we engaged in a robust scholarly debate on African-centred schooling in the pages of a national academic journal, and have long been aware of his outstanding social justice work in schools and communities.

Over the course of the last two decades I have been involved in a number of projects dealing with anti-racism education, a concept that has consistently evolved over time. There are many scholars, including my colleagues and students and researchers that I have worked with, who recognize the intersectionality of race, class, gender, sexuality and other forms of difference. Many other scholars and colleagues across the country, some of whom are represented in this book, have continued to work toward inculcating a more critical, meaningful, and relevant formulation of anti-racism. I believe that race is a fundamental marker of lived experience in Canada, as well as internationally and, at the same time, like the others in this book, I feel that so many other factors contribute to how race manifests itself.

My own work in Canadian schools and the academy, in general, has pointed to the politics and denial of race and difference even as race and racism stare us in the face. As racialized/minoritized students articulate their concerns about racism I have also encountered the denial and silencing that many others have often embarked upon, not simply to protect their privileges, but to mask any sense of complicity and responsibility for social oppression. What I have found over time, and one reason this book is such a timely and necessary addition to the literature on racism and racialization, is that many of the people most imbued with its orchestration and manifestation, namely White people, maintain the power and privilege to ignore and dissociate themselves from the experiences of others who are more directly affected or marginalized by racism. It is destabilizing, troublesome, and problematic to hear White people vigorously refute the notion that there is racism in society. We see this in Canada in many ways, and in education we have long heard of the *de facto* policy of "colour-blindness." Many people of good will, however, have become engaged in trying to make for a better society, but many others challenge the foundation and legacy of racism. The fact that most of the decision-makers are White, and that it is these people who control the funding, laws, programs, and policies, means that it is often an uphill battle just to get racism formally identified as a concern. Thus, a book on Whiteness, led by two academics who are White, is an important contribution to the discussion about how power works in society.

This book includes contributions from some well-known and critical theorists in the area of racism in this country—as well as some new voices in the field. The impressive range of approaches, methodologies, theoretical perspectives, and experiential vantage-points provides for a comprehensive and engaging text for students, researchers, and others interested in exploring how Whites are intensely implicated in perpetuating the racial project. I think the question of whether Whites should talk about race is "no brainer." As this book suggests, racism can best be addressed when everyone addresses their role in maintaining the *status quo*, even if difference is still considered to be a strategic consideration in how race manifests itself and is experienced. There is place at the anti-racism table for White scholars. For the dominant, the entry-point is the investigation of Whiteness and White identity.

There are many excellent chapters in this book addressing the specific concerns of those most marginalized by racism (i.e., Aboriginal peoples, Black/African Canadians, and other people from minoritized racial groups), and these works explore the myriad contradictions racialized peoples face in their quest for human dignity and rights. Until now, we have not seen a book within the Canadian context with such obvious relevance at the international level—one that effectively brings to light the curiously implausible contradictions of Whiteness. Paul and Darren's undertaking to gather such eloquent and thoughtful voices to fill this void provides an important catalyst for all people to reaffirm our engagement in living out equity and social justice, and toward an authentic and critical pluralism that surpasses the trivialized and romanticized versions of diversity and multiculturalism that seem limited to spicy food and coloured clothing on the dance floor. Racism is about maintaining White dominance and supremacy. It is about the power to produce and validate knowledge about particular experiences while subjugating other concerns.

In this regard, I would like to engage the dialogue with additional readings on Whiteness and White identity. I remember not long ago teaching a graduate class on the "Principles of Anti-racism" when a student asked why there was a focus on Whiteness and White identity in the course. It was not the usual concern about re-centring the dominant group's issues in anti-racist practice. In fact, what the student was alluding to was whether an anti-racist practice should today not be preoccupied foremost with the ways to empower racialized and minoritized bodies (spiritually, politically, and intellectually) to come to terms with our social oppression and, ultimately, to suggest ways to resist dominance.

Race is a powerful divide in contemporary society. Whiteness as a form of racialized identity helps frame much of the discourse and social practice. The universalism of

Eurocentric experience points to the bankrupt ways White racialized identities are held up as the norm to which everything else is measured and accounted for. The authority of Whiteness rests upon how, in everyday practice, the tropes of White supremacy scripts the lives of the oppressed and minoritized. In a racialized society to be White does not simply mean to be privileged. It also implies owning up to complicities and responsibilities for the maintenance of oppression. Consequently, it can be argued that there are limits to how we can deconstruct White identity without falling into the easy slippage of acknowledging responsibility and complicity.

White racial identity is about White privilege. Learning about Whiteness, and teaching about White identity and Whiteness are some of the many challenges facing anti-racist and dominant educators today. Discourses on race and anti-racism cannot avoid a discussion of White identities and white privilege. When we fail to do so we are merely reproducing the dominance of Whiteness. When certain bodies enter into our institutions they carry the institutional weight of Whiteness. These bodies can easily reproduce their dominance freely if they choose to use their positions to work for change. It is a choice that is often not afforded to all groups. Dyer (1997, p. 10) long ago observed that, in looking at Whiteness, the goal is to "dislodge it [Whiteness] from its centrality and authority, not to reinstate it." In order to dislodge Whiteness we must first understand the insidious ways it maintains dominance through the ideology of White supremacy. A supremacist ideology ensures that Whiteness guarantees racial privilege irrespective of gender, sexuality, and class. Consequently, Whiteness has become a system of dominance. In fact, Howard (2004) is correct in arguing that Whites cannot escape their implication and complicity in Whiteness in a White supremacist society. To claim otherwise negates or compromises the ability of Whites to do serious anti-racist work as "it espouses a gross misunderstanding of the structural and embedded nature of racism" (p. 8). Anti-racist Whites must clearly acknowledge and demonstrate the tensions and difficulties of their grappling with racism in order to gain credibility, and to solidify the ground for anti-racist coalition politics.

To my reading and experience, Whiteness is never invisible to those who daily live the effects of White dominance. Many Whites may see their Whiteness, and yet they are able to deny the dominance associated with it. This denial is not unconscious, nor is it accidental; I believe it is deliberate. Critical anti-racism maintains that we will only do away with racism when Whiteness no longer infers dominance and Whites acknowledge and work towards this end. In noting this I also agree that there are contradictory (and sometimes competing) meanings of Whiteness, as in the way Whites and subordinate groups understand contemporary Whiteness (e.g., the perception of Whiteness as anything but positive). As I have argued elsewhere (Dei, forthcoming), a critical study of Whiteness and White identity means bringing certain considerations to the fore of our anti-racist practice. For example, how individuals choose to inhabit their bodies (claiming a racial identity) ought to be distinguished from the concept of Whiteness as a system of domination conferring privilege upon White bodies at the expense of racial minorities. We must also look for what is being gained when distinctions between White identity and Whiteness is vigorously maintained. And, at whose expense and to what intents and purposes do we uphold such distinctions? At times we make distinctions to absolve us on individual and collective responsibilities, and not simply for the sake of intellectual scholarship. Personal accountability, and collective responsibilities and complicities, cannot be avoided or skirted around by focussing on how White bodies are trapped by the system. Consequently, while we may be seduced into separating "White identity" and "Whiteness," there is a link that must not be denied. In fact, White identity and Whiteness work together allowing dominant groups to become immune to the system. We know that certain bodies have the privilege to opt out by default through inaction.

The idea of practice of "disembodied identity" (which, for the purpose of this essay, I would interpret as "Whiteness without bodies") can be problematic as it fails to uncover how race is embodied and how race, gender, class, and sexual politics intersect to create and maintain social differences. As alluded to, Whiteness cannot itself be essentialized, especially when embodied Whiteness intersects along gender, class, and sexual lines. As Deliovsky (2005) notes in articulating an "embodied femininity," White women do not have the same relationship, access, or subjective experience to Whiteness as their male counterparts. Notwithstanding these complications, however, it is also equally important to reiterate that there is a systemization and structuralization of dominance within social institutions that perpetuate White privilege and other forms of oppressions "inter-generationally" and/or through time and space, irrespective of class, gender, religious, language, and sexual differences, particularly among dominant groups. The structural dynamics of Whiteness work with broader socio-economic forces as well as within the institutional aspects of structure/society as evidenced in everyday discursive practices and social scripts/texts to place Whites in a "positional superiority" (Said, 1979) at the expense of "Others." Such "positional superiority" of Whites is also fed constantly by the ideological system based on White supremacy (see Deliovsky, 2005, p. 12).

This collection has come at an opportune time. It fills a gap in the Canadian literature on the ways Whiteness masquerades in our institutions and within Canadian mythologies. Naming Whiteness and White identity is a political project as much as an intellectual engagement, and the co-editors of this collection must be commended for creating the space for such naming to take place in public and academic discourses. To some, while Whiteness can be said to be an "unnamed," "unmarked," and yet "marked racial practice" (e.g., Frankenberg, 1993; Mercer, 1991, pp. 205-206), its material and symbolic consequences are all too real irrespective of the intersections of class, gender, and sexual differences. We know that throughout history the power and ideological privilege of Whiteness has allowed working-class Whites to associate themselves more with their oppressive middle-class counterparts than the working-class of colour (see the pioneering works of duBois, 1975; Cox, 1958). The reason is not far fetched to the critical scholar interested in the political economy of race. Dyer (1997, p. 19), among many others, has also observed that Whiteness has proved more successful than class in bringing White people together across ethno/ cultural boundaries, often against the best interest of working-class peoples. There is no contradiction here. In fact, Harris (1993) got it right in her careful, astute, and eye-opening analysis of "Whiteness as property."

In effect, what I am leading to is the fact that the anti-racist discursive framework articulates a link between race, identity, and representation in educational and political practice. In the context of an anti-racism discursive practice, "bodies matter." White identity has powerful currency in social settings. In fact, in anti-racist work, "bodies matter" when we come to think of the ways knowledges are read and encoded on different bodies and how learners engage in/with processes of schooling and education. But as noted by others, bodies matter in anti-racist work also because of the "rootedness [or, I would say "embeddeness"] of racist ideologies in bodies" (Howard, 2006). I cannot agree more when Howard (2006) contends that the White body is potentially prone to racism, and this profoundly complicates any engagement in critical anti-racist work. The White body itself gives rise to certain liabilities in any work that would be deemed "anti-racist." Yes, this liability is attached to the body. However, this does not mean White bodies cannot do anti-racist work. In fact, as I have repeatedly noted, the critical question today is not "Who can do anti-racist work?" but whether we are all prepared to face the risk and consequences of doing this work! And the risk and consequences are different for who the bodies are. Engaging self in anti-racist schooling and education work, and what it means to bring an embodied experience, as well as the consequences for this, are all crucial components to such work. Because White bodies are invested in systems of privilege, the importance of dominant groups questioning their self-appointed and racialized neutrality is always critical and transformative. For far too long we have witnessed how White society has conscripted and choreographed the idea of a fractured Black community that avoids taking responsibility.

In the context of bodies, and the politics of educational transformation, Doyle-Wood (2006) reiterates that "it is not a question of the color of the person but the color of the person's politics" is on the mark. This is precisely because of the kinds of damage that minoritized bodies can engender when their politics are socially conservative. At the same time, if we are speaking about bodies whose politics must be libratory and transformative in anti-racist ways to begin with, then we must acknowledge that it is crucial that such bodies must substantially (but not exclusively) be bodies of colour. There is a psychologically liberating aspect for students when, in this context, a Black or racially minoritized teacher is present, and experienced in positions of knowledge production and learning. At the same time, location is a critical factor when we are speaking about issues of race and power. A minoritized gaze, and the knowledge produced from that gaze and experience, is a different gaze than that of the dominant White, supposedly normative view. It provides an alternative paradigmatic way of seeing and knowing. To give a concrete example, it should matter greatly who teaches what (e.g., race, anti-racism, Black Canadian Literature history, or Aboriginal knowledge). There is a powerful and symbolic reading of anti-racist work evoking Whiteness and different bodies.

Together, Darren and Paul have brought together a project that seeks to frame and foster debate, analysis and, most importantly, social change in relation to race, difference, and identity in society. Is it noteworthy to acknowledge that both Paul and Darren are White, and that they are overseeing this work on Whiteness? I believe that it is, not because others cannot write about the subject with clarity and insight, as is clearly evident in the diverse range of contributors to this book. Rather, naming their positions as White allies embracing a rigorous conceptual and analytical discourse in the social justice field is an important signal that White society must also become intertwined in the entrenched racism that infuses every aspect of our society. As Paul and Darren correctly point out, race is still a pivotal concern for everything that happens in society, and especially in schools. The beauty of this collection under the leadership of these two editors is that the engagement allows readers to bring healthy interpretations and contestations to critical anti-racist work.

REFERENCES

Cox, O. (1948). *Caste, class and race: A study in social dynamics*. Garden City, NY: Doubleday.

Dei, G. J. S. (forthcoming). Racists beware.

Deliovsky, K. (2005). *Elsewhere from here: Remapping the territories of White femininity* (Unpublished doctoral dissertation). Department of Sociology, McMaster University, Hamilton, ON.

Doyle-Wood, S. (2006). *Unpublished comments on a scholarship grant application*. Department of Sociology and Equity Studies, Ontario Institute for Studies in Education of the University of Toronto, Toronto, ON.

duBois, W. E. B. (1975). *The world and Africa: An inquiry into the part which Africa has played in world history*. New York, NY: International.

Dyer, R. (1997). *White*. London, England: Routledge.

Frankenberg, R. (1993). *The social construction of whiteness: White women, race matters*. Minneapolis, MN: University of Minnesota Press.

Harris, C. (1993). Whiteness as property. *Harvard Law Review, 106*(8), 1710–1791.

Howard, P. (2004). *Reflections on a reading course: Interrogating whiteness in critical/anti-racist and other ostensibly equitable spaces*. Unpublished paper, Department of Sociology and Equity Studies in Education, Ontario Institute for Studies in Education, University of Toronto, Toronto, ON.

Howard, P. (2006). *Unpublished comments on a thesis proposal*. Department of Sociology and Equity Studies, Ontario Institute for Studies in Education, University of Toronto, Toronto, ON.

Mercer, K. (1991). Skin head, sex thing: Racial difference and the homoerectic imaginary. In Bad Object-Choice collective (Eds.), *How do I look? Queer film and video* (pp. 169–210). Seattle, Washington, DC: Bay Press.

Said, E. (1979). *Orientalism*. New York, NY: Vintage Books.

ACKNOWLEDGEMENTS (2014)

Revisiting our book project these seven years later has been a provocative and sometimes challenging journey.

I (Darren) am immensely grateful to my family and to my many colleagues and mentors who inspire and challenge me in this and my other work. My hearty thanks go to my good friend Paul Carr, who has provided such a wealth of positive energy and wisdom to this project. I would also like to thank my amazing graduate and undergraduate students for all of their exciting ideas and quality work; I have been privileged to work with each of you. I dearly miss my parents, both of whom have passed away since the first edition was published, and whose many lessons on the importance of love, commitment, and hard work still resonate.

I (Paul) am sustained in this part of my life (the never-ending academic part) by those closest around me, especially Gina, and want to thank my family for their unwavering support. Many individuals have been present over the years to encourage me, and also to provide invaluable insight and inspiration, including Darren Lund, and I gratefully acknowledge their support as well. I would like to thank my research assistants – Lauren Howard, Gary Pluim, and Franck Potwora – for the wonderful contribution to the research project I have been leading related to democracy, political literacy and transformative education these past few years, which also connects to the Whiteness project.

We would both like to thanks our friends at Sense Publishers, who have supported us and our ongoing work for the past several years. We are also grateful for a broad range of support that we have received from colleagues in the Paulo Freire special interest group at AERA, who have contributed in myriad ways to our thinking and scholarship in relation to Whiteness, radicalization, and social justice.

ACKNOWLEDGEMENTS (2007)

Putting together a book that attempts to tackle the intensely personal and intractable issue of Whiteness has required a range of experiences over a period of years. We are grateful to a number of people who have supported us directly in this project as well as in our academic pursuits in general. This book has benefited from the moral and intellectual support of the other authors in the book, and especially from Joe Kincheloe, George Dei, and Peter McLaren, who generously offered their time to be part of this project.

I (Paul R. Carr) was supported in my work on this book by colleagues at Youngstown State University, and I would like to mention specifically Jim Pusch for his insight and camaraderie, as well as Dick McEwing, Bob Beebe, and Phil Ginnetti. Special thanks to my graduate assistant, Kinga Orban, who ensured that everything was in order. Three professors at the Ontario Institute for Studies in Education, where I completed my doctorate in 1996, deserve mention for their inspiration and support over the years: Richard Townsend, Jim Ryan, and George Dei, who introduced me to antiracism education some fifteen years ago. Lastly, and perhaps most importantly, I am grateful for the support of my family, especially my parents (Chris and Bob), my partner (Gina), my daughters (Chelsea, Sarah, and Nathalie) and Noah, the most recent and, undoubtedly, most original of the clan.

I (Darren E. Lund) would like to acknowledge the ongoing support of my colleagues and students at the University of Calgary, and the encouragement of my mentor and former supervisor, John Willinsky, from UBC. I am also indebted to Keith McLeod from OISE/UT for his initial encouragement of my doctoral studies, and to Kogila Adam Moodley for her guidance with my work. Jim Banks and Carl Grant have continued to inspire and inform my pursuits in social justice research and education. I am in awe of Kirsten Spackman, my dear friend and energetic colleague in student antiracism activism, and all of the teachers who do this collaborative work in schools and communities. Thanks to my all of my family and friends who have supported and encouraged my work over the years, especially my sister. I am grateful to my spouse and children for being the highlights of my life, and to my parents for their love.

DARREN E. LUND & PAUL R. CARR

INTRODUCTION (2014)

Reframing Whiteness

In so many ways, not much has changed since we first published *The Great White North? Exploring Whiteness, Privilege and Identity in Education*, and yet, so much has changed. One of our contributors has passed away, our dear friend and colleague, Patrick Solomon. Most chapter authors have carried on with their academic work, many within the broad field of social justice work. Both of the editors have attained new positions and new duties, and taken on additional commitments both inside and outside of the academy. The topic of Whiteness remains contentious and contested, rarely evokes a neutral response, and we understood the difficulty for our authors of revisiting their chapters some six or so years later. We made the decision to retain the original chapters wherever possible, and include in this edition an opportunity for the authors to reframe their chapters in light of new understandings and experiences since its original publication. It has been a pleasure and an honour to reconnect with the good people who have made this book an award-winning bestseller in this field.

It was an honour to be recognized by our peers for the first edition of this book, with an *Award of Distinction* from the Canadian Race Relations Foundation (CRRF), and with the *2008 Publication Award* from the Canadian Association of Foundations of Education (CAFE). In the meantime, we have often been called upon to write and speak about the book and its related projects. Invitations for community and academic conferences and journal articles (e.g., Lund & Carr, 2010), and edited book chapters (e.g., Carr & Lund, 2009; Lund & Carr, 2012) have seen us talking about aspects of White privilege with a variety of professional, academic, and lay audiences. Appearances on regional and national radio broadcasts have included right-wing radio shows, local and national news stories, and phone-in questions from members of the public. Following the publication of a seemingly innocuous article about our book in a national newspaper (Church, 2007) covering a presentation about our research at a national conference, the reader responses were immediate and many of them vicious. In the first few hours alone, over 160 written items were posted to the newspaper's online "Comments" page, most expressing racist, xenophobic, or otherwise hateful viewpoints. It is no understatement to say that there remains a very high level of resistance to the very notion of White privilege, especially among White people.

D. E. Lund & P. R. Carr (Eds.), Revisiting The Great White North?, 1–10.
© *2015 Sense Publishers. All rights reserved.*

Emotional responses to our ideas, and those of our contributors, have ranged from incredulous, to angry, to defensive, to curious, to bemused. People in the West and Global North remain immersed in Whiteness like fish in water. There remain dozens of embedded metaphors, analogies, images, and cultural icons that all speak to the sanctity, beauty, and the hypnotic predominance of the colour white in the Western world. Not merely the opposite of black, the colour white remains a signifier for global racial supremacy—good against evil, lightness versus darkness, and benevolence over malevolence—and symbolizes purity, cleanliness, kindness, serenity, and youthful innocence. White is associated with being the "good guy," the savior, and the empires of Europe and the UK as well as France, Spain and other Euro-colonizing forces, while Black is inexorably fused to colonial notions of the "bad guy," the villain, and the forbidding "dark continent" of Africa.

White supremacist groups have coalesced in North America, and continue to thrive and adapt around virulent hatred based on the false premise of biological superiority. Canada has long been a welcome home to the Ku Klux Klan and numerous other hate groups (Baergen, 2000; Kinsella, 2005; Pitsula, 2013). White supremacist propaganda has been used historically in a sophisticated manner to soften the message of xenophobia to reinforce White hegemony (Daniels, 1997). Slavery, colonialism of First Nations and other peoples, neo-colonialism, imperialism, and a host of other political, economic, and cultural strategic maneuvers and mindsets have all been buttressed by the grandiose conceptualization of the White man as morally enlightened (Dei & Kempf, 2006). Supported for centuries by the Christian religion and the drive to expand the Empire, White people have colonized and ravaged much of the planet. Willinsky (1998) reminds us that the racialized divisions of the past still shape our educational institutions, and that exposing privileges and inequities is part of what we owe our students. Further, he explains that students

> need to see that such divisions have long been part of the fabric and structure of the state, including the schools, and they need to appreciate that challenging the structuring of those differences requires equally public acts of refusing their original and intended meanings. (p. 5)

Rather than regarding this as a sensationalistic depiction of the legacy of a diverse group of people, one need only look at the history of indigenous peoples in North America (Carr, 2008; Churchill, 1998) to understand the present day privilege and power held by White people (Dei, Karumanchery, & Karumanchery-Luik, 2004; Fine, Weis, Powell Pruitt, & Burns, 2004; Lund, 2006a). Throughout the past few years, it has become evident that Whiteness cannot be separated from many other critical areas of inquiry, including neoliberalism, globalization, and democracy (see Carr, 2011).

The collection of writings originally assembled within *The Great White North?* speaks to the idea that Canada is an expansive country, richly diverse in its geography, shaped by the mesmerizing landscapes crafted by the Group of Seven artists in the early 1900s, with an undercurrent of the pioneer spirit defined in the literature of generations of great Canadian writers in the latter part of the twentieth century. One feature that defines the Canadian experience is the complex, and often antagonistic, relationship it has had with the United States since before Confederation. A common sentiment that continues to bind Canadians together is the self-assured notion that Canada does not suffer from the same racial problems as in the US. We believe we are less segregated, less discriminatory, less racist, and less divided, and we often remind ourselves of Canada's status as the first nation to have its multicultural identity entrenched in its constitution. The Americans, on the other hand, reveal endless visible warts, including a long history of racial tensions and civil rights struggles, and we strive to convince ourselves that we Canadians have not followed their destiny (Lund, 2006c, 2012).

As educational researchers interested in the sociology of "race" and identity in education, the editors of this book have become aware of the intricate, systemic, and pervasive nature of racism in Canada. Many well-known antiracism scholars have taken up the work of acknowledging and documenting this racist past and present (e.g., Dei, Karumanchery, & Karumanchery-Luik, 2004; Fleras & Elliot, 2003; Henry & Tator, 2005; James, 2003; Trifonas, 2003). Starting with the first European contact with the Aboriginal peoples, through the existence of slavery in Canada—about which many Canadians have no information—to the undulating waves of immigration, through the razing of Africville in Halifax, to the internment of Japanese Canadians during the Second World War, through the experience of Jamaican-Canadians in Toronto and Haitian-Canadians in Montreal, the history of racism in Canada is as rich as it is shrouded with resistance and denial (Lund, 2006b). While there have been hundreds of studies on race relations and racism in Canada, there have been few, if any, scholarly works exclusively dedicated to exploring Whiteness in Canada.

We decided to compile such a book examining the multiple perspectives and vantage points on Whiteness in order to challenge the current complacency in the Canadian state and nation, and particularly among educators, to address deep-seated inequities and injustices. This volume builds on a growing desire to examine Whiteness without reifying its centrality in the antiracism and other social justice movements. We have been, simultaneously, inspired by critical White scholars in the US who have undertaken critical self-examination of their own privileges as they take up the work of unlearning racism in their schools, communities, and faculties of education (e.g., Bush, 2005; Howard, 1999; Jensen, 2005; Lea & Helfand, 2004; McIntosh, 1988; McIntyre, 1997; Rodriquez & Villaverde, 2000; Sleeter, 2005; Sullivan, 2006). Questions emerge that seem self-evident and yet confound our work: Do most White people even know that they are White? Do they use their privilege to deny or ignore their racial identity and, simultaneously, infer inherent racial attributes to the "Other"? If White people do not know that they are White, how can those who are in positions of power, many of whom are White, effectively understand and challenge racism and unearned privilege?

We realize the oversimplification entailed in placing into one White category such heterogeneous ethnic, cultural, linguistic, religious, and other groups. Certainly, there are myriad international examples of nuanced experiences of oppression and struggle within and across nations of White people. For example, Francophones have historical differences with Anglophones in Canada, the Catholics and the Protestants have been at loggerheads for years in Northern Ireland, the Hungarian minority has not had a favourable experience with the majority Romanian population, and the Basque population has been involved in a separatist movement in Spain for generations, with all of these conflicts, struggles, and complexities involving White people. It would seem extremely unusual, and perhaps even unacceptable to most people, to hear news anchors speak of "the White community" during a daily newscast in North America, yet we commonly refer to the "Black community," the "Asian community," the "West Indian community" and so on, as if these racialized groups can so easily be confined within a tightly defined and coded category of identity and social experience.

This second volume asks the question: What does Whiteness look like, in general, and in Canada, in particular? It also pushes contributors to consider how we can challenge, disrupt, and alter power and privilege relations imbued within the Whiteness project. The Canadian context is highly complex with the number and variety of exogamous relations and blending of peoples with complex and shifting ethnic, cultural, and racial identities. Almost infinite individual experiences make for a confusing notion of "race" in Canada; for example, two of the last three Governors General are women from racialized minority groups, coincidentally with each being a former journalist married to a White husband. Is it a coincidence that there has never been a non-White Supreme Court judge or Prime Minister? Who maintains the predominance of power in Cabinet, at the CBC/Radio-Canada, in boardrooms of the large corporations, the Senates of Canadian universities, and so on? Power does have a colour in Canada, despite official multiculturalism, making our nation appear superficially to be a harmonious society in which anyone can be successful with the right attitude and effort. The meritocratic myth has worked against racialized non-White people in Canada for hundreds of years. It is problematic that many White people so effortlessly invoke deficits in individual efforts as an explanation of underachievement by some racial minorities.

Despite recent significant gains for (mainly White) women in the workforce and political life, there still remains an important and visible privilege gap between Whites and non-Whites in Canada and elsewhere. Clearly, women as a group still face numerous barriers and challenges in society, and for non-White women the inequities are multiplied. The tumultuous rift and near dismantling of the *National Organization of Women* (NOW) in the 1980s is illustrative of the tension between White and non-White women. The latter did not see their needs being addressed, nor their voices being heard, through an organization dominated by middle-class White women, which eventually led to non-White women assuming leadership positions in the movement.

Are people generally overtly racist in Canada? While it is unlikely that blatant racist behavior is currently condoned or tolerated by most Canadians, there is ample evidence that widespread systemic racism is a reality. Part of the problem in documenting trends is the absence of useful data collection. Many people resist indicating their racial origin on census forms, for a variety of reasons. People from racialized minority groups know that a chance at employment may later be tainted with the accusation that the employer simply wanted to "fill a quota." Playing the proverbial "race card" is perhaps most insidious when considering the trivialization and maligning of employment equity in Canada (Klassen & Cosgrove, 2002) and affirmative action in the US (Feagin & O'Brien, 2003). At some level, racial identity is obvious to everyone and, at the same time, is obscured by the false notion that human rights legislation, common decency, and religion all negate its existence, often culminating in the deleterious notion that we are all "colour-blind." Where people live, the positions they ultimately attain, who they may befriend, employ, and marry, the types of associations, clubs, and organizations they belong to, and other markers of social integration all may have a racialized component. Who most often attends private schools, private golf clubs, and private business circles, has traditionally depended on, among other things, unspoken racial categories. How people choose to understand their own implication in racism relates to privilege and power, and ultimately, Whiteness is shrouded with justifications and denials that allow people to avoid discussion of how oppression continues to benefit White people in Canada.

Therefore, we begin once again with the premise that "race" and racial identities are highly contested and problematic ideas for our consideration. Just as with politics and religion, these topics are not comfortably addressed openly in polite company. For this revised volume, we insist that Canadian society cannot be understood without stripping away the layers of the "race" onion. Clearly, social relations are infinitely more complex than race relations. The social construction and intersectionality of identity provide a medium in which Whiteness can be deconstructed and problematized. Whether we are speaking about sexual orientation, ability, religion, gender identity, cultural group membership, or some other aspect of our identities, the racial template always affects the power relations inherent between groups and individuals (McLaren, 2007).

The birth of this Whiteness project stems from a chance encounter of the co-editors at the *National Association for Multicultural Education* (NAME) conference in Atlanta in November of 2005. Sharing a table at lunch, we were both surprised to learn how much we have in common: We are two White males from Canada of about the same age who have been involved in antiracism education for a number of years. One is from Calgary (Darren), one from Toronto (Paul), and both have had a rich experience outside of the academic world—as a high school teacher (Darren) and as a government policy advisor (Paul). We enjoyed the talks, workshops, and especially the Freedom Ride, which traced the roots of the civil rights movement through Spellman and Morehouse Colleges, the Ebenezer Church, and the Martin Luther King Memorial Center. Against this poignant and moving backdrop we discussed the state of racism in Canada, and agreed that being White and not saying so, or failing to strive to understand the ways in which it works to subjugate others, serves to undermine the antiracism movement.

We wished to produce a book with people from a range of cultural and racialized identities, and with a variety of perspectives on Whiteness, with the stated desire that each author problematize Whiteness through inquiry that was both personal and critical. We are aware of the highly contentious and discriminatory history facing a number of White immigrants over the years in Canada (e.g., those of Jewish, Italian, and Ukrainian origin) but we wanted to focus on the power and privilege of Whiteness in this volume. This requires changing the paradigm, forcing the issue of who really holds the power, and interrogating the Canadian identity.

One scholar wanted to revise her original piece for this volume, and of course we respected that request. We have also included one new piece, by Gina Thésée, who works and conducts research in the province of Québec.

The book remains unique in that each of the writers addresses his or her personal implication in Whiteness, and for all but the new one, a reframing of their original piece, seven years later. We strongly believe this enhances these accounts of rich, subjective, and politicized experiences of Whiteness. All of the authors of chapters making up the core of this collection are Canadians, with the exception of Brad Porfilio, who taught Canadian students across the border at a university in Buffalo, New York. We are pleased that we have representation from almost all of the provinces, contributing a range of pieces—theoretical, conceptual, and applied—that collectively represent a range of interdisciplinary perspectives.

OVERVIEW OF THE BOOK

There are five sections in the book, each containing three to five chapters. All of the chapters approach Whiteness and race from a critical vantage point, problematizing identity within the Canadian context, and also providing linkages to the international arena. We would like to emphasize that this book need not be discounted as only addressing Canadian issues; on the contrary, it relates to common concerns everywhere, and Carr has used the book in a doctoral course in the US when he taught there, receiving much support and appreciation from the students once they surmounted the initial shock that the book did, indeed, originate in Canada. Education is a central focus to this volume, and is approached from a broad perspective. The range of authors, in terms of racial identity, ethnic origin, gender, region, discipline, and experience builds on our belief that Whiteness is multi-faceted, complex, and permeates human experience in this society. For far too long, many White people have believed, or have been led to believe, that race and racism are concerns only of those who are directly affected by it as its targets, and we challenge that notion through the book. George Sefa Dei's wonderfully critical and engaging Foreword, both for this second edition, and for the first edition, helps set the tone for the entire volume.

The first section sees authors conceptualizing Whiteness. The chapters presented therein provide an array of examples and insights as to how White identity is constructed and reinforced in Canada from the moment of birth. We need to understand how our own biographies and experiences shape and limit our identities and consciousness, and the path we must take to transform them. The barriers to teaching and learning are documented in this chapter, and the concept of power is underscored as being key to understanding how to achieve equity as well as, importantly, breaking the silence of Whiteness.

The second section is entitled "Whiteness and Second Peoples." As a society, we are so confident of the validity in the normative actions of White Christians that it will surely come as a jolt to some to hear of the colonizers of the First Nations as "Second Peoples." These chapters present important concepts of how we should deal with Whiteness once we have unearthed it, examining the place of both White people and non-White people in the struggle for social justice. This section opens the problematic of White people doing research on Whiteness and others, a common concern among antiracism workers: Who should be researching whom, and how? It can be painful to face White privilege and White guilt; and it can be frustrating to deal with issues related to Whiteness and White identity in a diverse nation such as Canada. Nevertheless, the quality of the relationship with disadvantaged groups depends on being vigilant about the many implications of positions of privilege.

The third section examines developing and de-constructing White identity, including the ability to be colour-blind and not colour-blind simultaneously as the hallmark of the achievement of a mature, anti-racist, White identity. There is never an endpoint to White racial identity development; the work continues as it transforms itself but, significantly, this work must be rendered visible. Attempting to achieve a more critical consciousness of lived and societal experiences through structured programs is one way of laying the groundwork for difficult, but necessary, conversations about race. Emphasizing that individuals and groups experience racism differently, the authors in this section warn against avoiding tackling race issues because of the illusion of colour-blindness, which deflects and denies the lived experiences of racial minorities.

The fourth section deals specifically with teaching, learning, and Whiteness. Ultimately, this analysis of Whiteness unearths and confirms the problem of over-generalizing about identity. Protecting and nourishing ethnic, cultural, and linguistic identity, as is the case for Francophones in Canada, is a complex enterprise, and the connection to Whiteness may, therefore, take on different shapes and forms. These chapters expose the deeply entrenched beliefs of White, middle-class university students, many of whom adhere to flawed beliefs about Canada as a pure meritocracy. The goal remains to implicate privileged students personally in an interrogation of their own roles in oppression.

The last section of the book deals with the institutional merit of Whiteness, building on the previous sections with chapters and dealing specifically with contentious educational issues related to identity and race. For school administrators and teachers, questioning their own predispositions and identities is a necessary component to understanding the educational experience of the students in their school. There remains a need to focus on accountability in how contentious school-based situations and policy development are handled, emphasizing the inequitable power relations framing school codes and policies used to assert Whiteness.

CONCLUDING THOUGHTS

We feel honoured once again to have our good friend George Sefa Dei involved in the book for the intensely critical pedagogical perspectives he brings to his work, and to attend to some of the pitfalls encountered when researching and writing about Whiteness. In reading this revised volume, it is inevitable that some will still contest specific aspects of these analyses of how Whites are fully immersed in the swamp of inequitable power relations. As a living and vibrant field, the community of researchers need not speak with a single, consensual voice. We hope that the plurality of views put forward here, and the reframing of the original pieces, will foster deeper conversation and stimulate further activism in eradicating racism and other forms of oppression and inequity. The authors of each of these chapters critically examine diverse perspectives and contexts as well as the construction and application of societal and institutional practices that underpin inequitable power relations and disenfranchisement based on racial identity. Each chapter concludes with a series of Questions for Reflection to foster further analysis and self-critique in readers as they continue to interrogate Whiteness. The relevance and salience of this text, we believe, extends far beyond the Canadian context, and we hope those in other global settings will find abundant and poignant lessons for their own transformative work in education with a particular focus on promoting social justice. We are very open to continuing the debate, and to stimulating new forms of inquiry and critique, and we welcome any and all follow-up aimed at making Canada and the world better places.

REFERENCES

Baergen, W. P. (2000). *The Ku Klux Klan in Central Alberta*. Red Deer, AB: Central Alberta Historical Society.

Bush, M. E. L. (2005). *Breaking the code of good intentions: Everyday forms of Whiteness*. Lanham, MD: Rowman & Littlefield.

Carr, P. R. (2008). The "equity waltz" in Canada: Whiteness and the informal realities of racism in education. *Journal of Contemporary Issues in Education, 3*(2), 4–23.

Carr, P. R. (2011). *Does your vote count? Critical pedagogy and democracy*. New York, NY: Peter Lang Publishing.

Carr, P. R., & Lund, D. E. (2009). The unspoken color of diversity: Whiteness, privilege, and critical engagement in education. In S. Steinberg (Ed.), *Diversity and multiculturalism: A reader* (pp. 45–55). New York, NY: Peter Lang.

Church, E. (2007, May 31). White people need to face role in racism, academics say. *Globe and Mail*, p. A5.

Churchill, W. (1998). *A little matter of genocide: Holocaust and denial in the Americas, 1492 to the present*. San Francisco, CA: City Lights.

Dei, G. J. S., Karumanchery, L. L., & Karumanchery-Luik, N. (2004). *Playing the race card: Exposing White power and privilege*. New York, NY: Peter Lang.

Dei, G. J. S., & Kempf, A. (2006). Anti-colonialism and education: *The politics of resistance. Rotterdam, the Netherlands: Sense.*

Daniels, J. (1997). *White lies: Race, class, gender, and sexuality in White supremacist discourse.* New York, NY: Routledge.

Ellsworth, E. (1997). Double blinds in Whiteness. In M. Fine, L. Weis, L. Powell & M. Wong (Eds.), *Off White: Readings on race, power, and society* (pp. 259–269). New York, NY: Routledge.

Feagin, J., & O'Brien, E. (2003). *White men on race: Power, privilege, and the shaping of cultural consciousness.* Boston, MA: Beacon Press.

Fine, M., Weis, L., Powell Pruitt, L., & Burns, A. (2004). *Off White: Readings on race, power, and society* (2nd ed.). New York, NY: Routledge.

Fleras, A., & Elliot, J. L. (2003). *Unequal relations: An introduction to race and ethnic dynamics in Canada* (4th ed.). Toronto, ON: Prentice Hall.

Henry, F., & Tator, C. (2005). *The colour of democracy: Racism in Canadian society.* Toronto, ON: Nelson Thompson.

Howard, G. R. (1999). *We can't teach what we don't know: White teachers, multiracial schools.* New York, NY: Teachers College Press.

James, C. E. (2003). *Seeing ourselves: Exploring race, ethnicity and culture* (3rd ed.). Toronto, ON: Thompson.

Jensen, R. (2005). *The heart of Whiteness: Confronting race, racism, and White privilege.* San Francisco, CA: City Lights.

Kinsella, W. (2001). *Web of hate: Inside Canada's far right network* (2nd ed.). Toronto, ON: HarperCollins.

Klassen, T., & Cosgrove, J. (2002). Ideology and inequality: Newspaper coverage of the employment equity legislation in Canada (Working Paper Series # 28). Toronto, ON: Centre for Research on Work and Society at York University.

Lea, V., & Helfand, J. (Eds.). (2004). *Identifying race and transforming whiteness in the classroom.* New York, NY: Peter Lang.

Lund, D. E. (2006a). Everyday racism in Canada: Learning and teaching respect for Aboriginal people. *Multicultural Education, 14*(1), 49–51.

Lund, D. E. (2006b). Rocking the racism boat: School-based activists speak out on denial and avoidance. *Race, Ethnicity and Education, 9*(2), 203–221.

Lund, D. E. (2006c). Waking up the neighbors: Surveying multicultural and antiracist education in Canada, the United Kingdom, and the United States. *Multicultural Perspectives, 8*(1), 35–43.

Lund, D. E. (2012). Multicultural education in Canada. In J. A. Banks (Ed.), *Encyclopedia of diversity in education* (pp. 296–301). Thousand Oaks, CA: Sage.

Lund, D. E., & Carr, P. R. (2010). Exposing privilege and racism in the great white north: Tackling whiteness and identity issues in Canadian education. *Multicultural Perspectives, 12*(4), 229–234.

Lund, D. E., & Carr, P. R. (2012). Disrupting white privilege in teacher education. In P. C. Gorski, K. Zenkov, N. Osei-Kofi, & J. Sapp (Eds.), *Cultivating social justice teachers: How teacher educators have helped students overcome cognitive bottlenecks and learn critical social justice concepts* (pp. 108–125). Sterling, VA: Stylus.

McCarthy, C., Crichlow, W., Dimitriadis, G., & Dolby, N. (2005). *Race, identity and representation in education* (2nd ed.). New York, NY: Taylor & Francis.

McIntyre, A. (1997). *Making meaning of whiteness: Exploring racial identity with white teachers.* Albany, NY: SUNY Press.

McLaren, P. (2007). *Life in schools: An Introduction to critical pedagogy in the foundations of education* (5th ed.). Boston, MA: Pearson Education.

Pitsula, J. M. (2013). *Keeping Canada British: The Ku Klux Klan in 1920s Saskatchewan.* Vancouver, BC: UBC Press.

Rodriquez, N. M., & Villaverde, L. E. (Eds.). (2000). *Dismantling white privilege: Pedagogy, politics, and whiteness.* New York, NY: Peter Lang.

Sleeter, C. E. (2005). How White teachers construct race. In C. McCarthy, W. Crichlow, G. Dimitriadis, & N. Dolby (Eds.), *Race, identity and representation in education* (2nd Ed.). New York, NY: Routledge.

Sullivan, S. (2006). *Revealing whiteness: The unconscious habits of racial privilege.* Indianapolis, IN: Indiana University Press.

Trifonas, P. P. (Ed.). (2003). *Pedagogies of difference: Rethinking education for social change*. New York, NY: RoutledgeFalmer.

Willinsky, J. (1998). *Learning to divide the world: Education at empire's end*. Minneapolis, MD: University of Minnesota Press.

SECTION 1

CONCEPTUALIZING WHITENESS

KATHLEEN S. BERRY

EXPLORING THE AUTHORITY OF WHITENESS IN EDUCATION

An Auto-Ethnographic Journey

INTRODUCTION

Using certain archeological premises of Foucault, the task in this chapter is to examine, track, deconstruct, excavate, and critique the existence of Whiteness in informal and formalized educational locations. The purpose is to reveal how the power and privilege of Whiteness has been created, circulated, and sustained through a socio-historical process of hegemony that questions, if indeed, Canada is a location for racial diversity and pluralism at the individual, societal, institutional and national levels. To examine and expose hegemonic practices of systemic and epistemic racism in Canada, I author an auto-ethnographic text as a White, Canadian woman privileged mainly by my immersion in the invisible constructs of Whiteness. Through my auto-biography as an ethnographic, historical process (not linear or chronological) that constructs and locates me in several discourses and practices, I am able to disclose not only the authority of Whiteness in Canadian society but discuss how the very invisibility of Whiteness works to generate, circulate and maintain racism in Canadian society and its institutions. The spaces and times of the auto-ethnographic text show where Whiteness hides in ancestral and inherited grand narratives, such as Euro-centric history and rationality, Christianity, and Colonization, that have constituted modern, Western education.

METHODOLOGY

In a manner similar to *bricolage* (Denzin & Lincoln, 2005; Kincheloe & Berry, 2004), I employ a mixture of analytical tools to dig and connect the personal to the political authority of Whiteness in Canada. The methodological *bricolage* includes elements of Foucault's archeological analysis (Frankenberg, 1993), auto-ethnography and axiology. In addition, the theoretical *bricolage*, taken mainly from the field of Critical Studies, is threaded throughout my auto-biography as interpretive discourses to further move the personal into the political. A criss-cross of these discourses attempts to prevent a simple chronological unraveling of a personal history. Instead, an archeological analysis of an auto-ethnographic text (Jones, 2005) surrounds the personal in the political, social, and economic powers of the time and space in which

D. E. Lund & P. R. Carr (Eds.), Revisiting The Great White North?, 13–26.

the story takes place. I borrow from Carolyn Ellis' *The Ethnographic I* (2004) as a way to present and write autobiographical research.

I purposely selected certain excerpts from my autobiography that best expose the invisibility of Whiteness. Although not a disclosure of all the invisible locations of Whiteness in Canadian life, I use the selected excerpts to move the personal in and out of the individual level to indicate where Whiteness exists at its most seductive levels of concealment—the societal, institutional and Western civilizational levels.

Another researcher, Frankenberg (1993), to whose work on Whiteness I often turn for theoretical and pedagogical assistance, has generated a useful research process that helps me focus my thinking yet avoid a totalizing "grand narrative" that seeks unity, coherence, and closure. Frankenberg guides the researcher through: (a) an *examination* of products of Whiteness; (b) a *tracking* of whiteness as it moves into formal and institutional, political processes; (c) a *deconstruction* of ways whiteness marks literary, cinematic, and scholarly practices; (d) an *excavation* of the limit points of whiteness, enabling reflection on the disciplinary practices that reinforce race as a historically constructed system of differentiation, exclusion, and belonging; (e) a *critique* of white complicity with reproduction of racial domination along a continuum from conscious to unselfish conscious enlistment; and finally (f) an *articulation* of strategies/action for development of antiracist, activist, and [transformative] practices (p. 70). In the limited space of this chapter, I have only scratched the surface of these different areas.

Another area of the *bricolage* known as axiology (Kincheloe & Berry, 2004) is also threaded throughout my autobiographical texts. In education, for example, the cloak of Whiteness generated by Western rationality and European Imperialism are handmaidens to capitalistic driven economies that need individualism and competition for material goods as human capital and subject formation. In turn, these organizing "grand narratives" are intersected by other discourses such as Christianity, patriarchy, and heterosexuality that serve to privilege Whiteness. This criss-crossing of grand narratives and shifting contexts is known as axiology. I include axiology as an attempt to avoid essentializing, normalizing, generalizing, and abstracting locations of Whiteness from the lived world. In other words, the power and privilege of Whiteness does not apply in all contexts or to all people at all times; neither is power and privilege stable, constant, or unified. In the modern world, however, Whiteness acts as a dominant construct for assigning power and privilege in Canadian society and institutions.

EXPOSING WHITENESS

Patterson (in Frankenberg, 1997) defines Whiteness as:

> the culture that the dominant peoples of the world possess; it was created
> socially and structurally by a society. Whiteness can be defined by several strong
> features including, capitalistic market society structure; belief in progress and

science, possession of modern concepts of family and societal group structures based on individualism, competition, social mobility, and belief in Eurocentric cultural, philosophical, and economic superiority. In a phrase, whiteness refers to ways of living that are discursive practices that were formed out of a culture associated with western European colonial expansion. (p. 104)

The difficulty of spotting Whiteness in educational arenas is that it is the invisible epistemological and ontological construct against which all others are compared and marginalized. Many of us are accustomed to studying about the oppression, silencing, and marginalization of other races without a critical awareness of the race that is camouflaged by White complicity and privilege. Dyer (1997) argues that, looking, with such passion and single-mindedness, at non-dominant groups has had the effect of reproducing the sense of oddness, differentness, exceptionality of these groups, the feeling that they are the departure from the norm. Meanwhile the norm [whiteness] has carried on as if it is the natural, inevitable, ordinary way of being human (p. 141).

Assumptions that White is right are packaged covertly in several locations of education. Teachers' subject formation, parents' desires, administrators' agendas, literary and subject area texts, curriculum artifacts, and government policies are all players in the circulation of Whiteness as authority.

The "grand narratives" of Western Enlightenment: namely, European imperialism and history; Christian spirituality, morals, and ethics; immigration; capitalism; individualism; the globalizing (Americanizing) of the world though modern technologies and media; and the compatible wars of positioning, discourse, and agency constitute a few of the organizing devices of modern education. At the time of conception, these frameworks provided the philosophical foundations that, in the context of their creation, structured modern society's systems of epistemology, subject formation, economics, politics, and public and private institutions. Since the structural frameworks of modern education were developed and circulated mainly by Western Europeans in the earlier part of modern life, these frameworks were established in order to unite, advance, support, control, and organize the population. The assumptions generated at conception were discursively producing Whiteness as power in many domains, from politics to education. In other words, as Daniels (1997) claims, "White supremacy is a central organizing principle of social life and systems... historically developed as institutional privilege and as ideological justification" (p. 11).

I grew up in a post-war, all white community in Maritime Canada but was told long ago stories, jokes, and rhymes (i.e., "enee, menee, minee, mo, catch a n___ by the toe") by friends and relatives, including the racist discourse that shaped my knowledge about the Other. I was read to or read stories of Other and of me-ness: *Huckleberry Finn, The Hardy Boys, Charlie Chan, Ann of Green Gables, Little Black Sambo, The Bobbsey Twins, Uncle Remus stories, The Five Chinese Brothers*, and would sneak peeks at the National Geographic pictures of "foreigners" while visiting neighbours' cottages or hiding under the stairs at the public library. Some readings engaged my imagination with overtly recognizable racial characters but covertly, I realize now, identified with Whites, like Ann and the Bobbsey twins, both in terms of their privileges and their agency. I had to read *Uncle Tom's Cabin* because I inherited an antique salt dish from Gram Berry. It was from the Doctor Lincoln who tended to Harriet Beecher Stowe's children when they were sick. Gramp, a self-taught man, taught me to work hard; he had five jobs during the depression, one of which was for the Canadian National Railways. He pointed out the black conductors but I don't remember talking to them. Mi'kmaq women came to the door selling their hand-woven willow baskets, but I hear that warning "Don't let them in the house Roy, they'll steal everything we have" [at the time for me it was legitimized by a voice (Grandmother's) of authority, circulated and consented to by the society in which it was spoken as truth]. I watched ten-cent Saturday matinees of John Wayne's cavalry and cowboys, fighting for the rights of Whites against those damn Indians. If I was lucky and finished my homework, I got to stay up an extra half hour to listen on the radio to the Jack Benny Show. I still can hear the black butler's raspy voice. "Dad, why do negro [a discourse used then] people talk funny!" My mother took Dad's shirts to the Chinese laundry to have the collars starched and we ate at the Chinese restaurant on special occasions. There were only two or three Chinese families in town. I can't remember where they lived or if they went to school or church.

That was the extent of my early surface exposure to a racialized world and, if noted, it was mainly through symbolic texts such as conversations and books. It seems that I was very comfortable and safe in that world, unknowingly because I already was carving out a stake in Whiteness. There were some contradictions, an occasional resistance, and those were primarily because of a difference in gender, body, and class. There were few reasons to resist or loathe family knowledge, values, history, or activities. The family's position and positioning of me in Whiteness was compatible, in most cases, with the Canadian societal and civilizational knowledge and values of the times that still reverberate today. Racism and the privileging of Whiteness still echo throughout that community today, but the latter is made even more invisible by the assumptions that multiculturalism and anti-racist policies have eradicated racist discourse and practices. The invisibility of Whiteness has been pushed even further to the background and allows complicity with the privilege of Whiteness to continue. For example, recently in my community a neighbour (White), angry at another neighbour (White), said he called him everything but "White," implying all other races are inferior and stupid. When I mentioned that was a racist statement, he passed it off, saying "I'm not racist... I have a friend who is Black."

Family is the first location where we learn our position because of Whiteness. Although the contexts and discourses vary, Whiteness and its axis with gender and class, for example, are constantly present. The discourse of racism that I learned covertly and overtly from story-tellers, books, media, popular culture, and joke-tellers operates quite differently for me in my privileged status of Whiteness. The Other is delegated to a powerless, degrading position while I, as a naive but privileged subject, have little need to question the inherent racism. I can laugh at the jokes; they work to confirm how I am superior at the expense of the constructed "Other" as inferior. The childhood of my auto-biography partially tracks the forces of Whiteness that were experienced as natural, neutral, and normal. The "lived experience of race emerges as a political taxonomy of the subject" (Phillip as cited in Hill, 1997, p. 330). In the case of Whiteness, it emerges as invisible power.

How this and other constructs of power and oppression positions me in relation to my practices, materials, and students is the key to being a critical pedagogue. I know and experience the same constructs of racism today mainly by the blindness to White privilege. When attempts to raise the assumptions underlying White privilege, the Maritime communities in which I live are predominantly White raced. Unlike the large metropolitan and urban areas of Canada, resistance to complicity with Whiteness is not always fore-fronted when the majority of the population lives off the benefits of Euro-centric society and structures. Nothing is served by denial, guilt, or blame except continuing to uphold current power structures, to which I either contribute or resist in the entangled web of cultural hegemony. How do we examine the very fabric we created? Is this really transformative pedagogy (Ellsworth, 1989)?

Whiteness as invisible coincides with postmodern and post-structural notions of erasure. Derived from Derrida's methods of deconstruction, erasure is the removal of truths and knowledge garnered from the margins or the silenced. Used mainly as a deconstruction of text, erasure is applicable to the multiple locations of Whiteness in education. The question of how Black, how White, how yellow, how grey, how red has always seemed to disappear into the great Canadian national, rather than racial, identity; that is, it has been erased by the discourse of Canada's cultural mosaic and liberal multicultural discourse. Race is left unchallenged when consumed by the seductive discourse of the benefits and existence of "how lucky we are to be Canadian," or "there's no other place I'd rather be," "we've got the second highest quality of life." But we forget, erased by assimilation, that racial differences become over-powered by national identity; that is "White" as the norm, the standard. For example, the removal of the Lord's Prayer occurred in public schools as a supposed removal of religion in schools. However, nationalism still exists to erase the presence of racism, which becomes collapsed in discourse such as "Oh Canada."

The subject formation of teachers as a location of Whiteness is cultivated beyond the family and individual levels into the broader societal levels. The process continues: Also mingled in my cultural mosaic were four Jewish kids (sometimes we played street ball together but never had sleepovers, and a dozen Catholic friends (we had sleepovers). With no Jewish troop available, Janet joined our Anglican girl guides; the Catholics wouldn't let any Jewish girls join their troop. Church Street had four Protestant churches, where every Sunday, some friends were United, some friends were Baptist, some were Anglican, and the friends from the "other side of the tracks" were Salvation Army. The class distinctions were clearly marked both within and between churches by what "big names" belonged to what church, the amounts in the church funds, and who wore what on Sundays. I memorized the

Anglican catechism so I could win a trophy, read the Bible so I wouldn't go to hell, and was taught that Jesus drove the Jews from the temple for money-lending. I believed in Jesus as a "real" man, so much so that I wanted to be an Anglican nun until, in training, I was told by the Reverend that church law said women couldn't be ordained. Catholic friends had to go to confession every Friday before they could go to the Young Men's Christian Association dances. The Y. M. C. A. had a swimming pool, dances, lots of money, and a huge building. The Y. W. C. A. only had ballet, tap, and a small, donated building down the street. Girls went to the YMCA but boys never went to the YWCA. Homophobic discourse was learned in jive joints and jokes; "Are you going to Alice's party?" "Alice who?" "Alice in Wonderland, all fairies are invited." This was told without any realization that gay and lesbian friends and family members were standing there; they only existed in jokes and the silence about homosexuality.

The host of cultural constructions that guides my positionality through Whiteness materializes further in the preceding second section of my auto-biographical narrative. Beyond the family, my privileged positioning by Whiteness was furthered by the expectations, rituals, clubs, rules, and standards established by participation in societal and institutional activities such as Girl Guides, Young Men's Christian Association, Protestant churches, community sports, and dating. The process of shaping constructions of gender, class, religion, relationships, sexuality, and how I am positioned in them are apparent. Where Whiteness locates me in privilege is not so obvious.

My Baptist and Anglican upbringing telescoped my knowledge, beliefs, and identity to read the world as a White Christian, including relationships and how I teach. In most incidences, my Christian history was compatible with the Christian foundations of Western education. Although I mentally and bodily left those institutions in 1962 (a reverse conversion!) because of their denial of feminism, I know that even today I still approach my daily life steered, in part, by Christian principles. Sometimes I recognize its tenets in my actions and decisions, such as "turn the other cheek," "save the children," or my Good Samaritanism for those "less fortunate." I remember now that, although we all played together, there were definite visible boundaries between Protestants, Catholics, and Jewish children as well as an absence of other religions. What was also being established were the invisible boundaries that empowered Protestant Christians over all others; that is to say a positioning of privilege by a "White" Euro-centric, state-initiated religion (Anglican) formalized by the institution of church.

My taken-for-granted thinking and actions are indicative of larger unexplored systems of Whiteness, such as Western rationality and Christianity. These grand narratives continue to circulate among educational history, ideas and artifacts, further institutionalizing Whiteness. Since a major mainstay of Christianity is conversion, not just in spirituality but in policy and principle, cultural differences of the converted are soon contaminated and consumed by the world of Whiteness, masquerading as saviours, deliverers from evil (a binary construct), redeemers, rescuers, and forgivers. With the bible as the guiding-light and European colonizers as the sailors, Christianity positioned the colonized as savages, ignorant, and uncivilized; in other words, inferior. These initial teachings became formalized in educational sites such as churches and schools. Christianity became invisible in the defining processes of colonization and emerged as a signifier of Whiteness, "a conversion to civility, social mobility, economic security, and cultural refinement" (Babb, 1998, p. 12).

In my childhood, going to the Protestant churches was another source of values, morals, and ethics, but it was also a silent source of knowledge about gender, class, and race, and an agent for positioning me in Whiteness and racial privilege. For my parents, school and church were connected to privileges, especially the Anglican church with its British, middle/upper class ambiance. Although public school policy denounces Christian teachings as part of the school curriculum, I sense, like Dyer (1997), that "its ways of thinking and feeling are none the less still constitutive of both European culture and consciousness [and educational institutions] and the colonies and ex-colonies (notably the USA) [and Canada] that it has spawned" (p. 15).

Finally, my auto-biographical narrative moves further into formalized education, including high school, university, and teacher education. In school, Dick and Jane were my first readers. I could dramatize "Look, look, look" so well that I got As on my report card. "This girl shows promise" was stated, now in retrospect, because of my complicity with text. My identity was confirmed by these readers; I related to Jane and I had a really nice Mom and Dad just like her and—some days—brothers like Dick. My Mom and Dad talked about how when Dad gets a promotion, we will be able to get a bigger house just like Dick and Jane. Even today, I have a copy of my grade four readers and the social studies textbooks from which I learned about how my Protestant relatives of long ago were driven out of Europe and came to fight for land from the Indians, but peacefully, and for freedom from religious persecution, by either Catholics or other Protestants. I learned how the ancestors of our town's nearby Acadian French communities wouldn't leave the country to make way for the British to access Lower Canada. In 1776 their families were split up and sent in many directions especially to the French territory of Louisiana. I was taught at home and school to believe that my relatives and textbooks were right and the French were wrong. If I challenged or disagreed, I would fail the provincial exams. In 1966, my English grandmother was horrified I dated a French boy and a "Catholic to boot"! I believed that my relatives were wrong but the societal pressure for a Protestant, English-speaking girl to not marry a French Catholic boy decided our relationship so we parted. The textbooks in high school, even today I can see the covers—history, math, geometry, literature anthologies, science, physics, music, art—but none for gym classes.

Whiteness existed between the covers; Greek battles fought against everyone so we could have a democracy; all the adventures of colonization—sword fights and sailing ships—to conquer and rescue "backward" people. Not only were the heroes male but White. In World War I and II, where all my British ancestors and Canadian relatives appeared on the pages as the good guys while the bad guys were everyone else from those "other" countries. Whiteness entered my knowledge and values through Greek math—Pythagoras' theorems and base ten numbers; British poets and authors, the scientific revolutions of Galileo, Copernicus, Newton, and Einstein, and Madame Curie; the art of Rembrandt, Picasso, Van Gogh, and Monet; the history and music of Chopin, Beethoven, Bach, and Handel. And when I hear this knowledge in the classrooms of 2006, I know Whiteness is still being circulated. If I learned anything about Eastern culture and history it was either because Europeans or Americans invented it (Said, 1978), discovered it, conquered it, or wrote about it. In teachers' college and university, I learned more about White supremacy, not consciously, but covertly in the theories of Locke, Rousseau, Dewey, objective lesson planning, (confirming scientific rationality) behaviour management, (confirming grand narrative of big business' need to control, manage human capital) and standardized (whose?) testing.

Schools are major sites for the discursive practices found throughout my auto-biographical narrative. Confirmation of Whiteness as dominant structures that creates epistemological, ontological privilege is confirmed in reading series such as Dick and Jane at the early level and social studies textbooks to the high school texts of geography, history, and literature. When Boyko (1998) reviewed the content of textbooks prior to the 1980s, he found the development of Canada was essentially of Ontario and Quebec and the French and English people, a reproducing of a Euro-centric history that invisibly privileges Whiteness. So over the decades since the 1940s of my childhood, it appears Whiteness continues to hegemonically superimpose its power.

Teacher education is another location for the perpetuation of the Whiteness of Western Enlightenment through foundation courses based on the ideologies of Kant, Locke, Rousseau and other western European philosophers who, in the case of Locke, very specifically states the superiority of the White race (Eze, 1997). Their thoughts are the major foundations that underpin the content and practices of education. Furthermore, these constructs that shape educational theory and practice are among the social forces that influence language, knowledge and ideology around the notion of the European Enlightenment. Compatible with the Enlightenment, today's teacher education programs still pay homage to the principles and structures of knowledge such as subject disciplines, objective outcomes, and standardized testing/courses. Even mathematics is based on Greek and Roman perceptions of the world. Time, measurement, angles, geometry and arithmetic, with its base ten configurations, are created out of the need for early Western rationality to manage, control, unify, shape, and govern a diverse population with its plurality of nation states, languages, cultural knowledge, and values. Cultural groups who construct time, place, organize family and spiritual centres, and build connecting artifacts such as tunnels and bridges did so without Western rationality. When asked to consent and conform to a different consciousness, however, the Other is positioned on the fringes of power or silenced. Those students with a Non-Eurocentric ancestry sit before me as they are forced to consent to time and space configurations that were created and enforced by Western rationality.

One of the prime influences shaping the dominance of Whiteness is the philosophical roots of Western thought. As a system built on the ideas and practices of early European philosophy, the Western Enlightenment created a history of traditions that empowered the dominance of White, middle-class, Christian, male, heterosexual culture evolving out of scientific rationalization, binary oppositions, objective consciousness and the rise of modern life. These elements of Western European Enlightenment have saturated our present-day educational system to the point that Whiteness lies invisibly dormant in the recesses of modern education as a set of neutral, taken-for-granted, hegemonic practices (Latouche, 1996). In so doing, education has structured a set of cultural practices that have, to date, advantaged White, middle-class, Christian, male, European-descent knowledge, values, traditions and so forth. The question becomes where do these practices fit in education? The philosophical foundations are "linked to unfolding relations of dominance" (Frankenberg, 1993, p. 6) which not only systematically privilege those with cultural and historical membership, but position everyone in relation to standards of Whiteness as the norm. Exposing and examining Whiteness, however, is not meant to "reconfirm the centrality, normalcy and authority of whiteness but to recognise the power and privilege thus preventing its continuance... its power to include and exclude" (Dyer, 1997, p. 10). Education is both a breeding-ground for the logic of Whiteness and the sets of structuring devices that circulate and maintain the *status quo*. In other words, Canadian education maintains unequal relations and contributes to social injustices, locally, and nationally.

The over-abundant standardization of educational systems by a dominant way of knowing, organizing, and being, such as the Enlightenment and its legitimation by hegemonic practices, including the predominance of Whiteness as neutral and invisible racism, extinguishes any postmodern wish for plurality, diversity, and creativity. Plurality as a postmodern construct demands the eradication of standardization/ standards. This move to plurality is diminished if not eliminated, in the constructs of Enlightenment projects. Just as oppositional binaries and Euro-centrism have defined rationality, scientific objectivity, and the separation of mind (as cognitive, biological), body (as object), and spirituality (as metaphysical waste), so to as modern education. The public (ignited by the likes of publishers, government interests, and media) and educational professionals (fuelled by fears of loss of power, control and Whiteness) whine about diminishing "standards," the need for "standards," plus more and earlier "standardized" testing. What, in fact, is happening is a need to maintain control over the privileges that come with a society based on Whiteness, which is similar to what Claude Steele (1999) found upon his return to a small liberal-arts school. What he mainly heard from the African-American students of the 1990s was, like his visits thirty years ago, "the curriculum was too white, they heard too little black music, they were ignored in class, and too often they felt slighted by faculty members and other students" (p. 44). In other words, racial integration still means assimilation into the "standards" designated by Whiteness. In 2006, Canadian education is not without the same invisible privileging of Whiteness.

History, as presented in modern times, is actually the history of White privilege and power. It was not until the rise of the Greek and Roman states and the expansion of Europe through colonization and imperialism, as Rodriguez (in Kincheloe & Steinberg, 1998, p. 61) points out, that "in the convergence of colonialism, capitalism, and subject formation," that Whiteness became a major signifier of power. To legitimize the creation of Greek and Roman states, European colonization and the supremacy of colonial imperialism, the racialized Other was born, a self-justification for Whiteness to emerge as an overarching ideology. Before that time, borders existed but they were based mainly on tribal, linguistic, religious, or ethnic divisions. Not only did the beginnings of Euro-modern times establish racial categories as border capital but it also established a Eurocentric culture of Whiteness that shaped a modern history of the East/Oriental (Said, 1987). To legitimize Western ideology and expansion, history is told/written/portrayed in such a way that continues to hide White imperialism while simultaneously circulating and maintaining its superiority, a similar set of discourses and practices initiated by Bush's war. In this "us" against "them" or "they" need "us" war of positioning, the historical consciousness is shaped as a judgment on the past in the name of a present truth (most often the legitimized truths of Whiteness, in addition to male, Christian, heterosexual, and so on). Counter-memory suggests "that the process of remembering can be a practice which transforms history... [that] combats our current modes of truth and justice, helping us to understand and change the present by placing it in a new relation to the past (p. 75). For my racialized memory, there was no call for counter-memory at the individual, societal or institutional levels. Even my memories positioned me in the privileges of Whiteness.

Memory and erasure are key points to include in the dominance of Whiteness as a history of imperialism and colonialism. As a person of European ancestry with limited, if any, interracial background other than White, I easily identified with the history lessons taught throughout my schooling, by my relatives, and by the racial sameness of my White community activities. My historical memory is informed by the great stories of heroes and their beginnings in Greek and Roman Empires, European nationalism, world wars, and Canadian contributions to the rise of Euro-American power. How my historical memory is shaped is more evident and trackable. Why it was shaped around these stories and erased certain other stories was, and still is, less obvious. Only in retrospect, though is the privilege of Whiteness made visible in my autobiography.

However, totalizing the privilege of Whiteness is as dangerous as ignoring its invisibility. This is where axiology draws in the multitude of contexts and experiences that shift the privilege of Whiteness. In other words, I am not always privileged as the politics of difference move me to the margins. Somewhere throughout all the social, historical shaping of who I am and how I read the world is the major event that initiated me into the politics of difference. Messages and signifiers of a difference that was not acceptable seeped into my life at the same levels of racism and exclusion that Scheurick (1997) mentions: individual, institutional, societal, and civilizational. I learned the politics of difference, like the racial Other, at a very early age: my fourth birthday looking out the window of an "isolation" ward of the hospital. I had contacted polio and, in those days before the 1956 salk vaccine, isolation (today it's called exclusion) was played out daily at all levels. Today, at the end of the glorious modern age, difference of any kind, still is put in the "isolation wards" of society or excluded from institutional regulations. I live in practice what for many is sometimes only theories of difference. At the individual level, parents pulling their children off the street when my mother and I walked down the street my interior monologue asking, "Why us Mom?" Parents, like the McManuses, who came to take my parents for a drive and deliver winter coats in spite of the quarantine sign on the apartment door. There was no socialized medicine so medical care was a handshake and good will by Dr. Cox and several nurses. Institutional locations I tried to enter were very clear on the regulations but individual interpretations and political implications for the institution varied in their degrees of inclusion based on a difference from the *normal*. The regulations and attitudes that prevented or allowed entrance into institutional structures were manifested, both overtly and covertly, at the individual or societal levels. In some cases it might have been my gender; my lack of middle-class articulation, educational qualifications or related work experience; or, quite simply, my appearance. It was clear to me that it was "the physical disability," as the applications for work and universities claimed. When refused entrance and interviews, my parents secretly (they thought) argued with employers and teacher college deans that I was not "crippled."

Although the word has changed to physically handicapped, physical disability, and differently-abled, it still acts in many ways as a totalizing discourse. Individuals and institutions trope physical disability with the images and facts that everything else must as well (e.g., intellect, interest, abilities, integrity, passion, ethics, and so on.) Interviews for teaching jobs, if I got one (the application asked if I had any physical disabilities), were mixed. Nuns said outright: "No, not in our school because of your arm" (in that context, I thought not being Catholic was a disability) or, that for special education school, "we think because of your arm you don't have the emotional stability to handle these types of children." I learned to lie, cheat, deceive, self-loathe, wear long sleeve puffy blouses and short skirts. It worked in many cases. I lied on that certain line on the application form, kept silent when the manager asked why, with a teachers' college education, I wanted a bank job. I cheated on the air stewardess application about my physical body, was accepted but was caught when I had to jump out of the simulator to rescue simulated passengers; a few drowned. I accepted my first teaching job on an isolated Northern Canadian armed forces base. There were very few applicants so I had a chance after several rejections (based on the continued categorization and discursive practices of physical disability) in the "big city" of Montreal.

The politics of difference thread their way through my auto-biography at several levels from individual and institutional to societal. A difference from the status quo and the discursive practices of essentializing and normalizing the body has served individual, society and institutional practices throughout many aspects of Canadian life. Borders of many kinds have prevented a difference from entering the mainstream for a variety of reasons, and I can guess it is because they are a threat to the established structures that maintain privilege. My major, visible difference disrupted knowledge, values, and structures that were in place, historically, and socially. That difference caused contradictions that challenged democratic participation, Christian charity, inclusive education, and community institutions. In my case, my difference pushed me to the margins of society and educational institutions. Those lessons I learned were not taught explicitly but discursively. Although privileged by Whiteness, at one level, for other reasons, I was not always privileged in Canadian society and institutions.

THE GREAT WHITE NORTH?

Through an auto-ethnographic journey, I have attempted to expose the invisibility and privileges of Whiteness assigned to many people that pass through the discourses and practices of Canadian life, especially that of education. The socio-historical passage through individual, societal and institutional levels of Canadian life opens doors for many based on the discourses, history and constructs of Whiteness. As discussed, however, it is not a matter of anger and guilt to expose the authority of Whiteness in Canada, but an awareness of where it exists as an invisible marker of privilege. To do so interrupts the assumptions that Canada is a multi-cultural society with equity, inclusion, and social justice for all.

As my autobiographical journey continues, I teach courses on Whiteness and introduce readings on the topic in other critical studies courses. Former students, like Mia and Ruby (pseudonyms), remember how annoyed they were initially when confronted with their Whiteness and its privileging of the raced subject in Canadian society. They, however, said that the course readings and discussions "opened their eyes about their contribution to [complicity] racism mainly by their lack of awareness of the role Whiteness plays" in the continuance of racism without the exposure of Whiteness in their everyday activities and practices, especially in their teaching. Ruby talks about "how schools in Atlantic Canada pay lip service to the cultural knowledge and values of Others [than Whiteness]." Mia remembers her rage at the beginning of the course, "thinking I was non-racist but then realized I took-for-granted my privilege [in Canadian society] by my complicity with Whiteness."

When I interviewed Mia and Ruby, they echoed what many researchers have found to be the initial response when students of any age are awakened to the privileging of Whiteness: anger, guilt and blame. But Mia wanted me to know that she attempted to change how she taught her elementary grade students to read a text for the privileges assigned by Whiteness, "very hard and dangerous." She elaborated further on how "we (White teachers in Atlantic Canada) have to start with ourselves even though it hurts too much at first."

Ruby expressed similar beginnings of anger and guilt as Mia. Ruby did try to evoke sensitivity to issues of privilege and marginalization based on a raced society.

She phoned a local newspaper reporter to alert her to how she had failed to decentre from her position of White privilege when reporting on the birth of the first New Year babies in the province. Ruby pointed out how the reporter positioned the White family as agents and superior, and devalued the birth of the child to an Aboriginal family by her discourse and erasure of the father (who was present at the birth). Ruby said she continues to follow the columns of the reporter, and has seen no evidence of her insensitivity to the privileging of Whiteness.

Until the invisible structuring devices, discourses and authority of Whiteness in Canadian society are exposed, the nation will continue to contribute to the circulation and maintenance of racism. The myths of multiculturalism, antiracism and the Canadian mosaic will continue to hide the privileges of Whiteness until the focus is shifted. At the same time, however, exposing and examining constructions of Whiteness is not meant to "reconfirm the centrality, normalcy and authority of Whiteness but to recognize the power and privilege thus preventing its continuance... its power to include and exclude" (Dyer, 1997, p 10).

QUESTIONS FOR REFLECTION

1. In what ways did/has Whiteness entered your life in Canada as either privilege and/or oppression?
2. In what times, materials, and spaces of your teaching moments does Whiteness hide and continue to circulate and maintain power and privilege?
3. What are the limits of the privileges of Whiteness in your daily life?
4. In what ways, and in what locations do individuals of non-Eurocentric ancestry, read Whiteness?
5. In what ways can you and your students/clients/family work to articulate and transform the authority of Whiteness at the individual, societal, community, and institutional levels of the local and national levels of Canada?

REFERENCES

Babb, V. (1998). *Whiteness visible: The meaning of whiteness in American literature and culture*. New York, NY: New York University Press.

Boyko, J. (1998). *Last steps to freedom: The evolution of Canadian racism*. Winnipeg, MB: Watson & Dwyer.

Daniels, J. (1997). *White lies: Race, class, gender, and sexuality in white supremacist discourse*. New York, NY: Routledge.

Denzin, N., & Lincoln, Y. (2005). *The Sage handbook of qualitative research*. New York, NY: Sage.

Dyer, R. (1997). *White: Essays on race and culture*. New York, NY: Routledge.

Ellis, C. (2004). *The ethnographic I: A methodological novel about autoethnography*. Walnut Creek, CA: Altamira Press.

Ellsworth, E. (1989). "Why doesn't this feel empowering?" Working through the repressive myths of critical pedagogy. *Harvard Educational Review, 59*(3), 297–325.

Eze, E. C. (Ed.). (1997). *Race and the enlightenment: A reader*. Cambridge, MA: Blackwell.

Foucault, M. (1982). *The archaeology of knowledge and the discourse on language*. New York, NY: Pantheon.

Frankenberg, R. (Ed). (1997). *Displacing whiteness: Essays in social and cultural criticism*. Durham, NC: Duke University Press.

Frankenberg, R. (1993). *White women, race matters: The social construction of Whiteness*. Minneapolis, MN: University of Minnesota Press.

Jones, S. H. (2005). Autoethnography: Making the personal political. In N. Denzin & Y. Lincoln (Eds.), *The Sage handbook of qualitative research* (pp. 763–791). Thousand Oaks, CA: Sage.

Kincheloe, J. L., & Berry, K. (2004). *Rigour and complexity in educational research: Conceptualizing the bricolage*. Maidenhead, UK: Open University Press.

Kincheloe, J. L., Steinberg, S., Rodriguez, N., & Chennault, R. (Eds.). (1998). *White reign: Deploying whiteness in America*. New York, NY: St. Martin's Press.

Latouche, S. (1996). *The westernization of the world: The significance, scope and limits of the drive towards global uniformity*. Cambridge, UK: Polity Press.

Said, E. (1978). *Orientalism*. New York, NY: Pantheon Books.

Scheurich, J. (1997). *Research method in the postmodern*. London, UK: Falmer Press.

Steele, C. M. (1999, August). Thin ice: "Stereotype threat" and Black college students. *The Atlantic Monthly*, pp. 44–54.

REFRAMING: KATHLEEN S. BERRY (2014)

With educational sites being consumed by involvement in the digital age, it seems that discussions around gender, race, sexuality, and other social issues are slowly disappearing into the neutrality and distancing of cyberspace. In addition, if educators forget the political history and struggles that began in the 1960s along with the limited gains made; if the political conservatism, far-right-wing rhetoric and religious/fundamentalist backlashers continue to gain strangleholds on the public social conscience; if media continues, with its powerful ability, to sell very carefully edited debates and hegemonic ideas to all political sides of the public by silencing or sensationalizing certain knowledge and truths; and if economic troubles dominate the consciousness, excuses, and actions of everybody in every facet of daily life; then perhaps it seems ludicrous even to reframe and reopen discussions of the privilege of Whiteness in Canada and, I add arrogantly, globally. Assuming, of course, they ever began or permeated educational sites, players, and practices?

Seven years since the publication of the *The Great White North? Exploring Whiteness, Privilege and Identity in Education*, is it important to reframe and foreground social ideologies and practices at the individual, societal, institutional and global levels? Definitely, more than ever. Based on the points presented in the first paragraph and several other factors, especially the global economic chaos in the first decade of the twenty-first century which allows the resurgence of blaming the Other and twisting or erasing crucial political and social truths, it becomes not a mere matter of exploring Whiteness but of a strong political commitment for societal, institutional and global members/leaders to somehow move the discussions, conferences, workshops and books into a wider political arena.

Since I wrote my chapter, *Exploring the Authority of Whiteness in Education: An Autoethnographic Journey*, I retired from academic life, and now spend six months in Canada and six in Florida. I enjoy the privilege of a comfortable life afforded to me by retirement funds and social Medicare and, obviously, without denial, my social and historical locations in Whiteness. Previously, my chapter explored, in an autobiographical style, the privilege afforded by my locations in sites of Whiteness. Furthermore, trying to escape sinking into the maudlin individualism that autobiographical accounts/research/writing often take, attempts were made to perform an archeological and genealogical exploration of locations and constructs of Whiteness, thus moving autobiographical history from the individual to societal, institutional and global locations.

Now: how to move my chapter from words to action, from the personal to the political? I cannot. Once retired, the connections to publishing as a way of circulating knowledge are diminished, if not nil. When retired, creating and circulating knowledge about critical pedagogy and ideas through teaching at any

D. E. Lund & P. R. Carr (Eds.), Revisiting The Great White North?, 27–29.

educational level, is impossible. Removed from the privileged circles of academia, I am afraid that, other than the readers and editors of my chapter, the words remain mere theory. What remains are two important questions. What responsibility and whose responsibility is it to enter the political arenas to reframe and invoke action to foreground how constructs of Whiteness have invisibly saturated every corner of history and life with its constructed ticket to privilege?

The critical retelling of the history of Western society and institutions is a starting point, however, not just in schools but inside families, textbooks, past and current media, inside churches, schools and economic institutions; from watching television and movies at home; from family trees to community archives; from schools to churches; from business to the public consciousness. Instead of retelling Western history as the binary constructs of conqueror and conquered brought on by colonization with the conquerors as, for example, heroes and deserving, and the conquered as, for example, uncivilized and the "Third World," we need to dismantle the knowledge that has circulated among families, textbooks, community, policies, and laws. And how does academia, a major source for generating and circulating critical knowledge and questions, move into those locations that have been stabilized through erased truths and hegemonic processes? We can talk racism and anti-racism, a problematic binarism in itself, yet actions tend to remain at the individual level or slip into the discourse and practices of quasi-academia.

Perhaps the cliché, "if you can't beat 'em join 'em"—referring in the case of critical theories and practices gaining access to the public social conscience—is where the debates and discourses of academia might out-source their own privileged location in Whiteness. Since the onslaught of popular culture and the pervasive presence of the digital world, here might be a way of inserting the debates and changing social conscience, laws, and practices. To fracture the binary status of academia and "Common Sense" (in itself, a socially, historically, politically constructed knowledge and truth) could argue with the social conscience at the same time as reframing it. Whether or not Michael Moore's movies did impact the far-right, conservative capitalists of their viewers, at least his movies entered mainstream popular culture and maybe influenced a few viewers and lawmakers.

For example, the APTN (Aboriginal Public Television Network) has foregrounded the culture, language, history, and so forth of the diverse world of Aboriginals. But there is not always a dismantling of the constructs, contradictions and conflicts lying invisibly below the surface. With the interactive possibilities of these types of digital communication, why not set up post-discussion sites and/or move these shows into schools where students can hear but also ask questions of the constructs? Mind you, a vast repertoire of questions that actually are informed by critical theory would need to be available for all viewers. Even within an ebook, a digital technology that I love, what if there were questions and possibilities on every page or chapter that had me re-read or respond to the book with a critically informed read? I think there are these possibilities already available but not necessarily with a critically informed mind.

Any changes in the future social conscience and practices from exploring Whiteness, privilege and identity? At the individual level, I look forward to a change when friends, family, neighbours, and colleagues respond differently to my comments on how, in North America, our wealth and power is *all* thanks to the land inhabited at one time by Aboriginal people. Instead of the complaints about tax exemptions and federal monies to "reserves," and all the other edited knowledge and mis-truths assigned by the conquerors through history, schooling, community mythologies, and so forth, hopefully the conversations will be changed. At the societal and institutional levels, hopefully the players will reframe the constructs through policies, laws, discourses, and history that will expose—not just explore— and then change the practices and politics of privilege.

TIM McCASKELL

BEFORE I WAS WHITE I WAS PRESBYTERIAN

INTRODUCTION

This chapter uses autobiography to examine the construction of White identities and their implications for anti-racist pedagogy. By reflecting on the development of my own understanding of race, racism and the role of Whiteness, first as a child in rural Ontario, then as a youth in a period of national liberation, as a young traveller, a gay activist and finally as an educator, I hope to cast some light on the development of individual White identities in Canada.

1955 TO 1958: A PRIMER

Beaverton, Ontario, where I live, is a village of 1200 souls nestled on the shores of Lake Simcoe, an hour and half north of Toronto. In Beaverton we are all Christian, and life revolves around church. Christians can either be Protestant (the best of whom are Presbyterians, the church that my family attends) or Catholic. My grandfather is an Orangeman and we always go to the Orange Parade to celebrate King Billy who defeated the Catholics and made the world safe for freedom and democracy.

There was once a Jewish family in Beaverton but they moved away when their daughter was old enough to date, because Jews are not allowed to go out with Christians. I get mixed up and tell a friend that our next-door neighbour—a Catholic—is a Jew, and my mother gets very upset. But I learn that even though Jews refuse to believe in Jesus you still shouldn't be mean to them. My father apparently even had a Jewish friend when he was in high school. Jews, however, are not allowed on the golf course in Beaverton because they are rich and noisy and would take over if you gave them half a chance.

Then there are French-Canadians. They are Catholic, live far away in Quebec and wouldn't fight in the war for the Queen, even though brave Canadian boys were dying. My father was in the army so he knew. It was their fault that nobody could read half the back of the cereal boxes.

The Italians, like the Jews, live down in Toronto, but they don't have cottages so they have to come to Beaverton to swim at our pier on Sundays. Although we kids regularly spend almost every waking moment swimming there during the summer, my friends won't go on Sundays because they say the *Eye-talians* make the water greasy. I'm never sure if it is because they use suntan oil or if it is something to do with their skin.

I want to be a cowboy when I grow up. Cowboys usually fight with Indians who, I am told, are Red, although you can't really tell on black and white television. My favourite, the Lone Ranger, has a sidekick named Tonto, who is an Indian, so it is possible to be friends. When I finally see Indians in colour at the movies, they aren't really Red after all, just light brown like a summer's tan. I am envious of Indians since they get to go around without their shirts on and ride horses bareback and have nice muscles. We, on the other hand, always have to wear clothes because we are civilized and Christian.

Indians live in tribes. There is a reservation called Rama[1] near Orillia, the town where my parents grew up. We drive past it to visit my grandparents but we never go in. My father says that Indians are always poor and on welfare because they drink too much beer. There are also some families in Beaverton who are on welfare even though they aren't Indians. My father calls them "tribes" too.

I soon learn that there are other parts of the world where people aren't civilized and Christian and they are of different colours. People in Beaverton don't really have a colour; we are White.

At *Children of The Church*, an after-school program held in our church basement, we sing a song called "Planting Rice Is No Fun." As we sing, we have to bend over and touch the floor and pretend to be planting rice which, when the song goes on for a long time, makes your back hurt. Then the missionaries come to save the children and we can stand up. My mother plays the music on the piano, and at the beginning and the end there are a series of funny musical chords that mean "Chinese." That's because the song is about Chinese people who are Yellow and always eat rice because they don't even have potatoes, and therefore, have to go to bed hungry. It's their fault you always have to finish your vegetables. We raise money to support the missionaries because that's what good Christians do.

Once a year the *Beaverton Lion's Club* puts on a Minstrel Show at the Town Hall. My father and all the other Lions put shoe polish on their faces and talk funny and tell jokes and sing songs like "Way Down Upon the Suwannee River." Sometimes they turn on special lights that make their eyes and lips and hats and bow-ties glow in the dark. Everyone finds it very beautiful.

Black people live in Africa. Even though they have nice muscles, Tarzan can always beat a whole tribe of them at once. He just picks one up and whirls him around over his head and throws him at the rest and they all fall down like bowling pins. Once, though, Tarzan has to fight a bad White man and it is more like cowboys fighting. They keep punching each other and falling down and getting up again. I wonder why Tarzan can beat a whole tribe of Africans but has so much trouble with one White man.

1959: THE SOUTH

I am eight and we drive to Florida for Christmas holidays. It turns out Black people don't really look like the ones in the Minstrel Show. The gas stations in the South always have three washrooms: Men, Women, and Coloured. I peek inside a Coloured washroom and it is really dirty. When I ask why Black people are treated so bad my mother says it's because White people think their skin is dirty. We are in a restaurant at the time and I ask if the White people think Black people are so dirty, why do they always let them wash the dishes. My mother looks confused and my father laughs.

A few years later in Sunday school we learn about Moses leading the Children of Israel out of slavery in Egypt in a big parade. We go to the movies and see it. My mother explains that in Florida Black people are parading so that they won't be treated like slaves anymore, just like the Children of Israel. Treating people bad just because of their skin colour isn't properly Christian, but a lot of the White people in the States don't understand that. We are lucky to live in Canada where nobody thinks that way.

1967 TO 1969: NATION

It's the hundredth anniversary of Confederation. We have our own flag and sing "O Canada" at school instead of "God Save the Queen." I spend hours at Expo '67 in Montreal, patiently waiting to see the different pavilions and even try to say a few words in French, because Canada is a bilingual country. Expo shows Canadians are fair, honest, liberal, peaceful, cosmopolitan, open-minded, modern, and welcoming. That's me. And anybody who wants to live like that is welcome to come here.

My final years of high school witness the assassinations of Martin Luther King and Malcolm X, the flowering of the Black Panthers, the Tet offensive against the Americans and their puppet regime in Vietnam, and the height of the anti-war movement. John Howard Griffin, author of *Black Like Me*, comes to speak at my high school. He talks about racism in the US, and links it to American intervention in Vietnam. It is the first time I consider that racism might be more than uncharitable acts by a few closed-minded people. While the talk stokes my self-righteous anti-Americanism, my Canadian identity shelters me from any sense of complicity with what the "Americans" are doing to Black and Yellow people.

At Carlton University there are some African students in residence. I have never really spoken to a Black person before. One day in an elevator I try to strike up a conversation by asking a young man if he is from Tanzania, a country I know is at the forefront of African liberation. He smiles and says, "That's interesting, last year people always asked me if I was from Kenya." I feel awkward, as if I have done something wrong.

1970 TO 1974: THE WORLD

I drop out of university and join the stream of "freaks" from Western Europe and America drifting overland around North Africa, the Middle East, and India. We pride ourselves on our rejection of the bourgeois lifestyle and move through the series of "exotic" landscapes, blowing our minds and always speaking English. Like modern day Tarzans, we are disdainful of our own "uptight" civilization and are much happier in strange, far-off lands. My journal entries of the time are peppered with romantic Orientalist descriptions on good days, and negative racial stereotypes on bad ones.

I am hitchhiking in the north of Argentina, and a truck driver picks me up. During the evening's conversation he says how upset he would be if his sister married someone Black or Indian, how lucky I am to live in a White country like Canada, and how he would like to go there. I look at him and say, "But in Canada, you wouldn't be White." Neither of us knows quite what to do with that information.

1974 TO 1978: POLITICS

Back in Toronto I join the Marxist Institute, a collective doing educational work. Someone suggests that we sponsor a lecture series on racism in Canada and I am bewildered. There is racism in the US, imperialist racism in the Third World, but surely in Canada racism is, at worst, a minor phenomenon. Over the course of the lecture series I have a kind of epiphany. For the first time I hear the voices of people of colour speaking about the petty, humiliating, life-destroying, infuriating, and sometimes violent and frightening racism they experience on a daily basis. Just as significantly, I finally begin to realize that I have been oblivious to all this because my colour has sheltered me from such experiences. I am White, not just when I travel, but in Canada, too.

I come out as a gay man. The quote that crowns the masthead of the local gay liberation journal where I volunteer states, "The liberation of homosexuals must be the work of homosexuals themselves." It is the experience of oppression that authorizes someone to speak about it, and to lead the struggle for change. The personal is the political. I learn not to speak for others.

Lesbians in the "gay movement" complain that gay men are just as sexist as straight ones. People of colour remark that whenever they talk about racism, White gay people always try to change the topic by bringing up homophobia. I learn to hold my tongue and not be so confident that I understand.

1979: ANTI-RACIST EDUCATION

I receive a call from a friend who is South Asian. He is working for the *Toronto Board of Education* (TBE) and has been asked to deal with a serious racial incident in a neighbourhood school. He feels he needs a White facilitator to work with him in the racially charged atmosphere. I begin to contemplate the utility of "speaking as" a White person. I can challenge other White people without being accused of having a chip on my shoulder or of being "racist against Whites." With me, White people can't play the race card.

By 1984, I am working for the TBE, facilitating antiracism discussions among students. Our working definition is "racism = prejudice + power." White people are the group with power. In one discussion, several Black youths have been talking about their experiences with police harassment. A White teen from Regent Park[2] becomes visibly angry. He says that he and his friends are being harassed by cops all the time, but since they are White and can't complain of racism, nobody cares.

As a facilitator should I challenge the "White guilt" that makes him defensive and prevents him from validating the experience of the Black youths? I opt to lead the group into an exploration of how social class also makes people vulnerable to mistreatment.

The core of my work at the TBE is organizing the twice-yearly anti-racist camps for secondary school students. Pairs of facilitators work with small groups of students to help them reflect on the impact of racism and other forms of oppression on their lives and in their schools. Each facilitating team is made up of a person of colour and a White person, one of whom is a man and the other a woman. Usually an experienced facilitator is paired with someone who has not facilitated the camp process before. That means that, as a White man with experience, I find myself consistently paired with less experienced women of colour. Is the fact that I often take leadership in managing the group a function of being a mentor, or a manifestation of white male domination? Can it be both simultaneously?

An exercise in the camp program asks participants to group with others of the same race, and to prepare a presentation on the significance of their racial identity. Students in the Black, South Asian, East Asian, Latin American, and Aboriginal groups usually emerge from the exercise confident, energized, and empowered, but the "White" group is always a problem. People literally don't want to go there. They express concerns that the exercise promotes "segregation." They worry about what others might be saying about them in the other groups. They are nervous about saying the wrong thing in their presentation. Sometimes Jewish participants form their own group although they "look White." That seems reasonable. Jews certainly have a history of racialization. Occasionally the "White" group divides, and the "Southern Europeans" go off on their own, claiming their experience is fundamentally different as immigrants to an "Anglo" Canada. At one camp some White female teachers go off on their own, asserting that as feminists, they don't identify as White either. It seems to me that a line is being crossed.

1992: EQUITY

The TBE establishes an *Equity Studies Centre* to bring together parallel work around racism, sexism, homophobia, disabilities, and class bias. We hope that a more intersectional approach will help us escape the dead ends of "identity-based politics" that often leave everyone competing to legitimate their oppression. There is a corresponding shift in emphasis away from the personal to the structural. For example, we try to incorporate the insights of Peggy McIntosh's (1988) notion of "White privilege" as a less threatening way of talking about racism to Whites, as well as sexism to men and heterosexism to straight people. We try to get learners to see that White privilege is something that White people acquire whether they want it or not. The choice is not having it, but whether to perpetuate it or address it.

We also begin to explore ways to talk about the "social construction of race" in order to challenge essentialist notions that shape commonplace ideas of what different "kinds" of people are "like." Talking about race as a social construction also helps expose reified racial categories such as those used in the *The Bell Curve* (Herrnstein & Murray, 1994), but puts us at odds with some anti-racist positions: the references to the four colours of peoples in some traditional First Nations teachings, the "sun people vs. ice people" dichotomy of Leonard Jeffries, (Appiah, 1994) or the racial ontologies of the Nation of Islam, for instance.

This new "equity" approach is still in its infancy when the Mike Harris *Common Sense Revolution,* the right-wing policy framework of the newly elected Progressive Conservative government, dismantles the TBE and its vision of progressive public education in 1997[3]. There is a public struggle over whether the policy of the newly amalgamated *Toronto District School Board* should reflect a strictly anti-racist approach, or a broader equity analysis – a battle between competing marginalities (Fumia, 2003). Although the broad equity policy is ultimately adopted, the ongoing crisis in public education means that among Toronto educators, the dialogue and the debates have still not recovered a decade later, while the problems we attempted to address have become more acute.

DISCUSSION

Among the basic principles of anti-racist education, (McCaskell, 2005) one especially relevant to this discussion is that anti-racist learning must be based on learners' experience. It follows then that the identity formation of White participants in an anti-racist process must be taken into account. These snapshots of my personal experience chart a range of White identities.

Research shows that children are capable of understanding racial identity at a very young age, (Goodman, 1964), but that does not mean they necessarily do so. For White children like myself, growing up in largely segregated communities, the racial "other" may have little more significance than cartoon characters on television. My identities for example, were located first in religion, and subsequently in nation and counter-culture left-wing politics. White privilege, which structured my life and opportunities, conspired to make the fact of my skin colour incidental to my consciousness. A pedagogy that seeks to engage White people requires that educators figure out the kinds of White identity that are present, and to identify their "zones of proximal development." (Vygotsky, 1978)

For example, in a world like that of my childhood, where Indians, Jews, Catholics, French Canadians, and Italians were conflated into one generalized category of "Other," and Black people were minstrel show caricatures, actual contact with real people from these groups was a precondition of any learning about race and racism on my part. My trip to Florida provoked my first questions about inadequate explanations for racial discrimination. My mother's linking of Sunday school Bible stories to the civil rights movement was, in retrospect, an appropriate and effective pedagogical strategy for a child of my age in the world where I lived.

The patronizing quality of my understanding of underdevelopment and race, grounded in the missionary tales of my childhood, continued to inform my Canadian nationalism as a teenager. Racism was something ignorant Americans did. At this point I needed to be introduced to a real history of racism in Canada and the forces that benefited from it. The clumsiness of my first attempt at conversation with the African student at Carlton was illustrative of the exoticization of the "Other" that continued to shape my understanding in my early travels. Simple contact was not enough. This young Canadian who considered himself progressive, anti-imperialist, counter-cultural, and anti-establishment had absolutely no notion of how the generalizations sprinkled throughout his diary, negative or not, were the building-blocks of a racist construction of the world. Although I certainly benefited from it, I still didn't think about Whiteness or privilege. For me at the time, the only people who thought that being White was important were racists, KKK members, and Nazis—and they didn't have anything to do with me.

A pedagogical strategy appropriate for my identity at the time might have built on my nascent understanding of imperialism while asking me to reflect how I personally benefited, and how the things I took for granted structured and limited my understanding of the world. The conversation I had with the Argentinian driver, if observed by an educator, would have been a stellar opportunity to investigate the social construction of race.

Coming out as a gay man deepened my understanding of the experience of oppression, but that understanding was limited by the tendency to think of oppression as one-dimensional. My friends and I needed to engage in a discussion of the similarities and differences between racism, homophobia, and sexism, and their intricate relationship to class. In the absence of such discussions, our world was troubled by circular debates about who was the most oppressed and jockeying to speak from the "victim" position.

My experience facilitating groups at the Toronto Board confirmed Mao's famous dictum about correct ideas coming from practice (Mao, 1963) It was in those discussions that I really learned about the contradictory ways that racism impacts young lives, and the strengths and limitations of my role as a White facilitator. Here I first began to struggle with the slippery slope between using Whiteness strategically versus catering to the discomfort of Whites. It was the practicality of those discussions that compelled me to integrate an intersectional approach. Sexism, class bias, and homophobia came up in our discussions of racism. They had to be worked through, or our groups would self-destruct. We had to recognize that race was not the only index of power.

The reluctance of White people to identify themselves as White remains an ongoing issue. An initial reflex in the early nineties was to talk about "White guilt," or in other words, the discomfort of identifying oneself with the power group. But it soon became clear that accusing Whites of exhibiting "White guilt" was not a particularly effective pedagogical strategy. It was just one more thing to be guilty about. Overcoming White people's difficulties and reluctance to recognize their Whiteness demanded an analysis of the identity and consciousness that gave rise to that reluctance.

First, we realized most White people, unlike people of colour, were unfamiliar with being singled out and grouped together by race. We needed to acknowledge that, and explore what it feels like to be identified by colour every day, despite individual differences. Second, we had to accept at face value that many of our White participants had really never thought of themselves as White before. Their identities were elsewhere. We could then spend time working with them to understand how those identities were constructed, the unseen benefits that White skin still bestowed on them, and *why* their Whiteness was invisible to them. Third, we had to recognize how privilege was distributed unevenly within the White group, and elsewhere, based on factors such as gender, wealth, class background, accent, origin, sexual orientation, religion, immigration history, and others. This was a springboard into the discussion of the intersection of different forms of oppression.

AUGUST 2006

I have been living with HIV for the last 25 years, and have just spent the last week as an activist at the *International AIDS Conference* in Toronto. The conference re-emphasized to me that my survival, when so many other have died and are dying, is also entangled with my Whiteness. Even in Canada I have access to medical care denied to many others. As anti-racists, our task is to fight to dismantle such material facts of White privilege and, in this case, ensuring equal access to treatment. As educators, then, part of our task is to understand the identities and consciousness engendered by White privilege, and to develop ways of transforming them.

For White people to become allies in anti-racist struggle, it is crucial that we understand not just the racialization of others, but our own Whiteness, both as a marker and a constituent element of our privileged cultural, national, and class location. We need to understand how our biographies and experiences shape and limit our identities and consciousness, (Bishop, 2002) and the path we must take to transform them.

QUESTIONS FOR REFLECTION

1. What is your personal trajectory of understanding White identity?
2. If you are White, how would you situate yourself in relation to the identity categories described in this chapter?
3. What do you feel is the relationship between racism and other forms of oppression?

4. Make yourself a list of the ways aspects of your social identity make you vulnerable to oppression, and secondly, the ways other aspects privilege you and potentially make you an oppressor.
5. How would you respond to the criticism that talking about Whiteness is just one more example of White people turning the focus of attention on themselves?

NOTES

[1] Rama is now known for its casino, and although much visited by gamblers of a variety of backgrounds from Toronto and central Ontario, there is still little connection between them and the lives of its Aboriginal residents.
[2] Regent Park, in downtown Toronto, was Canada's largest public housing development.
[3] In 1995, the Progressive Conservatives under Mike Harris swept to power in provincial elections in Ontario. They slashed educational funding and in 1997 forced the amalgamation of the Toronto Board of Education with five more conservative suburban Boards.

REFERENCES

Appiah, K. A. (1994). Beyond race: Fallacies of reactive Afrocentrism. *Skeptic, 2*(4), 104–107.
Bishop, A. (2002). *Becoming an ally: Breaking the cycle of oppression in people* (2nd Ed.). Halifax, NS: Fernwood.
Fumia, D. (2003). *Competing for a piece of the pie: Equity seeking and the Toronto District School Board in the 1990s* (Unpublished doctoral dissertation). University of Toronto, Toronto, ON.
Goodman, M. E. (1964). *Race awareness in young children.* New York, NY: Collier.
Herrnstein, R., & Murray, C. (1994). *The bell curve.* New York, NY: Free Press.
Mao, T. (1963/1971). *Selected readings from the works of Mao Tsetung.* Peking (Beijing), China: Foreign Languages Press.
McCaskell, T. (2005). *Race to equity: Disrupting educational inequality.* Toronto, ON: Between the Lines Press.
McIntosh, P. (1988). *White privilege and male privilege: A personal account of coming to see correspondences through work in Women's Studies* (Working Paper No. 189). Wellesley, MA: Wellesley College, Centre for Research on Women.
McIntosh, P. (1989). White privilege: Unpacking the invisible knapsack. *Peace and Freedom*, pp. 10–12.
Vygotsky, L. (1978). *Mind in society.* Cambridge, MA: Harvard University Press.

REFRAMING: TIM McCASKELL (2014)

Seven years is not a long time when talking about changes to notions of race and identity. But the seven years since the publication of *The Great White North* have been dramatic. The financial crisis of 2008 ushered in a period of prolonged recession, international instability, and growing social upheaval. In Canada it has accelerated an already alarming growth of disparity, and as The Colour of Poverty website (www.colourofpoverty.ca) points out, that disparity is increasingly racialized.

Landed immigrants are more marginalized and more exploited than immigrants were thirty years ago. Worse, Canada now receives more temporary foreign workers per year than immigrants. We are seeing the construction of a racialized underclass of indentured labourers without access to the most basic rights.

As racial disparities grow so does racism—on a popular level to make sense of those visible disparities, on a policy level to justify and excuse not dealing with them, and on a political level to shield those who most benefit from systemic injustice.

At the same time Whiteness is less and less a free pass. The Occupy Movement signaled the return of class when it identified the "one percent." Whiteness still provides me with privilege, but increasingly it seems to be of the "grandfathered" variety. Few young White people today can take the nonchalant approach to life that I did and still expect to succeed. As one young man pointed out to me recently, "When you were my age you could take risks; today things are much more competitive."

When I wrote *Before I Was White* it still seemed possible to assume a convergence of interests between liberal ideas of equal opportunity and more progressive notions of an egalitarian society. But what does it mean to have equal opportunity in an increasingly unequal society? Those two streams seem to be reaching a parting of the ways.

In Europe, the social contract is unraveling even more quickly. Entire populations are being reduced to poverty. At the same time, the continent continues to be a magnate for refugees fleeing economic misery, environmental degradation and political turmoil. We see there the predictable rise of xenophobic and racist sentiments and a resurgence of neo-fascist political formations. Monstrous identities once considered almost forgotten are being reactivated.

But this is not simply a return to the past, a slippage in the modernist trajectory of progress. Neo-liberal class disparities within racialized groups are also more and more profound. There *is* a Black president in the United States. His middle name *is* Hussein. In the White settler states especially, ruling elites *have* become more inclusive. It is no longer remarkable to hear "Brown, Black, and Yellow" speaking from positions of power. But they speak the same language as the more segregated elites before them, and to similar effect on those who do not share their privilege. Racial identities once spoke for class. Now they just as often obscure it.

D. E. Lund & P. R. Carr (Eds.), *Revisiting The Great White North?*, 41–42.
© 2015 Sense Publishers. All rights reserved.

This inclusion reflects a new slightly more integrated elite class structure, but also real shifts in balances of world power—economic, cultural and military. The echoes of colonialism and White imperial power are fading. New centres of power compete with declining imperialisms over finite resources. This produces not only a profusion of new identities and chauvinisms, but also increased instability and risk of war.

My article seven years ago focused on the evolution of my identity over the course of a lifetime. It mapped the development of broader social identities available to me. The concluding discussion examined the development of appropriate pedagogical principles to illuminate and challenge racism and other power relationships among white identities shaped by different social forces. But that discussion still assumed a relatively stable field of action, one that is now being increasingly disrupted.

In this new context, the meanings of identity are both more entrenched and less stable. They are also being innovatively deployed by power. Multiculturalism is used to justify homophobia and sexism. Secularism is used to police the behaviour of religious minorities. Gay rights are used to fuel the war build-up against Iran, and promote "ethical" oil from the Alberta tar sands. Feminism is enlisted to justify the invasion of Afghanistan. The Holocaust is mobilized to celebrate ethnic cleansing in Palestine.

Today's pedagogy must go beyond "challenging stereotypes." Prejudice + Power is no longer any more an adequate equation today than "Black Yellow Red White; Same Struggle Same Fight" was adequate for dealing with racism in the 1970s. How does our pedagogy grasp the new consolidation and fragmenting of power, the new profusion of identities, and the dangers of devastating war that they threaten? Do we consider our old certainties limited but heuristic propositions and try to build a deeper understanding on them? Or do we have to start someplace completely new based on the experience of learners today?

JAMES FRIDERES

BEING WHITE AND BEING RIGHT

Critiquing Individual and Collective Privilege

INTRODUCTION

I begin this chapter by discussing how Whiteness is a privilege that, while invisible to Whites, is hyper-visible to non-Whites. This discussion reveals why Whites resist analyzing the concept and the consequences of such resistance. I then focus on how I have dealt with Whiteness in my classes and discuss one strategy that has been used to overcome the silencing of non-Whites in the classroom. As a White male professor, Whiteness comes easy to support (as is the case for my White students) and I argue that only through conscious efforts can the classroom be a vehicle for inclusive dialogue that will facilitate learning for all.

WHITE PRIVILEGE

As long as White people are not racially seen and named, they function as the human norm. Other people are "raced"[1] while Whites see themselves as just people. Whites are individuals free from the constraint of being labeled a representative of a racial group. This raises the point that there is no more powerful position than that of being "just human," with the claim to speak for the commonality of humanity. Raced people can't do that; they can only speak for their race but non-raced people can, for they do not represent the interests of an entire race. The definition of Whites as non-raced is most evident in the absence of reference to Whiteness in the everyday language of White people. Even as I write this document, I find the term unusual and feel odd even writing self-consciously about Whiteness. It is a bit like taking your car to a mechanic, and when "he" takes off his hat and you discover "he" is a female. As one of my students stated, "it's just not natural."

Nevertheless, the assumption that White Canadians are just people, which is not much different than saying that Whites are people whereas other ethno-cultural groups are something else, is endemic to Canadian culture. Whites grow up[2] without having their racial supremacy being questioned. As Mills (1997) points out:

> White misunderstanding, misrepresentation, evasion, and self-deception on matters related to race are... psychically required for conquest, colonization, andenslavement... these phenomena are in no way accidental, but... [it]

D. E. Lund & P. R. Carr (Eds.), Revisiting The Great White North?, 43–53.

requires a certain schedule of structured blindness in order to establish and maintain the white polity. (p. 9)

Privilege is hard to see for those who were born with access to power and resources (Kendall, 2001).

At the same time, it is a very tangible and concrete for those to whom privilege is not granted. As such, it should be noted that White privilege is an institutional set of benefits granted to those who, by colour[3], resemble the people who dominate the powerful positions in our institutions and organizations. In turn, these become individual benefits (Manglitz, 2003). This system is not based on each individual White person's intention to harm but on a racial group's determination to preserve what they believe is rightly theirs. This distinction is, on the one hand, important, and, on the other hand, not important at all because, regardless of our personal intent, the impact is the same. Once a particular perspective is built into the laws, norms and mores of a society, it becomes part of the "the way things are." As such, Whiteness is defined as a part of human condition and it defines normality. Rather than actively refusing to comply with the law, individuals usually go along with the "norm," particularly if they think the law doesn't affect them personally. In summary, Whiteness functions as a large ensemble of practices and rules that give White people all sorts of small and large advantages in life, many privileges, and a major reason people have trouble giving it up (Jay, 1998).

White privilege is the ability to make decisions that affect everyone without taking others into account, and White people[4] set standards of humanity by which they are bound to succeed and others are bound to fail. Most of this is not done deliberately and maliciously. However, what they do is not seen as "Whiteness" but rather "normal." White privilege has nothing to do with whether or not an individual is "good" or not. Whites can be rude or unkind and still enjoy White privileges. At the same time, people of colour can be the most wonderful, giving, and brilliant individuals and yet they may not enjoy the same unearned privileges. Privileges are bestowed on Whites by the institutions with which they interact solely because of their Whiteness, and not because they are deserving as individuals (Hartigan, 2004). Often, it is not the intent of a White person to make use of the unearned benefits they have received on the basis of their skin colour. In fact, many go through their day-to-day activities unaware that they are even White or that race matters. In fact, many White students and faculty will argue that they don't have *any* privilege because of their Whiteness. Throughout Canadian history, White power-holders, acting on behalf of society, have made decisions that have affected White people as a group differently than groups of people of colour. White privilege allows people *not* to see race in themselves, and to be angry with those who do. Overall, Whites generally tend to live in the centre, while people of colour often live on the margins (Lopez, 2005).

Evidence of this can be found in Canada in the contents of the *British North America Act*, written by men believing that "our destiny" was to own the land previously was occupied by Aboriginal people, by removing First Nation's children from their homes and placing them in schools, and later, by placing First Nations' children in White foster homes and by manipulating immigration laws so that people of colour (e.g., Chinese, South Asians) were less free to immigrate to Canada than White Western Europeans. Everywhere we look, we can find Whiteness at the centre of Canadian society. Moreover, this perspective has been in operation for well over five centuries. However, with the recent entry of greater numbers of visible minorities into Canada (they now make up 13 percent of the total Canadian population), the issue of White privilege has become a topic of discussion. In summary, White people's privileges are bestowed on them prenatally, such that one cannot acquire them through behaviour, nor can one give them away no matter how much that individual may not want them.

WHITE INVISIBILITY

Whites do not recognize or acknowledge their unearned racial privileges because Whiteness operates by being invisible, so ubiquitous and entrenched as to appear natural and normative. As noted earlier, Whiteness operates as the unmarked norm against which other identities are marked and realized. On the other hand, while Whiteness is invisible to Whites, it is hyper-visible to people of colour who are always aware of Whiteness (Rothenberg, 2000).

Whiteness is a standpoint, a location from which to see and evaluate other individuals, ourselves, and the way institutions are organized. It is a product of history and is a relational category. However, Whites can, with extraordinary ease, slide from awareness of Whiteness to the lack thereof (Rasmussen et al., 2001.). White people rarely see their White privilege. The invisibility of these assets is part of the sense that Whiteness does not exist. White culture and identity have, as it were, no content and, having no content, White people can't acknowledge that they have anything that accounts for their position of privilege and power (Lipsitz, 2006). In the end, White people have created the dominant images of the world and cannot believe that they have constructed the world in their own image.

This sense of invisibility is a significant and taken-for-granted advantage for Whites in their day-to-day behaviour. Whites never have to speak for their race, not being viewed as the "White" teacher or lawyer. Moreover, non-Whites seldom see themselves as broadly represented in the media and educational curriculum (Doane, 1997). For example, I cannot remember ever reading a newspaper article in which the writer identified a "White community." Non-White students have to deal with the above issues and they experience, as a result, an important social and psychological cost. The advantage of being White is not to have to absorb this cost, nor even having to be aware of the benefits being received. This invisibility of Whiteness as a racial position in White discourse is of prime importance in analyzing how Whiteness provides a context for determining our behaviour (Dyer, 1992).

BARRIERS TO COMMUNICATION

Whiteness operates as a social force in mobilizing how people act and interact as well as in the ways they think of themselves and others (Nakayama & Martin, 2003). Moreover, Whiteness serves as a barrier to communication between Whites and non-Whites, making it difficult to effectively communicate and to resolve real or perceived differences. Furthermore, the hidden nature of Whiteness and White privilege enables Whites to participate in White racism that permits both individuals and structures to operate without calling it to the attention of anyone (Jensen, 2005). If Whites see themselves as the cultural centre of society, then the identities and cultural practices of others become something "different" that needs to be changed in order to claim full membership in the context, in the classroom, for example.

People of colour are expected to conform to the unspoken values of Whiteness, yet this is impossible because it is based on race. As long as Whiteness goes unacknowledged, anyone of colour will have difficulty in conforming. Much of White identity production swirls around the creation and maintenance of the dark "Other" against which their own Whiteness and "goodness" is necessarily understood. The social construction of this goodness, then, provides moral justification for privileged standpoints (Weis et al., 1997).

We also find that White people exhibit the optics of listening when dealing with people of colour. When people of colour try to make a point with Whites during a conversation, Whites have the ability and privilege to not understand the message being sent. Whites enjoy the privilege of assuming that they know best for everybody, and they may do what they want to do anyway. In many cases, people of colour will stop saying anything (invoking silence) that is then interpreted by Whites as agreeing with them. Besides silencing visible minorities, including Aboriginal people, most White educators are seldom aware that they have silenced the dialogue, and the silence is in no way a tacit agreement. Whites, both teachers and students, simply believe that their colleagues or fellow students of colour did, in the end, agree with them. After all, they stopped disagreeing (Delpit, 1988).

Whites control what others know about their own histories by presenting only parts of a story since Whites determine how and if historical characters and events will be remembered. For example, stories in our history books are replete with tales of White "battles" with Aboriginals versus "massacres" carried out by Aboriginals. The practice of "scalping" is generally associated with barbarous Aboriginal behaviour but it was actually introduced by Europeans who wanted to eradicate Aboriginals. Our knowledge of the Japanese internment during WWII is from the White perspective. We almost always forget that everything that happens in our lives occurs in the context of the supremacy of Whiteness, (e.g., being admitted to university, finding employment, and being able to live comfortably where one wants to).

We have been able to delude ourselves into thinking that all people come to the table having been dealt the same hand of cards and having played on a level playing field. We act as if there are no remnants of slavery that affect Black Canadians, that Japanese Canadians did not have to give up their businesses and assets, that Aboriginals did not have to give up their land or be denied access to the economy. Moreover, Whites can have a conversation about "race" without being questioned about their loyalty or being called an "Oreo," "Banana," "Apple," or "Coconut." In the end, Whites can speak up about racism without being seen as self-serving. In fact, some Whites are benefiting from the cottage industry known as multicultural training by speaking about racism.

EDUCATIONAL INSTITUTIONS

The *National Center for Education* (1999) has reported that over 80 percent of public school teachers throughout the country are White, while almost 40 percent of the students in public primary, secondary, and post-secondary schools are visible minorities. Moreover, the proportion of ethnically and linguistically diverse teachers is growing smaller as the diversity of the student population continues to grow (Sleeter, 2001). As such, there is a major "mismatch" between a teaching force that is White and a student population that is composed more and more of students of colour and non-native English/French speakers. As Cross (2003) notes, there is an enormous gap between post-secondary educational institutions that prepare teachers and who they will likely teach. This mismatch has resulted in a significant detachment of White teacher educators and White teacher education students from the children of colour who are in their classroom. Moreover, we find that predominantly our formal White educational institutions have generally responded very slowly to the growing racial and cultural gaps.

The intent of this brief introduction is to sensitize the reader to the issue of power differential, an example of "normed" positions and the invisibility of Whiteness. But how does this work out in the classroom and related interaction between students and professors? My focus on this issue will be on the post-secondary educational system since that is where I have worked for the past three decades. But more importantly, how does this "play out" in the classroom with a college/university environment?

White teachers need to undergo a profound shift, from viewing the world through a lens of dominance to a commitment to equitably shared power and resources (Dei, et al., 2006). To effectively counteract the pull and absorption of White privilege beliefs and behaviour of teachers, teachers need to understand how young people develop and react to racial identity and awareness as well as attitudes about race. Researchers have noted that, at a young age, White children begin to understand the power codes or rules of "White ways are right" (Ramsey, 2004; Ramsey & Williams, 2003). To be White in Canada means you do not have to think about differences or race. This invisibility of Whiteness leads to a general social tendency to assume that Whites do not have a "race" and diverts attention and analysis to "others" who do have a race (Doane, 1997). Most White teachers are unlikely to be reminded of social and cultural differences on a day-to-day basis. In fact, we find that White Canadian culture and practices are built into the post-secondary educational institutions and structures of Canadian life. The content of such educational institutions generally reflect White Euro-Canadian perspectives and standards.

WHITENESS IN THE CLASSROOM: A PERSONAL REFLECTION

Thirty years ago, when I first started teaching, I would look out into the classroom and it was predominantly young White males. While an occasional visible minority person would be in the class, by and large the class was White. Today, as I get ready for the next semester, I can count on a majority of the students in my class to be female, a sizeable number of the class to be a member of a visible minority group, and the age variation will range from 18 to 80 years.

When I arrived in the city of Calgary, it was a small prairie centre with roots in the oil and gas industry. The demographic make up of the city was nearly all White. Ethnic culinary choices ranged between "surf and turf" and Chinese food. Ethnic diversity was something that was happening elsewhere in the world and the few Blacks that one saw in the city were more than likely to be a member of the local professional football team. In all respects it was a White city. While the city is one of the fastest growing cities in the country, until the 1970s this growth came from nearby provinces or the United States. Also, all of the "immigrants" migrating to Calgary were White. Today the world has changed for Canadian educators.

What I find today is that many of my classes bifurcate along the line of "speakers" and "listeners." Within the speakers group, they are further divided into "seekers" and "challengers." Seekers are those individuals who require additional information to complete their understanding of the topic under discussion in the classroom. The seekers are simply trying to obtain additional information to fill gaps they feel they need to more fully grasp the complexities of the topic or achieve a better understanding of the material. The "voice" of seekers is generally directed toward that of obtaining clarification, additional information, or ensuring they are not misunderstanding the information presented. On the other hand, there are the challengers who adopt a more "confrontational" stance to the issue under discussion during class. Their challenges may or may not be ideologically based or theoretically relevant and, in many cases, it is difficult to sort this out. Nevertheless, these speakers feel it necessary to interact, question, and challenge the basic assumptions or conclusions being discussed in the classroom.

Those who are White tend to make up the speakers, while it has been my experience that generally the listeners in my class include all the visible minority members. In most classrooms I have taught or been a visitor in, I find that visible minority members seldom speak and rarely do they challenge their instructor. Moreover, I find that members of visible minorities tend to segregate themselves (or are covertly pushed into a segregated environment) both in and outside the classroom. What has always been of interest to me is the learning process and experience for those silent voices.

What happens in a class where there is a majority of visible minority students? Do they set new norms? Will the White students allow it? What are the interaction patterns of the class? Will the "silent voices" come forward? Can an instructor, through conscious intervention in the classroom, address the above questions and give voice to students of colour? Or do White instructors, willingly or not, reinforce Whiteness?

Over the years I have noticed that sometimes the class was vocal and articulate while at other times there were only a few students who spoke. As I reflected upon the ethnic makeup of each class, I began to see the picture as described above. As such, I began to search for ways to stimulate dialogue in the class, trying to ensure it was more inclusive for all members. For example, I began to break my class into small working groups and ensured that some groups were comprised of a majority of visible minority members. In these cases, I found that the listeners now turned into speakers and they occasionally would take on the "challenger" role. Miraculously, individuals from groups having a majority of visible minority members became articulate speakers who had no trouble in challenging the instructor or their colleagues in the classroom. How could such a transformation take place? What happened that allowed previously silent visible minority individuals to become articulate speakers?

My explanation is that the White normative position of the group was no longer appropriate as the "norm," and that members of the visible minority group established a new norm reflecting their own experiences. As such, the old rule of "White makes right" no longer applied to this setting, and new norms emerged that liberated visible minority students and gave them voice. At the same time, White students resented the new norm. Although they did not directly challenge the right of visible minority individuals in the class, they begin to look for alternatives to resist and to show resistance. Some of the White members of the class would request a transfer to another work-group and provide rationales such as "members of the group don't listen" or "members of the group don't take instructions." In other cases, White students would not show up for the group activities, citing conflicting commitments (e.g., family obligations or work commitments). It is clear that the establishment of new norms made White students uncomfortable. Their sense of superiority had been challenged and they were reluctant to acknowledge the challenge. What remains to be seen is whether or not these new norms that allow the individual of colour to speak can carry over to other classes and non-classroom situations. Of equal importance, do other visible minority students view the new "speakers" as mentors and role models that they aspire to emulate? Do visible minority students facilitate a richer and more in depth analysis of Whiteness so that White students are engaged in the dialogue?

I have found that, in order for teachers to be effective in their teaching efforts, they must first recognize and understand their own world views, as only then will they be able to understand the world views of their students (Marx, 2004). I also have found that most of my colleagues are not interested in discussing the role of Whiteness in the classroom. As such, it will typically be difficult to look to your colleagues to help support your inquiry on how you need to reconstruct your classes to deal with the privilege of Whiteness.[5] I have found, however, that one of the first steps White teachers need to take is to inform themselves of the concept of "White privilege," because many White people will argue they have never been bestowed the benefits of being White. White teachers need to see themselves as White, to see their particularity. In short, Whiteness needs to be made "strange." Most White teachers are unknowingly beneficiaries of White privilege (Gidluck & Dwyer, 2006) and resist the notion that they benefit from being White. When White teachers fail to acknowledge their own racial identity, this lack of acknowledgement becomes a barrier for understanding and connecting with the developmental needs of students of colour (Gordon, 2005).

Second, instructors need to appreciate that students of colour tend to bring rich experiences and perspectives to teaching, regardless of whether they are in arts and science, humanities, or education departments (Sleeter, 2001). This richness and these differential perspectives need to be fully utilized in teaching and learning about the subject matter. I teach in the area of statistics and methodology and I have found this richness of diversity stimulates a number of topics covered in the class. Teachers must not forget that the reason they teach is to explore both mundane as well as alien ideas. The goal of such activity is to expand our understanding of the diversity of human thought and *not* to expand our own specific hegemonic ways of thinking (Cordova, 2004).

Third, White teachers must understand the importance of context in order to properly understand that which lies outside her/his own context (Wittgenstein, 1968). Teachers cannot pretend that they can interpret a particular idea from an alien context without understanding that context. To do so without a grounded understanding will surely lead to misinterpretation and misunderstanding. Within the post-secondary educational context, to use such a strategy will result in only other White teachers having similar understandings that may or may not be accurate reflections of reality. White teachers will create "answers" to questions that are similar to other White teachers and have little linkage to non-White students. White teachers must be aware of the assumptions they bring to such interpretations, both in and out of the classroom. In the end, White teachers must address Wittgenstein's (1968) insistence on context as a source of meaning.

DISCUSSION

Why do White teachers not change regarding their perceptions, activities, and relations with students in their classroom? First of all, in assigning gains and losses with regard to change, it is often relative to the *status quo*. In addition, when teachers assess the prospects of future events, losses usually loom intuitively larger than gains. Finally, teachers experience an endowment effect where present and/or past experiences are given higher values than future prospects. As such, most White teachers define the transition from the *status quo* to a gain of some sort as not valued in the same way as the transition from the *status quo* to the loss of something (Schmid, 2006). As a result of such framing, outcomes deviating from the *status quo* tend to be evaluated in more negative terms and viewed as losses rather than gains.

Colour-blindness is neither blindness, nor an inability to see colour. Rather, it is a refusal, or what has been called "White resistance to seeing" (Helfand, 2006). This resistance is learned and nurtured to protect the *status quo* that privileges White people and occurs on both the individual and systemic levels. At the individual level, it allows for teachers to absolve oneself of racism. The systemic level of colour-blindness denies the institutionally mandated privileges and discriminatory practices associated with ethnicity. It denies the system of rules, procedures, and beliefs that result in Whites collectively maintaining control. Our education system perpetuates the pervasiveness of Whiteness and the passivity of White racism by failing to challenge and by reproducing this pervasiveness and passivity. By neither questioning nor challenging the neutrality of the White perspective, most post-secondary educational institutions and colleges of education silently condone it. This is so powerful it may indirectly carry more educational significance than the official curriculum. White teachers tend to focus on the individual level of colour-blindness that focuses on personal and professional dispositions, and becomes a good way of avoiding examining racism on the systemic level. It becomes a way to validate ourselves as "good" people without having to relinquish the privileges that we receive from the existing system (Gordon, 2005). Teachers must remember that Whiteness gives us advantages, some subtle and some obvious, some overt, some covert, some material, and some ideological.

Whiteness is an issue that challenges White teachers, and yet few have tried to come to grips with it. As White teachers, there is a tendency to shore up our sense of superiority, and I find myself never fully able to escape from an entrenched sense of White superiority. At the same time, students of colour understand how White professors' stereotypes impinge upon their performance in the class. White teachers have to take seriously trying to understand what it means for people of colour to live in a racialized world. Unfortunately, many White teachers try to maintain their status of "innocence" by not seeing their participation as privileged. However, there are many situations when actions by students and or White teaches can rupture the *status quo* and force them to experience a dissolution of a singular "moral self." White teachers need to work toward and recognize such events, and allow them to happen, rather than trying to "manage" the discomfort, or otherwise avoid discussion of these issues. These rupturing educative events can be profound teaching moments and create a new awareness of White people's complicity in perpetuating privilege and dominance, and can force teachers into accepting greater accountability for their positions of privilege. In the end, I am struck with my own naivety, discomfort, and lack of skill at responding to the issue of Whiteness, and with my students' attitudes about Whiteness and/or race, in ways that are truly effective in helping all students. However, I continue to struggle to deal with and confront students whose ignorance exposes my own.

QUESTIONS FOR REFLECTION

1. How would you know if Whiteness is a factor in silencing the voice of students in your class?
2. How do you deal with a student who makes a racist statement in the class, whether or not he or she is aware of it?
3. Can you name ten White Canadians and ten non-White Canadians who have made a major contribution to science, culture, and life of Canada (excluding sports figures)?
4. Do all White students benefit from Whiteness? Explain your answer.
5. How does Whiteness emerge in any of your class readings? Provide examples.

NOTES

[1] The term "race" is not being used in a biological sense. Rather it refers to the socially defined set of attributes (usually phenotypic) that people use to categorize people. It is a term that refers to the social construction of social and biological attributes that allow people to place individuals into broad biological groupings referred to as "races."

[2] Skin colour recognition is our first functioning perceptual system. Skin is a signed façade and is one of the first sign systems we learn to read (Taylor, 2005).

[3] We use terms such as "race," "colour," and "visible minority" interchangeably. However, it should be noted that in Canada, the term "visible minority" is a legal term and 13 ethno-cultural groups, excluding Aboriginals, are included in the legal definition.

[4] It should be noted that social class is an important factor in differentiating White privilege as not all Whites benefit the same.

[5] The implications for faculty obtaining tenure, carrying out research and student evaluations of their courses is noteworthy. However this is a subject for another time and place.

REFERENCES

Cordova, V. (2004). Approaches to Native American philosophy. In A. Waters (Ed.), *American Indian thought* (pp. 27–33). Malden, MA: Blackwell.

Cross, B. (2003). Learning or unlearning racism: Transferring teacher education curriculum to classroom practices. *Theory into Practice, 42*, 203–209.

Dei, G. J. S., Karumanchery, L., & Karumanchery, N. (2006). *Playing the race card: White power and privilege.* New York, NY: Peter Lang.

Delpit, H. (1988). The silenced dialogue: Power and pedagogy in educating other people's children. *Harvard Education Review, 58*, 234–257.

Doane, A. (1997). White identity and race relations in the 1990s. In G. Carter (Ed.), *Perspectives on current social problems* (pp. 151–159). Boston, MA: Allyn and Bacon.

Dyer, R. (1992). *White: Essays on race and culture.* New York, NY: Routledge.

Gidluck, L., & Dwyer, S. (2006). *Families of Asian children adopted by White parents: Challenges of race, racism and racial identity in Canada.* Unpublished paper, University of Calgary.

Gordon, J. (2005). Inadvertent complicity: Colorblindness in teacher education. *Educational Studies, 38*, 135–153.

Hartigan, J. (2004). *Odd tribes.* Durham, NC: Duke University Press.

Helfand, J. (2006). *Constructing whiteness.* Retrieved August 16, 2006, from http://academic.udayton.edu/race/01race/white11.htm

Jay, G. (1998). *Who invented White people?* Retrieved July 8, 2006, from http://www. uwm.edu/%Egjay/ Whiteness/Whitenesstalk.html

Jensen, R. (2005). *The heart of whiteness.* San Francisco, CA: City Lights.

Kendall, F. (2001). *Understanding White privilege.* Unpublished paper, University of Calgary.

Lipsitz, G. (2006). *The possessive investment in whiteness.* Philadelphia, PA: Temple University Press.

Lopez, A. (Ed.). (2005). *Post colonial whiteness.* Albany, NY: State University of New York Press.

Manglitz, E. (2003). Challenging White privilege in adult education: A critical review of the literature, *Adult Education Quarterly, 53*, 119–134.

Marx, S. (2004). Regarding whiteness: Exploring and intervening in the effects of White racism in teacher education. *Equity and Excellence in Education, 37*, 31–43.

Mills, C. W. (1997). *The racial contract.* Ithaca, NY: Cornell University Press.

Nakayama, T., & Martin, J. (Eds.). (2003). *Whiteness.* Thousand Oaks, CA: Sage.

National Center for Education Statistics. (1999). *Tables.* Retrieved April 10, 2006, from http://nces. ed.gov/pubs99/condition99/SupTables/supp-table-46-1.html

Ramsey, P. (2004). *Teaching and learning in a diverse world.* New York, NY: Teachers College Press.

Ramsey, P., & Williams, L. (2003). *Multicultural education: A resource book.* New York, NY: Garland.

Rasmussen, B., Klinenbert, E., Nexica, I., & Wray, M. (Eds.). (2001). *The making and unmaking of Whiteness.* Durham, NC: Duke University Press.

Rothenberg, P. (2000). *Invisible privilege.* Lawrence, KS: University Press of Kansas.

Schmid, G. (2006). Social risk management through transitional labour markets. *Socio-Economic Review, 4*, 1–35.

Sleeter, C. E. (2001). Preparing teachers for culturally diverse schools. *Journal of Teacher Education, 52*, 94–106.

Taylor, G. (2005). *Buying whiteness.* New York, NY: Palgrave Macmillan.

Weis, L., Prowleller, W., & Centrie, C. (1997). Re-examining "a moment in history": Loss of privilege inside working-class masculinity in the 1990s. In M. Fine, L. Weis, L. Powell & L. Wong (Eds.), *Off White: Readings on race, power, and society* (pp. 210–228). New York, NY: Routledge.

Wittgenstein, L. (1968). *Philosophical investigations*, G. E. M. Anscombe (Trans.). New York, NY: Macmillan.

REFRAMING: JAMES FRIDERES (2014)

I have been asked to reflect upon my experiences and activities in the classroom over the last while. What has brought even greater clarity to the issue is that, as I write this, I am working with the Ministry of Education in Kabul, Afghanistan. Having been to the Teacher Training Colleges across Afghanistan, working with the "experimental primary and secondary schools," and talking to teachers across the country, have reinforced my beliefs about how White ethnicity is seen as unproblematic as an ethnicity except as a potential source of racism. Nevertheless, it is clear that some Whites are seen as less White than others within a hierarchy of Whiteness.

This means that as the demographic transition continues in Canada and the number of "visible minorities" increases, Whites have recognized that they need to redefine who is White. This has meant that Whites, over the years, have begun to expand their membership to other groups previously not defined as White. As such, White Canadians have developed an ethno-racial identity that has expanded and acts as a kind of lifeline but remains hidden from their view. This new "White ethnic revival" is so evident in the media, film, and novels, and captures the essence of the new redefinition of Whiteness. The production of films like "My Big Fat Greek Wedding" and "Angela's Ashes" attest to the popularity of such a revival. In these productions, the expanded definition of White is depicted as the preferable norm, a cultural model that others should endorse; a kind of dance with Canadian diversity.

By not having to live behind a "veil" of differentness, Whites do not understand how the consequences of this identity benefit them and harm others. At the same time, Whites have the ability to utilize their power through the process institutional discrimination and political means, to delegitimize the racial identity of other groups, and to use racial ideologies to explain the failings of others. White people still do not know what it is like to experience a "double-consciousness," or the duality between being of a member of a visible minority group and a White.

So how does this all relate to education, teaching, and students? First, who is White and who is not has become fuzzy, and it complicates the relationship between teacher and student. It also poses problems for institutions that are being asked to become more "sensitive" to race issues and to put those sensitivities to the test. Post-secondary educational institutions are being asked to hire professors from underrepresented groups (e.g., visible minority and Aboriginal). These efforts are partially a result of government policy and the desire of educational institutions to provide employment opportunities for groups that have been traditionally discriminated against. Perhaps more important is the belief that low admission rates, poor academic performance, and high drop-out rates of visible minority students is a result of these students not having visible minority instructors at post-secondary educational institutions. There is a belief that visible minority instructors will more

D. E. Lund & P. R. Carr (Eds.), Revisiting The Great White North?, 55–56.

effectively interact with them, have more favorable attitudes toward them and, in turn, will enhance the learning environment. In short, these instructors will be better role models than White instructors.

Previous research showed that, for the most part, the racialized identity of a teacher has little impact on how much students learn in the classroom. The evidence seems overwhelming on this issue. Nevertheless, a teacher's "race" is still a crucial factor in teacher-student relations in that it is more likely to influence their subjective evaluation of their students. As such, this subjective evaluation of students is crucial as they are reflected in the encouragement provided to these students or that they encourage them to aspire. The question now turns to "Can White professors engender that kind of encouragement and aspiration in visible minority students?"

The notion that the classroom dynamics between teachers and students make a substantive contribution to the academic achievements of students already has a wide currency among educational researchers. However, the achievements are not a direct function of similar demographic traits between the teacher and student. In short, the passive teacher effects on the students are relatively benign. On the other hand, the role-model effects do produce changes in student performance through the teacher raising a visible minority student's academic motivation and expectations. When there is a lack of role model, visible minority students seem to experience an apprehension that reduces their academic identification and subsequent achievement. There may also be unintended biases in their expectations and interactions with students who have different demographic traits. In the end, it is important that visible minority students have appropriate role models, but it is equally important that visible minority students also come into contact with White teachers in their post-secondary education. White teachers, in their attitudes and behaviors, need to become aware of their biases and strive to overcome them in their relations with visible minority students. This is not an easy task. However, when correctly implemented, diversity management increases the engagement of all students by building the culture that demands equity in outcome. When people feel they're being treated fairly, they will be more engaged, and engaged people are more innovative and productive.

SECTION 2

WHITENESS AND SECOND PEOPLES

HERBERT C. NORTHCOTT

GOING NATIVE

A White Guy's Experience Teaching in an Aboriginal Context

INTRODUCTION

I was born White, and grew up in Winnipeg in the 1950s in a suburb dominated by White Anglo-Saxon protestants (WASPs). As a young idealistic baby boomer in the mid-1960s, my desire to help the disadvantaged led me to study Sociology at the University of Manitoba. One day, representatives of the Aboriginal peoples of Manitoba made a presentation at the University. In the discussion that followed, I asked how I could help. While I don't remember the exact words, the answer stuck in my memory as: "White boy, we don't need your help. We'll take care of our own problems." As discouraging as this answer was, I recognized the wisdom of the speaker. White people's efforts to help had done little good; consider, for example, the residential school system and its misguided attempt to assimilate Aboriginals (Hare & Barman, 2000; Milloy, 1999; Schissel & Wotherspoon, 2003). In many ways, White paternalism and the efforts of Whites to help Aboriginal peoples was the problem. Nevertheless, I wondered if some day I might be able to offer a helping hand.

I started my career as a sociologist at the University of Alberta in Edmonton in 1976. As Canada increasingly became a multi-cultural and multi-racial society, Asians, Blacks, and brown-skinned students joined the White students on campus. Notably absent were Canada's First Nations peoples. When the Faculty of Extension asked for instructors to teach Aboriginal students, I jumped at the opportunity. Education is a key resource, I thought, that empowers people to help themselves. I hoped that in some small way I could help First Nations peoples as an educator.

TEACHING IN AN ABORIGINAL CONTEXT

While I was advised that I should be "culturally sensitive," both the University and First Nations colleges expected me to teach the University's course as it was taught on campus; it was to count for University credit. There was a problem, however. When I delivered the course exactly as I taught it on campus, with lectures, textbooks, and multiple-choice examinations, the Aboriginal students did not perform as well as students at the university. One of the reasons was that First Nations colleges had more open admission policies. Nevertheless, I suspected that the problem had more to do with Aboriginal students' lack of familiarity, and perhaps resistance, to White

D. E. Lund & P. R. Carr (Eds.), Revisiting The Great White North?, 59–68.

pedagogy, given the discrepancy between White and Aboriginal models for teaching and learning (Frideres, 1998; Hare & Barman, 2000; Schissel & Wotherspoon, 2003; Te Hennepe, 1993). I chaffed under the nagging realization that I was a White guy, using White textbooks and a White pedagogy that did not seem to serve Aboriginal students well (Bailey, 2000; Schissel & Wotherspoon, 2003).

In 2001, I was asked to teach a course on social stratification and inequality for First Nations (primarily Cree) students. As I reviewed possible textbooks, it struck me that the texts were written for the most part by Euro-Canadians about a society dominated by Euro-Canadian social structure and culture. I decided to engage in a "radical" experiment (for a provocative discussion of radical pedagogy, see Sweet, 1998a and the accompanying discussion of his article: Gaianguest, 1998; Long, 1998; Sweet, 1998b). I concluded that I would not impose any text on the class. Instead, I set out to ground the curriculum in the students' own culture and experience (Schissel & Wotherspoon, 2003, p. 129). Furthermore, because I am a "White guy," I determined to remove myself from the classroom dynamic as much as possible and to replace Euro-Canadian pedagogy (e.g., lectures given from the front of the classroom) with a more Native-centred pedagogy. My limited insights into Aboriginal pedagogy stemmed from comments made to me by Aboriginal students, including a few Native elders, who I had taught previously. My view of Aboriginal pedagogy involved not lecturing and instead facilitating discussion in as non-obtrusive a manner as possible, having students and instructor sit in a circle (actually two concentric circles given the number of students), and emphasizing oral communication and personal (student) experience (Schissel & Wotherspoon, 2003, p. 40; for a discussion of the difficulties and opportunities involved in moving the instructor away from the centre of the classroom, see Finkel & Monk, 1999). A review of the literature indicates that my experiment in teaching reflects a "critical" pedagogy (Friere, 1970; see also Jakubowski, 2001); nevertheless, my teaching strategy was pragmatically chosen rather than motivated by a prior reading of pedagogical theory.

"Mature" students tend to be rare on campus; however, First Nations students were generally mature adults. Mature adults who have experienced life more than young adults may find memorization of textbook "facts" for the purpose of writing multiple-choice exams largely irrelevant, and, accordingly, may not be motivated to "play the game." Because of my sense, based on past experience with Aboriginal students, that multiple-choice exams were hostile to their preferred way of learning, I determined that there would be no multiple-choice exams. Instead, I decided that the central purpose of the class would be to write an Aboriginal-centred text as it emerged from classroom discussion and student essays. Indeed, students performed better on these written essays than they had done previously on multiple-choice exams.

In each three-hour weekly meeting over a 13-week period, the class explored a different aspect of social stratification and inequality. I minimized my involvement by giving each student the opportunity to speak as we moved around the circle.

I encouraged students to assess each day's topic in comparative terms comparing Aboriginal society with non-Aboriginal society and comparing past with present.

Each week, students wrote a 400- to 800-word summary and analysis of the topic of the day. Grades were based on these essays as well as on attendance. I graded attendance rather than participation so as to not make the discussions competitive. Each week a selection of the graded papers was distributed anonymously for the benefit of the class. This strategy was consistent with Aboriginal culture, where each person is expected to contribute to others, each according to her or his strengths, but without being elevated. I tried to spread the honour of being chosen around but was warned not to be too democratic. Students told me that a paper had to have merit, and could not be chosen simply because the author had not had a turn at being chosen. I worried that this introduced an element of competition that I understood to be inconsistent with Aboriginal ideals and wondered if I lacked insight into the intricacies of Aboriginal culture or if students had internalized to some degree Euro-Canadian values. In any case, by the end of the course, the class had produced a "text" which was grounded in the Aboriginal experience as interpreted by the students themselves.

In this class, learning became a cooperative exercise. While Aboriginal culture acknowledges differential strengths, these are to be used for the benefit of the community and not for individual self-aggrandizement. The Euro-Canadian ethic of individualistic competition for the purpose of identifying the strongest seemed foreign and hostile to the Aboriginal students (Frideres, 1998, pp. 156-158). Consequently, while academic grades reflected differential strengths, the dynamic among the students emphasized an equality derived from mutual respect, sharing, and communal assistance rather than individualistic competition.

EXCERPTS FROM MY TEACHING DIARY

Day 1. I walked into the classroom and stood before 35 sitting students. I said, "This course is about inequality and social stratification. What do my standing and your sitting facing me say about inequality?" The class observed that the way the classroom was organized claimed authority and superiority for the instructor while the students were defined as inferior. I asked, "How did teaching and learning occur in Cree culture in the past." It was observed that in the past teaching often involved storytelling and example, and learning was experientially based. Furthermore, communication often took place in a circle where all were considered to be more-or-less equal. We reorganized the classroom by moving the tables into a circle, and I found a place to sit in the circle. This overly filled the room and later students found it more convenient to have half the tables facing the other half. I then suggested to the class that we would spend the rest of the day designing the course from the point of view of their experiences and culture.

The Cree at the beginning of the twenty-first century lived in two worlds, aware of the traditions of their ancestors, and at the same time exposed to the individualistic, consumer capitalism of Euro-Canadians. As the class discussion unfolded, the distinctiveness of Aboriginal culture and experience quickly became evident. For example, it was pointed out that traditional Cree society was egalitarian, both ideologically and structurally (see Dickason & Calder, 2006, p. 29). Trying to be provocative, I asked: "Well, what about the term Chief?" I added, suspecting a linguistic divide, "Does the word Chief mean the same to the Cree as it does to the Europeans?" An older student said that, in Cree, the concept of chief was contained in a phrase rather than a word. The phrase was rendered as "the person who is temporarily in charge in this particular situation." Furthermore, it was expected that the "headman" would put the interests of all others ahead of his own (see Dickason & Calder, 2006, p. 12). He ate after all others were fed; he spoke after all others had spoken. The wellbeing of the community was emphasized and individual aggrandizement was socially sanctioned. In short, equality and communalism were emphasized. I realized that this was going to be an interesting experience.

Day 2. Our second discussion focused on social class. I asked how social class was manifested in Aboriginal society. It was argued that traditional Cree society was not hierarchical, but was egalitarian. It was pointed out that a nomadic hunting-and-gathering economy was not consistent with the individual accumulation of property. Furthermore, an ethos existed which encouraged individuals to share for the benefit of the group. When we turned to a discussion of present-day Aboriginal society, I was puzzled by the students' continued emphasis on equality rather than inequality. Surely, I thought, the past is being idealized, and the ideology of the past is resulting in a denial of reality. However, when the students themselves launched a passionate critique of consumer capitalism, I began to realize that the very idea of social class was foreign. The students criticized consumer capitalism as wasteful, a violation of Natural Law, the rape of Mother Earth, and the disrespectful promotion of greed and selfishness instead of caring and sharing.

Day 3. We examined age as a basis of social inequality. While age differentiation existed in traditional Aboriginal society, I had a hard time getting the class to focus on age-based social inequality. I noted that elders were highly respected in traditional Aboriginal society, but students spoke of the circle of life, and noted that each age was respected and no age was elevated above the others. There were differences, but an ethic of respect prevented the ranking of these differences and, instead, emphasized equality.

Day 4. We discussed gender as a basis of social inequality. Surely, I thought, patriarchy has been universal. Surely, we will get beyond the ideology of equality and focus on structures of inequality affecting men and women in Aboriginal society. The students acknowledged that men and women are different physically and are assigned different social roles and different cultural metaphors. The students acknowledged that these metaphors, for example, exalt women in their roles as givers of life, nurturers, healers, and rulers in the tipi. Nevertheless, this construction was not patriarchy nor was it matriarchy. Instead, gender distinctions were discussed in terms of interdependence, mutual respect, and equality.

Epiphany! I realized that I had mistakenly thought that it was enough to dispense with Euro-centric lectures, textbooks, and pedagogy. I had mistakenly thought that, without these props, I could still conduct a course on inequality and social stratification. I had mistakenly assumed that the basic conceptualization underlying the course content was universal, and not itself socially and culturally contingent. But how do you discuss inequality and social stratification, and ground that discussion in the culture of the students when that culture does not acknowledge inequality?

Moniyaw they called me, teasing. This is their word for White person (LeClaire & Cardinal, 2002). More literally it means, "you are not us, you are different from us" (not *Nehiyaw*, an Aboriginal person). Because I am White, the discussion idealizes Native culture and does not readily admit to realities inconsistent with ideals. They will not run their culture down in front of an outsider. Accordingly, there is resistance to critical discussion (see Hedley & Markowitz, 2001). The contemporary academic goal of generating critical thinking may be inconsistent with Aboriginal cultural ideals given Aboriginal norms of non-interference (i.e., don't tell people what they should do) and not being judgmental (i.e., respect all persons and accept people the way they are). Nevertheless, although many remain silent in public, critical thinking is evident in their written essays and in private conversation.

Aboriginal people remember when they were nomadic hunting and gathering societies. This memory is evident in their worldview, stories and metaphors, references to the Creator and Mother Earth, emphasis on respect, equality, and communalism rather than individualism, and their relative incomprehension of modern consumer capitalism. In contrast, Euro-Canadians understand capitalism, inequality and stratification. Euro-Canadians have a long cultural memory to help them understand these concepts. It has been a long time since European tribes were egalitarian hunters and gatherers.

Day 5. Having become concerned that a relatively small number of voices were beginning to dominate discussion in the classroom, and that discussion was becoming increasingly "politically correct" (reflecting a particular contemporary Aboriginal point of view), I decided to do things differently. We were to discuss racism. First, I observed to the class that many had become silent observers in the classroom. I argued that this was acceptable if silence was freely chosen. However, to make sure that each voice which wished to be heard was heard, I said we would go around the circle and each tell a personal story about racism. A person could decline to speak without penalty or could tell a story that someone else had told to them. The stories were often poignant and moving, and the discussion based on these stories was thoughtful and filled with insight. I was pleased that the resulting discussion was more "representative" in that no voices or points of view emerged to dominate at the expense of other voices.

In a three-hour class, one might expect some boredom (yawning, clock-watching, inattention, misbehaviours, etc.). None was evident. Everyone was involved for the whole class-period, and students commented privately to me that the course was interesting, thought provoking, relevant, challenging, and memorable. Students said that they were glad that the course did not involve a focus on irrelevant and forgettable textbooks. "This is better, much better," said one student, "I am getting much more out of this course."

Day 6. Our discussion for the day was religion and inequality. Because churches had run the residential schools, I suggested that we go around the circle and give each person an opportunity to relate a story about their own or a relative's experience with residential schooling. A middle-aged man said that when he was a very little boy he was taken to the residential school. Immediately his braids were shaved. He began to cry, he said. (While recalling this event that had taken place decades ago, he became emotional and could hardly speak.) His older brother warned him in Cree, "Don't cry." His brother was immediately strapped for speaking Cree. The little boy cried even more. The two boys were then made to stand facing the wall with their arms extended perpendicular to the floor. When their arms began to sag, they were strapped. "I hated that place from that moment on," the man said.

Many of the persons in class that day spoke of their own religious orientation. I had a hard time, as was becoming the pattern, keeping the class focused on the connection to inequality and stratification. Once again, I was struck by the cultural emphasis on respect for social differences and the relative absence of a cultural lens and language to describe these differences in hierarchical terms, as Euro-Canadian culture and language do so readily.

Day 8. We were to discuss health as a criterion for social inequality and stratification. There had been an allegation that I was favouring certain voices in the classroom, so I decided to try yet another change. I had already taken the Eurocentric textbooks out of play. I had done away with Eurocentric multiple-choice exams. I had dropped the Eurocentric pedagogy of lecturer lecturing to students facing the lecturer. But I had left myself in play as the facilitator of discussion—a Euro-Canadian facilitator now accused of choosing which voices were heard and not heard. I decided to take myself out of play. Accordingly, I told the group that I would remain silent for the remainder of the class discussion. The class took a break. When I returned the class had already regrouped—the first time they had ever come back from their break early! One of the students was standing at the front of the room asking the class how they wanted to proceed. I sat down in a corner and took notes.

The first speaker introduced the topic of HIV/AIDS. Subsequent discussion addressed teen pregnancy, HIV-positive mothers, abortion, multiple sclerosis, rheumatic fever, alcoholism, Fetal Alcohol Syndrome, and depression. The discussions focused on social attributions of blame and responsibility as well as on issues such as criticism and stigmatization. As the discussion proceeded, some passed on their turn to speak, and increasingly others would jump in with the discussion going back and forth in free form. When a topic was exhausted, there would be a moment of silence, and someone would then ask whose turn it was to speak.

The topic of depression resulted in several speakers making personal disclosures. All in the room were intensely engaged, and there was a respectful and attentive silence when each person spoke. Sometimes probing questions were addressed to a speaker seeking elaboration or clarification. The stories told were significant from a pedagogical point of view. They got attention, were meaningful, and were remembered.

The discussion has gone very well. As I review my notes, I am impressed with the quality of the discussion in terms of illustrative content, analysis, and insight. We kid ourselves, as instructors. We assume that our textbooks, lectures, and pedagogy are more important than they really are. Sometimes I think that we manufacture ignorance in our students for our own egos. These students are doing just fine without the text, without constant lecturing, and without me!

Having them write a weekly essay has worked well. For one thing, the students often make points and offer analysis that they are uncomfortable making in the classroom discussion. Second, their writing is improving. Third, the essays allow the students to show their considerable talent. Many of these students learned Cree as their first language, so there are often problems with grammar, sentence fragments, paragraphing, and so on. These weekly essays are a means of addressing and overcoming these deficiencies. More significantly, though, the students are improving their analytic skills and their abilities to present a concise, coherent argument. The weekly grading takes time, but it is interesting as students each put their own spin on the weekly topic. Importantly, I learn things that do not come out in the discussion.

Grading the papers that dealt with family and social inequality (discussed on day 7) was reassuring for me. I had assumed inequality was pretty much a universal experience and, finally, students were acknowledging inequality. Nepotism is rampant on the reserves, and is deeply resented by those persons not related to those in power. Of course, it is noted that this is inconsistent with the old ways, which heightens the sense of injustice and outrage.

Day 9. I wondered how effective our discussion about lifestyle and sexual orientation had been today. The three students I questioned after class had no complaints. Indeed, all wanted to continue the discussion, talking about things that had been germane but had been too personal or risky to share with the entire class. It is a small community, and a person has to be careful about what they say in public.

One of the students spoke of her choice to give up drinking several years ago, and to ban alcohol from her home. Another spoke of her choice to leave a relationship after years of abuse. There are many stories of redemption on the reserve. The stories of redemption begin with the all too frequent tragedies, but end with the successes of many who have transcended difficult situations—who have overcome histories of abuse, alcoholism, drug addiction, residential schools, abandonment, foster homes, discrimination, imprisonment of loved ones, death of loved ones, widowhood, lone parenthood, poverty, welfare dependency, and so on.

Day 13. This was our last day together. While the course title contains the term "inequality" rather than "equality," the discussions of the past 12 weeks have made me realize that equality is as important a concept as inequality, and that the two concepts have to be examined together. Euro-Canadians focus on inequality; Aboriginals emphasize equality.

We spent the second half of the class today evaluating my attempts to ground the course in the experience of the students. We acknowledged the limitations of this strategy: a lack of distance between subject matter and students, risks involved with speaking out and with personal disclosure, suppression of voices and points of view, and occasional hurt feelings. While all of the students said that they had learned a lot, and I too had learned much, we all felt that a combination of our experimentally grounded pedagogy with more conventional pedagogy (including textbooks) would be less risky for both students and instructor. Just the same, we all recognized the need for textbook material that was not solely Euro-centric; increasingly there is an emerging Aboriginal literature that should be utilized.

I spent the afternoon at the college grading the papers handed in on this last day, and compiling the grades. Two things stood out in comparison to previous courses I had taught in this community. First, student grades tend to show improvement over the term where in previous classes this trend was not as evident. With 12 weekly essays and lots of regular feedback, most students improved their skills and performance. In previous classes, three multiple-choice exams over the course of the term tended to brutalize them each time. Second, final grades tended to be higher.

DISCUSSION

Despite my attempts to remove Whiteness from this course, Whiteness remained. I, the "White Guy," was clearly responsible for the course, was the person who graded each essay, and assigned the students' final grades. Further, because I frequently "facilitated" classroom discussions, I retained considerable influence over the dynamics of the class.

The success of a course like this depends on disclosure by individual participants, and a willingness to examine issues publicly from a variety of perspectives. However, public discussion is constrained by political correctness, that is, by an awareness of the perspectives that are more or less acceptable in the local community. Furthermore, disclosure by individuals is constrained by the risks involved in telling personal stories and revealing personal points of view. In a small community, disclosure about oneself and about others can have negative social consequences. Indeed, students reported being sanctioned, threatened, etc. for comments that they had made in class and that were relayed to others outside of class. While such intolerance and oppression run counter to the ideals of traditional Aboriginal culture, this was a sad reality of contemporary life on this reserve.

It seems that there is some advantage to having a curriculum and pedagogy that is "distanced" to some safe degree. One of the "functions" of using a text and lectures is that these methods of instruction allow students to distance themselves from the subject matter and to insulate themselves from the risks of personal disclosure and interpersonal scrutiny and criticism. White textbooks and a White guy giving lectures can inform without risk because both can be dismissed as irrelevant when it is expedient to do so. Distance, in the form of Whiteness, is then both problematic and functional.

Ironically, a Euro-centric pedagogy also protects the instructor. By remaining the racial and cultural other, one is excused, ignored or dismissed, but by trying to de-colonize and de-racialize the curriculum, the instructor invites scrutiny and may be judged, fairly or unfairly, as racist. An outsider who tries to infiltrate an in-group is often met with resistance. Building a curriculum from within the experience and culture of the Aboriginal community may be perceived by some as an intrusive attempt to "go native" by an instructor who is clearly not native.

EPILOGUE

I have always disliked the pedagogical tradition of a lecturer lecturing to a large and relatively passive audience of students. While my course evaluations suggest that I am fairly good at lecturing, I have long felt that students are short-changed by lectures, and that they learn far more when they actively participate in their learning. I have accumulated evidence over the years I have taught in First Nations colleges that Aboriginal students do not do as "well" as non-Aboriginal students in lecture-based courses with multiple-choice examinations; nevertheless, I have long been convinced that such courses are in the best interests of neither Aboriginal nor non-Aboriginal students. Nevertheless, when I am required to teach an overview course to 150 or more students, I reluctantly but pragmatically, and with considerable guilt, choose the lecture format given the shortages of time, personal energy, and institutional resources.

On those relatively rare occasions when my university has agreed to assign me to small-enrollment senior undergraduate seminars, usually with about 25 students, I have delighted in dispensing with lectures and examinations. Instead I facilitate a student-centred course where students select the topics they wish to pursue within the broad parameters of the course, make a series of oral presentations to the class, and write a series of papers, with their grade based wholly on their own active learning. This student-centred, professor-de-centred, experientially based, egalitarian, and cooperative classroom structure reflects many of the ideals of traditional Aboriginal pedagogy. The one thing that I learned most from my attempt to deal with Whiteness in pedagogy, is a confidence and willingness to de-centre a class, that is, to push myself as the professor to the sidelines where I function as a coach, and occasionally cheerleader, watching and marveling as students learn, largely and effectively, on their own. It is my impression that Aboriginals have valued the teacher who teaches by example, in humility. It goes against Whiteness that too often places the expert in a dominating position on centre-stage. We are better teachers when we teach less and thereby allow students to learn more. Aboriginal elders, it seems to me, figured this out a long time ago.

QUESTIONS FOR REFLECTION

1. How is being White problematic for an instructor who is teaching Aboriginal students?
2. Can a White instructor become "culturally sensitive" and, if so, how can cultural sensitivity be practiced in the classroom?
3. In what ways is the social construction of the Aboriginal and White as a dichotomy problematic?
4. How should Aboriginals and Whites negotiate pedagogy in a changing world?
5. How should an instructor deal with ideology (White and Aboriginal) in the classroom?

REFERENCES

Bailey, B. (2000). A White paper on Aboriginal education in universities. *Canadian Ethnic Studies, 32*(1), 126–141.
Dickason, O. (2006). *A concise history of Canada's First Nations* (Adapted by M. Calder). Toronto, ON: Oxford University Press.
Finkel, D. L., & Monk, S. G. (1999). Dissolution of the atlas complex. In B. A. Pescosolido & R. Aminzade (Eds.), *The social worlds of higher education: Handbook for teaching in a new century* (pp. 117–127). Thousand Oaks, CA: Pine Forge Press.
Freire, P. (1970). *Pedagogy of the oppressed*. New York, NY: Herder & Herder.
Frideres, J. S. (1998). *Aboriginal peoples in Canada: Contemporary conflicts* (4th ed.). Scarborough, ON: Prentice-Hall Canada.
Gaianguest, K. (1998). Radical pedagogy is social change in action. Response to "Practicing radical pedagogy: Balancing ideals with institutional constraints." *Teaching Sociology, 26*(2), 123–126.
Hare, J., & Barman, J. (2000). Aboriginal education: Is there a way ahead. In D. Long and O. Dickason (Eds.), *Visions of the heart: Canadian Aboriginal issues* (2nd ed.) (pp. 331–359). Toronto, ON: Harcourt Canada.
Hedley, M., & Markowitz, L. (2001). Avoiding moral dichotomies: Teaching controversial topics to resistant students. *Teaching Sociology, 29*, 195–208.
Jakubowski, L. M. (2001). Teaching uncomfortable topics: An action-oriented strategy for addressing racism and related forms of difference. *Teaching Sociology, 29*, 62–79.
LeClaire, N., & Cardinal, G. (2002). *Alberta Elders' Cree dictionary*, E. Waugh (Ed.). Edmonton, AB: University of Alberta Press.
Long, D. (1998). A radical teacher's dilemma. Response to "Practicing radical pedagogy: Balancing ideals with institutional constraints." *Teaching Sociology, 26*(2), 112–115.
Milloy, J. S. (1999). *A national crime: The Canadian government and the residential school system, 1879-1986*. Winnipeg, MB: University of Manitoba Press.
Schissel, B., & Wotherspoon, T. (2003). *The legacy of school for Aboriginal people: Education, oppression, and emancipation*. Don Mills, ON: Oxford University Press.
Sweet, S. (1998a). Practicing radical pedagogy: Balancing ideals with institutional constraints. *Teaching Sociology, 26*(2), 100–111.
Sweet, S. (1998b). Reassessing radical pedagogy. *Teaching Sociology, 26*(2), 127–129.
Te Hennepe, S. (1993). Issues of respect: Reflections of First Nations students' experiences in postsecondary anthropology classrooms. *Canadian Journal of Native Education, 20*(2), 193–260.

REFRAMING: HERBERT C. NORTHCOTT (2014)

In this reframing exercise, I will discuss briefly four topics: writing a chapter on "aging and ethnicity," being white in Mexico, "white lies," and (un)parallel White and Aboriginal lives.

First, during 2012, I worked on a chapter on "Ethnicity and Aging" for the seventh edition of a Canadian social gerontology textbook. This new chapter was an addition to a long-standing textbook (Novak, Campbell, & Northcott, 2013) that had gone through six editions previously without a chapter focusing on ethnicity and aging. As I worked on the chapter, I wrestled with the issue of race. I wondered if the chapter should be titled "Race, Ethnicity, and Aging." However, reviewers of the initial outline of the chapter had warned that race was a problematic construct. Further, I had the notion in my mind that if Canadians are to de-construct racism, writers have to stop re-creating it in academic discourse. I wrestled with a dilemma; it seemed to me that highlighting race perpetuated racism but ignoring race perpetuated White privilege.

While working on the chapter, I noted that in Canada authors of official publications no longer used the term "race." Instead, non-White persons were termed "visible minorities," as if Whites were invisible. Of course, the term visible minority is a euphemism for race. Ironically, the Canadian government excludes Canadian Aboriginals from the definition of the term visible minority. Nevertheless, I refused to organize the chapter around the racialized constructs of "visible minorities" and "Aboriginal peoples." Instead I focused on ethno-cultural diversity and let race enter the discussion in terms of cultural diversity rather than skin colour. Nevertheless, the chapter tends to highlight the cultural diversity of culturally exotic others and once again falls into the trap of privileging Whiteness by taking White culture as the standard against which all others are contrasted and evaluated.

Second, I spent the month of August 2012 as a visiting professor at a university in Mexico near Mexico City. I was struck by the lack of racial and cultural diversity in Mexico. Being White (and not speaking Spanish) made me stand out. Nevertheless, I was only called "Gringo" twice (that I know of), the second time partly in jest. Being visibly White in Mexico contrasted my experiences with being invisibly White in Canada. One gracious Mexican colleague passed me the maple syrup at breakfast without my asking and then reflectively commented on his acting on a stereotype about Canadians. As un-Canadian as it is to admit it, I don't particularly like maple syrup.

This brings me to my third point. We all have myths we believe about racialized ethno-cultural others. Steckley (2009) explores this notion by reviewing various myths that White people tend to "know" about the Inuit. Steckley examines how these myths came into existence and how they continue to be perpetuated. Steckley calls

D. E. Lund & P. R. Carr (Eds.), Revisiting The Great White North?, 69–70.

this mythic knowledge "White lies." When teaching First Nations students, I was struck by some of the myths First Nations people had about White people. I suppose we all tell "lies" about the other. We also tell lies about ourselves. "White lies," then, encompass the lies White people tell about others but also the lies White people tell about themselves.

A Dene elder spoke to a class recently at the University of Alberta. As he told his stories, I realized that he and I were born in the same year (1947) and in the same country (Canada). Nevertheless, I was struck by the drastic differences in the lives we had lived. We had lived very (un)parallel lives. This is my fourth point.

The Dene elder had been separated from his family at an early age and forced to attend residential school. There he witnessed and experienced abuses that over a half century later he could only speak of with great emotion. I went to school in Winnipeg and have pleasant memories of my family, friends, schoolmates, and teachers, of whom none abused me in any significant way. He spoke of his later adolescence and adult years as a traumatized search for himself. He spoke of his anger and even rage as a young man and the distraction and damage of alcohol abuse. As a young man, I had no real difficulty finding my way. I went to university and started a career as a professor. In time he became an elder and his difficult life experiences formed the basis of his wisdom. Of seven whom he was close to in his early years, four "did not make it," dying prematurely. My brothers and sisters and most of my friends went on to live healthy and successful lives. It seems ironic to observe that he was one of the lucky ones. My "luck" as a privileged White person tends to be taken for granted.

REFERENCES

Novak, M., Campbell, L., & Northcott, H. C. (2013). *Aging and society: A Canadian perspective* (7th ed.). Toronto, ON: Nelson Education.
Steckley, J. L. (2009). *White lies about the Inuit*. Toronto, ON: University of Toronto Press.

TRACEY LINDBERG

ON INDIGENOUS ACADEMIA

*The Hermeneutics of Indigenous Western Institutional
Participation—Eleven Theorems (2014)*
(With Five Addendums, Four New Theorems, and Four Life Lessons)

INTRODUCTION

Participating in non-Indigenous, Western educational institutions requires anti-colonial approaches. This chapter addresses anti-colonialism in the daily life, and provides eleven theorems related to Indigenous peoples' survival in non-Indigenous institutions. As an Indigenous woman lives, celebrates, and thrives in the Indigenous community, it has been important to document survival tips for Indigenous people in White institutions. White institutions, to many of us, are governed by White rules and made by White people. White institutions are colonial tools. Surviving the ongoing and new colonization requires old as well as new strategies.

ARGUMENT/ANALYSIS

Case 1: Institutional Brutality and Responsibility

When I was in law school, there was a backlash against women's group where I went to university. A group of upper-year law students, responding to the personally and politically empowering group "Women and the Law," organized a stag party. The group, without law school sanction or promotion, organized the party. The stag party was, I suppose a response to the weekly Women and the Law meetings where potential women's rights advocates discussed recent case law and the impact the equality clause of the Canadian Charter of Rights and Freedoms on women's empowerment. The stag party itself, so the rumour-mill went, featured a prostitute from the city. The instructions, as we were told in gossipy corners around the school, were to retain a woman of colour. Let me assure you that no one used the term "woman of colour" to describe the prostitute they wanted to, and allegedly did, retain.

I tell you this story for three reasons. First, I want you to remember that the law is both empowering and disempowering. It can be used as a tool to unite or to divide. It can be used as a symbol of pride or as a tool to shame. Secondly, I want you to

D. E. Lund & P. R. Carr (Eds.), Revisiting The Great White North?, 71–87.
© 2015 Sense Publishers. All rights reserved.

understand that I thought myself to be outside of it: neither a member of the feminist group nor, of course, of that collective of men and the law.

As an Indigenous woman, my first and primary political, social, and cultural allegiance is to my people. Imagine, if you will, going to school each day with men that found your culture and race so despicable that they had to pay someone from that race, *own* them in a sense, to feel empowered. Further imagine, if you will, that the political group responding to the action of hiring an Indigenous or Black prostitute was so uninformed as to be incapable to addressing race or culture in this context in a meaningful way. You would be most likely to feel, as I felt, completely alone in a place in which you dreamed about being. Finally, and importantly, this story is important because it is an example of the impact that gender hate and race hate have on your ability to function adequately or respond appropriately to "intellectual" issues. We call them "intellectual" issues and are told "not to take it so personally." My lesson is that you only take it personally when it is about your person. You only tell someone not to take it personally when it is not about their person.

I felt outside of a system that I was supposed to be free to participate in. I felt objectified, labelled, and like a version of who I was, a perverted version placed on display. I tried to calm myself down by telling myself it was just gossip; it might not be true. One night, late at night, it hit me: If this was the gossip, there was horror in that someone could imagine this as truth.

Theorem Number One: most people you meet in academia will never have met an Indigenous person before. Almost all will have no Indigenous friends. As you are the only first Indigenous person that they will know, every statement you make becomes the "Indian position." Speak wisely. Be informed. Practice your principles that I learned in law school, and which I carry with me into my current job as professor: you do not belong here.

Theorem Number Two: survival here means visiting; do not make this your home. You are an observer, and to survive you have to treat this experience as a visit to a foreign land. Keep tightly bound to your family, friends, and community.

Addendum Number One (2014): The entire event that I detailed above – men and the law, law/men paying money for Indigenous women and/or black women's bodies triggered me on the day I heard about it, in the days that I wrote this, and today as I write this. When initially written, I could not deconstruct or name what this triggering was. My theorem – addressing Indigenous people as outsider/only/ the one is still something I understand. Additional meaning that has come to me over time is this: the objectification and dehumanization of Indigenous peoples, particularly women, contributes to the violence that faces us. It *is* a form of violence that we face. That violence – women murdered and missing, men murdered and missing, children murdered and missing and yanked from their homes – is embedded institutionally and in individuals. My terror and triggering from that event that I was not able to place in a theorem then, is this: when the collective dehumanization of Indigenous peoples and peoples of colour enters and institution, the potentiality for violence multiplies and morphs into forms which are very difficult to observe and unpack.

As a person with experience in a number of institutional contexts, I see and hear ideas, analyses, and conclusions that are seemingly benign on the surface, but which hearken to days when the brutality of Othering was politely entrenched in legislation. In my experienced self, I now can discern the brutality as politely entrenched in debate about where courses should be housed, who "owns" credentials, and who is appropriate to teach what knowledge/information. As someone who, in the intervening years, has been taught by knowledge holders, respectful presentation of information and true intellectual accountability, my understanding has changed.

Teaching Number One: We must remember our obligations when we get into rooms of privilege and prestige. We must remember our relatives, remember those who have no voices, remember those who were killed, disappeared, lost, taken away, and for whom sitting in those privileged rooms was never allowed. We don't speak for everyone, but we can speak for some. We have to. I mention the violence against our peoples in every conceivable room, in every speech that I can. I tie the privileged brutality of the institutions we create, replicate and reify to the ongoing physical violence we face as Indigenous peoples. If I work there and I do no different than my predecessors, I am a part of it and complicity in the impact on our peoples.

Case 2: Academizing the Indian

It is hard for me to write these days. Believe me, it is not because I am not as angry as I used to be. Mostly, I think that I am working my anger out in different ways now. I used to protest, write, and sing my anger to the world. Later, I found other ways to numb it; too much of anything will take away the tourist blues. Also, it seems to me that it is easy to dismiss the angry Indian. I do not want to be dismissed, and I am still angry. My anger should not defuse/diffuse the message. My anger is part of the message. Don't shoot the messenger just because she's enraged.

For the past nine years I have worked for non-Indigenous institutions. Primarily, I took the jobs because I have bills to pay and habits to support. Make no mistake, though; in this war in the workplace there is no such thing as a civilian Indian. I believe that the search that leads employers to me is of a value-added nature. I believe the perception is that *not only* am I hard working, educated and bright – I also happen to be Indigenous. Somehow this is perceived as adding to some sort of cultural milieu, and it also adds instant expert status to me.

I am expected to do my work – the same as everyone else does – and I am expected to field all questions Indigenous. Has the non-Indigenous academic been asked to translate the word "papoose," provide information about the hibernation patterns of bear, or to discern the phylum of plants in the everyday fulfillment of duties? (In the latter instance, I rudely commented that they did not teach that at Harvard.)

True, it is a hard line to draw; we are western educated and attempting to preserve and cherish our traditions. That people do not know what those traditions are is the alarming fact.

Secondary to that is this truism: there is a sense that we are personally indebted to those who hired us, to the degree that we are perceived as "uppity" or "angry" if we do not happily accept mentorship, gleefully appreciate inappropriate inquisitiveness, or dumbly accept ethnocentric standards and dialogue. That onus, that particular brand of race hate and the degeneration of Indigenous people's merit, more than our own will to remain strong diminishes us in the eyes of our peers. At every level of achievement that I have had – entry to law school, entry to graduate school, and my current position as professor – one person (in each situation, a non-Indigenous woman) has told me that I got the position, seat, or job as a result of their recommendation, influence, or good will.

I know that no person makes it in this world alone. I am so very thankful for and proud of the people who sacrificed their time, energy, and money to make sure that I was successful. These are my true friends and family, who drove me to interviews, rented houses for me that I could not, and who paid to ship my meager belongings from one country to another. Indigenous and non-indigenous women and men have let me camp at their place, mailed me sweetgrass, and talked me out of quitting school or job, and moving home. These peoples' sacrifices cost them, and were truly labours of love. How am I to compare these gifts to a letter, attendance at an interview, or a pleasing review of my resume? I am grateful to be viewed as accomplished, but these accomplishments are mine and my loved ones.'

When I am called upon to show gratefulness at having achieved the placement, gotten the interview, or even the job, I am required to acknowledge that I am not yet free of bonds of ownership. My accomplishments are supposedly good but they were not enough. I needed a favour from someone as brilliant as she was who could look and see that I had value added in my application. Why are the recently poor expected to be so personally indebted for success?

Addendum Number Two (2014): When I read this now and try to reflect upon what drove that anger, it seems a thousand years away, that experience of newness to institutions. I recall going home each night, wide open, like a wound. My sense of alone – aloneness – within the institution is what still pulses. It was isolating to work in the institutions that I did. My experience of that obligingly thankful worker had a flip side: because I was not, I think I might have been perceived as thankless. Merit and hard work, in my mind, were enough. There was a fair amount of gamesmanship and benefits to be gained from social machinations that I did not understand. The unwritten code of traded favours, protected turf and meeting mouth closed was lost on me. If I were in a reality show I would have been that person who said, "I did not come here to make friends" and "I do not have a strong social game" proudly.

It has also been to my disadvantage. Like any person, I have strong friendships and associations, welcoming and negative personal characteristics. I would have been so much better off had I found a group of people who were like-minded with regard to their own social concerns. Part of my isolation was pure will – I *would* do this on my own. Part of it was the arrogance of youth – I *don't* need anyone. Part of it was a real and valid response to being slotted, manipulated, and pushed and pulled in ways that were offensive and painful to me.

My experience of educational and some other institutions is that of violence; I understand the institutions as part of a continuum of colonization and I have responded with resistance and anger. They were necessary and survivalist approaches: they were not conducive to thriving. Sometimes I confused institutional with individual. This is no more an excuse than it is an apology; it's an awareness that I share.

I *did* and *do* get by with a little help from my friends. Mostly, I made friends in the local Indigenous community. Once there was a body of Indigenous peoples working within the institutions, I began to socialize and build my relationships with them. However, I have watched newer Indigenous colleagues *Academize* sooner, to a greater degree and with comfort that I have never had. They often get things done because they are institutionally savvy and because they built a non-Indigenous network. I do not regret having not made those choices. My work now is principally with Indigenous Nations, communities, and citizens. It is the best work I have ever done. I might not have been the person who could do the work had I spent my time building internal alliances and capacity.

More importantly, is the wish that I had known a different gentleness in my experience and character as I worked in non-Indigenous educational institutions. Certainly, I have faced aggression, bullying, and unkindness. In this respect, I did need to be tough. However, with a larger group of women, people of colour, people who experienced oppression prior to and once arriving at educational institutions, I might not have experienced it so directly, painfully, or singularly. My addendum: if you are going to play a social game, do it in a way that protects you, surrounds you with people who might understand your experience of institutional imperialism and brutality, and your natural inclination to resist both.

In my peripheral view, I can see the people who still insisted that I be thankful. In my read of that now, that need to be thanked (which is entirely different than grace and thankfulness) is a bit like the modern day pass system. I could travel the institutions freely, but always with the awareness that I wouldn't be there without *someone's* generosity. It is colonizing and it is abusive. This lesson was a hard one for me to learn and it visited me again and again until I understood: this kindness was not for me. It was for the person providing it. Eventually, over time, I began to work with and ask for support from people who did it not because they had some broad notion of social justice or neo-liberal support of oppressed peoples, but because they saw the worth and merit of the work I did. It was emancipating.

If I were to provide a script for the first two years of teaching that could be posted on the wall of a new academic's office, it would look something like this:

1. The only debt you have is to the family and community that supported you to get here. You repay that through advocacy, writing and building.
2. No one deserves this more than you.

Teaching Number Two: Those principles and values we are taught in the lodge, in the home, at kitchen tables, at gatherings are like a muscle: they must be exercised in order for them to be relied upon when you need them. You can academize[1] *those*, I think. It's a struggle and it is painful at times, but in order to get a good sleep at night, they will have to be what you do and how you do it. I don't always succeed. The pressure to give your stuff up, to open up your world and the sometimes shared understanding that you are obliged to *be* the systemized Indigenous person possesses the capacity to be soul chewing. My saving strength has been, in times of great stress, pressure and upset in the academy, those muscles.

Theorem Number Three: This success is not yours alone. Share your joy with family and friends. When you are required intrinsically to be thankful to those who perceive themselves as fundamental to your success, it is a level of supplication and subjugation that you should never have to live through.

Case 3: Indigenous Favouritism

In my experience in the non-Indigenous work-world, I have been told that I was not able to act impartially toward Indigenous clients, that I did not pay attention to billing Indigenous clients, and that I refused to see anything as anything other than an "Indian" issue.

Good for me. I am surviving, strong, and full of fight, I tell myself. The issue is a harder one than that, though. We are coming to a time when we will be able to build our institutions and staff them. Still, I see by the number of non-Indigenous consultants advising our Nations and their leaders that the dependency upon non-Indigenous resources, experts, and understandings exists. My fear is that we will have no place to come home to.

The principal political agency in my Treaty area is under the directorship of a non-Indigenous woman. There are several people from those umbrella Treaty Nations who are similarly educated and who do not have a chance at the position she has, because of the institutional preferences. After 10 years in a post-secondary training-plan (one in which I was cared for and mentored by many beautiful Indigenous people as well as some non-Indigenous peoples who told me to study hard) I wonder: When can we come home? Sure, there are positions available, but the preponderance of those still do not go to the people in whose homelands the positions were created.

Are we still so immersed in the effects of non-Indigenous economic domination that we cannot see beyond the immediate? How many Indigenous lawyers do you know who actually live on reserve? How many utilize the reserve as a tax shelter but maintain residence in the city? How many bands utilize the services of non-Indigenous firms? How many medical doctors live on reserve, train with traditional healers, and have been offered positions in their homelands?

So, we find ourselves relegated to academic and consulting positions in non-Indigenous institutions. How many of us train as lawyers, doctors, anthropologists, and historians to find ourselves working in Native Studies departments because we see everything as an "Indian issue"? How many of us look for the water spirits in the mainstream? I know of many Indigenous women and men trained in the same manner as I who end up living in the cities where our training is viewed as secondarily to our ethnicity as we take up the "Indian specialist" positions in the universities, colleges, and other institutions.

Addendum Number Three (2014): Ultimately, self-determination is about being about to build your own home. Metaphorically, in moving into western academia I was moving in to a foreign land. My home is not here. I consider myself as having taken a rental home. And, it is my feeling that I got in the academic door early and then complained about the accommodations.

Complaint is less valuable than concerted efforts to critique. Critique is less valuable than suggestions for growth and change. Suggestions are sometimes less valuable than building something. My Indigenous Studies experience has been beautifully challenging. Once here, once in the Indigenous Studies door, I started to think about what we could build, what we could challenge, and who we were doing it for. This, too, was at times painful. One of my colleagues told me a decade ago that another colleague offered public support for Indigenous Studies but critiqued the department and our efforts in small groups and in places where we did not attend. What I was expecting was a tough discussion about *why* Indigenous Studies programming is important, why we have to not just address enrolments, but the cultural programming as vital and revitalizing. What I got was silence. Silence does not allow for critique, change or growth. Silence is the space within which thought, debate and development dies.

In the autumn of my life and career, I think I am more peaceably able to entertain the notion of challenge for change. What I have seen happening is an increasing dependency within institutions on the *BIS* (bums in seats, registrations) math to justify the existence of Indigenous Studies. It is a frank discussion to have: we *need* to offer Indigenous Studies programs *because* of the devaluation and colonization of Indigenous Knowledge. We have to offer Indigenous Studies courses and programming precisely because of the racialized perceptions that it is not necessary, is not beneficial and belongs in some hybridity of Canadian/ethno/other studies. Institutions need to commit to Indigenous academics, the development of the Indigenous academy and a body of Indigenous knowledge within western academic institutions because the erasure (through *BIS* math, through defunding, through matrices which are set up to measure success based upon economic indicators) of Indigenous peoples is too easily embedded in "business" decisions.

Institutional commitment to Indigeneity starts with Indigenous peoples who are from the territory upon which the institution is located. It continues with the building of representative voices and participants who can look to the needs of the local, national and international Indigenous educational community to see what is needed: for Indigenous students and non-Indigenous students.

Theorem Number Four: Indigenous academics will be expected to be specialists in all that is Indigenous, regardless of the breadth of our training and experience. Do not take this responsibility lightly. If you do not know the answer, confer with those who do (Elders and Spiritual Leaders are a wonderful place to start).

This is not to suggest that we willingly accept the veil of Indigenous expertise. In my experience, whether we accept it or not, there is a presumption of expertise and we must do honour to our people by being informed, being involved, and following protocol in places which do not respect or are indifferent to the rules we live by.

We see a middle-class and upper-class Indigenous elite developing here and know that we are perceived to be, indeed may actually be, a part of it. We attempt to be true. We study the traditions and relish the traditions and learn the traditions. We are ready to come home. We are not victims. We are earning a living. Believe me, though; this can be easily distinguished from living well.

We are the first generation to witness the impact and effect of Indigenous training and education on the non-Indigenous workforce. We find ourselves turned away from academic and professional positions because institutions already "have an Indian."

Theorem Number Five: We may be the only Indigenous people that an institution feels it has "room" for. Part of our responsibility, even if we claim no representative status, is to educate the institutions that we work for in terms of inclusiveness and representative capacity. We need to participate in policy development, hiring committees and equity positions which have, at their root, the goal of encouraging both a welcoming environment for Indigenous participants and ensuring the successful recruitment of Indigenous participants.

I recognize the incredible affluence and privilege that comes with these positions-the ability to write this, stare out the window of my heated home, and drink my coffee while cogitating, is a gift. For that reason, I do not want to complain as, financially, I am part of an Indigenous elite that has tremendous buying power. This wealth, my education, and my urban life contribute to the potential alienation that I could still feel. Still, the restlessness runs within me, within many of us, as we pace over hardwood floors in concrete cities behind the velvet rope of academia. We must still ask: when can we come home?

For those of us who have trained extensively in the non-Indigenous academic institutions, who find relationship between non-Indigenous advisors and Indigenous governments solidly entrenched, we find that we are threatened by, and threatening, to the institutions, organizations and communities which we are no longer able to live (if indeed we have ever lived there) or work in. This is the colonial legacy: we are trained to the degree of outsider status, and perceived as sell-outs because we went to school and live in cities. We are perceived as (and sometimes are) elitist in our thinking because we have *eliticized* ourselves with education. We are perceived as thinking we are too good to be "regular Indians." We are hired and perceived as "lesser candidates" in Western institutions because of the stigma attached to affirmative action. We are perceived as "one of the good ones" (even though we are usually the only Indigenous person anyone in our faculties knows personally).

So, many of us live in cities and travel to our communities when work and circumstance allow. We gather remnants from the fabric of our Indigenous lives because colonization has devastated our economies. We piece them together in front of classrooms, in the absence of other Indigenous faculty-members, and in front of computer screens late at night when our colleagues are researching papers and our communities are celebrating, mourning, or gathering. We patch together memories and snippets of understanding that we are fortunate enough to be able to gather from each visit from a relative or to our communities. It is a beautifully onerous existence.

Theorem Number Six: Part of the teachings of egalitarianism includes the notion that we are to share out wealth with other members of our nations. This can include ensuring that Indigenous philosophies, understandings and notions are included in course development, programming and policy development.

In the old days, I would have followed the oath established by an older relative, spiritual leader, or mentor. Like many Indigenous academics, I find myself part of the first wave of Indigenous people who have successfully joined the non-Indigenous economy. Hopefully, I will break ground for others.

I like to think of us as word warriors. We battle in classrooms, boardrooms and faculty lounges across the borders. We are the scouts sent ahead to observe the terrain and the habits and strategies of the Second Peoples. We take the information back to our nations to strategize and equip us better in the continuing battle for self-determination. We are the translators at the negotiations for the peaceful coexistence of the First Peoples and the Second. Skilled and trained in both languages, we try to balance hermeneutics with humanism in this interpretive exercise.

Case 4: Resisting Institutionalization/Individualization or Building a Collectivity

I have had a number of *battles-royale* with faculty members in whom I observed what I understood to be preferential hiring, when I saw women and people of colour marginalized, where I believe that colleagues invested themselves actively in the fostering or development of conflicts or fissures between colleagues in order to establish themselves as "being on the right side," develop their reputation as being one who "helps" Indigenous peoples, and for reasons that seem to me to be predicated on the understanding that the Indigenous self-determining constituents of the institutions were not thankful, not reasonable, not amenable, not behaving in a way understood to be "Indigenous" enough.

In one instance, when I protested, pointing out to a colleague that the decision at hand was unfair, my colleague responded: "So, it's not fair. You can't always be fair."

This lesson taught me so much about the ethics and situational kindness rife within universities. It also taught me the distinct distinctly different philosophical underpinnings we are taught in Indigenous nations, and which makes our participation in academia so very difficult. When you are raised in the environment and with the ethic of balance and fairness, you are instantly searching for that balance and fairness in your life. Not finding it in your work place, you are viewed as utopian and unrealistic. As long as our realism is their optimism, we are still living in balance. As long as we are labeled idealists, we are closer to fairness.

Addendum Number Four (2014): Those royal battles (which I now think of as battling imperialism) pass in my memory today because there have been many. Those with whom I battled might not have the fleeting recall of it and hold them closer because they did not have as many battles. I don't think of myself as an aggressive person but I realize now, that for almost a decade I have felt like I was battling for my life. For the life of my family. For the life of our peoples. I took on every fight, jumped on every opportunity to address Othering, erasure, racialization, silencing, stereotyping, discriminatory treatment, or perceptions of the same. It. Was. Exhausting.

It also led to an understanding: I cannot fight every battle.

And another: not every person is oppositional.

And another: there has to be a better way. To thrive. To create space. To be sure we are included in decisions that impact our families, communities and Nations.

I had to learn not to think of my academic life as a struggle for our existence. I had to start to think of it as looking for ways, means and support to amplify the need, exemplify the approach (to anti-imperialism and anti-colonialism), and to welcome others into the struggle. There are often too few of us at any given western institution with too little access to resources and decision-making authority to develop a narrative of conflict politics.

Those muscles: of kindness, gentleness, courage, and fairness are best used when exercised and regularized, not when flexed in reflexive responses to battles and arising issues.

Those muscles are best exercised collectively. With your community. With your colleagues. Build something. Build something that is not reliant on money or favours. Build something that sustains and enriches and the academic stuff will follow: publications, kudos, institutional support and even funding. Build something. We have immense stores information, knowledge, resources and people. Look to where you came from to *act*, rather than where you are stuck to react.

For me, it started with this: we need to be able to smudge. We need to have a place where we can speak honestly. So we lobbied. We spoke with Executives.

We explained. We described. We showed. We invited. We built something: rooms on different institutional locations where we could smudge, gather, and speak full truths. From there – everything else is possible.

Theorem Number Seven: The principles of balance and the oft-stereotyped notion of harmony have their roots grains of truth and elemental understandings. Strive for the Indigenous in the everyday, particularly in spaces that are not welcoming to it.

Theorem Number Eight: You will battle every day for balance in your Western workspace. It will be hard. In the five years that I have been a professor, I have taught in classrooms that were filled with only a few or no Indigenous students. None of them particularly care that I struggle to ensure there is Indigenous content in courses and programming. None of them have thanked me for walking out of academic meetings to learn, and I am simply there to facilitate an environment in which they can find the material accessible.

Case 5: Remember Why You Are Here

My job is easy: I am there to make sure students are challenged and that they see themselves, their truths, their philosophies, and their actualities reflected in their courses, their professors, and their programs. This information does not have to be "All Indian," but it does have to be accessible. So, you struggle to ensure that stereotypes are eliminated and, further, that representations are respectful. You educate yourself and keep updating your skills to make sure that you are as responsive to your students, faculty and staff as you require them to be to the information and lessons that you teach. You eradicate polemics from your approach, develop new theories, and pay attention to the lessons brought to you, old and new.

This is painful. Having developed course-materials at an introductory level rife with generalizations, I realize I wrote them now to include all of the information that was missing from entire courses and curricula. Having lectured to law students, criminal justice students, Indigenous studies students, and general studies students, I can tell you that the most important lesson I have learned is to respect your audience. For the most part, they know they have learned very little accurate information about Indigenous peoples. This moment in the classroom, this opportunity in a lecture hall, and that chance to write curriculum is your moment to truly undo some of the damage that colonization has visited upon us.

Some people will reject out of hand any information or approach that you take to the information. Figuring out why the information is rejected and how to present it in a convincing and effective manner is one of the most useful skills you can acquire. Some people will be angry with you: learning that which is challenging should make you question the preconceived notions and analytical patterns you have subscribed over time. This is painful, and some people will respond to that in painful ways.

In one of my courses, an upper-year elective examining the traditional and contemporary roles of Indigenous women, one Cree woman told me she felt like she was being indoctrinated, that I was forcing her to believe something she did not personally believe in. I told her that was a lesson for each of us in that. For her, the lesson was that each instructor has a bias and a perspective *and* that they have, at least, tools that every student can choose to access and use or reject in the construction of their own ideologies. My lesson was two-fold: I had to learn to foster independent thought and to include information that was "value-free" for all students to access. My second lesson was a more difficult one: I had to make sure that the information and skills that I provide are simply that, a toolbox everyone can view and understand, and then determine whether or not they can avail themselves of the tools.

Theorem Number Nine: No one will thank you, nor should they. Your confidence and comfort will have to come from outside of the academic system. Those same friends and family who got you there will sustain you while you work to create a space in which you, and Indigenous students, can thrive.

I also learned about the resistance to change on an institutional level. When I started at one university I sat on a *Neheyiwak* ("the people" in Cree) caucus, a group of Indigenous faculty and staff at the institution who gathered as a collective to address concerns of inclusiveness, respect, and parity for Indigenous people who worked at and attended the University. Initially, we proposed a model of participation whereby Indigenous faculty and staff would work together in a center, department, or college. Our goals included the development of culturally respectful and responsive courses, programming, and institutional support. The report we tabled, and the recommendations we made, were for a five-year period. In retrospect, I can state that the proposal was broad and aggressive and, as a result, it was also not politically viable in the university environment. An ally in the institution told me that those of us who had written the proposal were called the "radical" Indians, labeled "troublemakers," and passed by individuals in the hallway who made aspersions about our racial "pedigree," urban residences, and lack of knowledge of the university political system. We gathered our strength, united our position and kept individuals in the institution who were supportive in the loop about our goals and aspirations. It was a very lonely time.

In a lesson garnered from my late friend and colleague, Patricia Monture, and as advised by one of our late Elders and colleagues, we decided to stop reacting and to act. We decided to build something new rather than critique something existing. With a very supportive institutional executive, we proposed and built an academic centre. Fully staffed by Indigenous people, our mandate included the development of partnerships with Indigenous institutions, organizations, and individuals. It also included the development of courses for the public and research materials accessible by Indigenous communities and other academic and administrative staff, both of which are respectfully developed with the inclusion of materials and information generated by Indigenous Elders, Spiritual Leaders, academics, and community members.

Addendum Number Five (2014): In retrospect, the relationship that we had with a fully committed institutional executive was key in our development as an academic entity within the post-secondary system. The executive encouraged us to meet with other academic centres, tell them about our proposal and to address the concerns raised by other faculty and staff members. We were yelled at in one instance. We were told that we were not supported by individuals who would not self-identify in another. But we were respectful and responsive as a collective of Indigenous peoples who wanted to build something beautiful.

We also were supported by many staff members and faculties. We had silent supporters and active allies who would speak to issues of relevance to Indigenous peoples and who supported a collective workplace.

We have had consecutive executives who allowed us room to grow, room to imagine and even room to make mistakes. That has made all of the difference. In only one instance have we faced open resistance to our autonomy and our attempts to build self-determining capacity within an institutional context. Had we faced this when the article was first written, my response would have been an immediate public discussion of the intent and impact of resistance to Indigenous independence. Now, with a better understanding of the challenge that we ask people to undertake and the goals of our institutional existence more firmly understood, we approach such resistance like water on a rock rather than a stone through a window. It is sometimes dreadfully slow and isolating, but with that patience has come institutional change, opportunities to learn from our mistakes (and those of others), and the development of the knowledge that we have work to do in order to find allies, people with shared understanding of institutional resistance and oppression.

All of the talk of supportive Executive leads me to this: they needed to have a united, prepared, self-determining collective of Indigenous activists/workers from whom to take advice. We worked hard on developing processes, spaces, and programs that reflected the principles of respect, reciprocity, and accountability. This was the hard work. Building a team with no institutional job descriptions, a full list of activities to undertake that are not acknowledged by the systems or processes the institution has already developed, and independence of institutionalization to the degree required not to subscribe to the institution's parameters of workload, work ethic and work responsibilities has been exceptionally challenging. None of our team accepted institutional standards as our guideposts and continue to advocate for self-definition and self-determination in the institution. This independence has led to allegiances and affiliation with communities and Nations that value the possibility of a mutually respectful and reciprocal relationship with a western institution.

It means we don't quite fit anywhere. We have a hundred telephone calls and emails a month that remind us: your work, your funding, your community project, your course, your staffing procedures, your flat management structure, your shared responsibility for decision-making do not reflect institutional policy. That is hard. But it is important that we do not. Fitting is temptingly close to cooptation.

I have rage-filled moments when I feel hurt, misunderstood, and silenced. But I also have reflective days when I am able to accept that institutional or individual resistance is an opportunity to learn. That opportunity to learn, I have found out, is so much easier to live through and in with a collective of Indigenous peoples who are kindly, gently and courageously living through it with me. Collectivity is key. In the best moments, we move in unity of purpose – even while not sharing absolutely our theories or practice of self-determination. Individually, we are committed. In that sense, we are a fantastically strong collective.

Theorem Number Ten: Institutional change starts with individuals who work in institutions.

Case 6: When the Institution Overwhelms

I have no time to write. I have no time to write this. In this mathematical equation in the university system which involvement I have found that not only does the community involvement not weigh equally in this equation, but that as (for a long time) the sole Indigenous faculty member, community involvement, and teaching was all that I had time for. In the day-to-day weighting of the priorities involved in being an Indigenous academic, writing has fallen to the wayside. Given that I became an academic because I love to read and write this has left me feeling bereft, like I am missing out an a part of myself that needs attention.

Insult follows the injury. You do not get tenure until you write. It often does not matter that we write briefs and reports for our governments at home, that we sit on every conceivable committee or that we generate memos for the university on the inclusion of Indigenous people its planning. There is a formula in place in academia, and it can find our credentials wanting.

My experience with the bar exams in Saskatchewan and Alberta has been quite similar to this. Not only am I not tested in the areas of law (Indigenous law, land rights, and land claims negotiation) that I specialize in, but also, neither is any lawyer who calls herself an "Indian law" lawyer in Canada.

In the utopian/Indigenous world that I envision, we have our own institutions to work at. A board of my peers can prove my competency and attest to my familiarity with and expertise in Indigenous law and government. The skills required for promotion in my expertise in Indigenous law and government. The skills required for promotion in my position include respect, kindness, and contribution to the nation. Indigenous people from all nations who practice an ethic of care, who understand that the world is supposed to be fair, and for whom equity is first nature, surround me. I struggle, admirably, to examine what post-colonial means in an historical context (now that there really is post-colonial). My agendas are written, known, and unthreatening. I do not walk out of Centre meetings, write memos of understanding, or create a paper trail for all of my activities to guarantee the authenticity of my work.

Self-determination is an adjective to describe what we have done, not a verb to describe what we will do. Sovereignty is not a dirty word. Elders and Spiritual Leaders fully participate in our formal education, and are acknowledged and honoured in the same way we honour learned people in other societies.

I work and live on the reserve. All of those disenfranchised by Canadian legislation have been welcomed home with open arms. We build. We pray. My children are healthy and happy. They learn our history in history class. I can sleep well. I can write. I have a few reasons to be angry. I am home.

Theorem Number Eleven: Until we assume our rightful positions in our nations, keep that anger. You will need it. Some days it will be all that can sustain you. The same thing that compels you to walk out that door will, surprisingly, sustain you and motivate you to effect change.

Case 7: Following the Path, Wherever it Leads[2]

It is August. 2014. A few leaves have started to turn. This paper is late to the editors. All papers are late to the editors. I still have no time to write. Thinking about this, I know that many of my colleagues are much more "productive" (read: published) than I am. My personal calendar changes from year to year, but I have tried to remain someone who speaks publicly as often as is possible. I went into academia because I know I have a story to tell that has not been told. I love writing. But, I haven't published much. Since I wrote this article I have written one novel and a fourth of a textbook. A handful of pieces. Forty or so speeches. A few distance courses.

There is within me, and I am certain within a number of Indigenous academics, a fear about putting the words into the world. Writing this piece initially cost me months of sleep and I am wringing my mouse over this updated piece, perhaps now for entirely different reasons. My fears in 2007 were about revealing painful things and putting something hard into the world. My pain, when I now read the first edition of the article, is so palpable that it hurts. "How could it hurt me and be of value to others?" I wondered.

Now, as autumn beckons – my own and the season – and guided by those muscles, I am less fearful of the pain that might come. Not because it is unimportant, but because if your intent is kind and your work is gentle, you are doing much more than publishing a piece. You are a microphone for someone or some place that wants their voice amplified. Looking back and forward, my fear was being understood to be *the* Indigenous voice. I didn't and don't want that mantle. There are many of us who can speak to our own experience. I just don't want mine to be taken as or understood to be anything other than my own. In being fearful of making mistakes, misinterpreting my experience or that of others, and recording a mistake forever I was doing the work a disservice. What if my logic is flawed, research is erroneous, or understandings are wrong? Well, it will serve as a humbling reminder of my understanding and development at one moment in time. My experience has led me to meet with some who feel like me: like our work in the communities we work for and with is so precious that we don't want to build our careers on the experiences of peoples who are still suffering. Moreover, there is a group of us, I am convinced, who slow down at the publication stage because we don't want to do harm.

What I have come to understand is this: keeping quiet may do more harm than amplifying the voices, with our inevitable mistakes. I started to read the theses and dissertations of other Indigenous scholars whose work I had taken to, or which I really admired. They made mistakes. Or didn't. They aggregated. Sometimes teetered on stereotypes. Generalized. Offended me.

They were brave enough to make mistakes. One Indigenous author, in his opening note, thanked a reviewer who had pointed out an error in his thinking. It was a moment of clarity for me. We. Those who have been dubbed the "word warriors" by some of our colleagues. We. Will make mistakes. We endeavor to be informed, be absolutely ethical and to amplify the stories as best we can. But we are human and humans are flawed, possess opinions, and make mistakes.

So, recently, knowing I was going to make mistakes – I started sending some of the things I was writing out to be reviewed. Not just to publish, mind you, but things that I thought had to be said. Things that have no footnotes (because our lives have been footnoted and I want us to be all over the page).

When I now think of why I became an academic and that story, that entirely different voice that needed amplification, I think of it as an obligation. People put their trust in me. People gave their time to me. People told me their beautiful, terrible, violent, and healing stories. It is my obligation not to leave the *wordgift* unopened.

Between the first edition of this work and this edition, I applied for and was awarded a research chair. My work is with individuals, communities and Nations who have faced colonial violence and whose stories have not been told. I am opening the *wordgift*. My work takes me on the road and to people most of the academic year. I record stories and then build them into books. In one community, they asked me to build the stories into a documentary. I have no idea how to do this. But I am doing it.

All of those things built: a good team of Indigenous scholars and staff, a supportive executive, strong relations with Indigenous communities, are the foundation for the work that I do now. It is hard. It is a privilege. And I will tell those stories. I will tell the hard stories and the lovely ones. I will tell my own and my family's. I will tell my Nations' and other Nations'. I have to. This is where the road led.

And. I finished this addendum.

Theorem Number Twelve: Remember what set you on this path; it may be the divining rod that guides you when it is hard to know what you are supposed to be doing.

Theorem Number Thirteen: There will come a moment or a series of moments when you have to make decisions about what you want to do with the gifts you have been given. If you do not listen, you will feel the absence of them, like a phantom limb. Listen.

Theorem Number Fourteen: Think not just about the classrooms you had as an Indigenous student, think about the readings you wish you had in front of you as you studied. You can write those.

Theorem Number Fifteen: You are going to make mistakes. Try not to. Don't become immobilized by the fear of them. Once you make them, take responsibility for them and learn from them. They may be our best teacher.

Teaching Number Three: An Elder told me this, when I was struggling with writing: "Smudge the page. Ask the grandmothers for help."

Teaching Number Four: Life can be fair. Make it so.

QUESTIONS FOR REFLECTION

1. Are institutions White?
2. How do the histories, employees, and policies of institutions reflect Whiteness and White principles?
3. In what way can individual Whiteness address institutionalized Whiteness?
4. What aspects of Whiteness are difficult to quantify? Is there a reason for the difficulty in articulating Indigenous responses to institutional colonization and racism?
5. What obligations do Institutions have to address Indigeneity? Individuals who work within them? What examples do you have?
6. What would you build / could you build in order to address Indigeneity with authenticity within a non-Indigenous institution?

NOTES

[1] In this sense, I mean "placing them gently into the academy," not colonizing them.
[2] This is an entirely new section. I wrote it because some things were not addendums. Some things were entirely new.

JULIE CAOUETTE & DONALD M. TAYLOR

"DON'T BLAME ME FOR WHAT MY ANCESTORS DID"

Understanding the Impact of Collective White Guilt

INTRODUCTION

"Although textbook authors no longer sugarcoat how slavery affected African Americans, they minimize White complicity in it. They present slavery virtually as uncaused, a tragedy, rather than a wrong perpetrated by some people on others" (Loewen, 1995, p. 138). The same rationalization applies to the internal colonization of Aboriginal people by White European Canadians and, indeed, this is precisely how the treatment of Aboriginal people is portrayed in Canadian history textbooks (Colavincenzo, 2003). Such a negative portrayal is certain to impact White Canadians' perceptions of their involvement, or their perceived lack of involvement, in the genesis and maintenance of racial inequality.

Many Canadians claim that culpability cannot run in their bloodline. As one participant in our experiment declared: "The sins of the father should not fall on the children." Young mainstream Canadians distance themselves from responsibility by emphasizing that wrongful actions were committed in the past by some distant European ancestors. However, many fail to consider that we are all accomplices in a society that perpetuates past wrongs in the present day. We don't appreciate that historical events are linked first, to societal barriers faced by Aboriginal people and second, to the unearned privileges White Canadians have gained as a result (Feagin, Vera, & Batur, 2001; Rothenberg, 2002; Tatum, 1997, 2000). As one of our research participants proclaimed:

> The effects of brutally unfair and racist treatment by European settlers are still being felt today; however, Canadians today feel disconnected from the past so they have trouble feeling responsible. They also have trouble accepting the fact that they are benefiting from previous transgressions. No wonder there is little support to make changes to redress social inequality.

Our own work with Aboriginal communities revolves around research and teaching, and we are fortunate to be allowed to share in their experiences. It also serves as a constant reminder of the historically privileged position we, as mainstream Canadians, find ourselves in. Most mainstream Canadians do not benefit from first-hand experience and thus are oblivious to the plight of Aboriginal people. Many

D. E. Lund & P. R. Carr (Eds.), Revisiting The Great White North?, 89–104.

Aboriginal people are destined to a life in the poorer, more invisible sections of our cities, or on reserves or isolated communities. Thus, most mainstream Canadians are unaware of their own relatively advantaged position compared to Aboriginal people, and unaware that the impact of centuries of colonization continues to this day.

At one level, we might expect high levels of collective White guilt among White Canadians when they are urged to reflect on the plight of Aboriginal people in Canada. Nevertheless, we have found surprisingly low levels of guilt in our research (Caouette & Taylor, 2005, 2006). In this chapter, we explore why this finding may not be so shocking and how White Canadians revert to a variety of psychological mechanisms to avoid possible guilt and, in the process, avoid any feeling of responsibility.

OVERVIEW

The present volume has evolved from the editors' observation that many Canadians do not realize or acknowledge the salience of their unearned White privileges in society today. Our own program of research (Caouette & Taylor, 2005, 2006) is designed to explore how White mainstream Canadians react when confronted with concrete evidence of their unearned privileges relative to Aboriginal people. Our particular focus is on the role of collective White guilt.

In social psychological terms, collective guilt is a group-based emotion experienced when people categorize themselves as members of a group that has committed unjustified harm to another group. More broadly, collective guilt is felt when the behaviour of group members is inconsistent with the norms and values cherished by the group, and foremost among the values that all groups respect is equality and fairness (Branscombe, Doosje, & McGarty, 2002). There is a growing interest in studying collective guilt (e.g., Barkan, 2000; Branscombe & Doosje, 2004) because it is a regulatory emotion that is strongly linked to support for corrective actions designed to alleviate intergroup inequality.

In this chapter, we present research findings that focus on one simple question: How can mainstream Canadians' belief in the egalitarian essence of society co-exist with obvious and persistent racial inequality? We found that, when confronted with evidence of racial inequality involving Aboriginal people, a majority of our young White Canadian participants experience surprisingly low levels of collective guilt. These same participants, nevertheless, strongly value egalitarianism. How can our participants endorse egalitarianism but not feel collective guilt, even when confronted with the reality of racial inequality? We argue that the explanation resides in how White Canadians interpret and understand the meaning of egalitarianism. Essentially, they have a particular interpretation of egalitarianism that paradoxically allows them to rationalize inequality and, as a result, avoid collective guilt.

The impact of collective guilt cannot be underestimated: it is a powerful psychological force. On the one hand, guilt motivates individuals to repair and make amends for their mistakes and transgressions. Importantly, such corrective actions are not undertaken as a consequence of external pressure, but as a result of self-regulation

(Mischel, Cantor, & Feldman, 1996). On the other hand, an absence of guilt is often made possible by psychological defence mechanisms, such as denial, dissociation, or distancing. In other words, the psychological avoidance of guilt is also a powerful motivator: the clearest example involves "blaming the victim" (Lerner, 1980).

We begin our analysis of White collective guilt by first exploring our own Whiteness, as White social psychologists conducting field research and teaching on the topic of racial inequality. Then we briefly explore how racial inequality is being maintained in Canada and review the social psychological literature on collective White guilt. Finally, we elaborate our own research findings related to egalitarianism and collective White guilt.

OUR WHITE PRIVILEGE... OUR WHITE GUILT

As mainstream social scientists and educators, our orientation no doubt originates from conscious and unconscious reflections on our own White privilege. For example, part of our involvement with disadvantaged groups includes research and teaching with a view to protecting and enhancing Inuktitut, the heritage language of the Inuit (e.g., Taylor & Wright, 2002; Wright & Taylor, 1995). In these contexts, our Whiteness is made very salient, and we are continuously compelled to contemplate our own White privilege. Although, at times, we feel angry, ashamed, or guilty about it, we remain resolved to continue studying group inequality. We hope it is because of our genuine conviction in the power of sound research to promote social justice, and not simply a rationalization on our part.

We acknowledge that there is always the possibility that our research is directly motivated by a need to assuage our own White guilt. If this is true, then we have to be careful that our research not be biased by our underlying motivation. If White guilt is the motivation, we may inadvertently be reproducing our position of privilege or, alternatively, we may inform policy through an overly optimistic representation of disadvantaged groups. Accordingly, we have a responsibility as scientists and as educators to be acutely aware of the underlying motivation behind our work, and to make sure to maximize the chances that it serves the genuine interests of disadvantaged groups, and not merely our need to deal with our own collective White guilt.

Conducting research, consulting, and teaching in disadvantaged communities may be one way that many mainstream White researchers and educators attempt to resolve their own distress about racial inequality, to come to terms with their own White guilt. In his book, Taylor (2002) points to an ongoing dilemma, and explains how defensive he initially was when writing about the plight of disadvantaged groups:

> I have been privileged to learn firsthand from peoples in culturally different disadvantaged communities. By writing about their reality, am I robbing them of their identity, am I breaking their code? I do not know the answer to these

questions except to feel a selfish need to share my observations in the faint hope that even if they are judged erroneous, they will have at least forced critics to confront the issues squarely. But I also know that I would feel equally distressed if I chose to remain silent. As an elder once said to me, "Please put a voice to our pain." (p. 6)

In a related vein, Steele (1989, 1991, 2002), an influential African American social scientist, has claimed that the motivation of many White individuals who champion the rights of racial minority groups is often more selfish than altruistic. He has argued that many White individuals are willing to capitulate to any requests from racial groups only in order to avoid potential guilt. He argues that Whites feel anxious when dealing with issues pertaining to racial groups, because they are afraid of what might be revealed about their deeper self:

The darkest fear of Whites is that their better lot in life is at least partially the result of their capacity for evil- their capacity to dehumanize an entire people for their own benefit, and then to be indifferent to the devastation their dehumanization has wrought on successive generations of their victims. (1989, p. 54)

One striking example in Canada is the effect that residential schools had, and continue to have, on generations of Aboriginal people (Milloy, 1999). For instance, there has been some recent speculation about a link between the legacy of residential schools in the 1960s and an increased risk for HIV/AIDS in Aboriginal populations today. The loss of culture and marginalization suffered by the survivors of residential schools, and its related intergenerational impact on subsequent family members, are believed to be contributing factors to the HIV/AIDS problem (Barlow, 2003).

Ultimately, even if our intentions are altruistic, our position as White social scientists, whose research hinges upon group inequality, will always remain paradoxical: our careers are fundamentally built on studying the plight of the most disadvantaged. Even though our intent is to curb inequality, we are, in fact, earning a respectful living out of other people's disadvantage. For example, Taylor recalls a unique experience, during the 1990 Oka crisis:

I was teaching on one of the reserves at the time and was shuttled back and forth across police lines by a group of Mohawk with a high-powered speedboat. During times of such high tension your own Whiteness becomes a complex and frustrating attribute. And yet I was still in a position of societal privilege! I had the advantage of being able to exit this thorny situation; I was able to leave, unlike people in the community who were left to deal with the tension.

Too often White individuals, including researchers and educators, think they share the same experience with their Aboriginal counterparts. They don't! White individuals need to fully understand the difference between occasionally experiencing a reality and the reality for Aboriginal people who have to continuously live it.

In sum, it can be painful to face our White privilege and our White guilt, and it can be frustrating to deal with issues related to our Whiteness and our White identity in a diverse nation such as Canada. Nevertheless, the quality of our relationship with disadvantaged groups depends upon our being vigilant about the implications of our position of privilege.

RACIAL INEQUALITY IN CANADA

Despite evidence supporting the reality of racial inequality, "historically, many Canadians have been reluctant to admit that they, their ideas and their behaviours have contributed to the social marginalization, denigration, and inferiorization of others based on the negative evaluation of 'race' difference" (Satzewich, 1998, p. 11). Indeed, most Canadians believe racism to be mainly an American problem. Reitz (1988) argues that such a myth could be based on the fact that while there might be less racial conflict in Canada, there is no less racial discrimination (for further insights on racism in Canada, see Henry, Tator, Mattis, & Rees, 2006).

One way racial inequality is maintained is through different ideologies that rationalize, legitimize, and sustain a pattern of uneven distribution of valued resources among different racial groups (Allahar & Côté, 1998; Curtis, Grabb, & Guppy, 1999; Li, 1999; Satzewich, 1998). Such legitimizing ideologies are effective because they are credible, and may even be partly true. One such ideology is the belief that our society is based on a meritocracy. In every life domain, from the world of work to intimate relationships, we believe that our outcomes are contingent upon our inputs.

For example, to be accepted into university you need to obtain good grades and by working harder you may even win a scholarship. On the surface, using grades as the sole criterion appears to be a prototypical example of a meritocracy at its best. Yet, it falls short of a genuine meritocracy when certain groups are denied entry to university because of systemic discrimination. Unfortunately, systemic discrimination is invisible and very difficult to document. Minority students often have parents with no experience with formal education, and may be surrounded by a school environment that is not very supportive of academic achievement. The social environment in which they find themselves systematically disadvantages these students. In this way, minority students are at a unique disadvantage when it comes to obtaining the grades they need to get accepted into university.

Another related legitimizing racial ideology is based on the belief among advantaged group members that members of racially disadvantaged groups are personally responsible for their lack of success in society because of their biological or cultural inadequacies (Barrett, 1987; Ponting, 1997). Suggesting that racially disadvantaged individuals could succeed by working harder and by developing further their personal assets legitimizes racial inequality. Such an ideology serves the interests of privileged White mainstream Canadians in two ways: (a) it legitimizes their own success as a result of their individual ability and hard work (meritocracy);

and (b) it denies the pervasive influence of structural forces at play that provide them with unearned systemic privileges, while systematically placing other racial groups at a disadvantage.

One obvious example of such discrimination is the institutional and cultural domination of mainstream White Canadians over Aboriginal people. This form of profound discrimination is difficult for many White Canadians to grasp since it is not intuitively obvious how past colonization still has a systemic impact today. For example, imagine how socially disruptive it was for nomadic Inuit people to be forced by the Canadian government to settle in permanent villages. This arrangement of permanent settlements was accompanied by the introduction of formal schooling. Inuit parents were forced into a hopeless dilemma; they could maintain their nomadic tradition, but this meant leaving their children behind at school for months at a time, or they could remain near the school and abandon their search for food. This forced choice undeniably contributed to the loss of tradition, culture and identity, undoubtedly affecting many Inuit today. For instance, one of the biggest issues today in Northern villages is coping with the fact that many young children seem to be left unattended in the village. Historically, there was no need to monitor children since they lived exclusively with their immediate and extended family. However, this lack of structure is problematic in a modern village now encompassing different clans or families, within the context of modern life, including education, work, and community obligations.

Another example is the negative impact of the rapid introduction of Western culture on the Inuit lifestyle, including media, culture and transportation. Western culture has had the luxury of many centuries to adapt to these technological changes; yet, many of us haven't adapted that well (e.g., increased in obesity and sedentary behaviours). We can only reflect on the massive challenge for Inuit to adapt to such changes, not only imposed by a foreign culture but also in the matter of a couple years (Taylor, 2002). Menzies (1999) has summarized the situation well by arguing that:

> the socioeconomic context of First Nations' people is one that is clearlydisadvantaged in comparison to mainstream society. Popular explanations of this imbalance of power and resources typically blame the victim…. Popular explanations deny the overpowering dominance of European traditions and economic processes that were forced upon Aboriginal people. An important and powerful set of explanations roots social inequality in the historical and cultural phenomena of colonialism, the expropriation of First Nations' land and resources, and government policies to undermine Aboriginal social institutions…. Mainstream Canadian society has to accept its collective responsibility for the legacy of colonialism. (pp. 239-240, 242)

Unfortunately, our research suggests that White Canadians are very reluctant to accept any collective responsibility. In a series of experiments (Caouette & Taylor, 2005, 2006), self-identified White Canadian students were presented with information about the impact of colonization by White Canadians on Aboriginal people. These students were recruited from a liberal metropolitan Canadian university, and different regions of the country were well represented. When we presented these White Canadian participants with actual evidence of racial inequality related to Aboriginal people, they evidenced only mild levels of collective guilt, as measured by a well validated scale of collective guilt (e.g., item: "I feel guilty about the benefits and privileges that I receive as a Canadian, compared to Aboriginal people.")

COLLECTIVE WHITE GUILT

Guilt is experienced when we perceive that our behaviour has failed in relation to a set of standards, norms, values, or goals. We will only experience guilt if we feel personally responsible for our failed behaviour. In understanding collective guilt, research in the field of social psychology, most specifically social identity theory (Tajfel & Turner, 1979, 1986), has pointed to the importance of distinguishing between two aspects of identity: our personal self (our individual unique attributes) and our social self (our shared group attributes). If my personal self is responsible for a wrongful act I will feel personal guilt. But if my social self is implicated in a wrongful act, through my membership with a wrongful group, I will feel collective guilt. Collective guilt can be avoided in two ways. First, I can distance myself from my group, or simply not categorize myself as a member of that group. Second, I can deny that my group is responsible for any wrongdoing, or also minimize the impact of the wrongful act.

In sum, we can categorize ourselves and our actions at either the individual or group level, and this categorization will influence how we think, feel, and behave. Accordingly, when we are placed in a situation where our social self becomes salient, for example when we need to face the historical transgressions of our racial group, our reactions or emotions will be experienced through our group membership, and the potential for collective guilt will be heightened (Branscombe & Miron, 2004).

Empirical evidence for the manifestation of collective guilt has been sought in a variety of contexts involving intergroup inequality (Doosje, Branscombe, Spears, & Manstead, 1998; Swim & Miller, 1999; for a review see also Branscombe & Doosje, 2004). Despite clear findings supporting the existence of collective guilt, the measured levels of collective guilt are typically quite low, as measured by a valid scale of collective guilt. For example, when Dutch students were presented with the historical reality about their country's brutal colonization of Indonesia, a few individuals experienced high levels of collective guilt, but the vast majority of participants only reported low levels of collective guilt (Doosje et al., 1998). Upon reflection, these low levels of collective guilt may not be so surprising. People are fundamentally motivated to avoid or escape negative feelings of self-evaluation, often to the extent of psychologically denying the precipitating events themselves (Kugler & Jones, 1992; Tangney & Salovey, 1999): "from a self-interest perspective, the unfairly advantaged are most strongly motivated to eliminate their guilt psychologically. If they do so, they need not redistribute resources, make more efforts, or treat those around them more fairly, to re-establish justice" (Tyler, 2001, p. 351). It is easy to alleviate collective guilt psychologically: Advantaged group members, such as White mainstream Canadians, need only deny that any real harm was done, argue that their group's privileged status is rightly deserved, displace any responsibility, distance themselves from their wrongful group, and deny group responsibility or dissociate themselves from any personal benefits as a result of their group's unjust actions (Branscombe & Miron, 2004).

Compared to personal guilt, collective guilt appears to leave open even more room for psychological maneuvering. Because, with collective guilt, the entire group is the perpetrator of the perceived wrongful actions, individuals can, with relative ease, escape any feelings of collective guilt. In the following section, we explore how even valuing egalitarianism can, surprisingly, still allow people to escape collective guilt.

COLLECTIVE WHITE GUILT AND EGALITARIANISM

Because egalitarianism is such a cherished value in North America, most people have internalized egalitarian standards; being non-prejudiced has become a personal value that is intrinsically important for most people (Devine, Monteith, Zuwerink & Elliot, 1991; Plant & Devine, 1998). However, recent research by Monteith and Walters (1998) suggests that the key issue may not be the extent to which a person has *internalized* egalitarian standards, but the *interpretation* of egalitarianism the person has internalized. They found that individuals who believe that egalitarianism is about meritocracy (based on their survey items; e.g., "Egalitarianism means that anyone who is willing and able to work hard has a good chance of succeeding") were not motivated to temper their prejudiced feelings. This belief in a meritocracy as an interpretation of egalitarianism is, of course, consistent with a racial ideology that legitimizes racial inequality.

A second interpretation of egalitarianism emphasizes a belief in equality of opportunity, and for many this interpretation appears to be more conducive to racial equality, although, as our results will show later, it is not. For example, many people advocate for the right of every child to have an equal chance to succeed at school and, accordingly, "special needs" children should be provided with special educational services to help them achieve. Achieving equality of opportunity is central to most liberal discourse. Interestingly, Feldman (1999) has argued that the meritocracy interpretation of egalitarianism, which we analyzed in terms of its relationship to the legitimization of racial inequality, is, in fact, consistent with an equality of opportunity interpretation of egalitarianism in North America. Thus, social inequality, in the form of socio-economic disparities, if based on hard work (meritocracy), appears to be quite acceptable to many people as long as there is parity in competition at the outset (equality of opportunity).

Accordingly, many North Americans believe that it is equitable if a person who works harder and who has more ability is rewarded with a higher salary, as long as that person initially had no better or worse an opportunity to succeed. Thus, although many people believe that equality of opportunity is the gold standard in terms of fairness, unfortunately many perceive racial inequality to be consistent with this interpretation of egalitarianism. They accomplish this by believing that while differential levels of hard work and ability produce inequalities, everyone has genuine equality of opportunity. For example, many mainstream White individuals may not realize the inherent power and influence afforded to their group because of their "normative" status in society. For example in business and politics, opportunities are more plentiful because these are prototypical mainstream institutions. Mainstream Canadians may well cherish equality of opportunity in principle but may not be conscious of the fact that there are social groups in society that do not enjoy equal access to all opportunities.

In fact, Kluegel and Smith (1986) have shown that people only need to perceive that there are *some* opportunities for advancement in society for them to believe that people achieve the success they "rightly" deserve. Unfortunately, the mere illusion of equal opportunity seems to make people oblivious to systemic inequality. Specifically, advantaged people believe that individual ability and hard work can actually produce opportunities, and then, paradoxically, argue that it is the responsibility of the disadvantaged individual to make up for any systemic barriers that confront them. This paradoxical reasoning places the burden of responsibility on the wrong agent: instead, systemic barriers should be fought at the mainstream societal level, not the individual level. This is why programs designed to promote social equality, by providing more and better education for disadvantaged racial groups, can produce unwanted effects. Specifically, this interpretation of egalitarianism points to disadvantaged group members as having the personal responsibility to increase their capacity for hard work and ability through education, with no consideration for the systemic discrimination they will have to face. Forgotten in the process is that society needs to be restructured so as to "level the playing field."

If the social system does not provide for a level playing field, then disadvantaged group members will always suffer from inequality, despite their best efforts to increase their personal skills and abilities through education. For instance, in their study on the advancement of visible minorities in contemporary Canada, Hou, and Balakrishnan (1996) conclude that, "most visible minorities receive less income return from their educational and occupational achievement.... Therefore, income inequality on the basis of qualifications is most probably related to discrimination" (p. 324). Clearly, their higher levels of education did not make up for the unequal playing field. Thus, one main challenge with the equality of opportunity interpretation of egalitarianism is the difficulty associated with perceiving the many layers of discrimination (individual, social, institutional, and systemic). On the surface, society seems to be based on a straightforward meritocracy: most individuals who achieve higher education will receive a higher socio-economic status. However, the danger resides in the layers underneath, where systemic advantage and systemic discrimination may operate.

In light of these observations, it is clear that holding an equality of opportunity interpretation of egalitarianism does not necessarily produce feelings of collective guilt with regard to racial inequality. Thus, advocating the virtues of equality of opportunity to the wider public, in the hopes of promoting social justice, may be destined to fail: it will not guarantee that individuals will perceive racial inequality as being unfair. In our program of research, we found that whether or not participants highly endorsed an equality of opportunity interpretation of egalitarianism had no influence on whether they would experience higher levels of collective guilt and, thereby, support compensation for Aboriginal people. This finding arose in the context of a series of experiments (Caouette & Taylor, 2005, 2006), where we presented information to White Canadians students about racial inequality between Aboriginal people and White Canadians in the form of essays from a reputable journal. In these experiments, we measured participants' agreement with different interpretations of egalitarianism based on a scale used by Monteith and Walters (1998) in order to explore which egalitarian belief (individualism, equality of opportunity, social responsibility) would most strongly predict feelings of collective guilt and compensation for Aboriginal people.

The basic question we address, then, is what interpretation of egalitarianism might be related to collective guilt? Our research supports the conclusion that a belief in the equality of opportunity interpretation of egalitarianism fails to produce collective guilt when it is imbued with individualism, and this interpretation was endorsed by a majority of our White Canadian participants. But collective guilt did emerge when an interpretation of egalitarianism in terms of equality of opportunity was coupled with a belief in social responsibility. Unfortunately, this interpretation was less likely to be endorsed by our White Canadian participants. Firstly, we found that an underlying belief in individualism leads to a passive interpretation of equality of opportunity, as people are reluctant to sacrifice their feeling of individual freedom in order to change the social system. For example, an individual can endorse equality of opportunity in principle, but may not feel compelled to assure its actualization for everyone else in society. Even though some individuals recognize that not everyone has the same initial chance to succeed, they may still not believe that they should be responsible to actually assure equality of opportunity for all.

Our analysis is corroborated by an independent survey that found that 63 percent of a representative sample of Canadians agreed with the statement, "while equality of opportunity is important for all Canadians, it's not really the government's job to guarantee it" (Reitz & Breton, 1994, p. 64). Furthermore, Kluegel and Smith (1986) have shown that many people do not perceive racism and inequality as a systemic problem, but rather, as the problem of a few bigoted individuals. Accordingly, most people feel no personal responsibility for group inequality, and they feel no need to engage in, or support, systemic actions to alleviate it. Participants in our study might have experienced low levels of collective guilt, despite endorsing a belief in equality of opportunity, because they did not feel that Canadian society, or they themselves personally, should be responsible for taking action to resolve what they perceive to be only occasional inequality between mainstream Canadians and Aboriginal people.

A second implication of individualism is exemplified by how many participants in our study seemed to legitimize inequality by emphasizing the importance of individual responsibility. As one participant expressed it:

> I agree that in the past Euro-Canadians have exploited Aboriginal peoples by taking their land, but I can't help feeling that they brought their problems upon themselves somewhat as well. I work hard, and am working hard so that I can live well in the future. A good life cannot be handed to you on a silver platter. Aboriginal people have to take responsibility for themselves.

It follows, then, that Aboriginal peoples are personally responsible for their socioeconomic disadvantage. In the words of Applebaum (1997), "this individualist understanding of moral responsibility functions to protect the privileges of certain groups of people and absolves them of any personal responsibility for their involvement in systemic oppressions such as racism" (p. 409).

Some White Canadians go even further by maintaining the belief that Aboriginal people are currently afforded even more opportunities than mainstream Canadians. They believe that Aboriginal people have special tax breaks that mainstream Canadians do not enjoy, and that Aboriginal people have all of their higher education paid for. These White Canadians are not likely to experience any collective guilt because of their belief that Aboriginal people are, in today's reality, actually in an advantaged position. One of our participants was surprised to learn that Aboriginal people are still disadvantaged today: "The suggestion that Aboriginal people are still in unfair conditions mixes me all up. I believed that Aboriginal people were receiving extra money all the time because of their ancestors. I think they are even better off than non-Aboriginal people." This belief is linked to an individualist understanding of responsibility. These mainstream Canadians believe that because Aboriginal people are provided with more opportunities than mainstream Canadians, it then follows that Aboriginal people are to be blamed personally for their disadvantage. As one of our participants claimed: "Aboriginals are not forcibly confined to reserves, but are free to be a part of mainstream Canadian society, just as everyone else, yet they are still granted many special rights. Thus they have all the opportunities of any other Canadian plus opportunities which are exclusive to their race." This excerpt clearly exemplifies the belief that Aboriginal people are provided with inordinate opportunities, that they are not disadvantaged by any external barriers and, accordingly, that their potential for achievement is maximized.

In this section, we have reviewed many interpretations of egalitarianism, and our research shows that none of them, taken individually or in combination, seems to be associated with collective guilt. In our research (Caouette & Taylor, 2005, 2006), there was only one interpretation of egalitarianism that did predict higher feelings of collective guilt. Only those participants who endorsed an interpretation of egalitarianism that emphasized *social responsibility,* while valuing the ideal of equality of opportunity, had elevated levels of collective guilt. Such people would strongly agree with statements such as: "The economic system of our country has to be drastically changed to bring about equality of opportunity," "We should be willing to pay higher taxes in order to provide more assistance to the poor," or "Every person should give some of his/her time for the good of his/her town or country." In addition, they would highly disagree with statements such as "Maybe some minority groups do get bad treatment, but it's no business of mine," "A person does not need to worry about other people if only he/she looks after him/herself," or "I have never been interested in thinking up idealistic schemes to improve society" (all items from Starrett, 1996).

In a surprising way, we have found that promoting the value of equality in our society may not necessarily produce more racial inequality. One recurring challenge is that a majority of individuals maintain a narrow understanding of egalitarianism, one that is generally very individualistic and passive in nature. To achieve social equality, we will need to promote an understanding of egalitarianism that emphasizes social responsibility and socially proactive attitudes. In terms of fostering group equality, we need to examine fundamental Canadian values and determine what aspect of equality is typically emphasized. We argue that usually social justice efforts focus on the idea of equality of opportunity, but our results suggest that we should be emphasizing an interpretation of equality that highlights social responsibility, in order to offset the damaging interpretation of equality of opportunity that is usually coloured with individualism.

DISCUSSION

"People generally think of themselves as egalitarian, but some people may construe egalitarianism in a way that can coexist comfortably with prejudice tendencies" (Monteith & Walters, 1998, p. 189). Our research suggests that, even though most White Canadians highly value egalitarianism as a justice principle, most construe egalitarianism in both a passive and individualistic way. This passive and individualistic interpretation of egalitarianism allows them to cope comfortably with racial inequality and escape any feelings of collective guilt.

Clearly, Canadian society will need to go beyond an individualistic interpretation and understanding of responsibility, such as "Be responsible to yourself!" in order to achieve far greater social equality. Espousing the values of equality and fairness, or more specifically, endorsing the ideal of equality of opportunity, will not necessarily produce a society where group inequality is minimized. We need to go beyond systematically believing that people are personally responsible and in control of outcomes in their life. We need to acknowledge that external contingencies shape people's lives, and that systemic and structural factors beyond a person's immediate control can limit opportunities for achievement. It is difficult to accept that systemic barriers limit opportunities for certain groups (including racially disadvantaged groups) and, by the same token, advantage others (including White mainstream Canadians). However, it is only by recognizing those limits that we will be able to change them. The rejection of an individualist understanding of responsibility is a necessary first step.

It would also seem to be important to shift our focus away from *attributing blame* and towards *taking responsibility*. Individuals often deny collective guilt by claiming that they are not personally responsible for what their ancestors did in the past, and that, therefore, they should not be blamed for their ancestors' actions, or the present consequences. However, "to say that it is not our fault does not relieve us of responsibility" (Tatum, 2000, p. 80). One does not necessarily need to have directly caused harm to another person in order to feel responsible for helping that person: "once we think about responsibility as having a duty to respond to one who has been harmed, the scope of responsibility widens considerably" (Radzik, 2001, p. 461). Put simply, we don't necessarily need to feel blameworthy in order to take responsibility for the well being of other individuals. Such a duty to respond may closely relate to feelings of guilt, but genuine care and concern for the other remains the core motive. Guilt comes from a sense of duty to respond.

QUESTIONS FOR REFLECTION

1. We have identified different ways to conceptualize egalitarianism. How do you define equality? How do you think other Canadians define equality? Would their definitions differ based on their race, class, gender, or ethnicity? Why?
2. Have you ever experienced or witnessed collective White guilt? If so, in which contexts? Can you recall how you coped with your guilt? Would you react differently after having read this chapter? If you have never experienced or witnessed White guilt, how did the present chapter make you feel?
3. Do you believe that most White Canadians would likely support actions to establish racial equality because they want to absolve themselves from White guilt, or because they genuinely care about the plight of disadvantaged groups, or a bit of both?
4. Besides White guilt, what other motivations do you think White Canadians could acquire that would lead them to support the interests of disadvantaged racial groups? How do those other motivations compare with White guilt?
5. Do you think that being motivated to fight racial inequality as a result of White guilt is necessarily a sign of an ill-guided motive? In which instances do you think White guilt could be beneficial, and, conversely, harmful?

NOTE

[1] The research presented in this chapter was supported by: scholarships to Julie Caouette by the *Fonds québécois de la recherche sur la société et la culture* (FQRSC) and by the *Social Sciences and Humanities Research Council of Canada* (SSHRC); and by research grants to Donald M. Taylor from the *Social Sciences and Humanities Research Council of Canada* (SSHRC) and from the *Fonds pour la formation de chercheurs et l'aide à la recherche* (FCAR).

REFERENCES

Allahar, A. L., & Côté, J. E. (1998). *Richer and poorer: The structure of inequality in Canada.* Toronto, ON: James Lorimer & Company.

Applebaum, B. (1997). Good liberal intentions are not enough! Racism, intentions and moral responsibility. *Journal of Moral Education, 26,* 409–421.

Barkan, E. (2000). *The guilt of nations: Restitution and negotiating historical injustices.* New York, NY: Norton.

Barlow, J. K. (2003). Examining HIV/AIDS among the Aboriginal population in Canada in the post-residential school era. *Aboriginal Healing Foundation: Research Series.* Retrieved from http://www.ahf.ca/assets/pdf/english/hiv_legacy.pdf#search=%22residential%20school%20aboriginal%20aids%22

Barrett, S. R. (1987). *Is God a racist? The right wing in Canada.* Toronto, ON: University of Toronto Press.

Branscombe, N. R., & Doosje, B. (Eds.). (2004). *Collective guilt: International perspectives.* New York, NY: Cambridge University Press.

Branscombe, N. R., & Miron, A. M. (2004). Interpreting the in-group's negative actions toward another group: Emotional reactions to appraised harm. In C. W. Leach & L. Z. Tiedens (Eds.), *The social life of emotions* (pp. 314–335). New York, NY: Cambridge University Press.

Branscombe, N. R., Doosje, B., & McGarty, C. (2002). Antecedents and consequences of collective guilt. In D. M. Mackie & E. R. Smith (Eds.), *From prejudice to intergroup emotions: Differentiated reactions to social groups* (pp. 49–66). Philadelphia, PA: Psychology Press.

Caouette, J., & Taylor, D. M. (2005, July). *"Don't blame me for what my ancestors did!" Factors associated with the experience of collective guilt regarding Aboriginal Peoples.* Paper presented at the 14th General Meeting of the European Association of Experimental Social Psychology, Würzburg, Bavaria, Germany.

Caouette, J., & Taylor, D. M. (2006, June). *A social psychological analysis of mainstream Canadians' attitudes towards compensation Aboriginal Peoples for the harmful effects of their internal colonization.* Paper presented at the 67th Annual Convention of the Canadian Psychological Association, Calgary, AB, Canada.

Colavincenzo, M. (2003). *"Trading magic for fact," fact for magic: Myth and mythologizing in postmodern Canadian historical fiction.* New York, NY: Rodopi.

Curtis, J., Grabb, E., & Guppy, N. (Eds.). (1999). *Social inequality in Canada: Patterns, problems, and policies.* Scarborough, ON: Prentice Hall Allyn and Bacon.

Devine, P. G., Monteith, M. J., Zuwerink, J., & Elliot, A. J. (1991). Prejudice with and without compunction. *Journal of Personality and Social Psychology, 60,* 817–830.

Doosje, B., Branscombe, N. R., Spears, R., & Manstead, A. S. R. (1998). Guilty by association: When one's group has a negative history. *Journal of Personality and Social Psychology, 75,* 872–886.

Feagin, J. R., Vera, H., & Batur, P. (2001). *White racism: The basics.* New York, NY: Routledge.

Feldman, S. (1999). Economic values and inequality. In J. P. Robinson & P. R. Shaver (Eds.), *Measures of political attitudes: Measures of social psychological attitudes* (Vol. 2, pp. 159–201). San Diego, CA: Academic.

Henry, F., Tator, C., Mattis, W., & Rees, T. (2006). *The colour of democracy: Racism in Canadian society.* Toronto, ON: Nelson.

Kluegel, J. R., & Smith, E. R. (1986). *Beliefs about inequality: Americans' views of what is and what ought to be.* New York, NY: Aldine de Gruyter.

Hou, F., & Balakrishnan, T. R. (1996). The integration of visible minorities in contemporary society. *Canadian Journal of Sociology, 21,* 307–326.

Kugler, K., & Jones, W. H. (1992). On conceptualizing and assessing guilt. *Journal of Personality and Social Psychology, 62,* 318–327.

Lerner, M. J. (1980). *The belief in a just world: A fundamental delusion.* New York, NY: Plenum.

Li, P. S. (Ed.). (1999). *Race and ethnic relations in Canada.* Don Mills, ON: Oxford University Press.

Loewen, J. W. (1995). *Lies my teacher told me: Everything your American history book got wrong.* New York, NY: New Press.

Menzies, C. R. (1999). First Nations, inequality, and the legacy of colonialism. In J. Curtis, E. Grabb, & N. Guppy (Eds.), *Social inequality in Canada: Patterns, problems, and policies* (pp. 236–244). Scarborough, ON: Prentice Hall Allyn and Bacon.

Milloy, J. S. (1999). *A national crime: The Canadian government and the residential school system.* Winnipeg, MB: University of Manitoba Press.

Mischel, W., Cantor, N., & Feldman, S. (1996). Principles of self-regulation: The nature of willpower and self-control. In E. T. Higgins & A. W. Kruglanski (Eds.), *Social psychology: Handbook of basic principles* (pp. 329–360). New York, NY: Guilford Press.

Monteith, M. J., & Walters, G. L. (1998). Egalitarianism, moral obligation, and prejudiced-related personal standards. *Personality and Social Psychology Bulletin, 24,* 186–199.

Ponting, J. R. (Ed.). (1997). *First Nations in Canada: Perspectives on opportunity, empowerment, and self-determination.* Whitby, ON: McGraw-Hill Ryerson.

Plant, E. A., & Devine, P. G. (1998). Internal and external motivation to respond without prejudice. *Journal of Personality and Social Psychology, 75,* 811–832.

Radzik, L. (2001). Collective responsibility and duties to respond. *Social Theory and Practice, 27,* 455–471.

Reitz, J. G. (1988). Less racial discrimination in Canada, or simply less racial conflict: Implications of comparisons with Britain. *Canadian Public Policy, 16,* 424–441.

Reitz, J. G., & Breton, R. (1994). *The illusion of difference: Realities of ethnicity in Canada and the United States.* Toronto, ON: C.D. Howe Institute.

Rothenberg, P. S. (2002). *White privilege: Essential readings on the other side of racism.* New York, NY: Worth.

Satzewich, V. (Ed.). (1998). *Racism and social inequality in Canada.* Toronto, ON: Thompson Educational.

Starrett, R. H. (1996). Assessment of global social responsibility. *Psychological Reports, 78,* 535–554.

Steele, S. (1989). The recoloring of campus life: Student racism, academic pluralism, and the end of a dream. *Harper's Magazine, 278,* 47–55.

Steele, S. (1991). *The content of our character: A new vision of race in America.* New York, NY: Harper Perennial.

Steele, S. (2002). The age of white guilt and the disappearance of the black individual. *Harper's Magazine, 305,* 33–42.

Swim, J. K., & Miller, D. L. (1999). White guilt: Its antecedents and consequences for attitudes toward affirmative action. *Personality and Social Psychology Bulletin, 25,* 500–514.

Tajfel, H., & Turner, J. C. (1979). An integrative theory of intergroup conflict. In W. G. Austin & S. Worchel (Eds.), *The social psychology of intergroup relations* (pp. 33–47). Monterey, CA: Brooks/Cole.

Tajfel, H., & Turner, J. C. (1986). The social identity theory of intergroup behavior. In S. Worchel & W. G. Austin (Eds.), *Psychology of intergroup relations* (pp. 7–24). Chicago, IL: Nelson-Hall.

Tangney, J. P., & Salovey, P. (1999). Problematic social emotions: Shame, guilt, jealousy and envy. In R. M. Kowalski & M. R. Leary (Eds.), *The social psychology of emotional and behavioral problems* (pp. 167–195). Washington, DC: APA Press.

Tatum, B. D. (1997). *Why are all the black kids sitting together in the cafeteria?* New York, NY: Basic Books.

Tatum, B. D. (2000). Defining racism: "Can we talk?" In M. Adams, W. Blumenfell, R. Castaneda, H. Hackman, M. Peters, & X. Zuniga (Eds.), *Readings for diversity and social justice: An anthology on racism, sexism, anti-semitism, heterosexism, classism and ableism* (pp. 79–82). New York, NY: Routledge.

Taylor, D. M. (2002). *The quest for identity: From minority groups to generation Xers.* Westport, CT: Praeger.

Taylor, D. M., & Wright, S. C. (2002). Do Aboriginal students benefit from education in their heritage language? Results from a ten-year program of research in Nunavik. *Canadian Journal of Native Studies, 22,* 141–164.

Tyler, T. R. (2001). Social justice. In R. Brown & S. L. Gaertner (Eds.), *Blackwell handbook of social psychology: Intergroup processes* (pp. 344–364). Malden, MA: Blackwell.

Wright, S. C., & Taylor, D. M. (1995). Identity and the language of the classroom: Investigating the impact of heritage versus second language instruction on personal and collective self-esteem. *Journal of Educational Psychology, 87*, 241–252.

REFRAMING: JULIE CAOUETTE & DONALD M. TAYLOR (2014)

Canada's Apology to Aboriginal Peoples:
The Role of Expectations and Collective White Guilt

The research outlined in our original chapter explored how White mainstream Canadians react when confronted with evidence of the harmful impact of the internal colonization of Aboriginal peoples. Our specific focus was on the role of collective White guilt. A number of research programs point to collective guilt as an emotion that can be a constructive impetus for actions aimed at rectifying past collective harm, such as compensation, financial reparation and public apology (for a review, see Wohl, Branscombe, & Klar, 2006).

Dramatically, since the publication of *The Great White North* in 2007, the significance of White guilt as an issue has become salient, in the form of a public apology made to Aboriginal Canadians. On June 11, 2008, the Canadian government officially apologized for its infamous residential schools, where many Aboriginal students, living in substandard conditions, were victims of physical and emotional abuse (see Annett, 2005; Milloy, 1999). But while many Canadians were quick to applaud themselves for such a commendable act of contrition, it is worth examining the implications of the apology more closely.

In the present reframing article, we will suggest that beneath the silver lining, a public apology may, unfortunately, provide an opportunity for many mainstream Canadians to let themselves "off the responsibility hook" and safely relegate feelings of collective guilt to a more distant, and less pertinent, past (see Caouette, Wohl, & Peetz, 2012; Peetz, Gunn, & Wilson, 2010). In stark contrast, for Aboriginal peoples, a public apology may signify merely a first step in a long reconciliatory process to heal past historical wounds. That is, perpetrators and victims often perceive a public apology very differently. Perpetrator groups may view an apology as resolution and closure for past historical harm, whereas victimized groups may judge an apology as signaling the beginning of a series of actions to mend past historical harm (Wohl, Hornsey, & Philpot, 2011). These contrasting interpretations can be highly problematic for future intergroup relations.

Almost as a warning, Mary Simon (President of Inuit Tapiriit Kanatami), an Aboriginal leader, offered the following comment in response to the statement of apology offered by the Ministers in the Canadian House of Commons:

> Let us not be lulled into an impression that when the sun rises tomorrow morning, the pain and scars will miraculously be gone.

D. E. Lund & P. R. Carr (Eds.), Revisiting The Great White North?, 105–107.

They will not. But a new day has dawned, a new day heralded by a commitment to reconciliation and building a new relationship with Inuit, Métis and First Nations.

By this statement, Mary Simon is voicing the position of the victimized group. The apology does not erase the past; it is a mere starting point for future, ongoing, constructive reconciliation.

Will mainstream Canadians hear this message? Based on social psychological research, we have every reason to dampen our enthusiasm but hope that the public apology will lead to genuine healing and reconciliation. First, there is mounting research evidence to show that people who have engaged in a good moral deed (such as providing an apology) then feel somewhat liberated to engage in more immoral or unethical behaviours in the future (for a review, see Merritt, Effron, & Monin, 2010). The rationale is that, as a consequence of performing a moral deed, a person or a group no longer needs to worry about feeling or appearing immoral. This phenomenon has been termed moral self-licensing. For example "when people are confident that their past behavior demonstrated compassion, generosity, or lack of prejudice, they are more likely to act in morally dubious ways without fear of feeling heartless, selfish, or bigoted" (Merritt, Effron, & Monin, 2010, p. 344). In short, engaging in good, moral behaviours disinhibit people from performing subsequent negative or immoral behaviours. Recently, Effron, Cameron, and Monin (2009) confirmed this hypothesis by showing that people who had voiced support for Barack Obama (a good deed "demonstrating" their non-prejudice) just before the 2008 election felt licensed to thereafter make ambiguously racist statements. Such less-than-commendable actions were "licensed" because people no longer needed to prove their lack of prejudice.

What are the implications in terms of the impact of the federal government's apology to Aboriginal peoples? The apology may well provide mainstream Canadians the opportunity for moral self-licensing. Thus, they may be less than committed to engage in serious efforts at reconciliation, or worse, they may feel freer to engage in more prejudice and discriminatory actions. For example, after the apology, some mainstream Canadians may feel more open about voicing qualms about providing tangible reparation or compensation to Aboriginal peoples, without fear of appearing racist or heartless: after all, "didn't we just apologize to them?"

In fact, recent data related to another Canadian public apology, the Chinese Head Tax, may lend credence to such a possibility. In July of 2006, the Canadian government offered a public apology for the "head tax" placed on Chinese immigrants during the early 20th century. In a longitudinal study, Wohl, Matheson, & Branscombe (in press) were able to examine both White and Chinese Canadians' perceptions and expectations of the Canadian government's apology both before and after the public apology was formally presented in the House of Commons. Even though, initially, both White Canadians and Chinese Canadians were optimistic about the consequences of the apology, at a one year follow-up, Chinese Canadians' willingness to forgive Canadians had waned. Also, those Chinese Canadians who assigned more collective guilt to White Canadians, that is, they strongly believed in the culpability of White Canadians (e.g., "Canadians have benefited at the expense of Chinese Canadians for generations") were especially likely to be unconvinced by the reconciliatory efforts following the apology. That is, their expectations of improved relations had not been met, and acts following the apology toward restitution were regarded as insufficient.

Were Chinese Canadians' expectations unrealistically high, or were White Canadians less than fully committed to reconciliatory efforts following the apology? We cannot answer this question yet, but it is clear that public collective apologies have a different psychological impact on perpetrators and victims. In our present context, it would be valuable to carefully research issues of expectations and collective guilt among Aboriginal peoples and White Canadians as the reconciliation process moves forward. Indeed, concrete answers to these questions are needed if the reconciliation process is to be mutually constructive.

In this reframing piece, we have considered the place of collective White guilt and collective apology in the establishment of a more harmonious relationship between Aboriginal Canadians and non-Aboriginal Canadians. Specifically, we have argued that for many mainstream Canadians, the offer of a public apology offers closure, and a chance to put behind any remaining feelings of collective guilt. However, for Aboriginal Canadians, beyond the immediate positive feelings and validation arising from having received an apology, an apology marks only the beginning of a process. The long-term consequences of this apology remain to be seen.

REFERENCES

Annett, K. (2005). *Hidden from history: The Canadian Holocaust.* Port Alberni, BC: The Truth Commission into Genocide in Canada.

Caouette, J., Wohl, M. J. A., & Peetz, J. (2011). The future weighs heavier than the past: Collective guilt, perceived control and the influence of time. *European Journal of Social Psychology, 42,* 363–371.

Effron, D. A., Cameron, J. S., & Monin, B. (2009). Endorsing Obama licenses favoring whites. *Journal of Experimental Social Psychology, 45,* 590–593.

Merritt, A. C., Effron, D. A., & Monin, B. (2010). Moral self-licensing: When being good frees us to be bad. *Social and Personality Psychology Compass, 4/5,* 344–357.

Milloy, J. S. (1999). *A national crime: The Canadian government and the residential school system.* Winnipeg, MB: University of Manitoba Press.

Peetz, J., Gunn, G. R., & Wilson, A. E. (2010). Crimes of the past: Defensive temporal distancing in the face of past in-group wrongdoing. *Personality and Social Psychology Bulletin, 36,* 598–611.

Wohl, M. J. A., Branscombe, N. R., & Klar, Y. (2006). Collective guilt: Emotional reactions when one's group has done wrong or been wronged. *European Review of Social Psychology, 17,* 1–37.

Wohl, M. J. A., Hornsey, M. J., & Philpot, C. R. (2011). A critical review of official public apologies: Aims, pitfalls, and a staircase model of effectiveness. *Social Issues and Policy Review, 5,* 70–100.

Wohl, M. J. A., Matheson, K., & Branscome, N. R. (in press). Victim and perpetrator groups' responses to the Canadian government's apology for the head tax on Chinese immigrants and the moderating influence of collective guilt. *Political Psychology.*

SECTION 3

DEVELOPING AND DE-CONSTRUCTING WHITE IDENTITY

CHRISTINE WIHAK

DEVELOPMENT OF ANTI-RACIST WHITE IDENTITY IN CANADIAN EDUCATIONAL COUNSELLORS

INTRODUCTION

My own sense of White identity developed during a decade-long sojourn in Nunavut, living and working in remote communities that are over 90 percent Inuit (Wihak, 2004a). When I returned to southern Canada, I discovered not only that I had changed, but that much had changed within the culture I had left so long before. Professionally, one of the most significant changes was the increasing emphasis on racial/cultural issues in the field of educational psychology in response to the changing demographics of Canadian society.

Psychology, a discipline little influenced to date by postmodern thought or critical theory, has been critiqued for its neo-colonial character (Duran & Duran, 2000). Nevertheless, psychologists of colour in the United States have pioneered the introduction of racial/cultural issues to the field (Ponterotto, Jackson, & Nutini, 2001). Under their influence, educational psychology has become sensitized to the need for practitioners to become *multiculturally competent.*

In this chapter, I begin by defining multicultural competence and discussing its importance in school counselling. I then introduce the topic of White Racial Identity Development (WRID), which is closely associated with the development of multicultural competence. After discussing existing theoretical WRID models, I use as an illustration examples drawn from a study (Wihak, 2004b) of White Canadian counsellors who had experienced extended and intense contact with the Inuit of Nunavut. The combination of theory and evidence is intended to assist educators to understand WRID as a developmental process requiring negotiation of an identity crisis. Such understanding will prepare them to support their students through the emotionally charged exploration needed to achieve a strong, anti-racist White identity.

MULTICULTURAL COUNSELLING COMPETENCE FOR SCHOOL COUNSELLORS

Students of colour now represent a significant presence in contemporary Canadian schools (Ghosh & Abdi, 2004). In the face of changing demographics, educational professionals from the dominant White culture need to develop multicultural competence, which is required for working with children from culturally and racially

D. E. Lund & P. R. Carr (Eds.), Revisiting The Great White North?, 111–122.

diverse backgrounds (Cole, 1998; Gopaul-McNicol, 1997; Gosine, 2002). While various conceptualizations of multicultural competence exist (Mollen, Ridley, & Hill, 2003), it is generally understood to encompass "the integration of attitudes and beliefs, knowledge, and skills essential for awareness of the impact of culture" on professional practice (Arthur & Collins, 2005, p. 48). In this definition, self-awareness and capacity to appreciate the worldview of self and others are essential for professionals in cross-cultural contexts. Multicultural competence models have been developed for both teachers (Taylor & Quintana, 2003) and counsellors (Arthur & Collins, 2005; Sue, Arredondo, & McDavis, 1992). The need for teachers to be aware of racial issues has been extensively discussed (Gosine, 2002; Kelly & Brandes, 2001; Solomon & Levine-Rasky, 2003), but the equal importance of such awareness for school-based counsellors is less well recognized (Wallace, 2000).

In North America, the majority of educational counsellors are likely to be White (Arthur & Januszkowki, 2001; Holcomb-McCoy, 2005). White counsellors typically report lower levels of multicultural competence than those who are themselves members of a visible minority (Vinson & Neimeyer, 2000; 2003). When educational counsellors lack multicultural competence, minority children and families may receive inadequate services (Constantine, 2001; Schwallie-Giddis, Anstrom, Sanchez, Sardi, & Granato, 2004). The impact on the school experiences of minority children and youth can potentially be profound.

Educational counsellors are typically responsible for conducting intellectual assessments that affect educational placement decisions, as well as for responding to students' academic issues, interpersonal problems, and mental health needs (Holcomb-McCoy, 2004). Lack of multicultural competence may contribute to the overrepresentation of children from minorities in special education classes (Myles & Harold, 1988; Reschly, 2005). Educational counsellors have a significant role in the development of socio-emotional competence in school children (Coleman & Baskin, 2003; Holcomb-McCoy, 2004). Higher rates of school disciplinary actions and suspensions reported for minority youth (Nichols, 1999; Ruck & Wortley, 2002) may reflect lack of understanding of racial/cultural factors in these students' lives. Educational counsellors who define their identities as independent individuals might make errors such as advising separation and individuation from the family and inappropriate expression of emotions and assertiveness (Constantine, 2001) when working with children and families from cultures that tend to define identity in terms of relation to their families and communities, including Aboriginal, Chinese, and African-American (Sparrow, 2000).

Despite the mandating of multicultural competence by professional counselling organizations, Canadian counsellors working in school-settings are likely to lack this expertise. Arthur and Januszkowki (2001) surveyed a random sample of Canadian counsellors concerning their multicultural competence and found that most needed more effective education and training to work with racially and culturally diverse clients. In a survey of Canadian training-programs for counselling psychologists, responses from Directors of Internship Training indicated that concern was warranted about the adequacy of diversity training in professional programs (Brooks et al., 2004).

Institutions that train educational counsellors have been making an effort to respond to the increased need for multicultural competence with courses and programs directed to that purpose (Arredondo & Arciniega 2001; Brooks et al., 2004). Although much thought and energy is being devoted to developing effective methods of training competent multicultural counsellors, these efforts are hampered by a lack of knowledge about the process of becoming multiculturally competent (Fuertes, Bartolomeo & Nichols, 2001). One promising research direction concerns the link between racial identity development and multicultural competency.

WHITE RACIAL IDENTITY DEVELOPMENT

An understanding of racial identity development and awareness of this facet of one's own identity is considered a key component of multicultural competence for educational counsellors (Holcomb-McCoy, 2004). The concept of racial identity encompasses both feelings of belongingness to a cultural/racial group and the internal, psychological process in which the individual makes a decision about the role of race in his/her life (Fischer & Moradi, 2001). For minority youth, many face the question of racial identity early in the developmental process (St. Louis & Liem, 2005; Sneed, Schwartz, & Cross, 2006). White adolescents, however, may never consider this facet of identity because Whiteness is not something that distinguishes them as individuals (Kroger, 2007). Thus, both White students in educational counselling programs and White professionals currently practicing in schools may have an undeveloped White identity, which will impact their multicultural counselling competence.

In a review of research studies exploring the relationship between racial identity development and multicultural competence, McAllister and Irvine (2000) found that higher levels of racial identity development were consistently associated with higher levels of multicultural competence, non-racist behaviour, and knowledge about other cultures and races. Graduate students who have participated in multicultural counselling courses generally show higher levels of self-rated White racial identity development on completion than at the beginning (Neville et al., 1996; Parker, Moore, & Neimeyer, 1998).

A number of White racial identity development (WRID) models (Helms, 1990, 1995; Sue et al., 1998) have been proposed in the United States as extensions of Erikson's (1968) developmental model of identity (Sneed et al., 2006). The models are based on an understanding that race is a social construct derived from differing histories of oppression and domination, rather than a biological fact (Helms, 1995). Although the White identity models differ in detail, they generally propose a series of stages leading from unawareness of racial identity to achievement of a strongly anti-racist White identity (Ponterotto, Utsey, & Pedersen, 2006).

Although Helms' (1990, 1995) WRID model is widely cited in the counselling and educational literature (McAllister & Irvine, 2000; Ponterotto et al., 2006), it has been criticized for lack of empirical validity (Fischer & Moradi, 2001). Sue et al. (1998) have further critiqued Helms' (1990, 1995) model as being context-bound. For example, Helms' model speaks exclusively about Black-White relations, without reference to other visible minority groups (Phinney, 1996). Further, Sue et al. (1998) noted that Helms' model does not include unachieved identity statuses, which are needed to reflect the lack of exploration of and commitment to racial identity characteristic of many White people.

As an alternative to Helms' (1990, 1995) conceptualization, Sue et al. (1998) proposed a 5-stage WRID developmental model. In the *Conformity* stage of that model, a White person has little awareness of the importance of race and culture. A person in this stage is likely to espouse colour-blind attitudes that minimize racial/cultural differences. Remarks such as "people are people" or "I treat everyone the same" are considered typical of this phase. Any problems that a minority person encounters are attributed to individual problems, such as lack of effort, rather than to systemic forces in society. Racial identity in this stage would be considered unachieved.

In the *Dissonance* phase (Sue et al., 1998), a White person encounters information that challenges his or her beliefs about the lack of personal bias towards minority individuals and the absence of racism in contemporary society. Such information may come from personal interaction that raises conflicting feelings, such as work-related difficulty with a visible minority co-worker, or it may come from a public event, such as Oscar Peterson being the target of racial harassment or attacks on Islamic mosques. The conflict of this information with personal beliefs produces a negative emotional reaction (e.g., guilt, shame, or anger). In response to this identity crisis, the person may either retreat further into the denial of the conformity phase or move forward into an exploration of racial issues.

Sue et al. (1998) termed the third phase of their model *Resistance and Immersion.* At this time, a White person will likely experience both "anger at having been sold a false bill of goods by family, friends, and society, and guilt for having been a part of the oppressive system" (p. 58). To compensate, the White individual may become a strong, liberal spokesperson for minority groups and/or seek to associate only with minority individuals, rejecting their own racial affiliation. Nevertheless, a thread of paternalism continues to run through this stage.

In the fourth phase, the White individual becomes *Introspective* (Sue et al., 1998) about Whiteness. It becomes easier to acknowledge the inevitable association between being White and both participating in oppression and benefiting from unearned White privilege. Although the person remains active in the struggle against oppression, defensive feelings such as guilt and anger about being White subside. Through active exploration of racial issues and association with minority individuals, the person thoughtfully considers what it means to be White. The process culminates in the fifth phase termed *Integrative Awareness.* At this point, the individual has achieved a non-racist White identity characterized by both an appreciation of multiculturalism and a commitment to ending oppression, even at the risk of being marginalized by White society.

Although the Sue et al. (1998) model needs further empirical investigation, it nevertheless highlights an important aspect of White identity development: the key role of cross-racial contact in catalyzing the developmental process. In the theoretical literature on WRID, contact with minority people is considered a necessary, if not sufficient, factor in the developmental process (Ponterotto et al., 2006). Nevertheless, empirical reports concerning cross-racial experience and White identity development in educational counsellors continue to be rare.

Boyle, Nackerud, and Kilpatrick (1999) reported on an experiment in social worker training that involved short international exchange programs with social work schools in Mexico for two small groups of students. Their results were so encouraging that the exchanges have now been institutionalized. DeRicco and Sciarra (2005) described how a ten-week immersion experience in a Black neighbourhood in the northeastern U. S. revealed to a White liberal counselling student that, "racism had taken up residence within her without her bidding" (p. 13). These two studies both involved short-term sojourns. Inspired by the profound effect of my own longer sojourn with the Inuit (Wihak, 2004a) on my own White racial identity, I conducted research with other White counsellors who had lived and worked for at least two years in school-settings in Nunavut's Inuit communities and since returned to southern Canada (Wihak, 2004b).

WHITE RACIAL IDENTITY DEVELOPMENT: THE EXPERIENCES OF CANADIAN COUNSELLORS

Nunavut offers the sojourning counsellor an unusual physical and social environment, one that is very different from southern Canada. The territory, which came into political existence on April 1, 1999, comprises two million square kilometers above the tree line north and west of Hudson's Bay. The population is approximately 29,000, of which about 85 percent are Inuit. Although Inuit employment is increasing, a majority of Inuit families live in public housing and rely on social assistance payments for income. This socio-economic situation is the consequence of the Canadian government's intervention in the Arctic after the Second World War when the official policy was to settle the formerly nomadic Inuit into organized communities. Settlement in permanent communities disrupted traditional reliance on subsistence hunting and gathering while the requirement for Inuit children to attend school interfered with generational patterns of cultural transmission. Many Inuit suffering from tuberculosis were also removed for treatment in southern Canada, further disrupting generational relations. Rapid social, political and economic change has taken its toll on the mental health of Inuit. Nunavut faces high rates of substance abuse, family violence, and suicide (Korhonen, 2002).

The White counsellors participating in my research had varying degrees of training in multicultural counselling and experience with cross-racial contact prior to going to Nunavut. The length of their sojourns also varied considerably, as did the intensity of their involvement with Inuit during their time in Nunavut.

Because of this variability, their observations on their White identities provided an interesting cross-section of the WRID developmental process. To illustrate thoughts and feelings characteristic of different developmental phases, I have related extracts from the participants' narratives to the Sue et al. (1998) WRID model introduced above. [Note: Some participants chose pseudonyms while other preferred to use their own names. To respect their preferences while maintaining confidentiality, I have not indicated which is a pseudonym and which is a real name.]

Conformity: Based on retrospective interviews, these participants cannot be characterized as unaware of the importance of racial and cultural differences. In describing their personal and professional interactions with Inuit, all participants showed awareness of belonging to a different culture/ through using terms such as *qablunaaq*, Southerner, and White in contrast to Inuit. Nor was there any evidence that the participants attributed their Inuit clients' presenting problems to individual failures, as Sue et al. (1998) suggest is typical of the Conformity phase.

Paradoxically, however, several of the counsellors expressed opinions that Sue et al. (1998) describe as indicating the colour-blindness of Conformity. Bev, who had married an Inuk man and learned to speak Inuktitut fluently, observed, "People are people and people and people. They have the same feelings. They have same ideologies. They have the same psychological make-up, basically." Danya, who was herself a member of the Jewish minority, echoed Bev when she said, "In so many things, we're the same. We're all humans." Meeka, who had grown up in Indigenous communities, had a long term relationship with an Inuit man, and learned to speak the language, added support to this view when she said, "There's more similarities than differences in people."

Dissonance: Several of the participants recollected really becoming aware of their White identity when they first moved to Nunavut, although they all had previous cross-racial experience. Their memories of their emerging awareness of being White and associated feelings of guilt and anger are characteristic of the Dissonance stage (Sue et al., 1998).

Patricia described becoming aware of her racial/cultural identity when her family moved to a small community that was over 90 percent Inuit. She explained that, "It was really one of the first times that I was ever a minority." She remembered the uncomfortable feeling of "being examined and stared at." Similarly, Rebecca felt that her racial/cultural identity came into being in Nunavut. It was a different experience for her, being "told how many times a day that you're *qablunaaq* [Inuktutut word for non-Inuit]." Her Whiteness seemed to be the most significant thing about her. Rebecca expressed mixed emotions about being White, "feeling very guilty to feeling kind of defensive." She sometimes felt that what had happened to the Inuit was not her fault; "What's happened, happened and I didn't do it."

Patricia and Rebecca commented on the difficulty of making a difference with regard to social justice, another characteristic of the Dissonance phase (Sue et al.,

1998). Patricia felt "very powerless to make changes, because some of them were major social things and you're one person." Rebecca's comments echoed Patricia's opinion: "Social workers in those northern communities who are from the South have done some good work…. Have they fixed some of the systemic problems, the broader issues? I don't think they ever can."

Resistance and Immersion: Many of the participants' comments about their immersion experiences reflected Sue et al.'s (1998) description of the guilt associated with this phase. Michelle, for example, explained that, "I needed to somehow make a difference or right a wrong for myself. There's just the privilege of my life, just seeing that privilege, just being aware of the fact that I have a different experience because I'm White."

Commenting on how her cultural/racial identity had been affected when she joined the Inuit in their struggle against Canadian government interventions in their culture, Fluff said, "It's a difficult thing to identify as being of a race and culture that is oppressive to a lot of the world, and to recognize that… one's culture exercises power in negative ways over other people."

Bev and Meeka, both of whom had relationships with Inuit men, also demonstrated the tendency to over-identify with the oppressed group, another characteristic of this phase. Bev described herself as becoming "quasi-Inuk" when she married into the culture and learned the language. After returning to southern Canada, Meeka remembered going to a meeting and thinking, "Wow! There's a lot of White people here… a lot of pasty White skin and yellow hair and pale eyes." When she visited a nearby Aboriginal reserve, she thought, "This is the community I want to live in.". [Approved Transcript, lines 815-820]

Introspective: Debbie had extensive contact with Indigenous people prior to moving to Nunavut, living as a child on reserves where her father worked and working with Indigenous bands earlier in her career. When asked how her identity had been affected by her Nunavut sojourn, Debbie commented that racial/cultural identity has "always been fuzzy for me… It certainly solidified my humanness, my perspective. But there's lots of humanness outside of the Native culture. So I do understand your question; I just don't have the answer." Reflecting her prolonged cross-racial contact, Debbie's response seems to portray the disconnection from the White world that Sue et al. (1998) said is typical of this phase. This disconnection is also apparent in the observations of Bev, who recollected that while she was in Nunavut, her bicultural family was never fully accepted by the other Whites.

Integrative Awareness: Several participants made comments that suggested they had internalized a non-racist White identity. Reflecting on what she had learned in Nunavut, Michelle observed, "I've gotten a lot of my White guilt out of the way, and in doing so… I'm feeling… more connected to people of different cultures as opposed to… that patronizing… view." On her return to southern Canada, Michelle continued to work and socialize with Aboriginal people, demonstrating the comfort with and commitment to minority groups that Sue et al. (1998) described in this phase.

Deborah's comments also illustrated a mixture of comfort with her own racial identity and commitment to working to end oppression. She described her own cultural identity in these terms: "I am undeniably the product of lower middle-class English people. I retain a lot of those values... and I'm very... comfortable in my cultural background." At the same time, Deborah learned a lot about working in solidarity with minorities from her experience in Nunavut, indicating that she had moved beyond a paternalistic, liberal approach. She explained:

> Women in [name of small Nunavut community] made it very clear to me that they don't need external spokespeople. Strategies? Yes. You can provide information, but women everywhere in the world advocate for themselves... They know what's wrong with their lives, and they take action on it when they're ready to.

Since leaving Nunavut, Deborah has worked with women's groups in Africa and Afghanistan.

Bev's perception of her identity changed after she returned to southern Canada. "Very definitely, I'm more *qablunaaq* now than I ever have been." She elaborated, "The kids blame me sometimes, 'Mom! You're too *qablunaaq*! Straighten up and be Inuk!' Look! You know, I'm White! This is me!" Bev has also continued her involvement with Aboriginal people in southern Canada.

TRANSFORMATIONAL EFFECT ON PROFESSIONAL PRACTICE

The counsellors in this study developed their White racial identities in the Nunavut context. Their deepened understanding of their own Whiteness, however, has continued to influence their professional practice when working with clients from other racially diverse groups in southern Canada.

Fluff brought from Nunavut an awareness of how capable people are to be healthy and to grow. She commented about her work with Aboriginal people in southern Canada:

> I think that in many of our schools that teach us counseling and therapy, there's quite an emphasis on what we do to assist other people and how we do that. But perhaps we don't really pay enough attention to acknowledging that it is the person who is healing themselves.

Michelle described how her Nunavut experience had helped her work with Aboriginal clients in the South: "I feel more... friendliness; there's a way to be with Aboriginal people that is different in the therapeutic professions. It feels more like... it's about creating friendships and being part of the community."

With visible minority clients, Patricia now recognizes that for some people, it's uncomfortable for them to say, "No, I want to challenge you." She doesn't accept that when they say "yes," they necessarily understand what she means. Patricia realized, "Sometimes I have to ask the same question in three or four different ways, and if I get a consistent answer, then I know that I've got the right information."

From her experience in Nunavut, Rebecca sees that most social work practice is based on a White European understanding and this may not be the best fit for everyone; "people aren't just all going to be the same, and you can't treat everybody the same way.... Just testing people out and asking them what they are comfortable with... that's just good practice."

DISCUSSION: WHITE RACIAL IDENTITY DEVELOPMENT AND GENERATIVITY

The comments of the counsellors who sojourned in Nunavut fit well into the phases of WRID in the Sue et al. (1998) model, with one notable exception. That is the participants' persistence in "seeing people as people," supposedly a characteristic of Conformity, even though other remarks indicate considerable progression beyond colour-blindness and conformity to liberal ideals. What accounts for this paradox?

The participants in this study were mature counsellors concerned with the question of "How can I help?" This question is the focus of the developmental stage that Erikson (1982) termed *generativity*, which encompasses much of adult life. That is, the sojourning counsellors were involved with the question of effective caring (McAdams Diamond, de St. Aubin, & Mansfield, 1997), rather than identity. Through their commitment to being effective helpers, their identities also expanded (McAdams, Hart, & Maruna, 1998) to incorporate caring for people from a different race and culture. Their descriptions of similarities between people of all cultures and appreciation of their realities reflect not conformity to liberal ideas but rather development of a universal-diverse orientation that is essential for effective cross-cultural helping relationships in today's multicultural schools (Constantine, Arorash, Barakett, Blackmon, Donnelly, & Edles, 2001).

In the spiritual life, there is a proverb: "First there is a mountain, then there is no mountain, then there is." The process of WRID is similar. Initially, a White person raised in a liberal, White country such as Canada cannot see the differences in life experiences and opportunities that come from race. As a White person actually gets to know members of oppressed minorities, she also starts to see her own Whiteness and the privilege that accompanies it. As she accepts responsibility as a White person to work for social justice, she once again can express her sense of shared humanity with minorities, a sense essential for making the end of oppression their common cause. That is, she has become able to do what Parker (1997, p. 297) asked her White friends to do: "The first thing you do is forget that I am Black... Second, you must never forget that I am Black." This ability to be colour-blind and not colour-blind simultaneously is the hallmark of the achievement of a mature, anti-racist White identity.

To support development of a mature White identity, effective educational programs need to ensure that White students have the opportunity for extensive cross-racial contact and, ideally, the opportunity for an extended immersion experience as a minority. Throughout this process, educators can use an understanding of the WRID model (Sue et al., 1998) to support students sensitively while they explore the conflicting emotions that characterize an identity crisis. Most importantly, educators need to recognize that White identity development is a process that may take months, if not years, to reach its mature expression in Integrative Awareness, and one that requires extended cross-racial contact to come to full fruition. Achieving Integrative Awareness is not, however, an end-point for White Racial Identity development. Although naïve colour-blindness and White guilt may disappear, the commitment to work collaboratively with minorities for social justice will continue to make learning about one's own Whiteness a lifelong task.

QUESTIONS FOR REFLECTION

1. What is your personal experience of developing a White Racial Identity?
2. How would achieving a mature White identity affect your professional practice?
3. How would you tell the difference between an individual who was expressing the colour-blindness of the Conformity stage and one who was expressing the colour-blindness/colour-vision of the Integrative Awareness stage?
4. How would educational activities to support White Racial Identity Development (WRID) differ for pre-service professionals in different phases of development?
5. Statistical projections indicate that in major Canadian cities (Toronto, Vancouver) White people will soon be in the minority. How might this affect the process of WRID?

REFERENCES

Arredondo, P., & Arciniega, G. M. (2001). Strategies and techniques for counsellor training based on the multicultural counselling competencies. *Journal of Multicultural Counselling and Development, 29,* 263–273.

Arthur, N., & Collins, S. (2005). Introduction to culture-infused counselling. In N. Arthur & S. Collins (Eds.), Culture-infused counselling: Celebrating the Canadian mosaic (pp. 3–40). Calgary, AB: Counselling Concepts.

Arthur, N., & Januszkowski, T. (2001). Multicultural competencies of Canadian counsellors. *Canadian Journal of Counselling, 35*(1), 36–48.

Boyle, D. P., Nackerud, L., & Kilpatrick. A. (1999). The road less traveled: Cross-cultural, international experiential learning. *International Social Work, 42*(2), 201–214.

Brooks, B. L., Mintz, A. R., & Dobson, K. S. (2004). Diversity training in Canadian predoctoral clinical psychology internships: A survey of directors of internship training. *Canadian Psychology, 45,* 308–312.

Cole, E. (1998). Immigrant and refugee children: Challenges and opportunities for education and mental health services. *Canadian Journal of School Psychology, 14,* 36.

Coleman, H. L. K., & Baskin, T. (2003). Multiculturally competent school counseling. In D. B. Pope-Davis, H. K. Coleman, W. M. Liu & R. L. Toperak (Eds.), *Handbook of multicultural competencies in counseling & psychology* (pp. 103–113). Thousand Oaks, CA: Sage.

Constantine, M. (2001). Multicultural training, self-construals, and multicultural competence of school counsellors. *Professional School Counselling, 4*, 202–207.

Constantine, M. G., Arorash, T. J., Barakett, M. D., Blackmon, S. M., Donnelly, P C., & Edles, P. A. (2001). School counselors' universal-diverse orientation and aspects of their multicultural counseling. *Professional School Counseling, 5*, 13–18.

DeRicco, J. N., & Sciarra, D. T. (2005). The immersion experience in multicultural counselor training: Confronting covert racism. *Journal of Multicultural Counseling and Development, 33*(1), 2–16.

Duran, B., & Duran, E. (2000). Applied postcolonial clinical and research strategies. In M. Battiste (Ed.), *Reclaiming Indigenous voice and vision* (pp. 86–100). Vancouver, BC: UBC Press.

Erikson, E. (1968). *Identity: Youth and crisis.* New York, NY: Norton.

Erikson, E. (1982). *The life cycle completed.* New York, NY: Norton.

Fischer, A. R., & Moradi, B. (2001). Racial and ethnic identity: Recent developments and needed directions. In J. G. Ponterotto, J. M. Casas, L. A. Suzuki & C. M. Alexander (Eds.), *Handbook of multicultural counselling* (2nd ed., pp. 341–369). Thousand Oaks, CA: Sage.

Fuertes, J. N., Bartolomeo, M., & Nichols, C. M. (2001). Future research directions in the study of counsellor multicultural competence. *Journal of Multicultural Counselling and Development, 29*, 3–12.

Ghosh, R., & Abdi, A. (2004). *Education and the politics of difference: Canadian perspectives.* Toronto, ON: Canadian Scholars' Press.

Gopaul-McNicol, S. (1997). A theoretical framework for training monolingual school psychologists to work with multilingual/multicultural children: An exploration of major competencies. *Psychology in the Schools, 34*, 17–29.

Gosine, K. (2002). Essentialism versus complexity: Conceptions of racial identity construction in educational scholarship. *Canadian Journal of Education, 27*, 81–100.

Helms, J. (1990). *Black and White racial identity: Theory, research and practice.* Westport, CT: Greenwood.

Helms, J. (1995). An update of Helm's White and people of color racial identity models. In J. G. Ponterotto, J. M. Casas, L. A. Suzuki & C. M. Alexander (Eds.), *Handbook of multicultural counselling* (pp. 181–198). Thousand Oaks, CA: Sage.

Holcomb-McCoy, C. (2004). Assessing the multicultural competence of school counselors: A checklist. *Professional School Counseling, 7*(3), 178–183.

Holcomb-McCoy, C. (2005). Investigating school counselors' perceived multicultural competence. *Professional School Counseling, 8*(5), 414–423.

Kelly, D. M., & Brandes, G. M. (2001). Shifting out of "Neutral": Beginning teachers' struggles with teaching for social justice. *Canadian Journal of Education, 26*, 437–454.

Korhonen, M. (2002). *Inuit clients and the effective helper: An investigation of culturally sensitive counselling* (Unpublished doctoral dissertation). Durham University, Durham, England.

Kroger, J. (2007). *Identity development: Adolescence through adulthood* (2nd ed.). Thousand Oaks, CA: Sage.

McAdams, D. P., Diamond, A., de St. Aubin, E., & Mansfield, E. (1997). Stories of commitment: The psychosocial construction of generative lives. *Journal of Personality and Social Psychology, 72*, 678–694.

McAdams, D. P., Hart, H. M., & Maruna, S. (1998). The anatomy of generativity. In D. P. McAdams & E. de St. Aubin (Eds.), *Generativity and adult development: How and why we care for the next generation* (pp 7–43) Washington, DC: American Psychological Association, Society for Industrial and Organizational Psychology.

McAllister, G., & Irvine, J. J. (2000). Cross cultural competency and multicultural teacher education. *Review of Educational Research, 70*, 3–24.

Mollen, D., Ridley, C. R., & Hill, C. L. (2003). Models of multicultural competence: A critical evaluation. In D. Pope-Davis, H. Coleman, W. Liu & R. Toporek (Eds.), *Handbook of multicultural competencies in counseling & psychology* (pp. 21–37). Thousand Oaks, CA: Sage.

Myles, D., & Harold, R. (1988). Teachers' bias towards visible ethnic minority groups in special education referrals. *B.C. Journal of Special Education, 1*, 19–24.

Nichols, J. D. (1999). *An exploration of discipline and suspension data.* Paper presented at the Annual Meeting of the American Educational Research Association, Montreal, PQ. Retrieved from http://www.eric.ed.gov/ERICDocs/data/ericdocs2/content_storage_01/0000000b/80/11/9d/68.pdf

Parker, P. (1997). For the White person who wants to know how to be my friend. In G. Anzaludua (Ed.), *Making face, making soul/haienda caras: Creative and critical perspectives by women of color* (p. 297). San Francisco, CA: Aunt Lute Foundation.

Parker, W. M., Moore, M. A., & Neimeyer, G. J. (1998). Altering White racial identity and interracial comfort through multicultural training. *Journal of Counseling & Development, 76*(3), 302–311.

Phinney, J. C. (1996). Understanding ethnic diversity. *American Behavioral Scientist, 40*(2), 143–152.

Ponterotto, J. G., Jackson, M. A., & Nutini, C. D. (2001). Reflections on the life stories of pioneers in multicultural counseling. In J. G. Ponterotto, J. M. Casas, L. A. Suzuki, & C. M. Alexander (Eds.) *Handbook of multicultural counseling* (2nd ed., pp. 138–162). Thousand Oaks, CA: Sage.

Ponterotto, J. G., Utsey, S., & Pedersen, P. (2006). *Preventing prejudice: A guide for counselors, educators, and parents* (2nd ed.). Thousand Oaks, CA: Sage.

Reschly, D. J. (2005). *Disproportionality in special education.* Retrieved from http://www.nasponline.org/culturalcompetence/index.html#powerpoint

Ruck, M., & Wortley, S. (2002). Racial and ethnic minority high school students' perceptions of school disciplinary practices: A look at some Canadian findings. *Journal of Youth and Adolescence, 31*(3), 185–195.

Schwallie-Giddis, P., Anstrom, K., Sánchez, P., Sardi, V. A., & Granato, L. (2004). *Counseling the linguistically and culturally diverse student: Meeting school counselors' professional development needs. Professional School Counseling, 8,* 15–23.

Sneed, J. R., Schwartz, S. J., & Cross, Jr., W. E. (2006). A multicultural critique of identity status theory and research: A call for integration. *Identity: An international journal of theory and research, 6*(1), 61–84.

Sparrow, L. M. (2000). Intercultural man: complexities of identity. *International Journal of Intercultural Relations, 24,* 173–201.

Solomon, R. P., & Levine-Rasky, C. (2003). *Teaching for equity and diversity: Research to practice.* Toronto, ON: Canadian Scholars' Press.

St. Louis, G. R., & Liem, J. H. (2005). Ego identity, ethnic identity, and the psychosocial well-being of ethnic minority and majority college students. *Identity: An International Journal of Theory and Research, 5*(3), 227–246.

Sue, D. W., Arredondo, P., & McDavis, R. J. (1992). Multicultural counseling competencies and standards: A call to the profession. *Journal of Counseling & Development, 70,* 477–486.

Sue, D. W., Carter, R. T., Casas, J. M., Fouad, N. A., Ivey, A. E., Jensen, M., ... Vazquez-Nutall, E. (1998). *Multicultural counseling competencies: Individual and organizational development.* Thousand Oaks, CA: Sage.

Taylor, G., & Quintana, S. (2003). Teachers' multicultural competencies (K-12). In D. Pope-Davis, H. Coleman, W. Liu & R. Toporek (Eds.), *Handbook of Multicultural Competencies in Counseling & Psychology* (pp. 511–527). Thousand Oaks, CA: Sage.

Vinson, T. S., & Neimeyer, G. J. (2000). The relationship between racial identity development and multicultural counselling competence. *Journal of Multicultural Counselling and Development, 28,* 177–192.

Vinson, T. S., & Neimeyer, G. J. (2003). The relationship between racial identity development and multicultural counselling competence: A second look. *Journal of Multicultural Counselling and Development, 31,* 262–277.

Wallace, B. C. (2000). A call for change in multicultural training at graduate schools of education: Educating to end oppression and for social justice. *Teachers College Record, 102,* 1086–1112.

Wihak, C. (2004a). Meaning of being White in Canada. *TESL Canada, 21,* 110–115.

Wihak, C. (2004b). *Counsellors' experiences of cross-cultural sojourning* (Unpublished doctoral dissertation). University of Alberta, Edmonton, AB.

REFRAMING: CHRISTINE WIHAK (2014)

In 2007, just as *The Great White North* (TGWN) was published, my intense involvement in research on racial identity development shifted as I took up a new administrative position at Thompson Rivers University (TRU) in British Columbia. TRU World, our international division, brings students from all over the planet to study in a small blue-collar city, Kamloops, in the interior of BC. These students inject a high level of racialized diversity into a hitherto predominantly White university context.

TRU has taken internationalization of the curriculum very seriously. Faculty members are regularly offered training sessions on how to internationalize their teaching, as well as an annual teaching award for excellence in this area, and students have the opportunity to earn a Global Competency certificate, the first credential of its kind in Canada. Most of these efforts are framed within the perspective of intercultural communication, particularly the work of Bennett (1986).

The issue of race is only intermittently addressed and is certainly not the primary focus. As a member of the committee responsible for guiding internationalization, I have found an invisible community in the contributors to *TGWN*. It is not an easy thing to raise the R-word, especially when no one else is talking about it.

While I remain convinced that White people in Canada, particularly those in the helping professions, must become more conscious of their White racial identity and associated privileges, I have become less enthusiastic about Helms' (1990, 1995) White Racial Identity model, which provided the analytical structure for my contribution to the first edition *TGWN*. As I observe contemporary students struggling with the concept of Whiteness in an increasingly multi-racial environment, as my own White identity continues to grow and change, I find that Helms' stages are too prescriptive and bound to the US context of Black/White relations. Scholars before me have made similar observations (e.g., Sue et al., 1998). But in 2004, when I did the research presented the *TGWN* chapter, there really was not any more satisfactory model to use.

Phinney (1989, 1996), the other major theorist influencing multicultural counseling at the time, focused on ethnic identity formation, which she defined to encompass both cultural and racial aspects of identity. Phinney, adapting Marcia's (1980) widely accepted extension of Erikson's (1968) developmental model of identity, offered a typology of identity statuses (*unexamined, moratorium, achieved*) characterized by different combinations of *exploration* (a period of active questioning about one's ethnic identity) and *commitment* (having made a firm decision about one's ethnic identity). Phinney's model was critiqued for combining of ethnicity and race into a single construct (Helms & Talleyrand, 1997).

D. E. Lund & P. R. Carr (Eds.), Revisiting The Great White North?, 123–124.

In 2005, Phinney did acknowledge that race and ethnicity are distinct facets of identity. In more recent work (Phinney & Baldelomar, 2011), Phinney has discussed the possibly curtailed process of identity formation for minority adolescents whose racial identities are ascribed to them by society. She had little to say about the identity development of dominant majorities, such as Whites in Canada, other than to point out that such individuals rarely explore this dimension of identity. Nevertheless, I think Phinney's (1989, 1996, 2005, 2011) emphasis on the process of identity development as an interplay of exploration and commitment is valuable for those of us who are trying to understand how best to encourage White students to consider the question of racial identity and racial privilege.

If we understand the process of identity development, it helps us focus on the importance of providing adolescents and young adults with provocative questions and experiences that will lead them to explore. It also helps us understand how threatening such questions can be to identities that are fragile while forming. Much research remains to be done on White identify development, and how we can intervene effectively to keep the process of exploration going. I encourage consideration of Phinney's theoretical work and associated measurement tools to guide such research in the future.

REFERENCES

Bennett, M. J. (1986). Towards ethnorelativism: A developmental model of intercultural sensitivity. In R. M. Paige (Ed.), *Cross-cultural orientation: New conceptualizations and applications* (pp. 27–70). Lanham, MD: University Press of America.

Erikson, E. (1968). *Identity: Youth and crisis*. New York, NY: Norton.

Helms, J. (1990). *Black and White racial identity: Theory, research and practice*. Westport, CT: Greenwood.

Helms, J. (1995). An update of Helms' White and people of color racial identity models. In J. G. Ponterotto, J. M. Casas, L. A. Suzuki & C. M. Alexander (Eds.), *Handbook of multicultural counselling* (1st ed., pp. 181–198). Thousand Oaks, CA: Sage.

Helms, J., & Talleyrand, R. (1997). Race is not ethnicity. *American Pscyhologist, 52*(11), 1246–1247.

Marcia, J. (1980). Identity in adolescence. In J. Adelson (Ed.), *Adolescent Psychology* (pp. 159–187). Toronto, ON: John Wiley & Sons.

Phinney, J. S. (1989). Stages of ethnic identity development in minority group adolescents. *Journal of Early Adolescence, 9*, 34–49.

Phinney, J. S. (1996). When we talk about American ethnic groups, what do we mean? *American Psychologist, 51*, 918–927.

Phinney, J. S., & Baldelomar, O. A. (2011). Identity development in multiple cultural contexts. In L. A. Jensen (Ed.), *Bridging cultural and developmental psychology: New syntheses for theory, research and policy* (pp. 161–186). New York, NY: Oxford University Press.

Sue, D. W., Carter, R. T., Casas, J. M., Fouad, N. A., Ivey, A. E., Jensen, M., & Vazquez-Nuttall, E. (1998). *Multicultural counseling competencies: Individual and organizational development*. Thousand Oaks, CA: Sage.

SUSAN A. TILLEY & KELLY D. POWICK

"RADICAL STUFF"

Starting a Conversation about Racial Identity and White Privilege

INTRODUCTION

Susan: I trace my interest in understanding Whiteness and White privilege to my doctoral research during which I conducted a critical ethnography with incarcerated women in a school housed within a prison. My experience was saturated with learning related to gender, sexuality, race, and class, and how they intersected and influenced the lives and experiences of the women I taught. I was forced to interrogate Whiteness[1] and White privilege, particularly the privilege I carried as a teacher/researcher who was "free" to leave the prison at the end of each day. This research reflects my continued interest in disrupting institutional norms that support the privileging of Whiteness.

Kelly: When I began my graduate studies, discussions on the changing demographics of Canadian classrooms, coupled with my prior teaching, prompted an initial interest in researching the experiences of immigrant children in schools. This interest, however, was challenged as I began to consider the implications of being a White researcher/teacher, and chose to readjust my research lens to shift away from immigrant students to instead explore the experiences of White teachers. Questioning what it means to be a White educator teaching in culturally diverse settings led to the completion of my thesis, *Conversations with EFL teachers: Toward an understanding of whiteness in the classroom*. In my current practices as a teacher talking about culture and communication, I continue to grapple with my own questions around racial identity and privilege. I struggle with how to provide educative experiences for other White adults while recognizing that many of my students may be joining this conversation for the first time.

In Canada, although efforts have been made in educational contexts to advance knowledge in areas related to antiracism (Dei, 1996; Short & Carrington, 1996; Solomon & Levine-Rasky, 1996) and multiculturalism (James, 2005; Moodley, 2001), and to support initiatives that have social justice and equity as goals, the local conversation has frequently been limited to language and concepts that maintain rather than disrupt dominant, White, liberal perspectives deeply embedded in educational systems. Programs are often developed and implemented with the intention of collapsing differences (James & Haig-Brown, 2000) and promoting principles of equality as primary outcomes. Although a focus on Whiteness and White privilege

D. E. Lund & P. R. Carr (Eds.), Revisiting The Great White North?, 125–136.
© 2015 Sense Publishers. All rights reserved.

is evident in a growing body of literature across academic disciplines, translation of principles and practices espoused in that literature to K-12 and/or postsecondary classrooms has not necessarily followed (Cochran-Smith, 2000; LeCompte & McCray, 2002; Sleeter, 2001).

A contributing factor to this lack of translation of principles into practice is that in the realm of teacher education instructors and students continue to represent the dominant, naturalized norm of who a teacher should be—namely, White, female, heterosexual, and middle-class (Schick, 2000; Schick & St. Denis, 2005), and for the most part, race talk is resisted (Tatum, 1992). What becomes disheartening in relation to the work of interrogating Whiteness and White privilege in postsecondary contexts, especially with individuals who are teaching in schools and are responsible for the education of students, or are being educated to do such work, is that opening up such conversation is still understood as "radical stuff."

We write this chapter as two White women who represent the "norm" and continue to work on developing knowledge about the ways in which White privilege, in general, and, our White privilege specifically, operate to support the institutional racism and inequities embedded in Western institutions like schools and universities. We trace our interests back to moments when it was difficult to ignore the privilege we carried and its material effects on others. Susan, in her work with incarcerated women, was forced to question why certain kinds of bodies were present in the prison while others were absent. Kelly, in her experiences teaching overseas, where her White skin equaled privileges not applied to her local colleagues, and translated into celebrity status she had not enjoyed back home, was pushed to consider the White privilege she had previously ignored. We cannot pinpoint the exact moment when, similar to Mathieson (2004), we "began to develop 'critical consciousness' about racism and [were] pushed to reflect on the ways that race, racism, and Whiteness shaped [our lives] and the broader social reality" (p. 236); we only know that it has happened.

THE RESEARCH

The qualitative research[2] informing this chapter centred on a course, *Culture, Identity and Pedagogy: Advancing a Lived Curriculum,* that Susan constructed and taught to graduate students completing a Master's of Education in curriculum studies. The students in that course grappled with difficult content that, among other things, examined the complex processes by which race, class, sexual orientation and other socially constructed categories intersect and influence children's and teachers' classroom experiences, with specific emphasis given to interrogating racial identity, Whiteness, and White privilege. Twelve graduate students, four racial minorities[3] and eight White students enrolled in the course and agreed to participate in the first phase of the research, which included a content analysis (Coffey & Atkinson, 1996; Constas, 1992) of all student assignments, instructor's notes, and student evaluations (See Tilley, 2006, for a detailed discussion).

This chapter reports on the second phase of the research. Of the 12 students (one international student had returned overseas) who participated in the first phase, three racial minority and two White students agreed to participate in conversations focused on their experiences since taking the course. We collected data through in-depth, open-ended interviews (Fontana & Frey, 2000; Merriam, 1998) approximately one year following students' completion of the course. In the following sections, we write of the "difficult knowledge" students emphasized in their interviews, and how they grappled with that knowledge later, attempting (or not) to translate it into their curricular and teaching practices.

DIFFICULT KNOWLEDGE

We were all starting out and we didn't know how to discuss [race] even. You know we had never done this [before], what are we supposed to talk about? (participant #1)

The 5 participants interviewed had originally enrolled in the course for a range of reasons, including "wanting to be challenged," "interesting course description," and "needing one last course to complete the program." As well, they had joined at various stages within their graduate program. Two participants were new to graduate studies and were taking this as their first course. In contrast, three other participants had completed more than six courses and were nearing the end of their program, anticipating their research exit requirement. As a group, they had classroom experience as elementary and secondary teachers, as well as in administration. Yet, in spite of their experiences and previous education, the participants admitted that many of the theories and concepts addressed in the course content were new to them. A racial minority participant with two decades of teaching experience spoke in amazement of never having been introduced to many of these core ideas before this course: "All of it, *all* of it was new. I'd never heard of this before, *ever* [emphasis on tape], never did it, you know in my undergraduate years... This stuff isn't even in *Professional Speaking*[4] those kinds of magazines" (participant #1).

The course was constructed to "push" students to address multicultural and antiracism education through a lens emphasizing racial identity. Participants highlighted as particularly difficult, material related to colour-blindness/colour-consciousness (Desai, 2001; Valli, 1995), racial identity formation (Cross, 1971, 1978; Helms, 1990), and White privilege (McIntosh, 1988; Strigel & Verhaag, 1996). A description from one White participant captures the psychological struggle for many students to think through these difficult concepts: "I remember leaving the classes and just my head hurt [participant laughs] because there was just so much... all the material was new to me and I was having troubles grasping all the content" (participant #5).

In interviews, participants were questioned specifically about the challenges they faced in working with/through troublesome course content. What emerged from participant responses was a stark difference in what was named as difficult. A White participant with both classroom and administrative experience acknowledged that the literature was "entirely new," yet what was repeatedly highlighted as a challenge was the volume of reading rather than the core concepts and ideas: "I think there were 1400-1500 pages there. It was massive. It was huge" (participant #4). Admittedly, there were limitations in the way the course was structured. Offered in the shortened summer term meant the reading requirements were heavy for all students. Yet, while this participant pointed to the amount of reading as being difficult, for racial minority participants the course challenges were different. Two racial minority participants spoke emotionally of the personal challenge it was to "sit back and listen" as their White classmates attempted (or not) to work through the theoretical concepts of racial identity and racial privilege:

> I can remember one day when I was totally frustrated, like dear God what are you thinking, right? But I remember walking away from that class despite the fact [I was] angry, just walking away thinking there's got to be a reason. There's got to be a reason why she thinks the way she thinks… I think the frustration for me was the fact that we were all doing the same reading. Why is there no enlightenment [participant laughs]? Or maybe there was but why is it not bluntly obvious yet? (participant #3)

Understandably, individual students engaged with course readings and took up particular concepts influenced by both their understandings of the theoretical knowledge introduced and the connections they were able to make to their lived experience. For example, not surprisingly, a White participant new to graduate studies and with three years teaching experience, she described as "all White," talked about the course content as "really opening my eyes to a whole bunch of information that I had never even thought about" (participant #5). Helms (1990) suggests that White people who have lived or worked predominantly in White settings may simply think of themselves as like the majority of those around them, paying little attention to the significance of their racial group membership. For this participant, who in the beginning of the course would whisper the word Black so as not to cause offense, participating in the class offered her the opportunity to begin to feel more comfortable using the language of race: "Even saying Black like that made me feel uncomfortable but after the course I didn't seem to have as much of a problem with it or feel as uncomfortable" (participant #5).

For racial minority students, concepts and ideas were taken up in more personal ways. Throughout the interviews, these students introduced stories of their parents growing up in a racialized society, retold personal encounters with racism, and even related course content to the schooling experiences of their own children. One participant spoke with relief of finally reading research with which she could identify. A racial minority participant talked about the idea of White privilege as "not really [new] because I've been confronted with it throughout my whole life that they [White people] are the dominant race" (participant #2), while White students often struggled with the idea that their group membership grants them unearned privileges not available to "others." Understandably, participants from racial minority groups articulated more awareness of the influence of race and culture on their identities and positions as teachers, but they also described becoming more aware of the *complexities* of racial identity (including White identity) by using their lived experiences of race to help inform their new theoretical understandings.

GRAPPLING WITH DIFFICULT KNOWLEDGE: SELF-CENSORING,
KEEPING SILENT

Several participants cited a need to be willing "to put it out there" as a necessary attitude for the success of class conversations centred on the difficult knowledge. Yet, all participants, whether in their first or last course, racial minority or White, at times, self-censored their contributions to maintain some level of comfort in the class.

> I don't think a lot of people even said what they believed a lot of times. I think people thought, "Okay, what I'm supposed to say so I'll say it".... I think that [the course content] did influence people and they may harbour other opinions but they are not going to say them. (participant #4)

Although not using the language of political correctness, this participant suggests that particular discussions may not have happened because students were concerned with saying "the right thing" and not causing offense. Two racial minority participants described the group dynamics and the un/willingness to speak up, and hints of "controlled" talk were also clear. Some people "hesitated" in large group discussions "because you weren't too sure how somebody else was going to take it" (participant #3); some "people weren't as open as they could have been… [and] were afraid to put themselves out there" (participant #2).

A racial minority participant explained how the difficult knowledge in the readings caused a critical pause: "[The articles] would make anybody kind of think twice before voicing an opinion" (participant #1), and a White participant spoke specifically of a hesitation and discomfort that others in the class also reported feeling in using the word *race* due, perhaps in part, to connections often drawn between talking about race and being racist: "I think people do feel uncomfortable when you bring it [race] up but I think it's only because being racist is so negative and no one wants to assume that they are racist" (participant #5)

The White participant quoted below explains her concern with examining race in a North American context because for Whites it brings up uncomfortable feelings of guilt and blame, giving "the wrong message":

> Whenever I read anything multicultural I tend to get this chip on my shoulder, you know somebody is just trying to blame me for something. So that's the one thing that I don't like when you examine race in this North American context.

I think it's the wrong context and it's the wrong message and I think that's maybe what turns [White] people off about wanting to study it. (participant #4)

The concern that talking about race provokes feelings related to blame and guilt on the part of White people is well documented in the literature (Helms, 1990; LeCompte & McCray, 2002). The participant quoted above continues on to suggest focusing on the global as a less guilt-ridden and more productive process for dealing with racism, in that the distance between the local and global provides a cushioning for White folks:

When we look globally, racism isn't something that's a White problem.... So I think if you have that more global context, I think the North American White people are going to get turned off less because that's what tends to happen is, you know: "You're a bad person. You oppressed me." Well, wait a minute; I've never even met you. Or these are events that happened hundreds of years before I was born. How am I responsible for that? These articles all tend to point out that you are a bad person. I don't know if that's all that productive. (participant #4)

This participant suggests here that racism is not a "White problem" in the global context, ignoring or not making connections between Whiteness and early and continuing colonization, highlighting her desire to grapple with the concepts of race and racism outside of personal implications. Our concern, however, is that White students' underlying feelings of guilt and embarrassment may work to limit their participation in these much-needed conversations. Thompson (2003) suggests there is a need to reframe such situations to include a sense of responsibility which might lead White people to take definite action, rather that simply feel like "you're a bad person."

US AND THEM

There is a lot of political correctness. We're [White students] not going to want to say something confrontational, you know we've got to be in class together. It's awkward. You sit right beside them [racial minority students]. Who wants to be in an argument?... I think a lot of things people let sit below the surface. It's a hard area to get people to be honest. (participant #4)

Observed in course interactions and in findings of the earlier content analysis was the often oppositional positioning experienced by White and racial minority students. The White participant above clearly articulates the us/them dynamic and the "political correctness" reasoning she employed for not confronting particular issues. Matching this cautious stepping into difficult terrain, other White participants spoke of changes made that, in effect, could be considered surface-level rather than the "deep" change for which instructors often (and perhaps naively) hope. For a White participant who declared she better understood diversity issues because of the course, her aim was to ensure her students (a majority of whom are White) were more accepting of people's differences: "I may be more aware of people's difference and make them [my own students] more accepting that people are different" (participant #5). Again, the racial minority (them) represented difference from the White norm (us), and could be dealt with by developing White students' acceptance of difference.

Curriculum was understood as a vehicle to "fit in" issues related to cultural difference and racial identity in ways that supported all children in classrooms, understanding what bodies represented the norm, and what bodies were different and needing to be accepted into the fold. However, only certain curriculum could be sacrificed for this task; as one participant said, "I know you can fit it [diversity-differences talk] in anywhere but I think a religion class is an easy place to talk about it and I wasn't teaching that. I was teaching math and sciences. It's hard to relate" (participant #5). Religion was a subject-area appropriate for conversation related to difference and acceptance while math and science were sanctioned knowledge, core content to be taught, tested, and regulated within school districts.

Racial minority participants were also hard-pressed to cover the standard curriculum. However, they spoke of their attempts to re-adjust their curricular lens. A racial minority participant vocal about her commitment to social justice described transferring course issues into her elementary classroom when facilitating a conversation around power with her students "first starting small and then taking it a little broader." Another spoke of bringing issues into the classroom "under the table." A racial minority participant spoke of how the course pushed her to think of ways to adjust her curriculum to explore notions of culture outside the "stereotypical box": "I found through the course it just gave a change to be able to look and say how can I actually get kids to understand what culture is outside of just the stereotypical box that even the curriculum allows for" (participant #3). While caught in the deeply embedded us/them institutional structure, racial minority participants attempted to make change in the classroom context, the arena where teachers, White or racial minority, often have the most say.

Racial minority participants found that addressing issues and making changes that moved beyond that relatively safe classroom space were much more daunting. They were painfully aware of the lack of colleagues' support:

You know to talk about it [issues of race] with the staff [would be difficult] because they would be, well, mortified. They wouldn't want to talk about it at all. They'd feel *so* upset, and you know, kooky about it. They would just shy away from it. (participant #1)

Another participant described a school atmosphere where "us and them" comments were present in conversations of colleagues, the "us" referring to White teachers and students, and the "them" consisting of racial minority students and the lone Black teacher. She was unsure if this dynamic could be changed but, as a possible option, was willing to consider developing workshops appropriate for staff development because the new principal "seemed open to conversation" and she had connected with one White colleague who was "on the same page" as she was. She was encouraged by what she perceived as administrative support that was previously lacking. She suggested, "if teachers could sit back and have these discussions [related to race and White privilege] it would set a totally different tone to the school where we are all truly accepting of each other, we can hear and identify with other people" (participant #3). Although we would argue that much more than a willingness to discuss issues is needed, and that structural change is necessary for any significant change to occur at the material level of the everyday operation of the school, such conversations may precipitate concrete, surface changes helpful to specific individuals.

The racial minority students described how the course content and conversations were often, even after the fact, close to the surface: "Away from the class, the course just leaves you thinking constantly. It still lingers" (participant #2). They spoke of an increased awareness of surveillance tactics that shaped what they could or could not do in their classroom/school contexts. Even when they felt students were capable of engaging in conversation related to social justice issues, and critique of dominant practices that might support inequitable treatment of particular individuals or groups, they had to "step lightly." This was the case particularly for a racial minority participant who taught in a White private school context. Parents kept a watchful eye over what transpired in their children's classrooms. She explains:

> This particular class that I've had this year is really, really mature. They can articulate well. They're very good at thinking aloud and no one shoots down another's opinion. So we always discuss things like this [poverty, homelessness]... But I am aware that I have to walk very, very carefully. I know a lot of their parents would be [participant pauses] upset even with us talking about that. (participant #1)

Even while choosing not to venture into territory related to race and racism, the participant was still concerned about raising the ire of White parents. Several times in the interview she described having to "bite her tongue" in classroom discussions for fear of having the comment go home and the possible repercussions. "This will get into this huge issue and then I'll say what I have to say and I'll get fired." The surveillance the racial minority participants experienced was a means by which they were constantly reminded that the easiest route for both themselves and their racial minority students was to find ways to fit into the established White norms of their schools. Taking this course encouraged them to question this thinking and to act, if only in *small* ways that seemed possible at the time.

DISCUSSION

> We were unaware of the significance of our racial positioning—of the privileged position whites had of entering and exiting the antiracism discourse at will, as opposed to people of color who "lived their race" everyday of their lives. Although we were grappling with issues of domination, white privilege,

and white supremacy, they were not clearly understood by us at the time. (Mathieson, 2004, p. 237)

Similar to Mathieson (2004), while researching the course, we also became more aware of the "privileged position whites had of entering and exiting the anti-racism discourse at will." However, we are not clear whether the White students completed the course with similar understandings. The White participants signaled they were quite at home in the world of White schools where they represented the idealized norm. The issues they were concerned with were those that all teachers deal with, whether White or racial minority (e.g., lack of time, covering curriculum). The personal costs of engaging with course issues addressed in class were less for those who were not "living their race" everyday.

A stark contrast existed between racial minority participants' description of experiences of surveillance, and the influence of being watched, on the ways they felt able to address issues related to what they learned in the course, and the total absence of any similar references by White participants. We suggest this is connected to the fact that White participants did not attempt to "rock any boats" when they returned to their schooling contexts. We did not expect that they would have the same experience of surveillance that racial minority participants did, but if even only "testing the waters," they would have at least felt the effects of speaking about race and privilege to those not interested in taking up the conversation, White or otherwise. Although often not visible in the surface talk and behaviours during this course, the us/them dynamic was in operation. Even with the purposeful structuring of the course and its goal of interrogating Whiteness and White privilege, White students (and Susan) continued to live their privilege in the daily workings of the class. White privilege is difficult to disrupt because it is so deeply embedded in the workings of school and university institutions where the expectation continues to be to find ways to shape difference to reflect White norms.

The three racial minority students who participated in the interviews described the influence the course had on their professional lives. One person described the course as influencing her practice "a great deal." She talked about how her level of comfort in talking around issues of culture has increased and is therefore more prevalent in her teaching now. "I'm very comfortable now in interjecting and I don't tolerate, there is very little tolerance for people talking negatively about difference" (participant #2). However, this participant went on to describe one incident in which her increased desire to address issues of culture in her class resulted in a challenge from parents. Another racial minority student talked about the course content encouraging her to be "more involved" in her teaching. She described how teaching had become "the same-old, same-old… it [was] like eating plain oatmeal all the time. There's a little cinnamon in it now. It's different now" (participant #1). For this participant, however, with her increased engagement also came increased internal tension: "It is harder for me now to justify where I work [at a private White school]…. I read much more into things. I'm hyper-sensitive about things." She

133

talks at length of this internal conflict-of wanting to do or say something but instead biting her tongue. Her increased awareness of race-related comments and how they "creep up," has translated into frustration and anger with herself and others.

For the racial minorities in the study there was no doubt that what they were doing in the course had wider implications for their work in schools and in their lives. They came to this class having "lived race" in their everyday lives. This work is difficult and there are heavy personal costs for racial minorities who feel compelled to take it up. For the White students, who continued to exercise their privilege, and for whom theory/practice connections were uninformed by ongoing critique of everyday experience, we have more doubts. We agree with Mathieson (2004) that, "our common task as whites remains to cast our gaze on our whiteness. Whiteness has been that unexamined, elusive part of ourselves that has remained very much taken-for granted, unquestioned and normalized" (p. 237).

For many teachers and students anti-racist teaching and learning will always be effortful and as Kumashiro (2000) argues, necessitate "*a particular kind of labor*" [italics in the original] (p. 42). As one racial minority participant suggested, "teachers might [be able to take up these issues] but it takes a lot and I don't know how many people have it in them" (participant #1).

CONCLUDING COMMENTS

Although our research is context-specific and findings are of local and very personal value, we argue that whatever the differences across post-secondary/public school contexts national and global, the interrogation of Whiteness and White privilege is work that needs to be done. For us the important question at this time is not the need for such an emphasis, but rather, *who* is able and willing to take up this radical stuff?

Through the process of constructing the course we were constantly reminded of the limitations of our knowledge, recognizing that our educational backgrounds included particular kinds of sanctioned knowledge that worked against, rather than supported this work. We recognized the need to acquire new, difficult knowledge to better understand what we needed to interrogate. The participants in this study also struggled to acquire new knowledge, some with more urgency than others. What we do with this difficult knowledge will be connected to the critical consciousness we develop through the process of acquiring new knowledge related to Whiteness and White privilege. Graduate study in education is one site where such work can take place. This is a context where practicing teachers have the opportunity to consider theory/practice relations, making concrete connections between their work in schools and the theoretical domain.

In this case we constructed a specific course to open up conversations on race and racism with teachers who work in classrooms where race matters—which we argue is *all* classrooms regardless of how bodies are "coloured." Our ultimate goal is to see such conversations taken up across courses and not isolated where only certain (kinds) of people choose to engage in the conversation. Although the limitations of coursework to actually effect deep change in the face of institutional barriers and social pressures cannot be dismissed, neither should the opportunities to take up radical stuff be taken lightly. If not here, then where?

QUESTIONS FOR REFLECTION

1. Think about how you self-identify. What connections can you make between who you are and how you teach?
2. How would you as a teacher and/or teacher educator develop understandings of the difficult knowledge necessary to interrogate Whiteness and White privilege?
3. In our daily lives as teachers and/or teacher educators, how are we complicit—intentionally or otherwise—in maintaining cycles of oppression?
4. As teachers and/or teacher educators, what should we say about race and racism? What should we have our students read, write, and do?
5. How can individuals work against the silencing of race discussions? What conversations need to happen? Where and with whom?

NOTES

[1] We understand the category "White" (like all racial categories) as a socially constructed and heterogeneous designation that includes various religious, cultural, ethnic, socioeconomic, and linguistic groups. Our use of the term is meant to underscore the dominant group in Canada which routinely constructs/positions itself as "normal," non-racialized and thus non-racist. We use the form "White" in this chapter with a capital W in accordance with the APA 6th edition guideline to capitalize names of racial/ethnic groups, including Black and White.

[2] Before initiating the research, we submitted a formal ethics application to, and received approval from, the university Research Ethics Board. Given that one of the researchers was also the teacher of the students being asked to participate, ethical considerations were important. Students' individual consent was also received before proceeding with any data collection or analysis. Additionally, because only one male student was enrolled in the course, to help ensure confidentiality, we have chosen to use the female pronoun "she" when referring to and quoting participants.

[3] Considering that this chapter focuses on examining race and racial identity, we chose to use the term "racial minority" to refer to all participants who are not "White." We recognize the potential problems of collapsing people of different racial, ethnic, and cultural backgrounds under the umbrella term racial minority and understand it is not necessarily representative of how these individuals would self-identify in terms of their race.

[4] *Professionally Speaking* is a broadly circulated Canadian education magazine. Published four times annually by the Ontario College of Teachers, the magazine provides articles on educational approaches, research issues, and resources.

REFERENCES

Cochran-Smith, M. (2000). Blind vision: Unlearning racism in teacher education. *Harvard Educational Review, 70*, 157–190.

Coffey, A., & Atkinson, P. (1996). *Making sense of qualitative data.* Thousand Oaks, CA: Sage.

Constas, M. A. (1992). Qualitative analysis as a public event: The documentation of category development procedures. *American Educational Research Journal, 29*, 253–266.

Cross, W. E., Jr. (1971). The Negro-to-Black conversion experience: Toward a psychology of Black liberation. *Black World, 20*(9), 13–27.

Cross, W. E., Jr. (1978). Models of psychological nigrescence: A literature review. *Journal of Black Psychology, 5*(1), 13–31.

Dei, G. J. S. (1996). *Anti-racism education*. Halifax, NS: Fernwood.

Desai, S. (2001). But you are different: In conversation with a friend. In C. E. James (Ed.), *Talking about identity* (pp. 241–249). Toronto, ON: Between the Lines.

Fontana, A., & Frey, J. H. (2000). The interview: From structured questions to negotiated text. In N. K. Denzin & Y. S. Lincoln (Eds.), *The handbook of qualitative research* (2nd ed., pp. 645–672). Thousand Oaks, CA: Sage.

Helms, J. E. (1990). *Black & White racial identity attitudes: Theories, research and practice*. Westport, CT: Greenwood Press.

James, C. (2005). *Possibilities and limitations: Multicultural policies and programs in Canada*. Halifax, NS: Fernwood.

James, C., & Haig-Brown, C. (2000). Reflecting on difference: A concluding conversation. In C. James (Ed.), *Experiencing difference* (pp. 294–318). Halifax, NS: Fernwood.

Kumashiro, K. K. (2000). Toward a theory of anti-oppressive education. *Review of Educational Research, 70*(1), 25–53.

LeCompte, K. N., & McCray, A. D. (2002). Complex conversations with teacher candidates: Perspectives of Whiteness and culturally responsive teaching. *Curriculum and Teaching Dialogue, 4*(1), 25–35.

Mathieson, G. (2004). Reconceptualizing our classroom practice: Notes from an antiracist educator. In V. Lea & J. Helfand (Eds.), *Identifying race and transforming whiteness in the classroom* (pp. 235–256). New York, NY: Peter Lang.

McIntosh, P. (1988). White privilege and male privilege: A personal account of coming to see correspondences through work in women's studies. In R. Delgado & J. Stefancic (Eds.), *Critical White studies: Looking behind the mirror* (pp. 292–299). Philadelphia, PA: Temple University Press.

Merriam, S. B. (1998). *Qualitative research and case study applications in education* (Rev. ed.). San Francisco, CA: Jossey-Bass.

Moodley, K. A. (2001). Multicultural education in Canada: Historical development and current status. In J. A. Banks & C. A. McGee Banks (Eds.), *Handbook of research of multicultural education* (pp. 801–820). San Francisco, CA: Jossey-Bass.

Schick, C. (2000). "By virtue of being White": Resistance in anti-racist pedagogy. *Race, Ethnicity and Education, 1*(3), 83–102.

Schick, C., & St. Denis, V. (2005). Troubling national discourses in anti-racist curricular planning. *Canadian Journal of Education, 28*(3), 295–317.

Short, G., & Carrington, B. (1996). Anti-racist education, multiculturalism and the new racism. *Educational Review, 48*(1), 65–78.

Sleeter, C. E. (2001). Preparing teachers for culturally diverse schools: Research and the overwhelming presence of whiteness. *Journal of Teacher Education, 52*(2), 94–106.

Solomon, P., & Levine-Rasky, C. (1996). When principle meets practice: Teachers' contradictory responses to antiracist education. *Alberta Journal of Educational Research, 42*(1), 19–33.

Strigel, C. (Producer), & Verhaag, B. (Writer/Director). (1996). *Blue eyed* [Video recording]. San Francisco, CA: California Newsreel.

Tatum, B. D. (1992). Talking about race, learning about racism: The application of racial identity development theory in the classroom. *Harvard Educational Review, 62*(1), 1–24.

Thompson, A. (2003). Tiffany, friend of people of color: White investments in antiracism. *International Journal of Qualitative Studies in Education, 16*(1), 7–29.

Tilley, S. A. 2006). Multicultural practices in educational contexts: Addressing diversity and the silence around race. In D. Zinga (Ed.), *Navigating multiculturalism: Negotiating change* (pp. 142–159). Newcastle, UK: Cambridge Scholar's Press.

Valli, L. (1995). The dilemma of race: Learning to be color blind and color conscious. *Journal of Teacher Education, 46*(2), 120–129.

REFRAMING: SUSAN A. TILLEY &
KELLY D. POWICK (2014)

A long time has passed since we wrote our chapter addressing issues of racial identity and White privilege in educational contexts. Susan used the text when working with three different groups of 12 elementary teachers enrolled in an ETFO sponsored 6-week Professional Learning Community entitled *Working across difference: Understanding identity, Whiteness, and critical pedagogy*. The chapters the groups read and discussed provided a vehicle for participants to make personal connections to the issues and experiences the authors explored in their chapters. Individuals were reading the text as they continued to teach so were often able to make theory/practice connections. The teachers indicated a desire to better understand how Eurocentrism and structural Whiteness affected their pedagogical and curricular decisions. Susan also used chapters in the book in her university teaching as a way to draw her students in to critical conversations.

At the time of writing the chapter, Kelly was teaching courses on cross-cultural communications to predominately White (adult) students and questioning how to encourage the students to engage in conversations related to race, culture, and White privilege and to take into account and respect individual and group differences. Since the chapter, her teaching responsibilities and her conversations have shifted dramatically. Presently teaching English to international students, she recognizes that the conversations she is having around race and racial identity are fewer and have moved out of the classroom and, are instead, taking place in the staffroom. Perhaps not surprising, most talks with her fellow teachers center around the sharing of effective teaching practices with respect to the diverse nature of the student population. Despite teachers' good intentions, these talks often take the form of how to help "those" students to better fit into "our" educational institutions. Three of Kelly's colleagues have read chapters from the *Great White North*. In discussions they have used what they have understood from the text to push beyond perceptions of international students as the *Other* to begin considering their own identities (racial and otherwise) and, in particular, how an individual's personal and professional identities intersect and shape each another.

Our more recent experiences addressing issues related to racial identity and White privilege have not been much different than what we described in our chapter. After teaching the course additional times, Susan repeated a similar process of data collection only to discover after analysis that findings reflected the first round of data. Teachers in the course described the normalizing of colour-blind perspectives, the structures in place to support Eurocentrism and White privilege, and the continued overriding and powerful influence of neo-liberal and dominant ideology. Again, individuals struggled with difficult knowledge the course explored, and we expect,

D. E. Lund & P. R. Carr (Eds.), Revisiting The Great White North?, 137–139.

as one of the earlier interview participants expressed, their heads often hurt at the end of a class. What has been hopeful in Susan's case is the number of graduate students who have indicated a desire to learn more about institutional Whiteness and the role the institutional structures and their identities, White or racialized, affect their pedagogical and curriculum decisions.

The student demographics in Kelly's current teaching context are changing. According to the Association of Universities and Colleges Canada (2012), the enrollment of international students in Canadian universities increased 12 percent in 2012, and approximately 110,000 students from foreign countries are currently attending Canadian universities. In response to the shifting educational landscape, several departments in her institution met to invite conversation around diversity topics. The us/them dynamic discussed in our chapter was exemplified by a panel of international students formed to encourage the predominately White teaching staff ("us") to ask non-White students ("them") questions about teaching practices and classroom styles in their home countries. The questions seemed be based in a belief that classrooms would operate more smoothly if educators and educational institutions could simply better "manage" the diversity in their classrooms.

When re-reading our chapter for this reframing task, Kelly was drawn to Question #5 in the reflection section, which asks how individuals can work against the silencing of discussions around race and racialized identity. This was an uncomfortable question for her to contemplate. Participants in our original study repeatedly acknowledged their reluctance to talk with others about such things. In thinking about her current teaching context, Kelly has come to recognize that despite having a degree of foundational understanding of these ideas and an awareness of the need for such conversations, she has, too often, also remained silent.

Moving forward to write a current companion piece, we would complicate our understandings of the discourse on Whiteness to a greater degree. We understand better now that this is far from an uncomplicated discourse. We would highlight more comprehensively, the intricacies of the intersections across race, class, sexuality, able-bodiedness, and culture. We also understand that in the Canadian context where the majority of teachers are White, middle-class women we need to find ways for them to continue their education so that they are knowledgeable enough to work respectfully across difference, remembering as they do, that they are not an isolated entity in their classrooms but part of the diversity present. While trying to reframe our discussion in light of the passing years, we concluded that not enough has changed and dissatisfaction with our progress continues.

In the Canadian context there is a push to reach out globally to create partnerships in educational initiatives that take various shapes. Universities are creating research opportunities for faculties and international study opportunities for students. We are crossing global borders in a variety of ways often without enough preparation. It is worrisome to think that many dominant perspectives applied daily to issues of racial identity and White privilege in the Canadian context will travel overseas as global collaborations continue to develop. Our chapter and other chapters in the *Great White North* are useful in supporting the development of a critique of structural Whiteness in the Canadian context. The text can serve as a starting point for those of us who will connect with international educational partners to build our knowledge but also, for those of us like Kelly who work with international students studying in this country.

REFERENCE

Association of Universities and Colleges Canada. (2012). *New university enrolment figures show increases in international, grad students*. Ottawa, ON: Author. Retrieved from http://www.aucc.ca/media-room/news-and-commentary/new-university-enrolment-figures-show-increases-in-international-grad-students-2

CARL E. JAMES

WHO CAN/SHOULD DO THIS WORK?

The Colour of Critique

INTRODUCTION

A primary element of the Canadian multicultural discourse is the idea that we live in a "raceless state" and as such, race does not factor into the ways in which we see and interact with each other, hence individuals' participation and achievements in the society are understood to be products of their own efforts. Insofar as race is identified or acknowledged—as in census data and/or equity census[1] reports—it is assumed that doing so is to find out about, or report on, the *representation* of the "cultural" make-up of our society. In this multicultural discourse, as I have written earlier (James, 2005), race tends to be acknowledged mainly because of its "visibility," and as such, "the behaviours, practices, values, attitudes, and aspirations of racial minority members are considered to be part of their race culture" and not a product of their *raced* experiences or racialization in the society (p. 11). In other words, in this discourse, it is culture and cultural differences—particularly those of racial minorities—that are at issue, not race. This is reflective of a colour-blindness paradigm, or more appropriately, "White-normed" ideology, in which taking up issues of race, and concomitantly racism and discrimination (as in our classrooms and/or interactions), would seem contrary to the notion of cultural democracy and harmony that is believed to exist in society.

Furthermore, that most of those who identify issues of racism and discrimination in the society tend to be those who are not members of the ethno-racial group (Whites) on which the norms are constructed, points to the ways in which racism is experienced. Indeed, as Lisa Delpit (1988) writes: "The rules of the culture of power are the reflection of the culture of those who have power.... Those with power are frequently least aware of—or least willing to acknowledge—its existence. Those with less power are often most aware of its existence" (p. 282). This notion is also captured in the old adage: "birds and fish... take the sky and water for granted, unaware of their profound influence because they comprise the medium for every act" (Barnlund, 1988, p. 14).

In this chapter, I explore the ways in which individuals take up issues of race, racialization, and racism in a context where Whiteness, which is embedded in notions of normalcy, is often taken for granted or ignored in prevailing discourses of race. In particular, I focus on the question: Who can/should do this work given

D. E. Lund & P. R. Carr (Eds.), Revisiting The Great White North?, 141–154.

our context in which particular bodies are "raced," consequently positioned and read as conveyers of race knowledge based on assumptions about their experiences with racism? I propose that Whiteness—structurally, culturally and institutionally speaking—functions as a lens through which all members of our society can expect to interpret and experience daily life, and as such "must be studied, named, and marked so as to uproot it from its position of normalcy and centrality" (Hytten & Adkin, 2001, p. 439; see also Kincheloe, 2005; Steinberg, 2005).

In the context of my work, and in this discussion, Whiteness serves not simply as an identity that is lived, learned, relearned, contested, and struggled-over, but as force within the institutional contexts in which I work as an educator and researcher. I recognize that Whiteness is mediated by and exists in relation to all other racial identities/identifications, and like all other identities, is not fixed, but is unstable and always in transition enmeshed in "conscious reflective struggle" and an active process of construction and reconstruction—the meanings and understandings of which continuously shift in relation to structural and cultural contexts (Beach, 1999; Presmeg, 2002; Levine-Rasky, 2000; Steinberg, 2005). The notion of transition is significant since, as a *learned* and *acquired* identity, Whiteness is embedded in a discourse characterized by subtle ambiguities and murkiness that is most powerful in its "embodiment of the normal as opposed to the superior" (hooks, 1992, p. 169). Furthermore, as Frankenberg writes: "Whiteness as a site of privilege is not absolute but rather crosscut by a range of other axes of relative advantage or subordination.... [and] the relationality and socially constructed character of Whiteness does not, it must be emphasized, mean that this and other racial locations are unreal in their material and discursive effects" (p. 76). Hence, in this discussion, I recognize that Whiteness and other race identifications and statuses are contextual, complex, and dynamic—always in an ongoing, relational process that is mediated by historical, social, political, and cultural factors (Aveling, 2004; Bedard, 2000; Kevil, 2002; Levine-Rasky, 2000).

In what follows, I use my experiences and references to students' comments to make Whiteness visible, noting how Whiteness instructs the ways in which issues of race, racial identification, racialization, and racism are viewed, interpreted, experienced, and engaged in postsecondary settings. I undertake this project with the knowledge that just as the issues I raise might contribute to the visibility of Whiteness, there are "mechanisms of Whiteness, especially privilege and 'rationality' [that] come into play" to disrupt or destroy that visibility (Hytten & Adkins, 2001, p. 435). Further, I expect that my discussion will reflect the limits, strengths, and specificity of my perspective as a Black-person and the subject positions from which I have been experiencing, observing, studying, and engaging Whiteness.

"IT'S NOT JUST ABOUT RACE"

Students come to our courses thinking that they are going to learn of the other, to learn how they can be helpers, to discover how to incorporate the dominant society's gestures of benevolence toward those designated as others. This is the assumption of superiority that whiteness permits: what we have is what the world needs whether it wants it or not. (St. Denis & Schick, 2003, p. 66)

Among the courses offered at many universities are ones such as: "Race and Ethnic Relations," "Race and Racialization," "Race and Racism," "Minorities in Canada," "Urban Education," "Culture, Identity and Pedagogy," and "Learning Anti-racism." It seems logical that through these courses universities expect to provide students with opportunities to examine the saliency of race with references to the experiences of the various racial groups and individuals that make up society. Usually, it is in these courses that the historical and contemporary issues of race in relation to racial minorities get taken up. While the inter-relationship among minority and majority groups might be explored, it is often the case that Whiteness is never taken up as a racial category, identity or identification. This approach to "race" courses, framed as they are within a White raceless paradigm, serves to re-inscribe and maintain White normativity and invisibility. This paradigm also informs the perceptions of some students, especially White students, who take these courses, causing them to complain that such courses "only" cover issues related to racial minority people.[2]

For some White students, participating in such courses tends to be for the purposes of getting to "know about minorities," and/or wanting "to learn about other cultures;" and for minority students, as one person said to me recently, "it is to learn about ourselves." This minority student went on to say: "Finally, there is a course about us." That she said "finally" is reflective of how much this student welcomes the chance to participate in such a course since, for the most part, despite the fact that today's universities are becoming more and more ethnically and racially diverse, the curricula have not changed significantly from when the student population was predominantly White and European. Consequently, today's students are continuing to get a diet of middle-class Eurocentric scholarship that marginalized students find to be removed from their experiences (Bramble, 2000; James, 2003b). In such a context, therefore, the courses that deal with race, racism or, more generally, issues of racial minorities, will be anomalies, and weekly readings and discussions on these issues will, before long, become "too much," particularly for those who lived and internalized the notion of "White neutrality." It is then that we are likely to hear complaints such as: "It is not only about race. What about gender, class, sexuality... " and other issues will be offered as students seek to make connections between their lived experiences and the scholarships with which they are expected to engage.

For example, during this past summer, I taught a course entitled, "Race, Diversity and Education," in which some 60 students participated, and about 20 of whom were White. One of the assignments in the course required students, in groups of three or four, to visit two communities in the urban and suburban areas of Toronto and observe the differences and similarities of both communities in terms of the racial, ethnic, economic, and religious (to the extent possible) diversity of the respective populations. Different groups of students visited the same communities. What was interesting is how the various groups of students read and reported on their observations. For instance, two groups of students—one all White and the other all Black—for their first community visit went to a low socio-economic community where the population was largely Black. When the group of White students presented, they told of a community that was characterized by low income evidenced in low-cost housing, limited recreational and shopping facilities, and a police station that was perceived to be making the community safe. The next day when the Black students presented they made a point of explaining that the police presence in the community was one of "surveillance" that was contributing to the criminalization of minority group members which was not a favourable situation and hence was a concern. The female whom the previous day argued that the police presence in the community was a "good thing," disagreed and suggested that reducing "everything to race" was a problem.

The ensuing class discussion reminded me of an earlier "Urban Education" class in which a group of racial minority students who sat at the same table in a class of largely White students, took on the role of challenging their White peers about the perspectives they brought to their reading of issues within the local low income, racially diverse "urban" community in which they were practice teaching. As one student wrote: "Throughout the course, the members of the 'centre table' passionately vocalized our positions on race and refused to allow the White students to remain neutral on issues of race," and in the process took on the role of "native informant which was the role many of us were forced into by virtue of the desire to continue discussions" (Campbell, 2006). But racial minorities do not all willingly take on the role of "native informant," for as one student in that "Urban Education "class related, "We take these courses to learn things related to our experiences, and the courses often become places where racial minorities have to teach Whites the importance and validity of this learning. We resent having to do this, that is why the *teaching* becomes fighting." This resentment and "battleground" atmosphere, as one racial minority teacher-candidate once explained, is because minorities hold the perception that their White peers are taking "race courses" not to get a "true understanding of racial issues in education" but to be able to "answer the diversity question [about teaching a diverse class of students] that is a staple of boards and school interviews."

The attachment of race to particular bodies and scholarships fosters a cultural discourse in which the idea of "race neutrality" persists. As such, White students will often maintain that race has little or nothing to do with the opportunities that they have – "It's not just about race," they claim; or as others assert: "I'm not defined by my Whiteness; I'm just me." Other statements include:

- "I don't see race. I see people as people instead of judging by external appearance."
- "I am fascinated by all the cultures. I love learning about them."
- "We weren't like some families. At our house we were taught to respect all cultures."
- "Why always bring up the past? I wasn't there."

These statements might be related to the fact that students are not encouraged, as Thompson (2003) wrote of White academics, to "read widely across races and, even if we do they tend to use the writings of scholars of color to bolster rather than interrogate our work. Insofar as we subordinate the work of scholars of color to our own intellectual projects and career advancement, we tokenize that scholarship" (p. 13).

PRIVILEGE—"NOT ASKED FOR"

> White privilege is vehemently denied by Whites who rely on a variety of tactics to justify and maintain their investment in the system of benefits and advantages conferred upon them. Rationalizations of White privilege spring from claims of meritocracy, individualism, and ethical neutrality, all buttressed by the same cultural and structural discourse of which they are a function. (Levine-Rasky, 2000, p. 274)

The issue of privilege in discussions of Whiteness, according to Levine-Rasky (2000), "commands a great deal of attention" (p. 274), pointing to, in the words of Leonardo (2004) "the notion that White subjects accrue advantages by virtue of being constructed as Whites" (p. 137). This usually occurs through the valuation of White skin colour and *approximate* attributes at individual and institutional levels.[3] Privilege is granted or assured even as individuals endeavor to "dis-identify" with Whiteness and/or fail to, or pretend not to, recognize how life is made easier for them (Leonardo, 2004, p. 137).[4] The notion of privilege is well referenced in essays by Peggy McIntosh (1995) and Barbara Thomas (2001) in which they delineate how the "unearned" package of privileges has functioned to their benefit. Hence, when students argue that "it's not just about race," or "I'm not defined by my Whiteness; I'm just me," they are, in effect, asserting their individuality and rationalizing that things, such as their achievements and opportunities, are a result of individual efforts. Moreover, through such claims, they are also demonstrating the extent to which the discourses of individualism, meritocracy, and colour-blindness (as embedded in multiculturalism) have operated structurally and institutionally, particularly at a time in their lives when they are engaging in an educational process which they expect to provide them the credentials to attain the opportunities and careers to which they aspire.

I recall, for example, a class in which we were discussing employment equity and university access programs with reference to women and racial minorities, a heated discussion ensued. In responding to a point that such programs were appropriate attempts to address institutional racism, Dominic (pseudonym), one of two males in a class of 30 education students, opined, in a very angry voice,

> I am tired of all this racism bullshit. I've never been handed anything on a silver platter... This is fuckin' scary. You're not good enough to get in like others... What about meritocracy? What about the esteem of people? You'd be seen as an equity quota, as a number. [Employment equity] undermines

what has been accomplished... It creates animosity and downright hatred. This means I'll be two years out of a job. I'm fed up of the bullshit. Is this what we call progress? (in James, 2003a, p. 190)

Dominic was expressing anger at what he saw as the compromising of his "inalienable right," a betrayal of his entitlement, and thwarting of his career ambition with programs that give racial minorities an "unfair advantage" over those who might have more to offer or have more experience in the field. It was also anger motivated by what many refer to as "reverse racism" (see James, 2003/2010).

Evident in the student's comments is his denial of, or blindness to, privilege (i.e., "I've never been handed anything on a silver platter") and his liberal stance that it is on the basis of individual efforts or hard work that individuals are able attain their ambitions regardless of race. Any other practices are perceived to be a violation of the principles of fairness, merit, democracy, and colour- blindness—the very principles on which universities are thought to function. It is little wonder, then, that Dominic would leave the class in anger—a form of resistance—since he was being invited to acknowledge his privilege while being presented with the fact that racial minorities have been disadvantaged by the very system that manufactures White privilege.

I recently witnessed similar acts of resistance in a group of White university students in an "equity" workshop that was facilitated by a woman of colour. The activities were designed to have students think about how physical appearance and other characteristics influence the assumptions we make about people, and how inequity functions to produce privileges and disadvantages. During a conversation afterwards with a group of participants, we heard their anger. They felt that the facilitator did not talk about equity nor give them any 'solid strategies' of how to be equitable. Claiming that they already knew about White privilege, participants went on to say that they "did not need a whole session to make them feel badly." Even as they were reminded that the facilitator repeatedly mentioned that she did not intend for them to feel badly, participants proffered that it was 'impossible not to feel bad.' They expected the workshop leaders and organizers to talk about and 'celebrate the strides that Canada has made as a multicultural society, instead of focusing on the negatives.' Reacting to an activity in which they were asked to get into groups on the basis of privileged attributes, participants said that they did not 'want or ask' for the privilege that came with Whiteness. And professing to feel badly for the minorities who were positioned through the activity at the back of the room, these White workshop participants maintained that they would "trade places with the minorities or bring them to the front of the room if they could." On this point, Thompson's (2003) observation is worth considering. She notes that White students may express a willingness to make sacrifices—such as "look at all the things that I'd be willing to give up, if I really had to," yet this "may seem to people of color like nothing more than new ways for whites to get comfortable with our whiteness" (p. 16). Quoting a student of colour, Thompson continues, "the discussion about sacrifice was a distinctly white way to think about change: social change conceived in terms of what whites, from their privilege position, were willing to do, rather than in terms of what needed to be done" (p. 16, see also Kivel, 2002; Miller Shearer, 2012).

Indeed, as McIntyre (1997) wrote, "talking about whiteness with white students is not easy. It generates uncomfortable silences, forms of resistance, degrees of hostility, and a host of other responses that many of us [instructors] would prefer to avoid" (p. 73). Furthermore, Tilley (2006) wrote that a common response of White students to discussions related to Whiteness or White privilege is guilt, something to which the workshop participants admitted. It is also likely that Dominic's comments and behaviour were motivated by guilt. However, as Thompson (2003) wrote, "guilt is indeed paralyzing. But I do not think it follows that the solution to White guilt is to help Whites feel 'good'" (p. 15). The solution, such as it is, should be to come to an awareness of the cultural and institutional nature of Whiteness that disenfranchises some and privileges others (structural racism) rather than exclusively focusing on personal expressions of racism (see Bérubé, 2001; Hytten & Adkins, 2002; Kivel, 2002; Thompson, 2003).

WHO SHOULD BE DOING THE WORK OF STUDYING AND RESEARCHING "RACE"?

Much of the education materials from which students obtain their perspectives on race are based on research that, in the tradition of "academic" scholarship, are perceived to be value-free, transparent, raceless, genderless, and objectively presented. Accordingly, neither the identity nor the epistemological location of the researcher/writer is revealed for it is perceived that these have no relationship to what is written (see Absolon & Willett, 2005).[5] Hence, as we try to engage students in our racially diverse classrooms in anti-racism work there are often issues about self-disclosure, voice and appropriation, voyeurism, "going native," and as one racial minority student said of Whites studying minorities, "playing anthropologists." Of course, in encouraging White students and colleagues to "study across race," we hope that they would be able to appreciate more fully, and hopefully, come to understand, the ways in which race functions in their own lives and those of others. In other words, there is the need to understand how the systems of power and domination contribute to the complex, contradictory, relational, and multiple ways in which "it's not just about race;" and "yes, it's also about race," including the race privileges Whites experience.

In relating to me her questions and skepticism about some White people doing cross-race work, one racial minority student recounted:

This is a no-win question for racial minorities. On one hand, there is resentment of the legion of White people who are making careers out of their scholarship on my history, literature, and oppression. In grad school, a couple of White girls in my post-colonial literature course were focusing on South

Asian literature and my first thought was 'Why are you making a living off of my people?' But then of course, to say that such scholarship is my right and responsibility is limiting to me. In fact, I have no serious scholarly interest in such issues. However, in the same class, when I tried to choose a Pakistani writer for my seminar presentation, I lost the bid to one of those White 'South Asianists.' I was pretty angry that the only Pakistani writer on the syllabus was not going to be presented by the only Pakistani in the class (and indeed, in the whole graduate program). I know my professor felt it too since the course was devoted to issues of appropriation and race but he didn't say anything. He never did. He could take on racial issues in readings, but never in the dynamics of the class. Anyway, I had to content myself with an Indian writer, which I guess was "close enough." Ironically, she turned out to be fascinating while the Pakistani writer's piece didn't interest me at all when I read it. So goes the dilemma of such issues. That there is no clear answer to them does not make any of the angles any less truly felt.

The above comment demonstrates that complexity and difficulties, for White and racial minority students and instructors alike, in doing anti-racism work and encouraging cross-race dialogues and activities.

The reservations and perplexing feelings expressed by this student about the motivation of some Whites in doing cross-race work seem, at times, well-founded if we consider Thompson's (2003) account of a White student "who displayed a sophisticated intellectual understanding of whiteness theory…, prided herself on her intellectual anti-racism and counted herself as a friend of people of color" (p. 16). The student admitted that if her anti-racism activities translated into her being "a race traitor" and "jeopardize her chances of being a professor; she could not do it…, she planned to play the academic game the white way." Thompson wrote:

> Such "halfness," as the abolitionist called it, makes for dangerous allies. In Isabel's case, studying the tools of whiteness provided her with ways to *further* exploit her white privilege. As Alec, Isabel's professor and a man of color, asked: "With allies like that, who needs enemies." (p. 16)

It is because of this "halfness" that some racial minorities and White anti-racism activists remain concerned, ambivalent, skeptical, suspicious and perplexed about the involvement and interests of some Whites who engage in cross-race studies/ activities while seeking to maintain White comfort, safety and privilege, especially in institutions like universities where the neoliberal framework or approach is sustained.

In light of the existing White structures, Absolon and Willett (2005) argue for researchers doing work with Aboriginal people to locate themselves and acknowledge the stake they have in the community, for there is no objectivity or neutrality to research "since all research is conducted and observed through human epistemological lenses" (p. 97). In other words, students have to come to recognize that the lenses through which they view subjects, or the interpretations given to their observations and/or materials, are all mediated and informed by their student/researcher's experiences and being. So the traditional idea, often communicated in research courses, that we should not get too close to our research subject—for doing so, will limit our impartiality and needed objectivity (if only in appearance) of giving way to our social, cultural and political interest—is neither tenable nor practical. All researchers and scholars need to become familiar with their subjects if they are to represent, if only partially, and speak to their subjects' experiences.

I have told students who choose to work across race and with, for example, members of the Black community, that they should be ready to answer questions such as: Is this another case of research for research's sake? What does it mean for me to add my voice to the issues, for instance, that Black youth are experiencing in schooling? Am I willing and ready to add my voice, and engage in the advocacy and activism sorely needed in addressing issues facing Black youth in our society and the educational system in particular? In what ways does my Whiteness mediate the possibilities of my participation in such advocacy work? Issues of voice and authenticity inevitably surface in these discussions. The questions put to me in response tend to be: "As a Black person, don't you think that you will have more credibility than me? How will people take up my work, especially if I am identified as an outsider?" By raising these issues, concerns, and questions, some White students seek to affirm that they are "not racist" and hence would not engage in work that ever suggests that race has something to do with the situation of minority youth including, for example, Blacks. The questions and concerns are also part of their privilege of choosing to avoid contentious issues related to race. For the most part, these students wish to play things safe and remove themselves from anything that would identify them as part of the racist structure (Hytten & Adkins, 2001). In other words, as Thompson (2003) suggested, they "desire to be and to be known as a good white person" (p. 9). However, as Susan Dion (2005)[6] point out, Whites are not "perfect strangers" to racial minorities, for they experience and are implicated in the racism (albeit in a different way) that defines the existence of minority people.

CONCLUSION: SO WHO SHOULD BE DOING THE ANTI-RACISM WORK?

Dialogue is critical to disrupting the normative power of whiteness because in order to see our own worlds differently, we must learn to listen to others and to some extent, see ourselves through others' eyes. (Hytten & Adkins, 2001, p. 441)

In this chapter, I took up the challenge of making Whiteness visible, which must be the task of everyone who engages in anti-racism work. With reference to commonly articulated statements, I tried to illustrate how the normativity of

149

Whiteness or White culture in our "colour-blind" and "colour-frightened" society sustains its invisible illusive and raceless character – a character rooted in the ideology of individualism evidenced in the statements in which individuals maintain that they are "not defined by my Whiteness" while denying the privilege they attain from skin colour. Though on the surface, concerns and questions of safety, credibility, identity, voice, authenticity, and essentialism that get raised by White students, may appear common-sensical, logical, and rational, they are part of the mechanisms of Whiteness that function to obscure the visibility, and maintain the system of privileges enjoyed by Whites. The statements are also part of what McIntyre (1997) called "White talk," which is, "talk that serves to insulate white people from examining their/our individual and collective role (s) in the perpetuation of racism" (p. 45). White talk also comes in the form of resistance, particularly as individuals attempt to assuage their guilt that, as Thompson wrote, "mourns a past that cannot be changed" (p. 23). All of these mechanisms serve to insulate Whites from examining their individual and collective roles in the perpetuation of racism.

In striving for social justice, fairness, and equity, anti-racism proponents need to work to disrupt the normativity and centrality of Whiteness as well as expose and challenge "White talk," both of which function to maintain White hegemony. Engaging in anti-racism work requires concerted efforts, creative dialogue and engagements, and imaginative exchanges with people who are ready to address racism, whether it is convenient for them or not. Instructors need to help students identify their own raced voices and those of the scholars they read. Addressing racism is not only the responsibility of those who are disadvantaged by it, but also those who are privileged by it. I admit that identifying who is disadvantaged and privileged is a complicated matter, since racism is experienced differently in relation to a number of demographic factors. Nevertheless, I contend that there are merits and advantages to approaching our work on the basis of "strategic essentialism" (Spivak, 1993; see also Dei, 1998; Gilroy, 1993; Martin 1994) – that is, we need to recognize and make assertions about the effects of racism on all racial groups understanding that the raced and racialization experiences and, consequently, the worldview and behaviours of group members do vary. In this regard, the idea of not wanting to "identify people by race," or, in the case of research, being concerned that the research is "not comparative" because it tells only of one group's experiences, would translate into doing nothing to address the "undiminished power of racism" and its effects on the people who "continue to comprehend their lives particularly through what it does to them" (Gilroy, 1993, p. 102). If in our teaching, scholarship, research, and community activities we engage, in our various ways, in political mobilization for social change, especially in the postsecondary educational institutions in which we work, then we would have played and should continue to play necessary and important roles in unsettling Whiteness and thereby do our part to make for more racially aware and equity institutions and society.

QUESTIONS FOR REFLECTION

1. What are some of the ways we might be able to avoid "tokenizing" the inclusion of racial minority (or non-White) people's experiences and/or scholarship into university studies and in "mainstream" society generally?
2. What are some of the mechanisms that are at White people disposal in their denial of race privilege? How are the respective strategies or mechanisms related to attempts to justify and rationalize their beliefs that their achievements are a result of their individual efforts? In your answer, take up the ideas of "halfness," essentialism, and "White talk" as presented in the essay.
3. Is it possible for racial minorities to gain equitable access to employment and educational opportunities without special structural and institutional programs like Affirmative Action and Employment Equity?
4. McIntyre (1997) wrote that "talking about whiteness with white students [and generally, some White people] is not easy. It generates uncomfortable silences, forms of resistance, degrees of hostility, and a host of other responses that many of us would prefer to avoid" (p. 73). Some of these responses result from a sense of guilt that often seems to be part of the process of recognition of race privilege. Discuss the extent to which these responses, including guilt, are unproductive to the project of addressing and effectively taking action against racism.
5. Ultimately, if racism is to be addressed, and indeed eliminated, the consistent, concerted and sustained efforts and actions of White people are necessary. It means recognizing (i.e., admitting to) "White privilege," dealing with the resulting personal or internal discomfort, tensions and conflicts, and challenging the very system or structures that contribute to the privilege. Discuss how best this state of being might be attained without developing the urge to give up or back down in the face of personal and interpersonal conflicts that could undermine the social, economic and political success for which everyone strives.

ACKNOWLEDGEMENTS

I am grateful to the editors, Paul Carr and Darren Lund, and to Brenda Johnston, Susan Tilley, Kulsoom Anwer, Melanie Kong, Howard Ramos, Bethan Lloyd, Krysta Pandolfi, as well as the many students who offered assistance, input, comments, and feedback to this work.

NOTES

[1] *The Toronto Star* (Brown, 2006) talked of a "new breed of 'equity census'" as part of a push of among educational institutions including universities such as Queens and Toronto "to understand their increasingly diverse array of students, and make sure the halls of learning are open to all" (p. A1).
[2] It should be pointed out that even these courses designed to teach about minority and Aboriginal peoples also structured within a Whiteness frame. For example, Patricia Monture-Okanee

151

(1995, p. 81), a Mohawk, relates that non-Aboriginals taught her university courses on Aboriginal peoples, non-Aboriginal peoples wrote the course materials in some cases, and even "the guest speakers were non-Aboriginal people." After a number of students "confronted the teacher" and expressed their concerns, they were "excluded, denied and marginalized."

3   It is important to emphasize that skin colour is not the only criterion for racial distinction; other whiteness factors or *approximates* operate at the individual level (e.g., hair texture, shape of nose, citizenship, language, accent) and institutional level (e.g., culture, language) to facilitate privilege or access to privilege (see Brodkin, 2004; Hunter, 2005; Ignatiev, 1995; Leonardo 2004).

4   Of course, class, gender, ethnicity, sexuality nationality all mediate white skin privilege, resulting in different experiences and circumstances for White working-class people, women, people with disabilities, and gays and lesbians. Hence, experiences with White privilege are complex and relational and, as such, it is impossible to make generalizations (Levine-Rasky, 2000). For instance, in an essay on "Whiteness in White Academia," Luis Aguiar (2001), an "immigrant working-class student" of Portuguese background uses the concept "Black" as "a political colour" to capture his experiences. He writes that feeling marginalized and silenced in his classes, and that class discussions, course content and pedagogy were rarely reflective of his experiences, but more of the cultural capital of bourgeois students and faculty members. He tells of having a "sense of dislocation" and feeling like an "imposter" in a "very privileged and exclusive milieu where [he] was not quite sure of the rules and practices of belonging" (p. 189).

5   In the White-normed masculinist context in which these scholarships are taken up, it is not surprising that materials written by women, racial and other minorities (including immigrants), with or without disclosures, tend be to perceived as written from the "biased position" of these writers. There is also a tendency to impute bias in works in which authors make personal disclosures.

6   Dion was referring to how White people, and teachers in particular, take the position that they are perfect strangers to Aboriginal people since they did not learn about them in schools and have little or no interactions with them.

REFERENCES

Absolon, K., & Willett, C. (2005). Putting ourselves forward: Location in Aboriginal research. In L. Brown & S. Strega (Eds.), *Research as resistance: Critical, indigenous and anti-oppressive approaches* (pp. 97–126). Toronto, ON: Canadian Scholars' Press.

Aguiar, L. M. (2001). Whiteness in academia. In C. E. James (Ed.), *Talking about identity: Encounters in race, ethnicity and language* (pp. 177–192). Toronto, ON: Between the Lines.

Aveling, N. (2004). Being the descendant of colonialists: White identity in context. *Race, Ethnicity and Education, 7*(1), 57–71.

Barnlund, D. C. (1988). Communication in a global village. In L. A. Samovar & R. E. Porter (Eds.), *Intercultural communication: A reader* (pp. 22–32). New York, NY: Wadsworth.

Beach, K. (1999). Consequential transitions: A sociocultural expedition beyond transfer in education. *Review of Research in Education, 24*, 101–139.

Bedard, G. (2000). Deconstructing whiteness: Pedagogical implications for anti-racism education. In G. J. S. Dei & A. Calliste (Eds.), *Power, knowledge and anti-racism education: A critical reader* (pp. 41–56). Halifax, NS: Fernwood.

Bérubé, A. (2001). How gay stays white and what kind of white it stays. In B. B. Rasmussen, E. Klinenberg, I. J. Nixica & M. Wray (Eds.), *The making and unmaking of whiteness* (pp. 234–265). Durham, NC: Duke University Press.

Bramble, M. (2000). Being me in the academy. In C. E. James (Ed.), *Experiencing difference* (pp. 271–282). Halifax, NS: Fernwood.

Bridkin, K. (2004). How Jews become white folks and what that says about race in America. In P. S. Rothenberg, N. Schafhausen & C. Schneider (Eds.), *Race, class and gender in the United States* (pp. 37–53). New York, NY: Worth.

Brown, L. (2006, August 2). Schools scramble to take colour count: Stats collected to boost diversity. *Toronto Star*, A1, 18.

Campbell, M. (2006). *My urban education class.* Unpublished e-mailed reflections on the class, York University, Toronto, ON.

Dei, G. J. S. (1998). The denial of difference: Reframing anti-racist praxis. *Race, Ethnicity and Education, 2*(1), 17–37.

Delpit, L. D. (1988). The silent dialogue: Power and pedagogy in educating other people's children. *Harvard Educational Review, 58*(3), 280–298.

Dion, S. (2005). From 'perfect strangers' to creating a new imaginary. In D. Barndt (Ed.), *Voices of diversity and equity: Transforming university curriculum* (p. 2). Toronto, ON: Faculty of Environmental Studies, York University.

Frankenberg, R. (2001). Mirage of an unmarked whiteness. In B. B. Rasmussen, E. Klinenberg, I. J. Nixica & M. Wray (Eds.), *The making and unmaking of whiteness* (pp. 72–96). Durham, NC: Duke University Press.

Gee, J. D. (1996). *Social linguistics and literacies: Ideology in discourses.* Bristol, PA: Taylor and Francis.

Gilroy, P. (1993). *The Black Atlantic.* Cambridge, MA: Harvard University Press.

hooks, b. (1992). Representing whiteness in the Black imagination. In L. Grossberg, C. Nelson & P. A. Treichler (Eds.), *Cultural Studies* (pp. 338–346). London, UK: Routledge.

Hunter, M. L. (2005). *Race, gender, and the politics of skin tone.* New York, NY: Routledge.

Hytten, K., & Adkins, A. (2002). Thinking through a pedagogy of whiteness. *Educational Theory, 51*(4), 433–450.

Ignatiev, N. (1995). *How the Irish became white.* New York, NY: Routledge.

James, C. E. (2005). *Race in play: Understanding the socio-cultural worlds of student athletes.* Toronto, ON: Canadian Scholars' Press.

James, C. E. (2003a/2010). *Seeing ourselves: Exploring race, ethnicity and culture.* Toronto, ON: Thompson Educational.

James, C.E. (2003b). Becoming "insiders": Racialized students in the academy. In K. S. Brathwaite (Ed.), *Access and equity in the university* (pp. 139–164). Toronto, ON: Canadian Scholars' Press.

Kincheloe, J. L. (2005). Reinventing and redefining whiteness: Building a critical pedagogy for insurgent times. In L. Karumanchery (Ed.), *Engaging equity: New perspectives on anti- racism education* (pp. 149–162). Calgary, AB: Detselig.

Kivel, P. (2002). *Uprooting racism: How white people can work for racial justice.* Gabriola Island, BC: New Society.

Leonardo, Z. (2004). The color of supremacy: Beyond the discourse of "white privilege." *Educational Philosophy and Theory, 36*(2), 137–152.

Levine-Rasky, C. (2000). Framing whiteness: Working through the tensions in introducing whiteness to educators. *Race, Ethnicity and Education, 3*(3), 57–71.

McIntosh, P. (1995). White privilege and male privilege: A personal account of coming to see correspondence through work in women's studies. In M. L. Anderson & P. Hill Collins (Eds.), *Race, class and gender: An anthology* (pp. 70–81). Belmont, CA: Wadsworth.

McIntyre, A. (1997). *Making meaning of whiteness: Exploring racial identity with white teachers.* Albany, NY: State University of New York Press.

Miller Shearer, T. (2012). Conflicting identities: White racial formation among Mennonites, 1960-1985. *Identities: Global Studies in Culture and Power, 19*(3), 268–284.

Monture-Okanee, P. (1995). Surviving the contradictions: Personal notes on academia. In The Chilly Climate Collective (Eds.), *Breaking the anonymity: The Chilly Climate for women faculty* (pp. 11–28). Waterloo, ON: Wilfrid Laurier University Press.

Presmeg, N. (2002). Shifts in meaning during transitions. In G. de Abreu, A. J. Bishop & N. C. Presmeg (Eds.), *Transitions between contexts of mathematical practices* (pp. 213–228). London, England: Kluwer.

Spivak, G. (1993). *Outside in the teaching machine.* New York, NY: Routledge.

St. Denis, V., & Schick, C. (2003). What makes anti-racist pedagogy in teacher education difficult? Three popular ideological assumptions. *Alberta Journal of Educational Research, 49*(1), 55–69.

Steinberg, S. (2005). The dialects of power: Understanding the functionality of white supremacy. In L. Karumanchery (Ed.), *Engaging equity: New perspectives on anti-racism education* (pp. 13–26). Calgary, AB: Detselig.

Thomas, B. (2001). Learning from discomfort: A letter to my daughters. In C. E. James & A. Shadd (Eds.), *Talking about Identity: Encounters in race, ethnicity and language* (pp. 193–211). Toronto, ON: Between the Lines.

Tilley, S. A. (2006). Multicultural practices in educational contexts: Addressing diversity and the silence around race. In D. Zinga (Ed.), *Navigating multiculturalism: Negotiating change* (pp. 142–159). Newcastle, England: Cambridge Scholars' Press.

Thompson, A. (2003). Tiffany, friend of people of color: White investments in antiracism. *Qualitative Studies in Education, 16*(1), 7–29.

REFRAMING: CARL E. JAMES (2014)

It is worth noting that this chapter was written before Barack Obama was elected president of the United States of America – an 'evidence' for neoliberals that skin-colour, if it did influence an individual's achievement, is a thing of the past; hence the ensuing talk of post-racial America. And those many Canadians who enthusiastically supported Obama's run for the White House, a reading into their support, especially those of White Canadians, might be that Obama presidency represents further evidence that does not matter. But I am more persuaded by the argument that rather than being a boost to the work of anti-racist advocates, Obama's presidency has made it even more challenging to make more visible, or convince neoliberals of, the entrenched realities of Whiteness and its concomitant properties of privilege. Furthermore, I find Canadians' support of Obama's presidency a paradox, in that the recognition of Obama's presidency is based on the notion that he is America's first "Black president." This supposed suspension or setting aside of Obama's race is contrary to Canada's claim of colour-blindness (à la the multiculturalism discourse) – something about which Canadian media seem all too willing to report.

This Canadian paradoxical relationship to race was made evident in news reports on the November 2012 U.S. elections. Take for example, two reports carried in Canada's so-called national newspaper, *The Globe and Mail*. On November 7, the day following the election, Thanh Ha (2012) wrote, under the headline, "Obama's victory delivered mostly by minorities, women, young voters," that "the Democrats retained enough support in their core demographic groups, with women, younger voters, Hispanics, the less wealthy and Jewish voters siding clearly with Mr. Obama" (n.p.). A week later, on November 15, writing from New York in a "special to" the newspaper, Chrystia Freeland (2012) wrote, under the headline, "Obama's election shows how diversity can provide an edge," (n.p.) and that, "for America, 2012 will go down in history as the year of the Latinos, the blacks, the women and the gays. That rainbow coalition won President Barack Obama his second term. This triumph of the outsiders is partly due to America's changing demographics. And it is not just the United States that is becoming more diverse. Canada is, too, as is much of Europe" (n.p.). The point is, while Canadians are able and willing to identify and report on how race operates in American society, the same is not done for Canada. Hence, it seems that it will be a long time before the media, and Canadians generally, will advocate for racially diverse parliament, legislatures, judiciaries, and corporate boardrooms, and even longer for a Prime Minister who is a racialized Canadian. That Canadians would support the efficacy of having a Black man in the White House, but not even question what we do in Canada to promote social mobility for racialized Canadians is indeed a matter of concern.

D. E. Lund & P. R. Carr (Eds.), Revisiting The Great White North?, 155–156.

The idea of "keeping things as they are" – that is, having Canada's symbols and images White – was recently demonstrated in Canadians' reaction to the new $100 bill which on one side revealed an image of a woman who appeared to be Asian looking into a microscope. Putting aside the criticism of some that the image could be seen as representing "a stereotype of Asians" (as people largely in technology and sciences), of concern here is the objection of some focus group participants from across Canada that "the image didn't represent Canada" (Robertson, 2012). The response of the Bank of Canada was to redraw the image "to give the woman 'neutral' ethnicity," suggesting that "the image was not designed or intended to be a person of a particular ethnic origin," since it is not the Bank's policy to have images of particular ethnic groups on banknotes. But as reported, the image, "with her stripped Asian features and light skin tone, it's arguable that she now appears Caucasian" (Kalinauskas, 2012, n.p.).

It is within this local, national and international context that as anti-racists we must carry out our work to address the ways in which normativity of whiteness operates in to obscure and maintain the status quo (St. Denis & Schick, 2003). So, for example, despite the many Canadian Employment Equity and Affirmative Action programs that claim to welcome "visible minorities" into workplaces, there is very little evidence that today's workplaces reflect the racial diversity of the Canadian population. This situation is able to persist, in part, because there are no data to help us make the case for *real* commitment to equity – and there is no obligation to collect race data as we do with gender (see James, 2012). What this says to me is that much work is left to be done, and in this regards, this book, *Revisiting the Great White North*, is a necessary and important reference in helping us to carry out this work at the local and national levels of our society, as well as at the global level.

REFERENCES

Freeland, C. (2012, November 15). Obama's election shows how diversity can provide an edge. *Globe and Mail*. Retrieved from http://www.theglobeandmail.com/report-on-business/international-business/us-business/obamas-election-shows-how-diversity-can-provide-an-edge/article5349872/

James, C. E. (2011, June). Canada: Paradoxes of 'visible minorities' in job ads. *University World News, 171*, pp. 1–4. (Reprinted from *FedCan Blog*). Retrieved from http://www.universityworldnews.com/article.php?story=20110513185935314

Kalinauskas, N. (2012, August 17). Bank of Canada bans image of Asian-looking woman from new $100 bills over ethnicity criticism. *Daily Brew*. Retrieved from https://ca.news.yahoo.com/blogs/dailybrew/bank-canada-bans-image-asian-looking-woman-100-170239135.html

Robertson, G. (2012, August 17). Bank of Canada slammed over 'racist' move to scrap Asian image from $100 bills. *Globe and Mail*. Retrieved from http://www.theglobeandmail.com/news/national/bank-of-canada-slammed-over-racist-move-to-scrap-asian-image-from-100-bills/article4485307/

Thanh Ha, T. (2012, November 7). Obama's victory delivered mostly by minorities, women, young voters. Retrieved from http://www.theglobeandmail.com/news/world/us-election/obamas-victory-delivered-mostly-by-minorities-women-young-voters/article5037640/

SECTION 4

LEARNING, TEACHING, AND WHITENESS

CYNTHIA LEVINE-RASKY

THE PARENTS OF BAYWOODS

Intersections between Whiteness and Jewish Ethnicity

INTRODUCTION

Dorothy Smith (1990) encourages us to write our own lives as they are situated in "conceptual practices of power." In this spirit, I begin this essay by describing a personal experience that influenced a trajectory in my research career. While formally initiated by a Social Sciences and Humanities Research Council (SSHRC) grant in 2000, its inspiration occurred years earlier. The data that arose from the project shape a path of reflection and a synthesis of ideas about social inequality, schooling, race/ ethnicity/class, and power. This essay maps a good portion of that path, beginning with an individual interaction, proceeding to a formal study of parents' responses to cultural diversity and analysis in a context of Whiteness and middle-classness, and ending up with an exploration of Jewish ethnic identity. The overarching theme is that the intersectionality of race, ethnicity, and class matters when it comes to understanding school relationships, not only in relation to marginalization where the concept of intersectionality has usually been applied, but also in relation to the exercise of power. What we hear from these parents reflects the intersections of middle-classness and Whiteness, but Whiteness as refracted through Jewish ethnic identity. The complexity of this "map" is undeniable. Indeed, I hope to embrace that complexity as integral to the parents' identity formation and to the very way they struggle with their responses to social difference.

In the fall of 1992, the third year of my Ph. D., I was working as a teaching assistant in the academic writing centre at a large university. The centre offers undergraduate students individual assistance in essay writing and research skills, and is staffed by tenured and contract faculty and graduate students from many departments. Pam[1] was a graduate student in fine arts; I was in sociology. We discovered that we had a great deal in common. We lived in the same part of the city, almost in the same neighbourhood; we were close in age, married with young children; we were Jewish and middle-class; we were graduate students at the same university; and we were financially dependent upon our husbands who both worked in business. I assumed that we shared a liberal perspective on things. As friends and colleagues, we spoke about our children and other aspects of our personal lives. Pam told me that her daughter had been attending the neighbourhood public elementary school but that she had recently placed her into a private school because "Pinecrest" had changed.

D. E. Lund & P. R. Carr (Eds.), Revisiting The Great White North?, 159–173.

Since the arrival of a large number of children of diverse ethnicities, the school was no longer desirable to Pam despite its strong 50-year reputation in the community. She told me that there were too many children who spoke English as a second language and that she was troubled by what she perceived to be a deterioration in the quality of teaching for her child. Her decision to remove her daughter from the school was presented as obvious. When I asked her to elaborate, she simply said to me, "I *had* to take her out. Wouldn't you?"

Wouldn't I? Through sociology, I feel that I have adopted a critique of the social structures that shape inequalities. I have also come to reflect on the significance of being socially located in the world through the ways in which I identify myself. I like to think that my understanding of the context for making such decisions as school choice liberate me from a self-centredness in my decisions concerning my children. But I'll never know for sure how I would have responded had it been my daughter who attended Pinecrest. As it was, my children went to another public school in a nearby neighbourhood that was almost exclusively White and middle-class, and I had always thought of *that* as undesirable. Despite my own contradictions, I like to think that I would have valued the diversity ushered in by the new children as a positive change in my children's school. I believed that I was different than Pam. Pam's question to me, however, presumed a shared intelligibility between us based on an acknowledgement of everything we had in common. She assumed that we shared a set of values about the kind of schooling we desired for our children who she understood to be distinguishable from the others now found at Pinecrest. Her question was a request for confirmation that I was a member of her group; it signified that a qualification of her decision to abandon the public school was unnecessary. This experience and others stimulated a set of research questions that led me far beyond my own reflections. Clearly I was a member of Pam's group, but the sociologist in me propelled me to learn more about the actions taken by parents like her to secure advantages for their children through their choice of school. Pinecrest was of great interest to me since I was aware that it had only recently become "multicultural." My sociological imagination was piqued. I embarked upon a research project that would bring together questions of social positionality and the problem of school choice for the reproduction of social inequalities.

This chapter explores some of the findings of that project. Specifically, it forges links between the literature of inequalities in school choice and Jewish ethnic identity. Well developed in the UK, knowledge of parents' school choice concentrates first on the effects of social class, and then "race." With the exception of some work on Asian parents, there is a near absence of research on ethnic differences in the way families negotiate their choices. Yet Pam's story highlights the importance of ethnic identity and the significance it can take on for some parents considering school options. While Pam did not name her Jewishness, I heard her words to signify not only the English-speaking difference she did name, but those that she did not name: her social class and her White ethnicity. In her neighbourhood, as both she and I knew, those elements ineluctably converge. The way that these categories escape articulation reveals much about their power, both ideologically (in that they're hegemonic and need not be articulated) and structurally (in that they make a concrete difference in people's lives).[2] The sense they make was confirmed, moreover, by their contrast with the other set of differences she didn't describe: those embodied by the children from the adjacent neighbourhood that I call "Kerrydale."

AN OVERVIEW OF THE LITERATURE

It is possible to consolidate relevant conclusions drawn in the literature on school choice and middle-classness: (a) Through their decisions about school, White, middle-class parents make their children into classed subjects. This process is propelled by the logic of the free market in which the school is becoming another commodity. A language of individualism and competitiveness in turn stimulates the desire of middle-class parents to secure advantage for their children in unpredictable conditions (Whitty, 2001a; Brown, 1997); (b) White, middle-class parents support the principle of inclusion in schools *and* they desire their child's success in a competitive environment. Values and actions are in conflict. One serves the conservation of distance and difference; the other serves integration and equity. In practice, these parents often end up working against the principle of equality in order to ensure their class interests (Ball, 2003; Holme, 2002); and (c) White, middle-class parents not only tend to be more involved in their children's schooling (Lareau, 1989), but their practices confer a particular selfhood upon their children in relation to their community. Moreover, they are associated with emotions such as confidence, fear, and pride (Byrne, in press; Gillies, 2005).

How is Whiteness interpolated in these debates? Few authors discuss Whiteness as a discrete category of analysis, assuming instead a Black/White racialized dichotomy among parents. This is particularly so in the US (e.g., Brantlinger, 2003; Goode, 1990). In the UK, Whiteness is usually placed as an attribute alongside middle-classness and simply becomes an element in the "White, middle-class" unit. There are exceptions, however. David Gillborn (2005), for example, refers to UK education policy as an act of White supremacy, and Whiteness has been conceptualized as both a form of cultural capital (Lareau & Horvat, 1999) and symbolic capital (Miller, 2000) in parents' differential involvement in school. While it's difficult to conflate Whiteness and privilege for White working-class parents, can this be said for White, middle-class Jewish parents? Intersectional theorizing may be of value here. Floya Anthias has recently asserted that intersectionality may allow us "to see ethnicity, gender and class, first, as crosscutting and mutually *reinforcing* systems of domination and subordination, particularly in terms of processes and relations of hierarchisation, unequal resource allocation, and inferiorisation. Secondly, ethnicity, gender, and class may construct multiple, uneven, and *contradictory* social patterns of domination and subordination; human subjects may be positioned differentially within these social divisions" (2005, pp. 36-37, italics in original).

From Anthias' perspective, the intersections of Jews' social class and Whiteness are clearly reinforcing in kind. However, that of their Whiteness and their ethnicity may be more contradictory. While a full consideration of Jewish racialization cannot be undertaken here, a cursory review of this subject shows that Whiteness takes on an ambiguous meaning for Jews. Historical and contemporary forms of anti-Semitism is an obvious factor, but ambiguity is also an outcome of invisibility for *Ashkenazim* (European Jews), of racism *within* Jewish groups (specifically against *Mizrachim* or Middle-Eastern and African Jews), of long-standing religious and cultural pluralism, and of the "new" anti-Semitism that even captures non-Zionist Jews in its wide condemnatory web. Despite high socio-economic among Jews and their sophisticated political organization, Whiteness and power/privilege are more complicated for Jews than is commonly thought. In the sections that follow, I will propose how the claims of these two sets of literature—class and Whiteness—intersect with White, Jewish ethnicity as represented by the participants in my research. The structure that follows is not intended to suggest an independence of factors. It should be recognized that the school marketplace, parents' contradiction and selfhood are as reticulate as their class and ethnicity.

While class and ethnicity are the focus of this discussion, I do not mean to discount the question of gender. The primary role of mothers in school choice has been the subject of work by Griffith and Smith (2005), Reay (1996), and others who show that preference for the generic term "parent" neglects the real gendered subjects engaged in these interactions. My project is not intended to imply a hierarchy of factors; it reflects only my curiosity at the time. Like all works in progress, it may be limited in breadth but hopefully it compensates for this in the richness of its data and in its contribution of ethnicity to the literature on school choice and social inequalities. Space permits only a very small selection of data in this chapter. For more, the reader should refer to my other work (see Levine-Rasky, 2008, 2009, 2011).

BACKGROUND

Pinecrest public school serves children from kindergarten to grade six. It is located in the centre of Baywoods, a neighbourhood distinguished by large, impressive, single-family homes. The most recent Census data provides some details about its residents. Using a program called P-Census that isolates a micro-geographic area drawn as a polygon around Baywoods' borders, I learned that Baywoods residents have household incomes averaging $160,000 and 71 percent of them are Jewish. Since its inception in 1941, the school was always well attended by virtually all of the Baywoods children. Growing up nearby, I recall the character of the general district as indelibly Jewish. I was to discover that among the participants we interviewed, there were a few former Pinecrest students who continued to live in Baywoods. These individuals confirmed their memories of Pinecrest's homogeneity and spoke of their fond attachment to it. We interviewed 25 individuals (23 were mothers), 21 of whom live in Baywoods. Of these, 20 are Jewish.

The 25 interview participants had 58 children among them and of these all but three attended Pinecrest for their elementary years some time between 1985 and 2001.

Four of the parents lived in another neighbourhood, "Kerrydale," with access to Baywoods—and hence to Pinecrest—via a bridge over a busy road. A cluster of high-rise apartment buildings characterizes Kerrydale; most of the residents are new immigrants to Canada. P-Census shows that their average income is $52,000, Jewish ethnicity is 10 percent and the immigrant population is 65 percent. The single largest groups in Kerrydale are Southern European (19 percent) and Eastern European (19 percent), but the majority is from countries in Asia, the Pacific, Africa, the Middle East, and elsewhere. The cultural diversity that Pam observed at Pinecrest was brought about by the change in immigration patterns in the city. As a result, by 2000, the primary language of 51 percent of the children at the school was something other than English. This was a tremendous contrast to the Pinecrest of the past, to the Pinecrest of personal memory for some of the participants and to the Pinecrest several others knew about and that motivated them to move to Baywoods. When Kerrydale changed, some of the Baywoods parents faced a challenge about how to respond. Some like Pam removed their children from the school; others stayed but voiced their concerns; others were happy to remain. Using what Alvesson and Sköldberg (2000) call a "data-oriented" method for the analysis of qualitative research (with some critical theory and postmodernism thrown in to enable a complex reading of subject positions, power, and contradiction), these social relations were the focus of my inquiry.

INTERSECTIONS BETWEEN MIDDLE-CLASSNESS AND WHITE JEWISH ETHNICITY

Middle-class formation and Whiteness intersect at the market. As the discourse of economic orthodoxy and political neo-liberalism permeates institutional life, the school becomes another product for sale in the marketplace. Ball observes that this works to the advantage of the White middle-class: "These small changes, financial and organizational, promotional and symbolic, bring about a reorientation of the education system as a whole to the needs, concerns and interests of middle-class parents. They work to embed class thinking into the policies of schools" (2003, p. 49). The individualism and competitiveness of the market stimulate the desire of middle-class parents to secure a future for their children in unpredictable conditions (Brown, 1997). This has particular implications for the maintenance of middle-class boundaries (Dehli, 2000; Whitty, 2001b). Class is subject to economic and social forces that prevent stability. Its reproduction is not assured and people are actively engaged in maintaining themselves in their classed location. Indeed, class is highlighted in times of crisis when the issue of its reproduction is in question. This is of particular relevance in discussions of schooling. Parents invest their children with class and their desire to maintain class.

For these Jewish parents, the process is inflected with their ethnic particularity. Using a language of cultural and family practices marked by favourable stereotypes in the excerpt below, Miriam distinguishes Jews from others. She uses this to legitimate her suspicion of difference and to conflate it with inferior parenting and teaching. Thus, she thus justifies her desire for teaching that benefits her children but that is jeopardized, in her view, at Pinecrest:

> It's a cultural thing. Education to a great extent—education is a cultural thing…In the Jewish religion, I mean, we're scholars. That's our background. It's a very important part of our upbringing to our children… and I think that it's not the case, in all cultural backgrounds, you know, you have people from all different worlds and their values are different and they don't get the kind of parental support when it comes to going to school… But I know we're high achievers and [pause] I know if I was to think myself, personally, that my son was in a class of kids that were not high achievers, the quality of education would have to be—you know, would drop. (Miriam)

Sander Gilman (1996) shows that the image of Jewish superior intelligence derives from the racial sciences in early anthropology and continues in popular culture and in science. To Miriam, her children's high achievement, Jewish scholarship, upbringing methods, values, and so on, are entirely normalized. In Miriam's remarks and in Wendy's below, we see not only a will to differentiate but also a claim of superiority for the children of Baywoods relative to those of Kerrydale. Unlike Miriam, Wendy frames herself in terms of class rather than ethnicity:

> The level of education went down. The level of achievement went down. And if you want, the best examples to compare, [are] Selby with Pinecrest. And with all—Selby has a lot of really, really bright kids. It kind of has, I'd say, the mix of kids that Pinecrest used to have. And it makes a difference. I'm not judging it as better or worse but if you look at say, inner city school versus mostly White Jewish middle-class with not working-class but educated professionals, there's a huge difference. (Wendy)

Wendy marks her group as White, middle-class, Jewish, educated, and professional by setting Pinecrest's past image against that of Selby, another public school. She denies judgment, but her preference is obvious. By claiming the children's superior potential and resources, these parents are negotiating their preferred position in the school marketplace.

Their assessments are made in direct relation to the Kerrydale children. In his struggle to locate Jewish identity and "election" of chosen-ness within the respect for alterity in others, Roger Simon writes, "this tendency to self praise based on the particularities of a people's founding mythologies and historical experiences is clearly not unique. Neither is the tendency to transmute this praise into chauvinism" (1999, p. 315). The danger is that Jews hold themselves up as the image of the self-made citizen who conquered barriers and made it. They attribute their success to qualities associated with Jewishness: hard work, dedication to education, high expectations, and independence. These are detached from considerations of when and where the Jews arrived here—the need for their skilled labour, the preference for professional occupations at a time when universities were opening up to Jews, benevolent societies to assist needy Jewish families, and experience with fighting discrimination and living in segregation (Steinberg, 1989).

Baywoods parents' responses to multiculturalism at Pinecrest can be described as a form of differentiation—an effort to impart a meaningful difference between themselves and the new immigrant families whose children attend the school. This is manifest in their disapproval of the "balance" of Jewish children and immigrant children at the school and in their negative evaluation of the quality of education. These views are not articulated with conviction, however, but with ambivalence. Participants in this study express self-consciousness and anxiety about making such statements, and represent contradictory and pluralistic positions on the question of multicultural classrooms. I suggest that these actors' perspectives may be read not only for the complexity of their positions, but also for the tensions attached to Whiteness as refracted through Jewish ethnic identity. Jews may be positioned unambiguously with respect to economic claims of White privilege, but because of historical purges and current resentment against them (partly due to fantasies of their links to Israel), the claim of unequivocal White privilege becomes difficult to make. This is not because Jews are vulnerable to systemic oppression, but because it contradicts their commitment to liberal humanism that has, after all, served Jews well. If an ethical Judaism is grounded in social justice emerging from a collective memory of oppression, how can Jews explain their success and others' relative lack of success? What happens when Jews need to extend their understanding of oppression and social justice to other groups? Is this possibility limited by their equally compelling desire to integrate, literally to be forgetful of who they are?

Below are two excerpts selected from others that reveal equivocal support for social difference in the school. They assess the benefit of diversity in teaching their children about integration against a possible risk of negative social influences:

> I guess, you know, on the one hand, my children aren't gonna grow up and meet only Jewish people. They're gonna have to work with people from all over 'cause Stafford's is a very cosmopolitan city. So, maybe it wasn't such a bad thing. It just wasn't what I had expected and what I had been led to expect. (Barb)

> Like I myself have always, like I always said—that was one of my main reasons for leaving my kids at a public school. I wanted them to be—I didn't want them to be submersed with only Jewish kids. I wanted them to have that exposure. I thought it was great. So, that was not the reason for to take [my son] out of public school. But yet, on the other hand, when all these immigrant kids started coming into the school, I started getting concerned. (Miriam)

Barb sees the diversity at the school as having negative repercussions. Miriam qualifies her choice of private school for her son. It was not, she insists, due to too many Kerrydale children at Pinecrest because "exposure" is a good thing. Heidi is more positive:

> It's funny. I always wanted my children associating with different ethnicities and not being so, you knew, having the blinders on. That's why I was so happy when my son—my oldest went to University A—and roomed with non-Jewish boys and I find I just don't want them to think this is how everybody lives. 'Cause we have a very good lifestyle. We travel and, you know, they don't want for anything. And I just love them to see how that not everyone in the world is as fortunate as we are. (Heidi)

Elaine is a Baywoods parent who raised her children in the 1980s, a little earlier than the others. She expresses a similar point of view to that of Heidi. She is describing the racism of some other Baywoods parents and contrasts them to her own tolerant views. Some details had to be omitted including her differentiations on the basis of purported poverty, Blackness, and single-parenthood that taken together spell "trouble":

> There were ethnic changes which [sic] we welcomed. Not everybody welcomed the ethnic changes. I think that a lot of people wanted it to be a White, upper-middle-class, homogenized school where most people were Jewish... Some people saw these kids as trouble. I thought, this was great, because I'd been telling them all along the whole world is not what's at Pinecrest. It's a big world out there and you've got to survive and co-exist. So I thought, fine. My kids brought home little Black kids for lunch. Who cares, you know? (Elaine)

The school is a venue for the learning of White, middle-class and in Baywoods, Jewish identities. In order to get that lesson right, these parents are vigilant in ensuring the optimal amount of "exposure" to cultural diversity. Exposure is good in principle but the risk is over-exposure. Parents express their desire to set the terms of achieving the best "mix" as they practice their social position. Some of the Baywoods mothers approve and even invite the kind of difference embodied by the Kerrydale children. Others do not. Throughout, we hear the moral dilemma in which desires for inclusion and for exclusion conflict.

Ball (2003) argues that middle-class parents neither defend class segregation in the schools nor ignore the impact their decisions have on reproducing social inequalities. He prefers to regard the parents as acting "within unclear and contradictory values systems which are complexly and unevenly related to our social practices" (p. 114). Exploring more deeply, psychoanalytic literature has potential value in explaining the resilience of contradictory positions and of the role that emotion plays in it. It is our very desires that are contradictory (Henriques, Hollway, Urwin, Venn, & Walkerdine, 1984, p. 224). In "splitting," a term borrowed from the psychoanalytic, a norm can coexist with its prohibition, and a social actor can perform both without sacrificing internal integrity, although perhaps with "guilt, anxiety and displacement" (Ellsworth, 1997: p. 94). This process impedes our capacity to make an ethical relation to the stranger, observed perhaps in the Baywoods parents' distance from the Kerrydale families. The contradiction lies in the preservation of an identity that is known to the self as liberal, tolerant, inclusive, and egalitarian. This theme is elaborated in the next section.

Beyond their generation of (contradictory) values and their negotiations for success, White, middle-class parents confer a particular selfhood upon their children. This is accompanied by emotions such as efficacy, fear, and pride (Byrne, in press; Gillies, 2005). British sociologists such as Diane Reay, Valerie Hey, Val Gillies, and Bev Skeggs have extended Pierre Bourdieu's concepts of *habitus* and cultural capital to include affective states in subjects. At the level of subjectivity, acquisition of middle-class cultural capital enables a sense of entitlement and legitimacy or what Skeggs calls an "emotional politics of class" (2005, p. 209). In Canada, Dehli (2004) asserts that middle-class and White "cultural repertoires" advantage the expressions of agency, resources, and ways of interacting characteristic of this group.

For these writers, class is understood *relationally*. That is, class becomes itself through differentiation and exclusion (see Savage, 2000) *and* through active identification or gestures of belonging (Ball, 2003). As Anthias (2005) points out, group membership involves the maintenance of boundaries. Defining a "we" is premised on constructing otherness. The same can be said for ethnicity. Below, Tracy oscillates between her desire for diversity and her (greater) desire for exclusivity. In her interview, she speaks of her preference for Jewish children and her disapproval of "too many" racialized children. Her daughter, however, has influenced her mother's rejection of a school for being too "jappy," a slur for a materialistic and emotionally shallow Jewish girl or "Jewish American princess." Tracy is struggling with the question of what kind of *Jewish* self she wants to cultivate in her daughter. Her anxiety is evident:

> We have another dilemma—where does she go for [grades] seven and eight?…
> I don't know 'cause Baywoods [Middle School] is—she says it's too "jappy" quote quote. She doesn't want—too many princesses there and she's not like that. So, we have a problem. I don't know where she's gonna end up, and Sunridge is not the greatest school in terms of a lot of things. The area has a lot of—see you worry about all these things as a parent—has an influx also of a lot of immigrants and a lot of Black children. So, I don't know. I don't know. I want a balance of both. (Tracy)

Tracy's open qualms about immigrants and Black children were rare in the interviews. But her words convey a moment in the making of raced and ethnic boundaries. Diane provides a different kind of insight into this phenomenon—one based on self-imposed boundaries and fear of jeopardizing those boundaries. In the following excerpt, she moves from risky boundary-making to the more acceptable language of ESL difference, a factor that can be measured at a safe distance from personal opinion

167

and emotion. She underscores her uncertainty and lack of justification for her claims that the Kerrydale children caused the departure of the Baywoods children:

> People are afraid of—I don't know. I'm not gonna say the Jewish community is any worse than a lot of other ethnic groups but, they tend to like to stay together and be together and keep themselves clustered. So, the neighbourhood, I guess, us moving in, you could think that that was what we wanted as well. But it surprised me—no one's come out and told me this—I have no one to say that this is true or documented back-up in any way. But I think that the immigrant population moving into the school has moved the Jewish population out. Fear of, I'm not exactly sure what. People believe that the education is going to be maybe jeopardized because of a lot of English-as-a-second-language children coming into the school. Their children will suffer because of them. (Diane)

Diane takes pains to qualify her statement and seems concerned about condemning her peers and Jews in general. She moves toward a deeper analysis of Jewish fear and ambiguity but then steps safely away from it. Still, her discernment of "clustering" evokes a Jewish specificity. Ruth also refers to aspects of a collective Jewish identity in explaining the practice of differentiation demonstrated by some of the Baywoods parents. She describes an insularism and standards for acceptable occupations for Jews rooted in a collective identity based on a persecution narrative and the urgency of financial independence:

> I think sometimes it has to do, I'm just guessing, with Holocaust survivors who have taught their kids that anything sort of outside of our group could be dangerous 'cause it was to them. Now I've, like that's like really specific, okay? But it's an example of a kind of upbringing that's closed. It's closed. It's like, you will never marry anyone outside of your group; you will, like, be, you will never have a job that is, like, not having money. Like it wouldn't be valued to be in the arts or to be a musician or an artist because like that's not what our group does. (Ruth)

Wendy refers to the same propensity for insularism. Here, she's trying to distance herself from it but she contradicts her liberal values in her negative assessment of the "balance" now available at Pinecrest:

> Even though I'm from a Jewish background, I really liked—I didn't want to be one of those Jews that lived in a little community, then look at my background, I'm not from here. I like to travel. I like my kids to be exposed to all kinds of cultures. So that's what I really liked. But the balance changed so that the education was really suffering. (Wendy)

Hal contrasts the school of today with its past character and attempts to modify parents' concerns about school quality. He refers to parents' fear as he challenges generalizations that immigrant children like those at Kerrydale will lower the standards at school. He points to my Jewish surname to support his claims:

For some reason, a lot of Jewish people, I think, and I see from your principal investigator that you probably have some insight, also think that a lot of immigrant kids just 'cause they're immigrant—they're not as bright and it brings down the level of the school—which I think is wrong. I think it's— what's the phobia it is when you're scared of other religions or races? I think with a lot of Jewish people that's very important—that they're almost scared to send their kid to a school...public school, the high school. There's not a high percentage of Jewish kids there. (Hal)

Diane's reference to clustering, Ruth's to the closure of the survivor mentality, Wendy's to the Jews' "little community," and Hal's to phobia gestures to the "ghetto thinking" described by Stratton (2000). For European Jews (Ashkenazim), their segregated communities provided refuge and safety from the chronic persecutions. Ghetto thinking is driven by Jewish memory of imminent persecution and is manifest in the post-Holocaust generation in various ways. Consider the stereotype of the overly controlling Jewish mother always fretting about the whereabouts of her children. I suspect many Jews of my generation will recognize this habit. Fearing an accident, my former in-laws refused to let their children attend summer camp. The parents of a Jewish boyfriend forbade their two children to fly on a plane together for fear that "god forbid something should happen." Stratton even suggests that the preoccupation with safety underpins the image of the well-appointed Jewish home whose occupants are preoccupied with commodity consumption. The home should always be a haven in an inhospitable world, or at least, one that may turn inhospitable at any moment. It is a kind of free-floating anxiety unmoored from an original trauma.

Jews were placed on the outside not only because of their religion, but because of their occupations as well. They had either to carve niches for themselves in which they could be independent, or they took up occupations that mediated between groups: moneylender, landlord, and tax collector. Such work was low in status but available to the Jews, yet it sealed their outsider identity. The legacy of this economic role has taught Jews that they cannot afford to become entirely comfortable with the terms of their membership in society (just as it led to an over-representation of Jews in business and the professions.) The problem is that this orientation gets interpreted as intolerance and it plays out as conservatism and insularism, even elitism. From their perspective, it may feel like prudent thinking or it is internalized as such. Yet if Jews only trust each other, what effect does this have on reproducing their ambiguous outsider status? Hal identifies one consequence of this in the excerpt below.

If you're Jewish, or my age, it was like my grandparents and their grandparents that immigrated. My mother was born here, my father moved here when he was two. It'd be a very similar to some of the small kids there [in Kerrydale]. My father was born in [Europe], he moved here when he was two. They didn't have anything. Were they stupid or ignorant because they spoke [a European language] and [the others] didn't? No, they worked hard and achieved something. Just like these immigrant people. But I think that's what my friends lose track of. (Hal)

169

Hal turns to the loss of the Jewish immigrant memory with its experiences of poverty, foreignness, and struggle. But there is an irony here. Jews retain collective memories of immigration, residential segregation, underemployment and discrimination, just as do the immigrant families living in Kerrydale. A selective withdrawal from such memories upholds commitments to individualism detached from history and biography (Simon, 2000). This forgetfulness about the material and cultural forces that produce a human subject may be a mechanism that supports the differentiation that Baywoods parents make of Kerrydale children. It underlies their negative expectations of them, and the relatively inflated image they have of themselves.

DISCUSSION

In this chapter, we have seen how a small group of Jewish parents differentiate themselves from the diverse families whose children attend the same elementary school. Some individuals were concerned with maintaining Jewish boundaries around their children's experiences while controlling an optimal amount of diversity. Neither absolute homogeneity nor heterogeneity was preferred, yet of course the power of assessing optimal "balance" lies with them. For some parents, an ideal arrangement would be a higher proportion of Jewish children with adequate numbers of others to teach their children to respect—perhaps even to normalize difference. Importantly, there are sufficient numbers of Baywoods parents who do not support this view so as to prohibit its generalization. We have representatives of both "sides" here: those like Miriam, who believe that Jews are superior and require more from Pinecrest teachers, and those like Hal, who are troubled enough by exclusion to stimulate some serious thinking in him about Jewish fear and memory.

Throughout, we hear the contradictions in the securing of advantages, the invention of difference, and the production of selfhood. We also hear an interpenetration of Whiteness and Jewish ethnicity as these complex human subjects negotiate the challenge of raising children to be successful yet ethical whose identities are both committed and formative. As I explain below, these identities are also ambiguous.

Some observers such as Stratton (2000) claim a resurgence of interest among Jews in 'activating' their identity in what Eric Goldstein calls a Jewish revival (2006, p. 212). Yet there is no distinctively Jewish ethnicity (Goldstein, 2006, p. 213). There is instead Jewish ethnic pluralism. This is reflected in the religious, ethnic, and linguistic differences among Jews from the Orthodox to the secular, Jews from Europe, Asia, and the Middle East, entirely assimilated Jews, to those with "mixed" heritage. This pluralism notwithstanding, there does appear to be a distinction among Jews in liberal values, political affiliation, and voting, and in attitudes toward gender roles, racial equality, and civil liberties. This pattern holds across intra-group divisions among Jews (Smith, 2005). So what happens when Jewish liberalism confronts its challenge? The answer may lie in the very act of making identity.

Jewish identity is ambiguous. Ambiguity is manifest in appeals for Jewish authenticity *and* for membership within the White, Christian majority. In general,

Jews want to sustain *dos pintele yid* (the Jewish essence) but within the framework of dominant Christian society. Jews may feel the risk of their difference or they can forget it, but they want to evoke Jewishness, too, by choosing schools and neighbourhoods that feel Jewish. Jewish narratives of immigration, struggle, and subsequent mobility influence these parents' regard of the "Other" embodied by the Kerrydale parents, since Jewish assimilation is accomplished through their ongoing project of differentiation from others. That is "we" are integrated only relative to others who are not. The problem of ambiguity in being both privileged and at the periphery induces Jews' contradiction with their liberal humanistic principles. Perhaps the solution is to exploit the moments Jews have in these postmodern times to realize their complex and multiple identities—their post-ethnic identities. Jews already animate these through intermarriage, inter-group pluralism, and their avid commitment to individualism. In embracing this, we could create new kinds of communities, yet again.

QUESTIONS FOR REFLECTION

1. Are Jews White? Are other European ethnic groups White? Or did they become White when they immigrated to North America? How did this process occur?
2. Why do parents (and students) choose one school over another? Do you observe any patterns of social class or ethnicity or "race" in these choices? Did everyone at your school exercise the same degree of "choice?" What is the impact of parent involvement upon student achievement?
3. How is Whiteness complicated by other expressions of ethnicity? By other religious identities? By sexual difference?
4. How is the Holocaust taken up in the curriculum? How does teaching about the Holocaust compare to teaching about Israel? About Palestinians and the Middle East? About other genocides?
5. In this chapter, the author makes the claim that White, middle-class parents confer a particular selfhood upon their children. Further, this is accompanied by emotions such as efficacy, fear, and pride. What is meant by this claim?

NOTES

[1] Names of individuals, schools, and communities are pseudonyms.
[2] My work is not intended to encourage anti-Semitism. Michael Lerner (1993), editor of Tikkun magazine, argues that claims of White Jewish privilege stem from an internalization of anti-Semitism. Yet, if Jews have achieved economic privilege, recognizing that doesn't make one an anti-Semite. Denying Jews' social position interferes with attempts to understand and bridge divisions among Jews and their neighbours. Jewish organizations' censorship of criticism is problematic for all Jews (and non-Jews) who advocate for peace and who exercise their democratic right to criticize state policy. Self-reflective criticism is, in my understanding, wholly compatible with a robust Jewish identity, and consistent with progressive and humanitarian approaches in Judaism to which I, as many other Jews, subscribe.

REFERENCES

Alvesson, M., & Sköldberg, K. (2000). *Reflexive methodology*. London, England: Sage.

Anthias, F. (2005). Social stratification and social inequality: Models of intersectionality and identity. In F. Devine, M. Savage, J. Scott & R. Crompton (Eds.), *Rethinking class: Culture, identities and lifestyles* (pp. 24–45). New York, NY: Palgrave Macmillan.

Ball, S. J. (2003). *Class strategies and the education market: The middle-classes and social advantage*. London, England: RoutledgeFalmer.

Brantlinger, E. (2003). *Dividing classes: How the middle-class negotiates and rationalizes school advantage*. New York, NY: RoutledgeFalmer.

Brown, P. (1997). Cultural capital and social exclusion: Some observations on recent trends in education, employment, and the labour market. In A. H. Halsey, H. Lauder, P. Brown & A. S. Wells (Eds.), *Education: Culture, economy, society* (pp. 736–749). New York, NY: Oxford University Press.

Byrne, B. (in press). *White lives*. London, England: Routledge.

Dehli, K. (2004). Parental involvement and neo-liberal government: Critical analyses of contemporary education reforms. *Canadian and International Education, 33*(1), 45–75.

Dehli, K. (2000). Traveling tales: Education reform and parental 'choice' in postmodern times. In S. J. Ball (Ed.), *Sociology of education: Major themes—Volume IV: Politics and policies* (pp. 1997–2015). London, England: RoutledgeFalmer.

Ellsworth, E. (1997). *Teaching positions*. New York: Teachers College Press.

Gillborn, D. (2005). Education policy as an act of White supremacy: Whiteness, critical race theory and education reform. *Journal of Education Policy, 20*(4), 485–505.

Gillies, V. (2005). Raising the "meritocracy": Parenting and the individualization of social class. *Sociology, 39*(5), 835–854.

Gilman, S. (1996). *Smart Jews: The construction of the image of Jewish superior intelligence*. Lincoln, NB: University of Nebraska Press.

Griffith, A. I., & Smith, D. E. (2005). *Mothering for schooling*. New York, NY: RoutledgeFalmer.

Goldstein, E. L. (2006). *The price of whiteness: Jews, race, and American identity*. Princeton, NJ: Princeton University Press.

Goode, J. (1990). A wary welcome to the neighborhood: Community responses to immigrants. *Urban Anthropology, 19*(1–2), 125–153.

Henriques, J., Hollway, W., Urwin, C., Venn, C., & Walkerdine, V. (1984). *Changing the subject: Psychology, social regulation and subjectivity*. London, England: Methuen.

Holme, J. J. (2002). Buying homes, buying schools: School choice and the social construction of school quality. *Harvard Educational Review, 72*(2), 177–205.

Lareau, A. (1989). *Home advantage: Social class and parental intervention in elementary education*. London, England: Falmer Press.

Lareau, A., & Horvat, E. M. (1999). Moments of social inclusion and exclusion: Race, class, and cultural capital in family-school relationships. *Sociology of Education, 72*, 37–53.

Lerner, M. (1993, May). Jews are not White. *Village Voice, 18*, 33–34.

Levine-Rasky, C. (2008). Middle-class formation and whiteness in parents' responses to multiculturalism. *Canadian Journal of Education, 31*(2), 459–490.

Levine-Rasky, C. (2009). The dynamics of parental involvement at a multicultural school. *British Journal of Sociology of Education, 30*(3), 331–344.

Levine-Rasky, C. (2011). Intersectional theorizing applied to whiteness and middle-classness. *Social Identities, 17*(2), 239–253.

Miller, B. A. (2000). "Anchoring" White community: White women activists and the politics of public schools. *Identities, 6*(4), 481–512.

Reay, D. (1996). Contextualising choice: Social power and parental involvement. *British Educational Research Journal, 22*(5), 581–596.

Savage, M. (2000). *Class analysis and social transformation*. Buckingham, England: Open University Press.

Simon, R. (1999). Election, ambivalence, and the pedagogy of Jewish particularity. In S. Shapiro (Ed.), *Strangers in the land: Pedagogy, modernity, and Jewish identity* (pp. 309–322). New York, NY: Peter Lang.

Skeggs, B. (2005). The Re-branding of class: Propertising culture. In R. Devine, M. Savage, J. Scott & R. Crompton (Eds.), *Rethinking class* (pp. 46–68). Hampshire, UK: Palgrave MacMillan.

Smith, D. E. (1990). *The conceptual practices of power: A feminist sociology of knowledge.* Toronto, ON: University of Toronto Press.

Smith, T. W. (2005). *Jewish distinctiveness in America: A statistical portrait.* New York, NY: American Jewish Committee.

Steinberg, S. (1989). *The ethnic myth.* Boston, MA: Beacon Press.

Stratton, J. (2000). *Coming out Jewish.* London, England: Routledge.

Whitty, G. (2001a). Vultures and third ways: Recovering Mannheim's legacy for today. In J. Demaine, (Ed.), *Sociology of education today* (pp. 206–222). Houndmills, Hampshire, England: Palgrave.

Whitty, G. (2001b). Education, social class and social exclusion. *Journal of Education Policy, 16*(4), 287–295.

REFRAMING: CYNTHIA LEVINE-RASKY (2014)

In the years intervening between the original and new edition of *The Great White North*, critical Whiteness studies has continued to evolve. I take note of two divergent directions in the literature and then suggest ways in which they may bear upon new research on educational inequality and school choice. To describe the two directions, I use the metaphor of fracturing what was at one time a conceptual whole: the power exercised through an enactment of White racefulness. As inquiry has grown, Whiteness theorists are confronted by an undeniable complexity of the analytic field. New questions about the practice of power are challenging the sphere of Whiteness studies as it was originally formulated. The first of these fractures I describe as outward, and the second as inward. Outward fractures of Whiteness are produced by its intersectionality with mutually constituted moments in power relations. Inward fractures are visible by peering through a psychoanalytic lens.

As Whiteness studies fractures outwardly into the universe of intersecting differentiations, the privileging of class over religions or ethnicity or gender becomes problematic. Brah and Phoenix (2004) define intersectionality "as signifying the complex, irreducible, varied, and variable effects which ensue when multiple axis (sic) of differentiation—economic, political, cultural, psychic, subjective and experiential—intersect in historically specific contexts. Different dimensions of social life cannot be separated out into discrete and pure strands" (p. 76). It is an arbitrariness of methodology to do so. The fact that class is salient in the UK and ethnicity is salient in Canada reflects something important about those societies and the kinds of national narratives with which their citizens identify. Multiculturalism is a robust set of ideas that, despite its waning status internationally, continues to command admiration in Canada. The deep roots of multiculturalism policy reverberate in the way Canadians present themselves. This is not a uniform phenomenon, but one that is thoroughly contradictory as seen in the writings of Mackey (2002), Chazan, Helps, Stanley, and Thakkar (2011), Thobani (2007), and Francis (2011), who have contributed immeasurably to our critical understanding of Canadian multiculturalism. Among the Baywoods parents, one can be for multiculturalism but only up to a point. The "mix" has to be conducive to positive relationships for those with the power to determine those limits. Yet Jews are part of Canada's multicultural blend. They were a signatory to Book IV, "The Cultural Contributions of Other Ethnic Groups" of the Royal Commission on Bilingualism and Biculturalism in 1969-70. Their arrival in Canada predates this by a century.

So what is more salient for these research participants as they weigh the balance of the dual principles of inclusivity and exclusivity? Ethnicity? Gender? Class? Religion? Culture? Piecing apart these dimensions is an artifice, for everyone

D. E. Lund & P. R. Carr (Eds.), Revisiting The Great White North?, 175–177.
© *2015 Sense Publishers. All rights reserved.*

is multiply situated. What is important to keep in mind is the not the fact of intersectionality, but its effects. As Anthias (2007) discusses, identity is as much a matter of positioning as position. Belongingness, and identity itself, is a process of negotiating advantage, risk, rewards, and trade-offs that are not so harsh as to disturb one's sleep.

The impulse to maintain peace with oneself despite alarmingly contradictory positions testifies to the workings of Whiteness' inward fractures. Charles Mills (1997) introduced the idea of an epistemology of ignorance, a willful un-knowing of the essential relationality between self and other. What mechanisms keep ignorance in place? My original chapter mentions the psychoanalytic mechanism of splitting, but this sets aside projective identification in which a distressed subject confers on the Other those components of herself which she cannot integrate. The process involves "the actual pushing of feelings onto others, making them experience aspects of the self in order to relieve the self of mental pain" (Rustin 1983, p. 60). It then becomes manageable to hate the other because it is perceived as wholly disconnected to the self (Frosh, 2005). Having divested itself of any relationality to the Other of its own imagination, the White psyche can freely express aggression towards what appears to be a deserving victim and a threat. The subject projects onto the hated object its desire to control, violate, or extinguish it (Britzman, 1998). But admission that the self intends harm is inconsistent with its integrity. Therefore, projective identification involves a fantasy that the Other is essentially bad, dirty, violent, or dangerous. To know oneself as White is to engage its essential relationality to Other. Yet Other is the very thing whiteness renounces; paradoxically it is "nemesis, fascination, and self" (Martinot, 2003, p. 186). This construction of the Other threatens our psychic stability (Clarke & Garner, 2005, p. 204), even our identity, power, control, "ego losses which threaten traditional identities of gender, class, ethnicity and nation" (Pajaczkowska & Young, 1992, p. 204). In White fear of the other, Ahmed (2004) identifies concern "with the preservation not simply of 'me,' but also 'us,' or 'what is,' or 'life as we know it,' or even 'life itself'" (p. 64).

Jews have long been objects of such fantasies. Yet when the parents of Baywoods explain their responses to the changes they observe at Pinecrest School, they are not drawing from a collective knowledge. The flow of memory has been cauterized. The consequences of this are complex as I indicated in my original chapter. In order to penetrate this complexity, a psychoanalytic frame has much to commend itself. This is the case whether we are reading about school choice in a Canadian urban centre, or in places such Europe, Australia, and the Middle East, where school choice research, and parental ethnicity and class intersections are growing.

REFERENCES

Ahmed, S. (2004). *The cultural politics of emotion.* Edinburgh, Scotland: Edinburgh University Press.
Anthias, F. (2007). Gender, ethnicity and class: Reflecting on intersectionality and translocational belonging. *The Psychology of Women Review, 9*(1), 2–11.

Brah, A., & Phoenix, A. (2004). Ain't I a woman? Revisiting intersectionality. *Journal of International Women's Studies, 5*(3), 75–86.

Britzman, D. P. (1998). *Lost subjects, contested objects: Toward a psychoanalytic inquiry of learning.* Albany, NY: State University of New York Press.

Chazan, M., Helps, L., Stanley, A., & Thakkar, S. (2011). *Home and native land: Unsettling multiculturalism in Canada.* Toronto, ON: Between the Lines.

Clarke, S., & Garner, S. (2005). Psychoanalysis, identity and asylum. *Psychoanalysis, Culture & Society, 10*(2), 197–206.

Francis, M. (2011). *Creative subversions: Whiteness, indigeneity, and the national imaginary.* Vancouver, BC: University of British Columbia Press.

Frosh, S. (2005). *Hate and the 'Jewish science': Anti-semitism, Nazism and psychoanalysis.* Hampshire, UK: Palgrave Macmillan.

Mackey, E. (2002). *The house of difference: Cultural politics and national identity in Canada.* Toronto, ON: University of Toronto Press.

Martinot, S. (2003). *The rule of racialization: Class, identity, governance.* Philadelphia, PA: Temple University Press.

Mills, C. W. (1997). *The racial contract.* Ithaca, NY: Cornell University Press.

Pajaczkowska, C., & Young, L. (1992). Racism, representation, psychoanalysis. In J. Donald & A. Rattansi (Eds.), *'Race,' culture and difference* (pp. 198–219). London, UK: Sage.

Rustin, M. (1983). Kleinian psychoanalysis and the theory of culture. In F. Barker, P. Hulme, M. Iversen, & D. Loxley (Eds.), *The politics of theory* (pp. 57–70). Colchester, England: University of Essex.

Thobani, S. (2007). *Exalted subjects: Studies in the making of race and nation in Canada.* Toronto, ON: University of Toronto Press.

LISA COMEAU

RE-INSCRIBING WHITENESS THROUGH PROGRESSIVE CONSTRUCTIONS OF "THE PROBLEM" IN ANTI-RACIST EDUCATION

INTRODUCTION

I take, as a starting-point, that the terms "White" and "Whiteness" refer primarily to race; however, I emphasize that race is not a biological category. Rather, the race category is a socially constructed one that intersects with other categories including gender, class, sexual orientation, (dis)ability, and so on, in ways that may influence the extent of dominance and privilege enjoyed by individuals who are marked as White. I situate this chapter within the growing literature that shows how Whiteness is constructed and maintained through very particular discursive practices. It is based on a recent study in Saskatchewan, Canada, in which White teachers were asked how they developed their sense of critical consciousness. Employing a discourse-analytic perspective, I explore the variable and often contradictory ways these highly educated, experienced, and well-intentioned research participants discursively construct and account for the problem of social inequality. My point is that the discursive production of cultural difference through racializing and racist discourse is complicit in re-inscribing both Whiteness and Otherness, thereby reproducing the social inequality that is claimed to be the object of transformative, anti-oppressive education. This chapter considers how White race privilege and dominance are perpetuated through Canadian educational discourses, policies and practices. Hence, it seems appropriate to I begin the chapter by reflecting on how I learned to become a "good White girl" (Moon, 1999) through my own experiences in formal and informal education.

HOW I BECAME WHITE

Education in Canada has been increasingly informed by liberal articulations of multiculturalism since it became official policy in 1971, and was later enshrined in law through the Multiculturalism Act in 1988. For many Canadians, multiculturalism is understood as an antidote of sorts to the blatantly racist ideology and practices of pre-WWII Canadian history. Although some Canadians have reservations about multiculturalism, the national embracing of multiculturalism permits individual Canadians, and the nation as a whole, to claim what Wetherell and Potter call the "moral identity of tolerance" (1998, p. 148). It is often taken as evidence of goodness and rationality in contrast to the mean-spiritedness and irrationality that

D. E. Lund & P. R. Carr (Eds.), Revisiting The Great White North?, 179–188.

is assumed to characterize racism when racism is equated with prejudice. This thinking has influenced me.

I grew up as a White, English-speaking girl who lived in an (almost) homogeneous White middle-class neighbourhood, and attended (almost) White homogeneous schools during the 1970s. As a White Canadian child, my schooling and socialization positioned me within what Cavanagh describes as a "colonial dyad... [in which I was] constituted as future agent of global care, [while] the Third World recipient of that care (who is both a living subject and a Canadian social fiction) [was] constructed to be in need of care" (2001, p. 402). As Willinsky (1998) suggests, I was taught to "divide the world," learning who I was by learning who I wasn't. I was *not* poor, uneducated, orphaned, disabled, and dirty, from the "developing" world, primitive, uncivilized, superstitious, or exotic. By contrast, I was Canadian, North American, middle-class, smart, pretty, talented, and clean. I learned that I was, in a word, "normal." I was taught that the life I lived was the kind of life all people aspired to, and indeed, had a right to. This was my education in what Rich calls "White solipsism" (cited in Moon, 1999, p. 178). The world was configured for me as if it were "White space," and Whiteness were a "normative and universal condition" (Moon, 1999, p. 178).

If I had been in school 30 years earlier, my White skin, Christian heritage and Western European ancestry would have been held up as evidence of my superiority to the brown-skinned, non-Christian and non-European Others in developing countries, and in the "degenerate" spaces *within* Canadian borders, namely, "urban slums" and Indian reserves. But during my education in the 1970s, overt references to skin colour and racial hierarchies were largely omitted. Instead, I was explicitly taught colour-blindness, along with such liberal and Christian ideals as the irrelevance of skin colour, and the equality of all people. Little reference was made to the obvious *inequality* of living conditions of the brown-skinned people that I saw on television other than to remind me of how much more fortunate I was ("there but for the grace of God..."). I don't recall any historical or political accounting for why people in some parts of the world seemed to continually face starvation, disease, and various forms of political unrest, and there certainly was no explanation that might have implicated the way I lived in other people's marginalization and suffering. This "evasion of Whiteness" (Frankenberg cited in Moon, 1999, p. 178) taught me not to see myself as White, and not to see Whiteness as a "specific structural and cultural location" (Moon, 1999, p. 179). My education to Whiteness rendered my own White dominance and privilege "invisible" (McIntosh, 1988), and allowed me to maintain my sense of myself as good and as disconnected from such irrationalities as racism. I learned not to see that Whiteness remains the (in)visible ruler against which all else is measured and found wanting. The de-historicizing of Whiteness prevented me from learning that I was able to become White through precisely those historical processes that subjugated my own French and Acadian heritage and that continue to exclude so many people from the privileges I enjoy because of my skin colour and a world built on an ideology of White supremacy.

THE RESEARCH CONTEXT

Evidence of White solipsism and White evasion can also be found in the following analysis of teacher discourses. However, I focus more specifically on participants' avoidance of discourses of race, and their use of discourses of culture to explain the specific forms of social inequality that are prevalent in Saskatchewan. Unlike other Canadian provinces with large populations of recent immigrants, Saskatchewan's entire population is slightly less than one million people (Saskatchewan Bureau of Statistics, 2006), and is comprised primarily of descendents of European settlers and Aboriginal people[1]. While Canada as a whole can rightly be described as a "settler society" (Green, 1995), the European colonization of Aboriginal people and territory continues to define contemporary racial politics in Saskatchewan. In Saskatchewan, as throughout Canada, Aboriginal people experience much higher than national rates of poverty, poor health, school incompletion, and incarceration (Royal Commission on Aboriginal Peoples, 1996). In response to the publication of *Indian Control of Indian Education* (National Indian Brotherhood, 1972), several Aboriginal teacher education programs (TEPs) have emerged with the mandate of preparing Aboriginal teachers to work with Aboriginal students in both provincial and Indian band-controlled schools. Specially designated "community schools" receive additional resources in order to address the needs of "at risk and Aboriginal and Métis students" (Saskatchewan Education, 1996). More recently, the inclusion of Aboriginal content throughout the curriculum has become mandated for all Saskatchewan students. This is the context in which teacher-participants in this study work.

Participants in this research are four White teachers (two men and two women), who self-identify as critically conscious and committed to social and racial justice through teaching. Two teach in rural Saskatchewan, and two teach in large urban centres in the province. Three have graduate degrees in education. They each have several years of experience as classroom-teachers, and in one case in administration, and all have taken active leadership roles in Saskatchewan education. They are considered experts in their field who speak with authority. Each participant consented to an interview of approximately one and a half hours in length. Prior to the interview, participants received a series of questions to consider. These were not meant or used as a formal interview schedule, but rather as guidelines for an informal, conversational style of interview. Pseudonyms were used for all participants. Following transcription, each participant received a transcript of their own interview, with the invitation to read, delete, or otherwise change the transcript to ensure that their own perspectives were represented as accurately as possible.

Participant-revised transcripts of interviews were analyzed from a discourse-analytic perspective. According to Wood and Kroger (2000), the defining feature of the discourse analytic perspective is that language is taken to be active. Thus, the discourse-analytic perspective permits an understanding of how language constructs, or produces social phenomena (Wood & Kroger, 2000, p. 9), such as the construction and explanation of a problem like social inequality. It is from this perspective that

I refer to the construction as opposed to the conceptualization of the problem of social inequality. Drawing on post-structural theorizing of the discursive production of subjectivities, I understand that, like me, participants are interpolated by social and cultural discourses already available. From this vantage point, I understand participants as "de-centred, not the author[s] of [their] own discursive activity and not the origin point of discourse" (Wetherell, 1998, p. 393). Colonial and racist discourses establish the framework for contemporary thinking about issues of social inequality. The Other—as internally, ontologically problematic (Said, 1978)—is a primary colonial discourse available for making sense of social inequality. Such discourses remain socially, culturally and professionally available discourses, and are authorized as "truth" when "expert knowers," such as these participants, re-cite them.

WHITE TEACHERS CONSTRUCT "THE PROBLEM": IT'S NOT ABOUT RACE...

Although not in explicit terms, participants speak against outdated and debunked notions of race as a biological category. In this framework, biological race had a causal quality about it, such that the assumed superiority of the "White race" was promoted as the explanation of the "European miracle" (Blaut, 1993) of imperialism and colonialism, while the supposed degeneracy of "subject" races accounted for their subjugation and legitimized their conquest (Said, 1993). Echoing the modernist liberal insistence that "*race* is 'a morally irrelevant category'" (Goldberg, 1993, pp. 5-6), participants in this study work hard *not* to name race as the source of the poverty and other examples of social inequality they see in the lives of their students and other people they identify as culturally different. As Howard says, "you can't say that because they're Indian, they're like that." Similarly, Janet insists that "the culture of poverty transcends all ethnic groups.... all those stereotypes that were out there for *Indian²*—aren't stereotypes for Indian, they're the stereotypes that go with the culture of poverty." Tim emphasizes that it's really about individual personality: "Teaching for a number of years in community schools... you have lots of people... who... were White, who I would not want to be friends with, and a lot of people who were Native... who were really nice people!... It was more personality based."

...IT'S ABOUT CULTURAL DIFFERENCE

Participants agree that race does not determine social conditions, such as poverty, or individual characteristics, such as likeability. Instead, they employ the "cultural differences" trope to explain social inequality. They speak of two categories of cultural difference. The first one is often described as "traditional" or "authentic" culture in public discourse. Sherry describes "a different culture... or a different way of looking at the world."

Without exception, participants valorize the cultural differences that are socially accepted as expressions of "authentic" culture. For instance, Janet often talks about "First Nation, Indian culture... [that] was honouring. It was respectful... It's this First

Nations culture that's to be honoured." Tim compares the relatively homogeneous White, middle-class, suburban school he currently works in, to the highly diverse community schools where he has worked for many years. Regarding the question of cultural diversity, he finds the homogeneous schools to be "missing" something important. Tim refers to "people's different practices and traditions, you know, the heritage festivals," and explains that:

> the kids will bring that to the school sometimes, just through what they bring, you know, in form of a lunch for example, or what they might do differently at a birthday party, or Christmas or something. They bring those traditions and expose the other kids to it.... because they make *friends*... you will go out to a friend's house and you'll see something entirely different.

By comparison, the students at Tim's current homogeneous school "don't know... how much they *miss*... [they] don't *have* that. Those little differences... that I think people can bring." Like Tim, Howard also cites what Hytten and Warren (2003, p. 78) call the "enrich me" discourse numerous times in his interview. For Howard, "multiculturalism isn't just that we allow a bunch of immigrants into our country that find a safe place to live or whatever. They bring with them a whole bunch of stuff that we benefit from." Echoing claims made on the Canadian Heritage web site (Canadian Heritage, 2004), Tim's and Howard's "food and celebration" understanding of diversity offers a richness, a spice to life. As bell hooks puts it, it offers a chance to "eat the Other" (1992).

My concern is that offering kids a chance to see "something entirely different," as Tim says, produces some groups of people *as* "something entirely different"—much like the language of biological race used to do (an idea some people still accept as true). Being made to contain difference produces some people as Other, essentially different from the White middle-class that is reproduced as the norm. Ultimately, the essential difference between White "homogeneous North American culture" (Tim) and racial and cultural Others must be reproduced in order for the richness of cultural diversity to be shared.

SOCIO-ECONOMIC CLASS AS CULTURE

Through their language use, participants also produce socio-economic class *as* culture through references to "the culture of poverty" (Janet; Tim), "White middle-class culture" (Janet; Sherry; Tim), and "the culture of the ultra rich" (Janet). This discursive culturalizing of class has many effects, including the essentializing of "authentic" culture and the denial of racism as a determining factor in some people's lives. For example, in the following excerpts Janet distinguishes First Nations culture from both the culture of poverty, and White middle-class culture. She says: "I started to see there's two distinct cultures here. There's the First Nation culture and then there's the culture of poverty.... But it was this culture of poverty that was screwing everything up." She amplifies this:

> But that's what that insidious thing was. It was trying to make them into White middle-class.... And to move away from that idea of assimilating, to how do I affirm their culture, cultural identity... but *equip* them for the dominant culture. So, *not* assimilate, but equip? And still honour the First Nations side (Janet, lines 729-762).

Concerned with this challenge of how to honour authentic culture while "equipping" for dominant culture without assimilating, Janet recounts a story about one of her First Nations students who, in his late teens, decided to make school success his "personal agenda." She speculates about whether "it's railing against the White man's culture? Or, they've come to realize that they need the tools to function in the White man's culture? Or, whatever it is—they're okay with who they are, and it's okay for them to learn these tools. And they do!" (Janet). In this narrative, learning to use the tools to function in the "White man's culture" is possible when First Nations students are "okay with who they are." In order that such learning not constitute assimilation, First Nations students must be able to maintain their "authentic" cultural identity in spite of learning the tools required to function in the dominant culture. Tim employs a similar formulation in a narrative about his friend, an Aboriginal person indigenous to an island nation, who mistook library deadlines as "*suggestions*...until he got his first $40.00 overdue fine!" Tim concludes, "That was a kind've a different nature," and offers his friend's academic and employment success as evidence that "he *must* have adapted;" at least "that's one part of his life that became like that." These productions of the cultural Other's essential difference resonates with Said's (1978) description of the imperialist understanding of the Other: "this object is a 'fact' which, if it develops, changes, or otherwise transforms itself in the way that civilizations frequently do, nevertheless is fundamentally, even ontologically static" (p. 32).

The culturalizing of socio-economic class also makes it difficult to hold racism accountable for class position. Recall Howard's insistence that "you can't say that because they're Indian, they're like that." He explains further that "they're like that.... because they're taken advantaged of and they're disadvantaged people, but there's disadvantaged White people too." In this excerpt, Howard makes it impossible to attribute disadvantage to racism because if racism were to blame, then there wouldn't be any poor White people. Disadvantage is recognized as a social reality, the cause of which is neither race nor racism, but is located in "those same kinds of conditions...same sort of upbringing or circumstances" (Howard). To blame disadvantage on race, one is *being* racist. To blame disadvantage on racism doesn't work if one equates racism with prejudice against dark complexioned people. If racism is understood as a system of power relations that benefit White people as a group at the expense of non-White people as a group, then blaming disadvantage on racism is to implicate oneself if one is White. Thus there is much pressure to deny racism as a powerful constitutive force in society.

Even as participants culturalize poverty, and locate the source of disadvantage in specific ways of living, they are also emphatic that these manifestations of inequality are *not* racially or culturally essential. Quite the contrary, Janet claims that her students live in poverty because of the choices they make. Employing the "culture of poverty" trope denies the salience of race and racism, while also leaving the responsibility for escaping poverty on the shoulders of the poor. Ultimately it is up to poor people to learn how to make choices that don't result in poverty, thus "bootstrapping" (Briskin, 1994) themselves out of poverty. This, in turn, opens the space for tolerant White teachers to help their Other students escape poverty by providing them with career information (Tim), helping students make the connection between going to school, doing well, and getting a good job (Tim), and as Janet suggests, helping them to make better choices that lead to a balanced life rather than a life of continued poverty. Kumashiro (2000) calls such pedagogical approaches "Education for the Other." They are forms of "deficit" education whereby giving Other students the knowledge they are assumed to be lacking is seen as potentially making all the difference in their lives.

IT IS ABOUT RACE, ISN'T IT?

In spite of their insistence on the richness of cultural diversity, participants also construct racial and cultural Others as problematic in schools and society. Some of this is apparent already in participants' talk about poverty. Recall Janet's claim that her students live in poverty because of the choices they make, and Howard's claim that "Indians" are "like that" because of their "upbringing and circumstances." Participants locate the source of inequality within Other's differences in various ways. For instance, Sherry is angered to hear colleagues use such derogatory notions as "Indian time" in explaining why "it's difficult for them" and "it's difficult for us to work with them." Ultimately, however, she accepts this construction as a cultural truth and wishes that it might be "reframed" in more positive language. Tim explains that in order to succeed in community schools, teachers have to be "very flexible… in a lot of cases you have to be a little thick-skinned because… some of the kids will come from a background where they don't have a respect for authority." Howard is concerned that government efforts must be made to help First Nations people "achieve a certain level… [or] as a province we're just sunk. 'Cause we can't go on supporting what's going to be maybe 25-30 percent of our population in the future if they haven't become integrated enough to be contributing citizens." Janet cites First Nations students' lack of self-trust and fear of success as reasons why these students don't participate on school teams.

My purpose in pointing out talk that constructs Aboriginal people as being inherently problematic is to show that even though participants claim that social inequality is about cultural difference rather than race, and whether they speak of cultural difference in valorizing or pejorative terms, what remains central in their talk is that "the problem" of social inequality is located within the difference that some people are made to contain. If there is no difference, there is no problem. In spite of their claims that social inequality is *not* about race, their productions of cultural Others as problematic echo very clearly the kinds of things that were once routinely said about the racial degeneracy of some people. As Razack articulates, "cultural differences perform the same function as a more biological notion of race... once did: they mark inferiority. A message of racial inferiority is now more likely to be coded in the language of culture rather than biology" (1998, p. 79). What these participants in Saskatchewan say also resonates with Wetherell's and Potter's observation that "race is still 'everywhere' in the discourse of [their White New Zealander participants], but... mainly as a kind of residual sediment" (1992, p. 123). Goldberg says that "the irony of modernity, the liberal paradox comes down to this: ...race is irrelevant, but all is race" (1993, p. 6). It seems to me that all is *still* race, even if some people call it culture.

DISCUSSION

In this chapter I have argued that culture is essentialized as race was (and many still assume it to be), and serves a similar function of maintaining White dominance and privilege. Racial and cultural Others are required simply *to be* their culture, appropriable as objects of knowledge, and available to be consumed and/or saved for the enrichment of dominantly positioned White people. In this can be heard a loud echo of Canada's imperialist and colonialist past. As Razack claims, "the cultural differences approach reinforces an important epistemological cornerstone of imperialism: the colonized possess a series of knowable characteristics and can be studied, known, and managed accordingly by the colonizers whose own complicity remains masked" (1998, p. 10).

Educational discourses that currently pass for progressive are often demonstrations of superior-because-sympathetic knowledge *about* racial and cultural Others. It is the sympathetic quality that marks progressive knowledge as superior to the irrationality of prejudiced knowledge about Others, and that positions the sympathetic knower as tolerant, therefore innocent of racism. Hence, demonstrations of progressive knowledge once again re-inscribe Whiteness as goodness and rationality, even if the tolerance that now constitutes goodness and rationality is quite different from the overt White supremacy and patriarchy of Canadian history. The power relations between dominantly positioned White people and marginalized people of colour continue to look a lot like colonial power relations of a century ago. It is *still* the dominant, authorized by their good intentions and superior rationality and knowledge, who *define* what—and who—the problems are, and what the solutions might be. Explanations of social inequality still turn on the production of the Other, who is made to contain the problem. In Fellows' and Razack's words, "the containment of the Other is a making of the dominant self" (1998, p. 343). White dominance requires a non-white Other.

What is required is to expose and disrupt the essentializing of categories of race and culture, and to see the construction of dominance as the problem of social inequality, rather than seeing those who are marginalized as containing, or even being, "the problem" to be fixed. I think it necessary that education name the tradition of White supremacy as well as the vested interest of White people in maintaining dominance, privilege and a sense of personal innocence in the perpetuation of racial injustices. This is not easy or comfortable work. In my experience, it is met with considerable resistance, both from my students as well as from within myself. Moreover, I am aware that even as I advance my own critique of progressive educational discourses (and my career in the process!), I am once again performing both goodness and superior rationality, and ultimately re-inscribing my own Whiteness. So I find myself caught in what Ellsworth calls the "double binds of Whiteness" (1997); I'm damned if I make the critique, and I'm damned if I don't because not doing anything permits the re-production of the racist status quo. I think that in the current historical moment, this double bind position is unavoidable for White people who want to disrupt racial inequalities. I take some solace from recognizing that my own sense of discomfort with my own complicity is *itself* a colonial legacy. For now, I remain convinced that working to reveal the mechanics of White dominance is important to anti-racist struggle.

QUESTIONS FOR REFLECTION

1. What are some of the characteristics of Whiteness referred to in this chapter?
2. What are some of the ways education works to construct Whiteness?
3. How might it be possible to explain social inequality without locating its source in the Other?
4. How might education work to disrupt rather than re-produce Whiteness?
5. (How) does Whiteness influence your own life?

NOTES

[1] According to 2001 Census figures, the total Aboriginal Identity Population of Saskatchewan was 130,185, or 13.5 percent, with the non-Aboriginal identity population being 86.5 percent (Saskatchewan Bureau of Statistics, 2001b). In the same Census, the total "visible minority" population of Saskatchewan was 27,580 or 2.9 percent, where "visible minorities" are defined as "persons other than Aboriginal peoples who are non-Caucasian in race or non-white in colour" (Saskatchewan Bureau of Statistics, 2001a). Nationally, the Aboriginal Identity Population was only 3.3 percent in the 2001 Census (Saskatchewan Bureau of Statistics, 2001b).

[2] Italics were added in the transcription process to denote participants' emphasis on certain words and phrases.

REFERENCES

Blaut, J. M. (1993). *The colonizer's model of the world: Geographical diffusionism and Eurocentric history*. New York, NY: Guilford Press.
Briskin, L. (1994). Feminist pedagogy: Teaching and learning liberation. In L. Erwin & D. MacLennan (Eds.), *Sociology of education in Canada: Critical perspectives on theory, research & practice* (pp. 445–470). Toronto, ON: Copp Clark Longman.

Cavanagh, S. L. (2001). The pedagogy of the pastor: The formation of the social studies curriculum in Ontario. *Canadian Journal of Education, 26*(4), 401–417.

Ellsworth, E. (1997). Double binds of whiteness. In M. Fine, L. Weis, L. Powell, & M. Wong (Eds.), *Off white: Readings on race, power, and society* (pp. 259–269). New York, NY: Routledge.

Fellows, M. L., & Razack, S. H. (1998). The race to innocence: Confronting hierarchical relations among women. *The Journal of Gender, Race and Justice, 1*(2), 335–352.

Goldberg, D. T. (1993). *Racist culture: Philosophy and the politics of meaning.* Cambridge, MA: Blackwell.

Canadian Heritage. (2004). *Canadian diversity: Respecting our differences.* Ottawa, ON: Government of Canada. Retrieved June 15, 2006 from http://www.pch.gc.ca/progs/multi/respect_e.cfm

Green, J. (1995). Towards a détente with history: Confronting Canada's colonial legacy. *International Journal of Canadian Studies, 12*, 85–105.

hooks, b. (1992). Eating the other. In *Black looks: Race and representation* (pp. 21–39). Toronto, ON: Between the Lines.

Hytten, K., & Warren, J. (2003). Engaging Whiteness: How racial power gets reified in education. *Qualitative Studies in Education, 16*(1), 65–89.

Kumashiro, K. (2000). Toward a theory of anti-oppressive education. *Review of Educational Research, 70*(1), 25–53.

McIntosh, P. (1988/1992). White privilege: Unpacking the invisible knapsack. In P. S. Rothenberg (Ed.), *Race, class and gender in the United States: An integrated study* (4th ed., pp. 165–169). New York, NY: St. Martin's Press.

Moon, D. (1999). White enculturation and bourgeois ideology: The discursive production of 'good (White) girls'. In T. K. Nakayama & J. D. Martin (Eds.), *Whiteness: The communication of social identity.* London, England: Sage.

National Indian Brotherhood. (1972). *Indian control of Indian education.* Ottawa, ON: National Indian Brotherhood.

Razack, S. H. (1998). *Looking White people in the eye: Gender, race, and culture in courtrooms and classrooms.* Toronto, ON: University of Toronto Press.

Royal Commission on Aboriginal Peoples. (1996). *Report of the Royal Commission on Aboriginal Peoples* (Vol. 1). Ottawa: Canada Communications Group.

Said, E. (1978). *Orientalism.* New York, NY: Random House.

Said, E. (1993). *Culture and imperialism.* New York, NY: Vintage Books.

Saskatchewan Bureau of Statistics. (2001a). *Visible minority groups, Saskatchewan, Regina and Saskatoon.* Retrieved November 9, 2006 from http://www.stats.gov.sk.ca/census/visible_minority1.pdf

Saskatchewan Bureau of Statistics. (2001b). *Aboriginal identity Canada, provinces and territories.* Retrieved November 9, 2006 from http://www.stats.gov.sk.ca/census/aboriginal1/pdf

Saskatchewan Bureau of Statistics. (2006). *Quick facts.* Retrieved November 9, 2006 from http://www.stats.gov.sk.ca

Saskatchewan Education. (1996). *Building communities of hope: Best practices for meeting the learning needs of at-risk and Indian and Métis students. Community schools policy and conceptual framework.* Regina, SK: Planning and Evaluation Branch, Saskatchewan Education.

Wetherell, M. (1998). Positioning and interpretative repertoires: Conversation analysis and post-structuralism in dialogue. *Discourse & Society, 9*(3), 387–412.

Wetherell, M., & Potter, J. (1992). *Mapping the language of racism: Discourse and the legitimation of exploitation.* New York, NY: Columbia University Press.

Willinsky, J. (1998). *Learning to divide the world: Education at empire's end.* Minneapolis, MN: University of Minnesota Press.

Wood, L. A., & Kroger, R. O. (2000). *Doing discourse analysis: Methods for studying action in talk and text.* Thousand Oaks, CA: Sage.

REFRAMING: LISA COMEAU (2014)

Shortly after the publication of the first edition of this book, I left academia and Saskatchewan to return to Ottawa and a position within the federal government. I reflect briefly here on some of the challenges of opening a serious public discussion on race and Whiteness in the Ottawa context and amidst political incentives to silence such discussion.

OTTAWA'S DIVERSITY

As presented in my original chapter, Saskatchewan has fewer new immigrants than Ottawa, a much larger Aboriginal population than most other Canadian provinces, and colonization continues to mark contemporary racial politics in that province. It is still true that in Saskatchewan, power, wealth, and opportunity tend to be enjoyed to a much greater extent by White people than by Aboriginal people. By contrast, the population in contemporary Ottawa, and within the public service, is far more racially and culturally diverse than both contemporary Saskatchewan, and the "(almost) homogeneous White" Ottawa of my childhood. Ottawa's diverse population is also relatively well educated and well paid because the largest employer here is the federal government. Other large employers include municipal government, crown corporations, IT companies and several post-secondary institutions – all requiring highly skilled employees, and all subject to federal employment equity legislation requiring them to proactively increase the representation among their employees of four designated groups: women, people with disabilities, Aboriginal peoples, and visible minorities. The result is that in Ottawa, the intersection of race and class is more complicated – the correlation between them less direct than in Saskatchewan. In Ottawa, there are plenty of poor, homeless, White people, and plenty of well-to-do people of colour. Unearned privilege and power held by people with lighter skin, gained originally by their ancestors through very explicitly raced-based policies, is less readily apparent in the context of Ottawa's well-educated and well-paid racially and culturally diverse citizenry. White privilege and inequalities along racial and cultural lines are simply less obvious and more easily denied.

Perhaps it is because of the ease of denial on a daily basis that more overt cases of racism tend to hit the news. In a recent example, Ian Campeau[1], a local First Nations man, launched a campaign to change the name of a local youth football team, the Nepean Redskins (complete with logo depicting a First Nations "warrior" with feathers in his hair), because he thought it was racist and offensive. Recognizing that the team recently invested several thousand dollars in new helmets, uniforms, and so on all bearing the logo, he proposed to negotiate

D. E. Lund & P. R. Carr (Eds.), Revisiting The Great White North?, 189–191.

a gradual change in order to offset the cost of replacing the name and logo yet again. His charge was met with considerable outrage and backlash on the part of some local personalities as well as individuals emailing and tweeting their comments to local media covering the issue. Even City Councillor Jan Harder publicly aired her opinion that the team moniker was neither offensive nor racist, and claimed the complainant was creating a problem where none existed. This story remained in the news for a week or so before fading away – the Redskins kept their name and saved their money.[2]

MULTICULTURALISM AND OTHER POLITICAL INCENTIVES TO SILENCE DISCUSSION

In addition to the fact of Ottawa's ethnic diversity, there are a number of political incentives to silence discussion. Multiculturalism, both the daily social reality and the legislation, works well to keep racial tensions below the surface. An important aspect of Canadian national identity revolves around our embrace of multiculturalism and our "celebration" of diversity. Many Canadians derive a (smug?) sense of moral superiority from our place as a global role model of tolerance in the midst of rising nationalist sentiments in several European countries and even within the province of Quebec. Sustained discussion of whiteness and racism would destabilize this element of Canadian national identity, and likely also the resulting social cohesion. It might also constitute a disincentive to highly skilled and educated prospective immigrants from "non-traditional"[3] source countries in Africa and Asia, whose human capital the Canadian government hopes to exploit in order to grow Canada's tax base and enhance GDP as the Canadian-born baby boomers are aging and retiring. A discussion of Whiteness and racism would be socially and politically divisive, and too easily interpreted as advocacy on behalf of "special interest groups" – something that the Canadian government claims it cannot, will not, and does not do – ironically, because its mandate is to serve *all* Canadians. The bottom line is that a serious confrontation with contemporary manifestations of racism in Canada is simply not politically expedient.

NOTES

[1] Aka DeeJay NDN, of music group *A Tribe Called Red*.
[2] Update: In the fall of 2013, the Nepean youth football team announced it would change its logo (CBC, 2013).
[3] The notion of "race" is embedded in this very phrase by virtue of its implication of "traditional" source countries and the historical race-based immigration policies that determined that White western and northern European immigrants were the most desirable immigrants. It is these policies that made the Canadian population White. The assumption that Canadians are White remains and surfaces in such government sanctioned terms as "visible minority," as well as in the recently publicized debacle in which the Canadian mint replaced the image of an Asian woman on the back of the $100 bill with a White woman deemed to present a more "ethnically neutral" image.

REFERENCE

Canadian Broadcasting Corporation. (2013, September 19). Nepean Redskins to change controversial name, logo. *CBC News* [online], Ottawa, ON. Retrieved from http://www.cbc.ca/news/canada/ottawa/ nepean-redskins-to-change-controversial-name-logo-1.1860795

R. PATRICK SOLOMON & BEVERLY-JEAN M. DANIEL

DISCOURSES ON RACE AND "WHITE PRIVILEGE" IN THE NEXT GENERATION OF TEACHERS

INTRODUCTION

In this chapter we explore the ways White and minoritized pre-service[1] teachers perceive the concept and practices of racism and White privilege from their racial locations in Canadian society. These discourses emerged within the context of a teacher preparation program that integrates antiracism and other social difference issues into its curriculum and pedagogy. As two persons of African heritage in a White supremacist society we have been knowingly and unknowingly marginalized and disenfranchised by White privilege. As teacher educators we have made it our professional project to bring to the consciousness of White and minoritized teachers the insights to critically analyze and expose the myth of White privilege masquerading as merit (Frankenberg, 2004), and to engage these teachers in the pedagogy of social reconstructionism. This will indeed be a challenging task since teacher education alone cannot reverse racial formations that lead to "race privilege" behaviours in schools and the communities they serve.

Emerging from the study we examine, in this chapter, interesting contradictory, contested and divergent discourses on racism and White privilege informed by pre-service teachers' racial identities and experiences. The chapter concludes with an analysis of these discourses and their implications for teacher education. We introduce the urgent need for a radically progressive preparation program for tomorrow's teachers destined for a racialized environment.

PRE-SERVICE TEACHERS

Pre-service teachers' engagement with issues of race and White privilege reflects that of their colleagues who had earlier completed the teacher education program. In the U.S., for example, the research of McIntyre (1997), Sleeter (1993, 2005), Swartz (2003), and Valli (1993) provides revealing insights into ways predominantly White pre-service teachers construct race in the process of learning to teach. The discourse they construct provide disturbing insights into the attitudes, assumptions and perspectives they nurture about the "racial other." McIntyre's (1997) study, for example, uncovered strategies White female pre-service teachers utilized to subvert and derail any critical interrogation of racism and White privilege. They employed "White talk" to absolve themselves of any individual responsibility for race privilege,

D. E. Lund & P. R. Carr (Eds.), Revisiting The Great White North?, 193–204.
© 2015 Sense Publishers. All rights reserved.

or any social and economic advantage that may accrue from the practice of White privilege in the broader society.

King's (1991) study of "dysconscious racism" among pre-service teachers provides insights into ways the mis-education of teachers persists and reproduces itself when programs fail to critically interrogate the dominance of White norms in society. According to the King, these norms "justify social and economic advantages White people have as a result of subordinating diverse others" (1997, p. 135). What has emerged from the research are themes of reluctance to interrogate White privilege, tacit acceptance of White norms, physical and psychological distancing from the socially different, (e.g., reluctance to work in urban, inner-city environments), the pretense of "colour-blindness," and the subversion of emancipatory pedagogies such as antiracism (King, 1991). McCarthy (2003) concludes:

> Strategic discourses can be used to deflect, displace, and disavow racial privilege.... In the case of "the discourse of connections," White pre-service teachers often speak a language of self-declared marginalization that allows them to fend off the moral entanglements with race privilege and racism. White students can, on the one hand "understand" racism and, on the other, reject any entailment in its proliferation. (p. 130)

These themes reflect the next generation of teachers in the U.S. as one that will reproduce and transmit racial inequality, and also teacher education programs that are unprepared to disrupt this transmission. Critics contend that without a rigorous program that includes reflection, internalization of new knowledge about social difference and cultural diversity, the next generation of teachers will not transform the social order (Kagan, 1992; Ross & Smith, 1992).

A review of the research on Canadian pre-service teachers reveals similar themes but introduces some unique issues (Levine-Rasky, 1998, 2000a, 2000b; Rezai-Rashti & Solomon, 2005). Levine-Rasky (1998, 2000a, 2000b) reveals a number of crucial issues surrounding pre-service teachers and their relationship with social difference and, more specifically, race, and Whiteness in education. She found these teachers' negotiation of social difference replete with tensions, contradictions and inconsistencies based on their individual identities, social locations, and value systems. Her 2000a study dramatically shifted the discourse on racism away from the pathology of the "racial other" and spotlighted "Whiteness" itself. She captures the tensions generated when Whiteness is problematized and White pre-service teachers are exposed to the various ways they are implicated in educational inequality based on race. What we find most compelling about Levine-Rasky's research is that it provides insights into the culture, the structures, the mechanism, and the social relations of Whiteness that produce racialized subjects (p. 271). Schick's (2000) research findings bear striking similarities to those of Levine-Rasky; they both found gross inconsistencies and contradictions in the way White pre-service teachers profess liberalism and distance from racism while engaging in discursive repertoires that maintain and reproduce race dominance.

Solomon, Portelli, Daniel, and Campbell (2005) unearthed strategies used consistently by White candidates to avoid interrogating Whiteness and its associated privileges. They support equity and social justice in principle but were reluctant to move from principle to practice. Their responses were firmly grounded in liberalist notions of individualism and meritocracy, arguing that those who work hard will be rewarded in an assumed meritocratic opportunity structure. They deny the existence of "White privilege" and its associated capital and material benefits, and continue to construct the racial terrain as one of equal opportunity for Whites and racialized minorities, not as a site where Whites possess unearned privileges. These findings raise serious implications for teacher education and its task of responding to cognitive dissonance, ideological entrenchment, contradictions, inconsistencies, and emotional tensions that surface in the exploration of race, White privilege, and antiracism pedagogy as a corrective enterprise.

An unexplored, under-researched voice on the issue of race and White privilege is that of racialized pre-service teachers. A recent Canadian study (Solomon, Portelli, Daniel, & Campbell, in press) of racialized pre-service teachers in two urban universities in Canada revealed the ways they deconstruct notions of racism and White privilege, and the impact of the "culture of Whiteness" on their personal and professional lives. From this study two primary responses emerged: (a) contesting the terrain of Whiteness, they perceived the emergence of critical Whiteness studies and the exposure of White privilege as a validation and affirmation of their marginalized existence in a racist society; and (b) re-inscribing Whiteness and White privilege. This is the case where some minoritized pre-service teachers uncritically denied the dominance of White privilege through their investment in the liberalist notion of meritocracy and "blaming the victim" of racism for their oppression. While the large majority of minoritized candidates held a more critical view of Whiteness, this sub-group, by virtue of their professional status has the power, authority, and influence to reproduce the "racial order" in the next generation of Canadians.

From this brief synthesis of the Canadian research have emerged some salient themes on predominantly White pre-service teachers and their attitudes and dispositions towards racism and White privilege. The White pre-service teachers engage in the discourse of denial, defensiveness, ignorance, and hostility, and demonstrate a variety of "counter-knowledge strategies" to avoid critical interrogation of the racial norms and beliefs from which they earn White privilege. In the next section we explore and make meaning of recurring themes on racism and White privilege among White and minoritized pre-service teachers. Their perceptions and practices have serious implications for teacher education curriculum and pedagogy.

RESEARCH SETTING AND DATA SOURCES

Data for this chapter were drawn from an ongoing study of pre-service teachers in a Canadian urban university with high racial and ethnic diversity in its population. This diversity is reflected in a special initiative that prepares teachers to work competently in multiracial schools. Specific objectives of such an initiative are to: (a) provide an environment in which teacher candidates of various racial and ethnocultural groups and abilities have extended opportunities to develop teaching competencies and professional relationships in a collaborative environment; (b) integrate issues of equity and diversity into the curriculum and pedagogy of the teacher education program and in the classrooms of practicum schools; (c) prepare teacher candidates to work in urban environments where the diversity that represents the current Canadian reality is evidenced; and (d) develop collaboration among practicum school staff, the candidates, and teacher educators from the university forming a community of learners.

Participants in this program were enrolled in a nine-month post-baccalaureate teacher education program and reflected the ethno-cultural and racial diversity of the larger urban community from which they were drawn. Candidates of colour were of African, Latino, South Asian, South-east Asian and First Nations heritages while White candidates were mainly of Western European and Jewish heritages. While most candidates were Canadian-born, the others were of immigrant and refugee status, many of whom were already teachers in their countries of origin.

Qualitative research methods (Guba & Lincoln, 1994; McCarthy, 2003) were used to collect data on an ongoing basis. There were several sources for the data: responses to class assignments in the Social Foundations of Education course that critically interrogates issues of race, racism and White privilege among other social difference issues; open-ended feedback questionnaires that gauged candidates' attitudes and perspectives on social issues taken up in the theory-driven readings; discourse patterns of candidates in collective electronic class folders; and individual portfolios and journal entries. McCarthy (2003) argues that these are the best moments to study issues of racial identity—when complex and contradictory feelings and White racial anxieties begin to surface; "Open-ended conversational context of the pre-service teacher seminar acts like a confessional in which the protective layer that often pastes over racial anxiety, prejudice, and antagonism of the pre-service teachers sometimes slip away" (p. 130). Observational data from candidates' interactions in field-based practicum schools and the racially diverse neighbourhoods served by these schools proved important. The most relevant and significant data for this study, however, were the responses generated from Peggy McIntosh's (1990) article: *White privilege: Unpacking the invisible knapsack.* This article exposes the many ways that taken-for-granted privileges are bestowed on White people, always at the expense of racialized bodies.

Analysis of data from these multiple sources took the form of searching for themes in candidates' responses to issues of race and White privilege. We searched for similarities and differences in the discourses of White and minoritized candidates. Emerging patterns in the data were triangulated with the observations of other course directors who work with candidates in various teaching and supervisory capacities in the program (e.g., school practicum and community development supervision).

FINDINGS

Two salient themes emerged from the data: (a) "Not here in Canada" reveals the extent to which the candidates remain unaware of the history of racism in the Canadian context; and (b) Discourses of Competing Oppressions, which centres gender and class, while de-centering race.

NOT HERE IN CANADA!

The theme of moral superiority over the Americans was pervasive in the responses of the teacher candidates to race-related course content that addressed issues in the U.S. context, but with theoretical relevance to multiracial societies. The teacher candidates denied the relevance of the data to a Canadian reality while constructing the situation regarding race in the U.S. as distinctly different from the situation in Canada. The authors and selections most frequently critiqued by pre-service teachers were: McIntosh (1990), *White privilege: Unpacking the invisible knapsack*; Delpit (1988), The *silenced dialogue: Power and pedagogy in educating other people's children*; Sleeter, C.E. (1992). *Resisting racial awareness: How teachers understand the social order from their racial, gender, and social class locations,* and King (1991*), Dysconscious racism: Ideology, identity, and the mis-education of teachers.* Respondents to these readings routinely perceived them as "anti-White" and "un-Canadian," and offered emotional critiques in the following ways:

> I feel this [McIntosh] article was meant to raise consciousness of racism in the United States. I think this article does not represent Canada in any way. [White male]

> I find it difficult to determine if my thinking is a result of my inability to accept my "White privilege," or if I truly disagree on the basis of concrete fact. I did notice that the [McIntosh] article was written 15 years ago and is based on American society, which immediately makes me aware of the possibility of some inconsistencies with the information and what is currently happening in Canada. [White female]

What is worthy of note is that both White and minoritized candidates were invested in this notion of Canada being the safe haven of freedom.

> I understand that economically many minority groups are at a disadvantage and that, in order to help them elevate their economic position, changes need to be made. I do feel, however, that the American perspective expressed in the article made it less relevant to me as a Canadian. I do not see Canada as a country that experiences the same intensity of racial tension and we do not have the same civil rights issues historically as the United States does. [minoritized female]

I would like to know how relevant these articles are to Canadian society. Are we to compare ourselves with the Americans and their way of thinking? Articles like these appear to be so one-sided. There is no mention of racism that Blacks inflict on other groups. [White male]

Are the perspectives and attitudes portrayed in this collection of papers relevant to our educational and social situation in Canada? Did the long and bitter history of black oppression as experienced in the U.S.A. affect public opinion and likely taint objectivity [in Canada]? [White female]

I know this statement is of common nature of people living in the United States, but I would like to believe that here in Canada it is not all too common. I am not saying that Canada is perfect in that there are not racists among us; however, at least in Canada different cultures and races are welcomed. [minoritized female]

Multiculturalism policies have played a primary role in constructing this belief in the equanimity of Canadian racial interactions, and have embraced and celebrated difference, primarily focusing on harmonious and celebratory cultural artifacts and practices. These practices have served to provide racially minoritized immigrant groups with the sense that their cultures are being respected and included, thereby creating a true mosaic versus the traditional American melting pot ideology. Canadian teacher candidates remain unaware of the way in which the historical and contemporary treatment of Canada's First Nations People can be identified as a form of apartheid. Canadians fought diligently to dismantle apartheid in South Africa; however, their continued failure to recognize its existence in their own front yard limits their ability to dismantle the social, political and ideological structures that maintain racial divisions in Canadian society.

The theme of distancing racism was a prevalent one among both White males and females. Teacher candidates continually dismissed the issues as being irrelevant to Canadian society, thereby continuing to create the "them" and "us" dichotomy, convincing themselves that they have generally exhibited a superior moral stance with regard to race. There was the generally held belief that racialized people in Canada were afforded similar opportunities and privileges as Whites, and, therefore did not experience the marginalization of the counterparts in the U.S. Consequently, teacher education course materials on racism and White privilege were perceived to be biased, provocative, controversial, racially divisive and "un-Canadian."

DISCOURSE OF COMPETING OPPRESSIONS: CENTERING GENDER AND CLASS—DECENTERING RACE

There was a tendency on the part of many of the teacher candidates to marginalize and minimize the effects of race and replace them with issues of gender and class. Anti-racism theory speaks directly to this notion as one rationale for developing an anti-racist framework. There is an unspoken tradition in Canada to marginalize or dismiss issues of race while seeking more "palatable" rhetoric to explain people's oppression.

Have I benefited from being a White middle-class woman, no doubt, my three closest friends have also received the same benefits, higher education, employment privileges and better police protection than most. The only difference is they are Spanish, Iranian and Indian. The thread that unites us is social class. I truly believe that class is a greater determinant of "success" or "privilege" than gender or race. [White female]

As a White female, or collectively as White females, do women really have this power? Can we weaken the hidden system of advantage that also disadvantages women of other groups? The fact remains that men are given more power in society. [White female]

As I read the [McIntosh] article... I was struggling with the concept of White privilege. I see that there are certain privileges that the population receives but is this idea a generalization? Is privilege the right term to be used here? Do people of other skin colours not receive privileges in life too? Could we consider this to be more of a class basis, rather than skin colour one? [White female]

I think it is inevitable that certain children will have more advantages in the school system and in life, not because of the colour of their skin but because of who their parents, or siblings are. [White male]

Although many immigrants and persons of colour (visible minorities) speak of the relatively fair treatment they experience in Canada... many more are disadvantaged because of other characteristics such as gender, sexual orientation, age, religion, etc. [minoritized female]

During the question-answer presentation [in a class exploring race and White privilege], most responses raised by the audience were concerning the guilt White people faced because of the privileges they have... I actually felt very guilty at one point that I had to apologize to the class for labeling White people as "White people." [minoritized female]

To say that "Whites" are always conferred dominance and advantage in all circumstances is incorrect. "White" people are not dominant in culturally specific neighbourhoods such as Chinatown or West Indian areas. They do not have the benefit of speaking the same language, and understanding the cultural connotations and references in these areas. (minoritized female)

In much the same way that the issue of race has been referred to as the ampersand problem within feminist discourses (Spelman, 2001), it appears to be addressed in a similar peripheral manner amongst teacher candidates. Canadian society continues to regard race as a discourse that should be closeted because of the assumption that the mere mention of the word retards human sensibilities and has the interesting repercussion of instituting feelings of guilt amongst minoritized candidates. The maintenance of the mythology of colour-blindness, irrespective of the fact that the lived realities of Canada's many visible racialized groups attest to the insidious challenges of racism, and serve to placate the ideology of the Canadian mosaic, whether they are members of the dominant or minoritized groups. Canadians appear to be more willing to admit to gender and class-based discrimination at least on a superficial level, and more recently, sexual orientation and ability have entered academic and colloquial conversations. The vagaries of political pundits have served to, at various junctures, include or expunge conversations about race or race-based policies such as the anti-racism, which then provides a platform for teachers to measure the importance of race-based dialogues.

The marginalization of race on a broader social front is replicated within Canada's classrooms. One possible explanation for the tacit willingness to discuss gender and race could be explained by the demographics of the Canadian teaching force. Canadian teachers continue to be overwhelmingly White, female, and middle-class (Solomon, Portelli, Daniel, & Campbell, 2005). However, many of them are also members of European immigrant stock who, in their initial experience on Canadian shores represented an underclass. The story then follows that their parents and grandparents, through hard work were able to establish themselves in the society and therefore the notion of hard work and not complaining about their circumstances, becomes marked as the step to success (the myth of meritocracy). The part of the story that seldom gets told is the fact that their ancestors were given land (often stolen from First Nation peoples), or allowed to purchase land for nominal sums of money. The fact that their ancestors Anglicized their names in an attempt to better fit in with the existing Canadian populace, or that within one generation, their White skin and the disappearance of their accent gave them the same access as the dominant group at the time, is another part of the story that that remains untold.

Conversations about class therefore continue to be framed within the construct of meritocracy:

> I lived and went to school in a small remote farming town in Northern Ontario. Almost all of the families were White, lower to middle-class inhabitants who had lived in this community for generations. I was a newcomer. Although not a visible minority, my last name was different, my parents barely spoke English and our customs and traditions were ethnic. [White female]

Teacher candidates also appeared to cling to the issue of gender discrimination as a way of reducing personal culpability in race-based discrimination.

> As a White female, or collectively as White females, do women really have this power? Can we weaken the hidden systems of advantage that also disadvantages women and other groups? The fact remains that men are give more power in society. Therefore, I find it difficult to take this knowledge as

a White person, and use it as a White female to evoke change. This does not mean that I am against change. But we must not forget that being White does not always mean having power. Within the White race there are many groups that also face inequalities. [White female]

I have taken women's studies and many other courses that touched on the subject of social justice issues--yet until now it was not explained to me as something that I am responsible for maintaining. [White female]

As a woman, I believe that there has been a shift in the balance of power, not that the genders are equal, but it is changing for the better. [White female]

As the above quotes indicate, the teacher education candidates were well aware of the issues that affected them based on their gendered self; however, they failed to transfer that experience of discrimination to other sites. Studies have shown that when people experience discrimination, they can sometimes develop the ability to transfer this experience to other forms of discrimination (Chang, 1999; Daniel, 2003). Although some participants in the study did experience a shift in their understanding of discrimination, especially that which is related to race, there was an obvious reluctance on the part of others to make that shift. This pattern provides an impetus for additional research aimed at identifying the differential response patterns evidenced amongst the candidates.

DISCUSSION

The research provides indications of two primary patterns of responses. Teacher candidates lack historical knowledge of race relations within a Canadian context. The failure of existing history texts to comprehensively address and contextualize historicity, as well as the continued failure on the part of Canadian society to acknowledge its painful past, serves to underscore the denial of the most nefarious forms of racism on the part of the teacher candidates. This erasure of history also buffers the political economy of Whiteness.

Whites continue to experience multiple economic, political, social and ideological benefits, which have been accrued through centuries of colonial ventures. Acknowledgement of these benefits also entails a tacit recognition of the process through which these benefits were acquired and the integral role that race and practices of racialization have played in monopolizing various forms of social capital. If those historical and contemporary factors are acknowledged, the myth of meritocracy becomes stripped bare; one can no longer claim ignorance, thereby creating a moral dilemma. The unfair achievement of benefits goes against some of the primary guiding principles of Canadian society, which strongly condemns inequitable and oppressive acts against humanity. Acknowledgement of history requires the acknowledgement of ill-gotten gains, and also the requirement that that which is unfairly achieved should be returned to its rightful owner. Ignorance, denials, anger, and resistance all become symptomatic of a larger moral issue: to acknowledge the past necessitates a significant change in the power dynamics of the future. This implies that Whites would have to relinquish significant benefits and privileges that Whiteness has afforded them. Denial then becomes a way of protecting their economic hegemony.

History has shown us that oppression is not possible without some degree of complicity on the part of those being oppressed, a truism that is highlighted and reinforced by the responses of the racially minoritized teacher candidates. The minoritized teacher candidates replicate dominant ideology regarding race and practices of racialization because they, too, have been educated and socialized in the same system as their White colleagues. Their school knowledge and popular culture convey the positive treatment of immigrants; they are seldom exposed to knowledge that elucidates the systemic and insidious nature of a system of race-based practices that are so firmly entrenched, normative and, at its worst, invisible.

The results of this study have multiple implications for the field of teacher-education. They highlight the importance of providing clear, consistent, and comprehensive documentation of Canadian history rather that the antiseptic version that is currently presented in textbooks and classrooms. Further to this, Canadian society needs to accept the multiple facets of its history and work to develop strategies for changing the future rather than using America as its evil antithesis. Canadian social and legal policies are rife with varied racist and exclusionary practices that have created a painful legacy for many of it people. The continued exhortations of "Canada the good" result in the continued denial of that history, and within contemporary spaces, and obfuscate the need for change. The failure to change will ensure that millions of Canadian children will continue to be schooled by teachers who fail to recognize the extent to which these children's lives are framed by historical legacies and institutionalized practices that limit possibilities.

To conclude, the continued discourse of competing oppressions which decentres race, will see an increase in the numbers of children who engage in varied forms of resistance to the school, increasing instability in the overall education system, an increase in the numbers of racialized youth being identified as "at-risk" and an ever-widening gap between the reality of the students and the competing ideology of the teachers. Within the field of teacher education it is imperative that the teacher candidates who enter classrooms are effectively prepared to *re-centre* race in its multiple manifestations rather than continuing to adopt the myth of colour-blindness.

QUESTIONS FOR REFLECTION

1. How may teacher educators use antiracism pedagogy to disrupt the discourse of denial, defensiveness, emotional tensions, ignorance, hostility, and "counter-knowledge strategies" that teacher candidates often engage in to avoid a critical interrogation of racism and white privilege?

2. The next generation of teachers demonstrates limited knowledge of Canada's racist history. Consequently, they demonstrate moral superiority toward their neighbours to the South. How do we work toward a comprehensive picture of Canadian history that highlights similarities between American and Canadian racial histories?

3. Structuring cross-race dyad partnerships in learning to teach (see Solomon, 2000) provides White teacher candidates exposure to the lived experiences of racism faced by their minoritized colleagues as well as insights into their own privileges. Speculate on the potential for interdependent learning of both groups and also the challenges of such a structure in teacher education.

4. How may we begin to explore racism with teacher candidates in a manner that unveils the political economy of Whiteness and grapples with the inherent moral dilemma of benefiting from other people's oppression in Canadian society?

5. Given Canada's colonialist history and the implications that are evidenced in contemporary social and schooling practices, how might teacher candidates' engagement with colonial and post-colonial discourses further their understanding of race and racial discourses?

NOTE

[1] We use the terms teacher candidates and pre-service teachers interchangeably throughout the chapter.

REFERENCES

Chang, M. J. (1999). *The impact of undergraduate diversity course requirements on students' level of racial prejudice.* Paper presented at the annual meeting of the Association for the Study of Higher Education, San Antonio, TX.

Daniel, B. M. (2003). *Cohort group membership and individual agency in teacher education: Implication for addressing issues of race, gender and class* (Unpublished doctoral dissertation). University of Toronto, Toronto, ON.

Delpit, L. (1988). The silenced dialogue: Power and pedagogy in educating other people's children. *Harvard Educational Review, 58,* 280–298.

Duesterberg, L. M. (1999). Theorizing race in the context of learning to teach. *Teachers College Record, 100*(4), 751–775.

Frankenberg, R. (2004). Growing up White: Feminism, racism and the social geography of childhood. In A. Prince & S. Silva-Wayne (Eds.), *Feminisms and womanisms: A women's studies reader* (pp. 139–165). Toronto, ON: Women's Press.

Guba, E., & Lincoln, Y. (1994). Competing paradigms in qualitative research. In N. Denzin & Y. Lincoln (Eds.), *Handbook of qualitative research* (pp. 105–117). Thousand Oaks, CA. Sage.

Kagan, D. M. (1992). Professional growth among pre-service and beginning teachers. *Review of Educational Research, 62,* 129–169.

King, J. E. (1991). Dysconscious racism: Ideology, identity, and the miseducation of teachers. *Journal of Negro Education, 60*(2), 133–146.

Lawrence, S. M., & Tatum, B. D. (1997). White educators as allies: Moving from awareness to action. In M. Fine, L. Weis, L. C. Powell., & L. C. Wong (Eds.), *Off White: Readings on race, power, and society* (pp. 333–342). New York, NY: Routledge.

Levine-Rasky, C. (2000a). Framing Whiteness: Working through the tensions in introducing Whiteness to educators. *Race, Ethnicity and Education, 3*(3), 272–292.

Levine-Rasky, C. (2000b). The practice of Whiteness amongst teacher candidates. *International Studies in Sociology of Education, 10*(3), 263–284.

Levine-Rasky, C. (1998). Pre-service teacher education and the negotiation of social difference. *British Journal of Sociology of Education, 19*(1), 89–112.

McCarthy, C. (2003). Contradictions of power and identity: Whiteness studies and the call of teacher education. *Qualitative Studies in Education, 16*(1), 127–133.

McIntosh, P. (1990). White privilege: Unpacking the invisible knapsack. *Independent School, 49*(2), 31–36.

McIntyre, A. (1997). *Making meaning of Whiteness: Exploring racial identity with White teachers.* Albany, NY: State University of New York Press.

Rezai-Rashti, G., & Solomon, R. P. (2004). Teacher candidates racial identity formation and the possibilities of antiracism in teacher education. *Education and Society, 22*(3), 65–89.

Ross, D., & Smith, W. (1992). Understanding pre-service teachers' perspectives on diversity. *Journal of Teacher Education, 43*(2), 93–103.

Sleeter, C. E. (1992). Resisting racial awareness: How teachers understand the social order from their racial, gender, and social class locations. *Educational Foundations, 6,* 7–32.

Sleeter, C. E. (1993). How White teachers construct race. In, C. McCarthy & W. Crichlow (Eds.), *Race, identity and representation in education* (pp. 157–171). New York, NY: Routledge.

Sleeter, C. E. (2005). How White teachers construct race. In C. McCarthy, W. Crichlow, G. Dimitriadis, & N. Dolby (Eds.), *Race, identity and representation in education* (2nd ed., pp. 243–256). New York, NY: Routledge.

Solomon, R. P. (2000). Exploring cross-race dyads in learning to teach. *Teachers College Record* (Special Issue on Multicultural Education), *102*(6), 953–979.

Solomon, R. P., Portelli, J. P., Daniel, B. J., & Campbell, A. (2005). The discourse of denial: How White teacher candidates construct race, racism and 'White privilege'. *Race, Ethnicity and Education, 8*(2), 147–169.

Solomon, R. P., & Levine-Rasky, C. (2003). *Teaching for equity and diversity: Research to practice.* Toronto, ON: Canadian Scholars' Press.

Swartz, E. (2003). Teaching White pre-service teachers: Pedagogy for change. *Urban Education, 38*(3), 255–278.

Valli, L. (1995). The dilemma of race: Learning to be color blind and color conscious. *Journal of Teacher Education, 46*(2), 120–129.

REFRAMING: BEVERLY-JEAN M. DANIEL (2014)

As I have continued to teach in the field of teacher education there have been various aspects of this work and this book that continues to be highly relevant in the discourse of whiteness in a Canadian context. The content of the work contained herein provides a uniquely Canadian lens for interrogating and reconceptualizing these issues, thereby limiting the site of resistance that marks these issues as American, while challenging the "Not here in Canada" ideological positioning that the late Dr. Patrick Solomon and I had identified in our earlier research.

There is a continued failure within Canadian classrooms to provide an integrated history of the different groups in our society in a manner that can truly engage and support the development of a thinking and critical citizenry. This partial story is a very strategic project upon which liberal capitalist democracy is built and designed to maintain the existing structures of power, domination, and control, while simultaneously maintaining a veneer of equality within the Canadian space. However, this smoke and mirror trick requires the presence of a foreign or "othered" site of oppression to act as the ultimate representation of oppression and domination to thereby create a Canadian space that appears to be relatively flawless. In so doing, this trick absolves those in power of any experience of guilt or need for change, because the populace does not demand it. As such, one is unable to deny what one is truly unaware of, and further, how can those of us who question and critique the status quo speak of resistance to these dialogues, when people are unaware of the world in which they are embedded? The maxim – "ignorance is bliss" is entirely *a propos* in this context. Genosco (2001), citing the work of Deluze and Guattari, speaks of the ways in which societies are structured to produce and sustain an illusory state of being. In an interview, Deluze and Guattari (1995) in an interview indicate that, "the problem of education is not an ideological problem, but a problem of the organization of power: it is the specificity of educational power that makes it appear to be an ideology, but it's pure illusion" (n.p.).

Based on these assertions I would argue that as we move forward in the field of teacher education, what is required is a stripping away of the illusory nature of the ideal Canadian state to reveal the machinations of power and oppression at work in and through educational discourses. Such a re-analysis of the data would allow us to ask and respond to questions such as: How does the recognition that there are significant aspects of Canada's historical practices of oppression left out of the curriculum in schools change the ways we need to work with teacher education students? And further, how does the failure to include a more comprehensive picture of Canada's history beyond the multicultural ethnic, limit the efficacy of fostering a true understanding of the need to engage in anti-oppression work amongst teachers? These understanding and practices, I believe, would facilitate a more comprehensive

D. E. Lund & P. R. Carr (Eds.), Revisiting The Great White North?, 205–206.

understanding and theorization of notions of resistance (Hollander & Einwohner, 2004) while exposing strategies for challenging it.

Updating this previous research project would benefit from analyzing the data much more comprehensively through the lens of historically embedded relations of power and dominance. As well I believe that such a lens would facilitate a more globally relevant reading of the work, given the tendency of the public to read current events without and informed understanding of the historical relations that have produced the patterns of engagement that we see today. As nation-states' borders and boundaries become increasing diffuse, the changes in the demographic complement of the nations across the globe requires a more nuanced approach to education, in order that works such as these can provide direction for educational development to limit the potential for discord in classrooms.

REFERENCES

Deluze, G., & Guattari, F. (1995). *Capitalism: A very special delirium.* Retrieved from http://www.generation-online.org/p/fpdeleuze7.htm

Genesko, G. (2001). *Deluze and Guattari: Critical assessment of leading philosophers.* New York, NY: Routledge.

Hollander, J. A., & Einwohner, R. L. (2004). Conceptualizing resistance. *Sociological Forum, 19*(4), 533–554.

BRAD J. PORFILIO

WHITE FEMALE TEACHERS AND TECHNOLOGY IN EDUCATION

Reproducing the Status Quo

INTRODUCTION

I was born in 1970 and grew up in a decaying area of the Northeast, Little Italy, Niagara Falls, New York, where my mother did the major share of raising my sister and me. My racial status, unjustly, provided many privileges in schools and on the streets compared to my working-class peers of colour. Unlike my Black and Latino counterparts, in school my skin colour positioned me to have entitlements and, *a priori,* to accrue power. White skin privilege is invisible to most citizens of the dominant culture, unless brought to the centre for examination and deconstruction. For instance, my Whiteness ensured I was placed in the so-called "high-ability," academic track, treated with respect and kindness by most schoolteachers and administrators, taught curricula speckled with historical figures from my race, and provided protection from physical assaults launched by White adolescent students against the "Other" students.

Outside of school, my Whiteness shielded me from being a scapegoat for the community's social and cultural ills, such as poverty, urban decay and blight, unemployment, crime, gang violence, and drug abuse, all of which became more pronounced when political and economic leaders plotted to commodify all social life during the mid-1980s. Rather than blaming the social actors, powerful business leaders and government officials who sought to increase their profits through liquidating organizations, vocations, and social practices to more economically "desirable" locations across the globe, many White working-class citizens, paradoxically, blamed the "Other" for the downsizing of their futures and for the deleterious effects wrought by the merging of deindustrialization, globalization, and capitalism.

Unfortunately, the school system, which bestowed upon me unearned power and privileges due to my skin colour, did little to disrupt the fact that minoritized[1] populations have served as scapegoats for problems emanating from corporate and political greed in North America for the past 400 years. Our teachers did not hold the critical mindset to make us cognizant of how the economic and political systems created by White citizens have "enslaved millions of Africans in the United States and still disproportionately exploits people of colour worldwide" or position us to make

D. E. Lund & P. R. Carr (Eds.), Revisiting The Great White North?, 207–221.

Whiteness visible, so as to show how it operates to provide unjust entitlements and privileges to members of the dominant culture in various social contexts across the globe (Fischman, 1999, p. 33). They also failed to link past historical injustices to how the realities at our school, in our communities and across the globe were structured, in great part, by the dominant society engaging in the "Othering" of minoritized peoples for the purpose of maintaining its power and privileged position. Instead, my schoolteachers engendered fictitious liberalist narratives, such as America is the "land of opportunity," the Civil Rights Era magically eliminated institutional racism, and social and political institutions are open and fair to all citizens. As a result, we were left with neither the critical insight nor the sense of urgency to work collectively with other concerned citizens to build life-forms free from White privilege, racism, sexism, and homophobia, where "joy and love can flourish" (Fischman, 1999, p. 33).

It is against this backdrop that I present a set of findings from a two-year qualitative research study, which unearthed twenty White Canadian female pre-service teachers' experiences and beliefs in relation to computing technology and male-centred computing culture. The study was launched at "Border College[2]," a small independent coeducational institution located along the US/Canadian border in the Northeastern part of the United States. The Canadian female pre-service teachers each took part in two in-depth individual interviews and one focus group session. Interview data were recorded, transcribed, coded and analyzed by the researcher[3].

CONTEXT: A COMMERCIALIZED SCHOOL OF EDUCATION

The recent shift of institutions of higher education embracing a commercialized approach to teaching and learning, scholarship, and hiring practices is prevalent at Border College. A "student as a customer" approach to teacher education is a modus operandi to structure and restructure educational practices. This is ironic in light of the fact that the College prides itself on how its religious heritage melds with its current programs to produce compassionate graduates who contribute actively to the betterment of the world community.

The College has designed specific programs that allow students to become teachers without giving up their full-time jobs. With this arrangement in place, teaching students about pressing social problems takes a back seat to developing courses and programs designed to maximize profits. In this case, the College must always think about keeping students "happy" before it examines how to educate future teachers to become more critical, caring educators. Moreover, since most future teachers have internalized the dominant discourse in the wider society, which configures education as merely a commodity that is acquired when students pay their tuition fees, many teacher-educators feel compelled to meet their students' demands. They often structure their courses devoid of content that may be unsettling to their "customers." In this context, teacher education is a breeding-ground for providing future teachers skills or behaviour strategies designed to help them survive on the "job" during their first-year of teaching. Not surprisingly, many students openly resist taking courses that require them to take inventory of how their frames of references are socially constructed, analyze how wider macro-level forces influence the day-to-day realities of schools, or reflect upon how they and their peers can design democratic classroom teaching practices. This form of resistance might ultimately play into the participants' perception of the function of social and economic institutions, the nature of computing technology, and its chief functions in contemporary society.

ORGANIZATION OF CHAPTER

In this chapter, I will show how the vast majority of participants' perceptions in relation to how North America's political and economic structures function at today's historical juncture veer little from my White teachers in Little Italy. The first part of the chapter pinpoints these women's non-critical views of computing technology and computing culture. Here, the participants' narratives illuminate how their racial status, block them from recognizing the social and economic processes behind the dominant, hegemonic commercial function of computing technology and computing culture. The next part of the chapter details how the pre-service teachers' view the nature of women's and girls' relationship to computing technology and male-centred computing culture. The future teachers' narratives show that their entrenched beliefs of North America's social systems—for example, as open and fair, of "the rules of society applying roughly the same to everyone," and of effort and merit accounting for the success of social actors in political, economic, and social institutions—block them from recognizing the structural forces along with the institutional barriers that perpetuate the gendering of computing technology and culture (Sleeter, 2002, p. 37)[4]. The chapter will end with a brief discussion of how the commercialized context of teacher education has impeded White female future teachers from accruing a counter-hegemonic understanding of the nature of social stratification, from recognizing the social nature of computing technology, and from understanding how computing technology can function as a conduit to promote social justice in K-12 classrooms. Suggestions will also be made in relation to how teacher-educators and critical scholars can work to uproot commercialized imperatives, values, and practices, which are thwarting transformative projects from flourishing in schools of education.

PRE-SERVICE TEACHERS' VIEW OF TECHNOLOGY AND ITS RELATIONSHIP TO THE WIDER SOCIETY

Although the future teachers individually possess various degrees of comfortableness and familiarity with computing technology, and have witnessed computing technology being used differently in educational and social institutions, these women have embraced our society's dominant myth surrounding computers—a contrived story that positions computers as neutral artifacts that indiscriminately cure our social ills (Bryson & de Castell, 1998; Scott-Dixon, 2004; Wajcman, 2004). Their beliefs about computers align with their entrenched beliefs of North America's social systems. Their narratives show that they, like many White teachers and citizens in North America, have failed to question modernist narratives created by political and economic leaders that continue to (re)frame North America's society as progressive, fair, just and democratic (Giroux, 1991). For instance, the participants have been sold on the idea that computing skills are required to be "successful" in today's society. The following narratives are illustrative of how the participants embrace techno-centric rhetoric that conflates "success" with possessing computing skills:

I think we need to start moving towards this idea that it is a technology-based society now and a lot of jobs are requiring us to know this. Within almost every field, you have to know the basics of computers. I know just being a waitress that I've had to know how to put everything in the computer. Everything is becoming computerized. Everybody should be taught. We got to make it available for everyone. (BP[5])

I think computers are going to become implemented more and more, particularly within elementary schools. We are almost forced into using them on a daily basis because they are used in almost every occupation. (CF)
Well, I think the main thing teachers should accomplish is to help create great human beings, but you are not going to accomplish something like that without computers because in order to make a good salary, in a profession, you need to know computers. (DD)

I am sure a lot of parents want their kids on the computer, but some parents are totally against the computer and don't want their kids to even go near the computer at all, which in my opinion is a bit ridiculous because that is where society is right now. If your kids don't even know how to use a computer and they don't get exposed to it, they will be at a disadvantage. (TR)

The pre-service teachers' visions of children needing computing skills "to be a good person" or to "land a job" seem to mirror techno-centric rhetoric espoused by corporate and political leaders, rather than reflect the reality of most children and workers in contemporary society. For instance, several critical scholars have looked beyond corporate-supported techno-centric rhetoric and have found possessing basic computing skills are neither necessary nor required for an individual to obtain or function in most jobs. In today's post-industrial era, only the fortunate few (a cadre of mostly White men) will be afforded the opportunity to parlay their computing skills into "good paying" stable jobs (Aronowitz, 2004; Nolan & Anyon, 2004). Information technologies are social artifacts that are affected by the social context of use. Echoing McLaren (2002), when information technologies are "embedded heart and soul in the capitalist marketplace," they exacerbate alienation for citizens across the globe (Rizvi, 2002).

More specifically, computers serve as the linchpin of transnational capitalists' desire to liquidate their organizations, social relations, and ideologies to the so-called Third

World regions. The globalization of capital has led to the disappearance of "good jobs" in most "developed" nations while at the same time creating jobs that imperil many global citizens in less "developed" countries toiling in the midst of poverty, pollution, and hopelessness (Aguirre, 2001). Digitized information systems have sped up the circulation and production of capital, which has concentrated more wealth and power in hands of transnational corporate giants. Computers are used by the global aristocracy "to expand the free market in the interest of quick profits, to increase global production, to raise the level of exports in the manufacturing sector, and to intensify competition among transnational corporations" (Rizvi, 2002).

Furthermore, Arnowitz (2004) makes it clear, despite popular perception, that high-tech jobs have not cushioned the blow of the loss of manufacturing in North America; rather, over the past decade the high-tech sector has been dealt a "death blow" by transnational capitalists fixated on reducing labour costs to yield more profits. Corporate leaders have instituted the processes of automation, integration and networking, which have resulted in the "massive erosion, deskilling and demeaning of work" (Millar, 1998; p. 11). For women and minoritized groups, the changing economic tide has been particularly pernicious, as more sophisticated computer technologies have been used to eliminate or degrade jobs staffed by the aforementioned populations (Bromley, 2001; Milllar, 1998; Wajcman, 2004).

Corporations also are the key beneficiaries of having future teachers and other members from the dominant society embrace the dire need for children to have computing skills because they reap a large profit from getting all citizens on the Internet (Kroker & Weinstein, 1994). Certainly, large-scale corporate leaders reap great profits by selling products in cyberspace. They also feed corporate coffers by wiring schools, selling computers, and selling computer games and computer-related products.

Ironically, several of the pre-service teachers who feel computing skills are needed to obtain "good paying" jobs in today's economy have experienced the fallout from corporate greed, despite possessing computing skills. In many cases, their bouts of unemployment or part-time employment served as a key factor in enrolling at Border College. According to one teacher candidate, she was forced to leave her position as clerical worker at a natural gas utility company because "they (the business leaders) were downsizing again for I think the fourth time and I had no seniority left and took the opportunity" to enter Border College (JM).

Despite being positioned as another "statistic" in the corporatist agenda to reduce costs and increase profits, the participants are led by the liberalist belief that the social structures are molded to the interest of all citizens. They feel unemployment and downsizing are only ephemeral problems for working-class citizens. Seemingly, the economy has the power to right itself and bring peace, happiness and prosperity to all global citizens. However, the "technological genie" will neither disrupt the deskilling of workers across the globe, nor clear away the blight associated with deindustrialization, globalization, and the service economy. Redundancy, restructuring, and downsizing are impediments all workers must face in their quest to find permanent, well paying jobs. It appears joblessness and underemployment will become more pronounced in "developed" countries, as casual and contingent labour become more widespread with the implementation of neo-liberal policies and practices (Aronwitz, 2004; McLaren & Farahmandpur, 2003).

The participants' view of computing technology as a neutral artifact is also witnessed in how they gauge computing knowledge. Several future teachers equate computing competence with understanding basic programs, turning off and on computers, burning CDs, and playing video games. They feel today's students are quite proficient at computing, and in many cases, even more proficient than their elementary teachers. One participant details how students' online chatting and video game playing have allowed them to "accelerate faster" with computers compared to their elementary teachers:

> I think kids are accelerating faster than teachers. It is just part of the world that is out there. So instead of writing or phone calling each other, kids are emailing each other.... I think every kid out there needs to know how to type and get into email if they don't have a computer. Just aside from the computer, kids are learning how to play computer games. (MC)

Although the participants seem to be excited that our youth have surpassed adults in internalizing computer "skills," their excitement has led them to believe, incorrectly, that being technology-competent merely consists of starting up a computer, controlling a joystick, and sending email. By merely equating computing knowledge with grasping a set of skills surrounding how the computer functions or picking up the intricacies surrounding computing games, these future teachers are not recognizing that we must educate our next generation to have a social understanding of the artifact. In other words, a mere understanding of computing skills does not bestow computing literacy on our "Net children" or teachers. Children, as well as our future teachers, must start to wrestle with some abstract questions in order to internalize the abstract qualities and power associated with computing and computing culture. For instance, to become "computer literate," one needs to reflect deeply upon a number of questions: "How the impact of a given technology varies with the specificities of different times and places: What is going on where technology is used? Who is deciding how to apply technology and what are the objectives? What agendas do the technology become attached to?" (Carr & Bromley, 1997, p. 17).

Indeed, without this critical understanding of computing, the participants were also blocked from recognizing how their computer-use along with their family member's computing activities does very little to improve the foundations of our society, but does a tremendous amount to benefit the stockholders of corporations. Several participants detail the trajectory of their family members' computing use, all of which is tied to the current commercial hegemony of computing technology. For instance, one participant feels her family is "blessed" because her daughters utilize commercialized software from a computing company:

My kids play on the computer and they have their own games, like how to know the (United) States from Canada. In the last year, we have had cereal promotions where on your cereal boxes you can find different computer games, so we are blessed there. We have already purchased reading programs and the math programs and Barbie…I think wow at this age, their computing knowledge is amazing. (AL)

Likewise, several of the participants mentioned their most typical uses of the Internet were doing banking, playing video games, and engaging in online shopping. Although the participants' and their family members' commercialized nature of computing use was not terribly surprising since the commercial sector has come to rule the content on the Internet, and, importantly, White males, who operate the video game industry, have sold billions of dollars of computerized video games to adults and children alike (Margolis & Fisher, 2003; Millar, 1998).

However, it was surprising that none of the participants detailed how they themselves, friends, or family members used technology to confront any form of social, economic, or environmental injustices in their social worlds, let alone confront similar problems existing in the wider society. Thus, their narratives show North America's commercialized culture is positioning more and more citizens to be spectators rather than active participants in the events that shape the degree of power and resources held by global citizens. The participants' limited insight in how computing consumption and computing culture is often tied to commercial imperatives operates at another level; as I will show in the next section, it appears to block them from guiding our youth to embody a critical perspective of the current sociopolitical environment, of the nature of computing, and of computing culture, a form of understanding needed to dismantle social and economic inequalities wedded to our racist, sexist, and classist social structures.

PRE-SERVICE TEACHERS' VIEWS ON GENDER INEQUITY AND TECHNOLOGY

The future teachers also shared their insights and experiences in relation to what is fueling the gendering of computing technology and computing culture. Despite several of the participants' narratives illuminating structural and ideological barriers that position many women and girls as "incompetent" with computing technology, they remained steadfast in their belief that North America's institutions are fair and open to all individuals. Their Whiteness leads them to attribute women's and girls' success or failure in the computer world, as well as in other social contexts, to solely their "effort and agency" (Solomon, Portelli, Daniel, & Campbell, 2005, p. 160). The future teacher's narrative detailed below is representative of several women who fail to see how macro-level power relationships twin together with micro-level cultural processes to foster the gendering of computing technology and culture. The participant states:

Now in my school women are computer technicians so I don't think there are any barriers, really. Computer courses are offered to anyone who wants them.

I think it is pretty equal, now. I don't think anything would hinder women. It depends on the person doing the hiring. (CW)

Do you think that there are barriers that prevent women from advancing in the technological field today? (BP)
No not really. I know when I worked at the bank there were a lot of women there, in the technology department. They were really, really, good. Actually, I think they're good at communicating with other women in the field. I didn't see any. (CW)

So you think that the educational system will promote a more equitable playing field for boys and girls when they grow up. (BP)

Yeah. (CW)

So there's not anything that needs to be done. (BP)

No, I think that they (government and educational officials) are pushing the sciences and that on kids, like as far as boys and girls equally. That's what I see in schools. It's pretty well equal. (CW)

Although the pre-service teachers have witnessed several women within the working world as being "really, really, good" at manipulating computers, and it is true that information technology has created economic and social possibilities for some women and girls across the globe, the participants downplay the institutional barriers that women must grapple with to either acquire computing skills or demonstrate their computing prowess. In other words, they mistakenly assume the technological "success" of a few women at a Canadian "bank" or at an Ontario "school" implies most women do not face structural or ideological constraints when demonstrating their computing competency (Leonard, 2003). They also fail to see how systemic barriers, along with the masculine nature of computing technology, hinder many women and girls from becoming computing experts (Jenson, 1999; Leonard, 2003; Margolis & Fisher, 2003). Finally, their Whiteness also blocks them from looking beyond their own social worlds to see the peculiar systemic barriers the vast majority of minoritized women and girls face to be successful in the computing domain. Unlike the majority of White citizens in North America, most women and girls of colour across the globe are not "literate, nourished, or disease protected," let alone have access to computers at home or school or manipulate them in the workforce (Chandler, 2002).

Interestingly, although these women do not acknowledge that many institutional practices continue to re-inscribe computing with maleness, their narratives point to micro-level practices that position boys as the computer-experts in schools. Here one participant, who served thirteen years as an educational assistant in Ontario schools, notes how school officials have normalized and acted upon the gendered stereotype that technological expertise is associated with maleness.

> Right now, I think they are equal. I think the girls do the same thing the guys are doing on the computer. Even in the classrooms they are taught equally. So the boys, if there are any problems, usually the boys know more about the computer than girls. They will know how to access things and more of them will know what websites to go on to. (MW)

Why does this happen? (BP)

> I don't know if they have more time on the computer or the girls choose to do something differently. Whether the boys have more initiative to want to learn more or because it is easier for them, I don't know. If I could think back to whenever I had a computer problem it was always, a male, boy that helped out *never* a female. The faculty knows them (boy computer experts). They will say ask Bob, ask Eugene, whoever, it is known. (MW)

In juxtaposition, several participants believe a gender-gulf does exists with computing technology, as they find more women and girls are reticent with computing technology than are men and boys. However, their solutions to eradicating the problem shows their racial status blocks them from understanding how the wider social structure functions as well as from evaluating the role computing technology and its culture play in consolidating wealth and power in the hands of the White global aristocracy. Four future teachers believe women's computing reticence will be washed away gradually, as more women gain access to the device. They have bestowed computers with the unbridled power to eradicate this deeply rooted social phenomenon. One participant states:

> I think things are improving for women. It's happening. I heard this morning on the news that 15 percent of corporate America is women. So you have the CEO of Ebay and HP, and Xerox. It's happening. I believe it's happening. It's just happening slowly. Women are more confident, and that's happening more quickly with computers and programs. It's a normal evolution that you can't stop. (CM)

The participants are correct that some women are very "confident" using computing technology and demonstrating their computing competency in various social contexts. However, many transformative scholars illustrate that there are entrenched systemic barriers operating underneath the surface to make it arduous for women to acquire computer skills or demonstrate their computing competency (American Association of University Women Educational Foundation, 2000; Jenson, 1999; Scott-Dixon, 2004). For instance, because computing has been a masculine domain for over the past 60 years in the business world, in media outlets, and within educational circles, many women and girls have actively resisted taking up masculinized forms of technology or venturing in occupations which use technology socially associated with men (Cooper & Weaver, 2003; Henwood, Wyatt, Miller, & Senker, 2000; Sofia, 1998). They believe their identities as feminine will be under heightened surveillance or undermined (Jenson, de Castell, & Bryson, 2003, p. 562).

It has also been shown by several scholars that providing more computing access to women and girls might, paradoxically, keep more women out of computing fields. Once girls and women become familiar with the dominant qualities associated with computing, they often find it to be toxic for humanity. Some feel that the general masculine love for computer equipment is unhealthy for all members in the wider society, while others take exception to how women and children are demonized on the "Internet's Superhighway" through advertisements, movies, and music videos (Millar, 1998; Sofia, 1998). A study conducted by the American Association of University of Women (2000) suggests many teenage girls often deliberately resist developing a better understanding of computers because they believe boys' attachment to technology is a "waste of intelligence," a social activity that does little to improve society, but does much to create an outlet where boys have full-reign to assert male-centred qualities of violence, aggression and control. Similarly, many women have left technological fields because they find male-centred computing culture shallow and unhealthy, which seems a healthy response to their male-techno counterparts, who often seem to be "locked inside" their computers. For instance, some male programmers spend days and nights fixated to the computer, situated alongside streams of empty soda cans and other junk food, without any form of human contact (Margolis & Fisher, 2003; Scott-Dixon, 2004; Ullman, 1995).

Some researchers have also documented how masculine computer culture intertwines with unjust social practices to shortchange women and girls in the computer arena (Bullen & Kenway, 2002; Jenson & Brushwood Rose, 2003; Littleton & Hoyles, 2002). Although women are online more often than their male counterparts, they are far less likely to acquire educational credentials that allow them to direct the technology in more sophisticated ways. Gorski (2001) warns we must not mistake women's and girls' growing Internet usage as the elimination of the sex digital divide that continues to plague our schools and society. He states

In the year 2000 when women became over 50 percent of the online population, only 7 percent of all Bachelors-level engineering degrees were conferred to women and only 20 percent of all information technology professionals were women. So, while equality in access rates reflects an important step forward, it does not, by any useful measurement, signify the end of the sex digital divide. In fact, the glaring inequities that remain despite equality in Internet access illustrate the urgency for a deeper, broader understanding of the digital divide and a deeper, broader approach for eliminating it.

Therefore, it appears the participants' solution to "promote technology a bit more" and provide "access" will not dismantle systemic barriers that position computers as boys' toys. In fact, women's computing reticence, paradoxically, might be exacerbated by more exposure to the socially toxic computing world (Margolis & Fisher, 2003; Scott-Dixon, 2004).

DISCUSSION

The study reveals White, Canadian, female pre-service teachers enter schools of education with a shortsighted view of how power, privilege and domination gird their own as well as other citizens' social relationships. The data indicate teacher educators did little in twelve graduate courses to broaden their perspectives so as to help them recognize how White privilege "class structures, racism, sexism, and/ or the globalizing economic in interpersonal and/or structural relations" (Weis, 2004, p. 113). For instance, virtually all the future teachers' narratives reveal that critical conversation around computers and schooling was not a priority or a concern of teacher educators at Border College. Teacher educators failed to provide any discussion in relation to the social nature of technology, provide research that documents how powerful social actors at today's historical moment use computing technology to alienate and disempower many global citizens, or provide alternative visions of how schoolteachers can use computers to promote equity and social justice initiatives in K-12 classrooms[6].

To reload the counter-hegemonic struggle of preparing future teachers to become transformative intellectuals, critical scholars must broaden their collection of perspectives and methodological tools to glean how neo-liberal policies and practices are invading all aspects of teacher education (Hinchey & Cadiero-Kaplan, 2005; Porfilio & Yu, 2006). For instance, critical scholars have seldom taken a narrative approach to make sense of how sociopolitical and economic processes braid together to commodity teaching and learning in schools of education. In the classrooms, teacher educators must educate their students about how corporate logics and values are "de-theorizing" teacher education, controlling the labour of schoolteachers across the globe, and undermining the progressive and humane nature of education (Giroux & Searls, 2003; Hill, 2004; McLaren, 2005). They must also make a concerted effort to help White teacher candidates come to a critical understanding of schools, technology, and society. Future teachers must get beyond embracing salutary myths suggesting that North America's political and social institutions are focused on ameliorating the lives of all citizens, and also recognize how the power structures spawn social relations of exploitation (McLaren, 2005). They must also recognize how information technologies are used to perpetuate White supremacy, racism, sexism homophobia and their own computing reticence, while concomitantly understanding that the very same technologies can be ratcheted to dismantle the structures of oppression and create a society founded upon democracy, social justice, and equity. If teacher educators and concerned scholars do not attempt to interrogate and subvert the current perniciousness path of teacher education, we are, arguably, preparing the next generation of future teachers to reproduce the *status quo* in schools and society.

QUESTIONS FOR REFLECTION

1. According to the author, most White citizens in the mid-1980s blamed minoritized citizens for social problems in his community. What is causing this similar dynamic to unfold in Canada today? What should be done in Canadian schools to unmask the normalcy of White privilege and the ideologies that support the status quo?

2. The White Canadian female pre-service teachers at Border College held non-critical views' of social stratification, of the role technology plays in structuring social relationships, and of the gendering of computing and culture. Please reflect upon how various institutions, such as the media, schools, and families, feed into their insights.

3. How do minoritized teacher candidates' views differ from their peers' in relation to the issues outlined in question number 2?

4. What problems, especially in relation to race, unfold when commercialized imperatives and practices are the chief forces structuring the day-to-day happenings in schools of education?

5. What are some steps schools of education must take to prepare future teachers to utilize computing technology for the purposes of excavating social and economic inequalities inside and outside of K-12 classrooms?

NOTES

[1] The term minoritized is borrowed from Solomon et al. (2005, p. 166) to document that Whites are members of a racial group, "however their racialization affords them benefits that are seldom available to minority groups."

[2] "Border College" is pseudonym for the institution.

[3] The data collection process was initiated in September 2002 and ended in May 200The first set of one-on-one interviews was conducted from September 2002-December 2002. Four focus group sessions, with five participants in each session, took place in February 2003. The last set of one-on-one interviews was structured from March 2003-May 2003. The length of each one-on-one interview lasted between 45 and 90 minutes, while the focus group sessions lasted between 100 and 190 minutes. After the first round of individual interviews, in December of 2002, the author started to analyze the data. He developed 'thinking units' to help scrutinize the data. Next, he compiled the data into specific categories of information to tease out the meaning of the findings. Third, he generated specific themes that either ran throughout the data or carried a heavy emotional or factual impact. Fourth, he pored over the transcripts to determine how the participants' responses were coloured by the dominant discourses, both in the past and in the present, surrounding computers, education and gender. Fifth, he determined whether any of the participants provided information that may disconfirm the veracity of claims made during any of the interview sessions. Sixth, he analyzed the data generated during the focus group sessions, looking for both similar and different themes that emerged during the one-on-one sessions. Finally, in the fall of 2003, he began to compile the findings and link the participants' narratives to extant literature surrounding the social nature of computing technology, gender, computers and education, and the commercialization of teacher education. It should be noted computer-generated software was not used to categorize or code data. The interviews' structure prefigured how some of the data were coded. The remaining were coded by hand.

218

4   To learn more about how White pre-service teachers view social stratification, see Sleeter's (2002) article, *Teaching Whites about racism.*
5   The initials represent the pseudonyms created by the participants. "BP" in this chapter stands for the identity of the author.
6   Please see Cummins' (1995) *Brave new schools: Challenging cultural illiteracy through global learning networks* for specific examples of how in-service teachers employ technology to guide youth to have a critical understanding of the constitutive forces causing poverty, war, and hunger, to help them develop a deeper understanding of the factors that shape their understanding of self and "Other,' and to mentor them in intercultural dialogues with students across the globe, which are aimed at creating an online community of learners who work together to solve world-wide problems.

REFERENCES

American Association of University Women Educational Foundation and American Association of University Women. (2000, April). *Tech-savvy: Educating girls in the new computer age.* Washington, DC: American Association of University Women Educational Foundation.

Aguirre, L. C. (2001). The role of critical pedagogy in the globalization era and the aftermath of September 11, 2001. Interview with Peter McLaren. *Revista Electrónica de Investigación Educativa, 3*(2). Retrieved January 22, 2004 from http://redie.ens.uabc.mx/vol3no2/contenido-coral.html

Aronowitz, S. (2004). Foreword. In N. Dolby & G. Dimitriadis (Eds.), *Learning to labor in new times* (pp. ix–xiii). New York, NY: Routledge.

Bromley, H. (2001). The Influence of context: Gender, power, and the use of computers in schools. In R. Muffoletto (Ed.), *Educational and technology: Critical and reflective practices* (pp. 23–67). New York, NY: Hampton Press.

Bromley, H. (1998). Introduction: Data-driven democracy? Social assessment of educational computing. In H. Bromley & M. Apple (Eds.), *Education/technology/power: Educational computing as a social practice* (pp. 1–25). Albany, NY: SUNY Press.

Bromley, H. (1995). *Engendering technology: The social practice of educational computing* (Unpublished doctoral dissertation). Madison, WI: University of Wisconsin-Madison.

Bullen, E., & Kenway, J. (2002). Who's afraid of a mouse? Grrrls, information technology and education pleasure. In N. Yelland & A. Rubin (Eds.), *Ghosts in a machine: Women's voices in research with technology* (pp. 55–70). New York, NY: Peter Lang.

Bryson, M., & de Castell, S. (1998). New technologies and the cultural ecology of primary schooling: Imagining teachers as luddities in/deed. *Educational Policy, 12*(5), 542–568.

Carr, A., & Bromley, H. (1997, Winter/Spring). Technology and change: Preservice perceptions on agency. *Teaching Education, 8*(2), 15–22.

Chandler, R. (2002, January 17). The digital divide: Racism's new frontier. *The Guardian.* Retrieved January 28, 2006 from http://www.guardian.co.uk/comment/story/0,,634547,00.html

Cooper, J., & Weaver, D. K. (2003). *Gender and computers: Understanding the digital divide.* New York, NY: Lawrence Erlbaum.

Cummins, J., & Sayers D. (1995). *Brave new schools: Challenging cultural illiteracy through global learning networks.* New York, NY: St. Martin's Press.

de Castell, S., & Bryson, M. (1998). Retooling play, dystopia, dysphoria, and difference. In J. Cassell & H. Jenkins (Eds.), *From Barbie to Mortal Kombat: Gender and computer games* (pp. 232–261). Cambridge, MA: MIT Press.

de Castell, S. Bryson, M., & Jenson, J. (2002, January). Towards an educational theory of technology. *First Monday, 7*(1). Retrieved January 9, 2004 from http://firstmonday.org/issues /issue7_1 /castell/index.html

Fischman, G. F. (1999). Peter McLaren: A call for a multicultural revolution. An interview with Peter McLaren. *Multicultural Education, 6*(4), 32–34. Retrieved June 26, 2006 from http://www.findarticles.com/p/articles/mi_qa3935/is_199907/ai_n8876168

Giroux, H. A. (1991). Postmodernism as border pedagogy: Redefining the boundaries of race and ethnicity. In H. A. Giroux (Ed.), *Postmodernism feminism and cultural politics: Redrawing educational boundaries* (pp. 217–256). Albany, NY: SUNY Press.

Giroux, H. A., & Searls, S. (2003). Take back higher education. *Tikkun, 18*(6), 28–32.

Gorski, P. (2001). *Understanding the digital divide from a multicultural education framework.* Retrieved March 20, 2005 from http://www.edchange.org/multicultural/net/digdiv.html

Hill, D. (2004). Critical education for economic and social justice: A Marxist analysis and manifesto. In M. Pruyn & L. M. Huerta-Charles (Eds.), *Teaching Peter McLaren: Paths of dissent.* New York, NY: Peter Lang.

Hinchey, P., & Cadiero-Kaplan, K. (2005). The future of teacher education and teaching: Another piece of the privatization puzzle. *Journal for Critical Education Policy Studies, 3*(2). Retrieved September 27, 2005 from http://www.jceps.com/?pageID=article&articleID=48

Henwood, F., Wyatt, S., Miller, N., & Senker, P. (2000). Critical perspectives on technologies, in/equalities and the information society. In S. Wyatt, F. Henwood, N. Miller, & P. Senker (Eds.), *Technology and in/equality: Questioning the information society* (pp. 1–18). New York, NY: Routledge.

Jenson, J., de Castell, S., & Bryson, M. (2003). Girl talk: Gender, equity, and identity discourses in a school-based computer culture. *Women's Studies International Forum, 6*(6), 561–573.

Jenson, J. (1999). *Girls ex machina: A school-based study of gender, culture and technology* (Unpublished doctoral dissertation). Burnaby, BC: Simon Fraser University.

Jenson, J., & Brushwood Rose, R. (2003). Women@ work: Listening to gendered relations of power in teachers' talk about new technologies. *Gender and Education, 15*(2), 169–181.

Kroker, A., & Weinstein, A. M. (1994). *Data trash: The theory of the virtual class.* New York, NY: St. Martin's Press.

Leonard, E. B. (2003). *Women, technology, and the myth of progress.* Upper Saddle River, NJ: Prentice Hall.

Littleton, K., & Hoyles, C. (2002). The gendering of information technology. In N. Yelland & A. Rubin (Eds.), *Ghosts in a machine: Women's voices in research with technology* (pp. 3–32). New York, NY: Peter Lang.

Margolis, J., & Fisher, A. (2003). *Unlocking the clubhouse women in computing.* Cambridge, MA: MIT Press.

McLaren, P. (2005). *Capitalists and conquerors: A critical pedagogy against empire.* New York, NY: Roman and Littlefield.

McLaren, P., & Farahmandpur, R. (2003). The globalization of capitalism and the new imperialism: Notes towards a revolutionary critical pedagogy. In G. Dimitriadis & D. Carlson (Eds.), *Promises to keep: Cultural studies, democratic education and public life* (pp. 39–76). New York, NY: Routledge.

Millar, S. M. (1998). *Cracking the gender code: Who rules the wired world.* Toronto, ON: Second Story Press.

Nolan, K., & Anyon, J. (2004). Learning to do time: Willis's model of cultural reproduction in an era of postindustrialism, globalization, and mass incarceration. In N. Dolby & G. Dimitriadis (Eds.), *Learning to labor in new times* (pp. 133–150). New York, NY: Routledge.

Porfilio, B., & Yu, T. (2006). Student as consumer: A critical narrative of the commercialization of teacher education. *Journal for Critical Education Policy Studies, 3*(2). Retrieved June 22, 2006 from http://www.jceps.com/index.php?pageID=article&articleID=56

Rizvi, M. (2002). A radical educator's view on the media. Interview with Peter McLaren. *Znet.* Retrieved April 22, 2003 from http://www.gseis.ucla.edu/faculty/pages/mclaren

Scott-Dixon, K. (2004). *Doing it: Women working in information technology.* Toronto, ON: Sumach Press.

Sleeter, C. (2002). Teaching Whites about racism. In E. Lee, E. Menkart, & M. Okazawa-Rey (Eds.), *Beyond heroes and holidays: A practical guide to K-12 anti-racist, multicultural education and staff development* (pp. 36–44). Washington, DC: Teaching for Change.

Sofia, Z. (1998). The mythic machine: Gendered irrationalities and computer culture. In H. Bromley & M. Apple (Eds.), *Education/technology/power: Educational computing as a social practice* (pp. 29–52). Albany, NY: SUNY Press.

Solomon, P. R., & Portelli, J., Daniel, B. J., & Campbell, A. (2005). The discourse of denial: How White teacher candidates construct race, racism, and "White privilege." *Race, Ethnicity and Education, 8*(2), 147–169.

Ulllman, E. (1995). *Close to the machine: Technophilia and its discontents.* San Francisco, CA: City Lights.

Wajcman, J. (2004). *Technofeminism.* Malden, MA: Polity.

Weis, L. (2004). Revisiting a 1980s 'moment of critique': Class, gender and the new economy. In N. Dolby & G. Dimitriadis (Eds.), *Learning to labor in new times* (pp. 111–132). New York, NY: Routledge.

REFRAMING: BRAD J. PORFILIO (2014)

It has been nearly eight years since I have helped position numerous White Canadian female pre-service teachers to become critical educators, social advocates, and multicultural educators. For over six years, I served as a teacher educator to mainly this specific student population. Since the Canadian government was unwilling to provide additional resources to allow the many students who yearned to become schoolteachers obtain their teaching credentials in Canadian universities, these students often completed needed coursework in teacher education programs located across the western New York region.

Central in the brand of critical pedagogy engendered in my graduate seminars was to help students recognize that unjust institutional arrangements, policies, and practices in schools and other social contexts that are responsible for creating asymmetrical social relationships along the lines of race, class, gender, sexuality, and (dis)ability in North America. Certainly, helping students unlearn the idea that Canada is a multicultural society where one's hard work and effort are the chief factors responsible for the social and economic standing of individuals often proved difficult. Many of my students were inculcated to believe, incorrectly, that the institutional structures in Canada are predicated on improving the lives of all individuals, irrespective of their racial class status. For instance, students were typically (mis)led to believe that political and economic leaders in Canada historically engendered treaties – and currently support Aboriginal "self-determination" – so as to improve the lives of members of this social group (Slowey, 2007; Tupper & Cappello, 2008). However, in reality, the policies supported by colonial members and contemporary political leaders are designed to keep in place settler colonialism, a structural relationship predicated on allowing the political and economic elite to exploit Aboriginal labour, land, and resources.

Not coincidently, many of my students also had an arduous time conceptualizing how computing technology is a social artifact that affects and is affected by the social context of its use (Bromley, 1998). They were blinded by modernist narratives that link computing technology with the sole power to solving social problems, to improving students' educational performance, and to saving human and ecological resources. Their racialized status also blocked many of them from pinpointing the web of power relationships behind dominant forms of computing use at today's historical moment. For instance, large-scale corporations currently use computing technology to move ideologies, relationships, and practices to the so-called "Third-World" region. This technology allows corporations to "achieve major gains in productivity" and affords them the ability to "restructure, 'flexibilize,' and shed labor worldwide" (Robinson, as cited in Fassbinder, 2013). In additional to helping the global elite amass profits off the labour power of mainly people of colour across

D. E. Lund & P. R. Carr (Eds.), Revisiting The Great White North?, 223–225.

the globe, computers have been used to help the elite to amass additional profits. Over the past several years, the elite have successfully generated a culture consisting of a "corporate-interest shopping-mall Web of eBay and Amazon.com" (Norris as cited in Ali, 2011, p. 185).

Although many other scholars have pinpointed the difficulty to move students who are privileged by their racialized status to unpack the forces, structures, and social actors behind the privileges they accrue due to their social status, behind oppression faced by the "Other," and behind the social nature of computing technology and culture, I found some of my students were on the road to deeper understanding when they left my classroom several years. However, contemporary social and economic conditions may challenge teacher educators, in unpredictable ways, in their quest to guide future teachers to become critical agents of change and transformation in schools and in society. For instance, White college graduates, who are more frequently experiencing a lack of well-paying jobs, health care, housing, and educational opportunities at today's historical moment, may funnel their alienation "into a passive revolt, depotentiating and enfeebling more militant forms of insurgency by militant trade unions, socialists, and environmentalists" (Fassbinder, 2013).

On the other hand, with the guidance of critical educators, White students may funnel their alienation into nascent forms global resistance, including the Occupied Movement, the Arab Spring, workers' and youth resistance in Europe, Idle No More, and teachers' strikes and protests across the globe, against the unjust practices and structures that privilege the few at expense of many. Since computing technology has been vital in developing networks of support and promulgating oppositional ideas and social and political movements, students may recognize how computing technology can become an emancipatory lynchpin in turning their alienation into collectivist movements aimed at improving the lives of workers, children, and the environment, instead of a conduit for allowing the elite to cement their wealth and power.

In any event, the future is not foreclosed. As a critical pedagogue and scholar, I believe in the potential of education in hope (Freire, 1995). Critical education has the revolutionary power to position our next generation of White schoolteachers to be agents of change and transformation, instead of individuals who unwittingly keep in place the status quo through their teaching and computing use.

REFERENCES

Ali, H. A. (2011). The power of social media in developing nations: New tools for closing the global divide and beyond. *Harvard Human Rights Journal, 24*(1), 185–219.

Bromley, H. (1998). Introduction. In H. Bromley & M. Apple (Eds.), *Education/technology/power: Educational computing as a social practice* (pp. 1–25). Albany, NY: SUNY Press.

Fassbinder, S. (2013, June 7). His work, his visit to Turkey and ongoing popular struggles: Interview with Peter McLaren. *Counterpunch*. Retrieved from http://www.counterpunch.org/2013/06/07/interview-with-peter-mclaren/

Freire, P. (1995). *Pedagogy of hope: Reliving Pedagogy of the Oppressed.* New York, NY: Continuum.
Tupper, J. A., & Cappello, M. (2008). Teaching treaties as (un)usual narratives: Disrupting the curricular commonsense. *Curriculum Inquiry, 38*(5), 559–578.
Slowery, G. A. (2007). *Navigating neoliberalism: Self-determination and the Mikisew Cree First Nation.* Vancouver, BC: UBC Press.

SECTION 5

THE INSTITUTIONAL MERIT OF WHITENESS

LAURA MAE LINDO

WHITENESS AND PHILOSOPHY

Imagining Non-White Philosophy in Schools

INTRODUCTION

It was 1998. A young student walked down the lonely halls of the university eager to collect the final piece for her graduate school application. Classes were out, and only a few stray students remained scattered across campus preparing for final exams. She quickened her step, pushing a twist out of her eye to check the office numbers. She knocked on the door of room 223. "Come in," a voice answered from inside the office. "Can I help you?" the professor asked as she opened the door and walked into the small room. She noted a distance in the professor's tone but chalked it up to the pressures of marking final papers and exams as well as the mountain of reference letters that he probably needed to complete for his many students, including her. He was the Graduate Program Director in the department of Philosophy, after all.

"Hi there," she began, "I just came by to grab the reference letters." She tried to sound as confident as possible but something wasn't right.

"What?" he barked abruptly. "I'm not writing a letter for you!"

She was shocked and experienced the unfolding scene in devastating silence. It was as though she was living this event from a third-person perspective. It was all she could do from fainting.

He continued: "You aren't university material, especially considering the schools *you think* you'll be applying to! There will be no letter coming from me."

She tried to remain calm. She tried to keep cool. She prayed that the tears that began welling behind her eyelids would not come pouring forth, but she was unable to pretend that what she was experiencing was not affecting her.

"Sir, I don't understand. You said you'd write the letters for me. My applications are due in a little over a week…"

He interrupted her, throwing a box of tissues across his desk. "Sit down," he commanded. In her shock she complied, not knowing what else to do. "Why do you want to go to graduate school anyway?" he demanded.

D. E. Lund & P. R. Carr (Eds.), Revisiting The Great White North?, 229–238.

"I want to become a professor and teach philosophy at a university. How can I do that if I don't apply for graduate school? I'm a straight A student and I haven't gotten less than an A in any of the assignments in your classes. How much more do I need to do to be university material?" She was still having a difficult time processing his tone and the language he used with her.

"Look," he said, collecting the box of tissues he had thrown and putting it away. "You are just not university material. Just because you got into an undergraduate program does not mean you can successfully make it through a graduate program. You would not cut it here. If you still want to try and get into graduate school you'll have to consider a lesser university such as …"

She had stopped listening. A single question struggled to be voiced, but she had been taught not to consider circumstances such as these to be connected to her own Black, female body. Such thoughts ran counter to the rigid vision of multiculturalism that she had been taught to accept since she was in elementary school. So she did the only thing that she knew how to do.

She collected her things. She thanked him for his time. She left the office, took a deep breath, and began making her way off campus, and out of the only intellectual embrace she had known in her entire university career: philosophy.

As a Black woman I have often thought about Whiteness in opposition to my own racialized body. This became even more pronounced when I found my first true academic love: philosophy. Struggling to create a space for myself within the discipline—one that has typically been envisioned as colourless—contemplations of Canadian colour-blindness and the denial of hegemonic Whiteness have been disconcerting. However, my research in the area of secondary school philosophy has offered me hope, for there I am able to envision a space where discourses of Whiteness can be overtly engaged. Thus, this chapter will begin with an analysis of the normative notion of the archetypal philosopher, considering how discourses of Whiteness continue to determine who can and cannot participate in "genuine" philosophy. I will then consider the implications of the normalized notion of the (White) social world on the philosophical enterprise. The discussion will focus on Ontario secondary school philosophy classrooms as a site for challenging discourses of Whiteness within the philosophical discipline.

PHILOSOPHY AND WHITENESS: A CRITICAL LOOK

Canadian multicultural discourses have promoted the notion that students, no matter their race or ethnicity, will be treated fairly within the Canadian educational system. Whether we examine examples of elementary, secondary, or post-secondary settings, one thing holds true: as a consequence of multiculturalism, most, if not all, educational institutions in Canada take pride in their "colour-blind" discursive practices and continued "tolerance" of people of all races. However, the notion of "colour-blindness," upon closer examination, often reveals a latent failure to racialize

230

Whiteness. Consequently, Whiteness becomes the normative backdrop upon which all other races are perceived. Examining the consequences of this practice, and being open to discussions of how Canadian discourses of Whiteness are reproduced within and outside of schools are important first steps, especially in light of suggestions that educational systems are microcosms of the broader society (Dei, 1996; Yon, 2000).

Consider a simple supposition: Often unstated discourses of Whiteness frame our understanding of the Canadian educational system. Consequently, a daunting wall forever indicating, whether consciously or subconsciously, who belongs within and outside of the educational gates is created and upheld. I propose that the same is true within the discipline of philosophy. How do Canadian discourses of Whiteness shape images of who is or is not considered "a philosopher"? What are the implications of this on curricula and pedagogy in philosophy? Might secondary school philosophy classrooms be used to challenge notions of Whiteness that are so deeply embedded in the discipline itself? In order to address these issues, I believe it is necessary to examine more generally the ideas of philosophical identity to ascertain the extent of epistemic closure that arises from current notions of who can and cannot be "a philosopher" (Gordon, 2000, p. 88).

THE CREATION OF THE PHILOSOPHICAL INSIDER

The African-American philosopher Robert Birt (1987) writes, "to this day a 'black philosopher' is commonly regarded as a contradiction in terms, an anomaly or an undesired intruder into a realm that does not concern him or her" (p. 116). George Yancy (1998) concurs, noting that African-American philosophers are part of a particular "othered" reality that shapes aspects of their "being-philosophically-in-the-world" (p. 11). I take this comment one step further and suggest that other "others" in the philosophical world—women, homosexuals, and Canadian "visible" minorities interested in philosophical activities—all experience this otherness.

Philosophy has often been presumed a "disembodied" practice resulting in a further assumption that philosophical pursuits are inherently separate from the racialized bodies doing the work. Explicit discussions of race would, therefore, pose a challenge to philosophical reflections assumed to be disembodied. Notably, this concern is intensified when envisioned within the broader boundaries of Canadian multiculturalism, because both the discipline and political framework within which the discipline is functioning reinforce "politically correct" notions of "invisibility" that paradoxically make the "other" highly visible in their otherness. This heightened visibility leads mainstream philosophers not only to shy away from the embodied "other" whose body alone posses a threat to the naturalized de-racialized conception of philosophy, but also, often ends in the avoidance of, and resistance to, explicit discussions of race within the discipline. More directly, philosophy creates "others" while erecting barriers between what can be communicated epistemically across these strictly policed boundaries. "Philosophical insiders," then, are granted epistemic and institutional authority to denote who can and cannot be considered a "philosopher," while ignoring the naturalized assumptions inherent in their decisions. Based on this model, philosophers form part of the dominant philosophical culture and they are, I argue, overtly presumed to be both racially and gender neutral while, at the same time, being (paradoxically) *implicitly understood* as both White and male. As Lewis Gordon (2000) proposes, labels such as man, woman and child carry with them a "prereflexive parenthetical adjective" (p. 87). Hence, when reading the words "man," "woman," and/or "child," it is implicitly understood that we are referring to (White)man, (White)woman and (White)child (Gordon, 2000, p. 87). I contend that the same is true for the philosopher, though in this case the philosopher has two separate prereflexive parenthetical adjectives: (White)(male)philosopher[1].

Canadian multicultural discourses appear to reinforce this understanding, hindering explicit dialogues of who the "norm" really is, while implying the answer to such queries in more manipulative ways. As Clifford Jansen (2005) writes when referring to the term "visible minority," "as at least one author has pointed out, this expression implicitly contains racist assumptions because it implies that those classified as such are 'visible' to Whites. While Whites are also 'visible' to non-Whites, we have no special term for them" (p. 26). Within the philosophical discipline, this also holds true if we consider that the philosophical undertakings of non-White philosophers are most often offered outside of the core philosophical courses, if they are offered at all.

I am not arguing for the presumed Whiteness and maleness of "the philosopher" as a necessary factor in making the philosopher what he (and within the realm of my argument, I do mean *he*) is. Rather, as Gordon (2000) explains, "it is that our life world, so to speak, is such that these are [the subtextual markers'] significations" (p. 81). In other words, like Gordon, I wish to emphasize the *sociality* of the markers, while showing that it is society that manipulates the lens through which we see the world; a lens that leads Canadians to presume that with neutrality, we assume Whiteness.

The importance of social markers also hold true for the philosopher and the philosophical discipline within Canadian multicultural contexts. This rationale can be supported by Birt (1987) who claims that, "Whites decide on the reasoning methods for arriving at warrantedly assertable claims or the methods of analysis purporting to correspond to the movement of things in the world. They decide the kinds of questions considered philosophically important or interesting" (p. 117). It is the power of the (White) social world that I will examine below in order to show how epistemic closure—the ending of a process of inquiry—is produced from this conception of the philosopher.

IMPLICATIONS OF OUR (WHITE) SOCIAL WORLD

There is a yearning in many people to understand how we, as individuals, are positioned in relation to the dominant culture. This is more than a simple desire to fit in—it is a longing to be a part of, and participate in, the knowledge produced by the dominant culture. However, membership in this group often means denying our differences and believing that we—the "They"—are all the same. I am referring here to Heidegger's (1962) conceptualization of the *they-self* as it appears to add an interesting layer to discussions of philosophical alterity.

For Heidegger (1962), *Dasein*, loosely interpreted as "person," is, for the most part, the condition of (all) others. This aspect of *Dasein*'s being is termed "being-with-one-another" and leads to a sense of "averageness" or being alike (Heidegger, 1962, p. 164-165). And here "the They" emerges with its particular mode of being-in-the-world. It is beneficial to quote Heidegger (1962) at length:

> Thus the "they" maintains itself factically in the averageness of that which belongs to it, of that which it regards as valid and that which it does not, and of that to which it grants success and that to which it denies it. In this averageness with which it prescribes what can and may be ventured, it keeps watch over everything exceptional that thrusts itself to the fore. Every kind of priority gets noiselessly suppressed... This care of averageness reveals in turn an essential tendency of Dasein which we call the "leveling down" [*Einebnung*] of all possibilities of Being (p. 165).

Heidegger (1962) continues,

> Distantiality, averageness, and leveling down, as ways of Being for the "they," constitutes what we know as 'publicness' *die Offentlichkeit*. Publicness proximally controls every way in which the world and Dasein get interpreted, and it is always right... By publicness everything gets obscured, and what has thus been covered up gets passed off as something familiar and accessible to everyone (p. 165).

The strength of this affiliation of sameness is undeniable and, more importantly, manipulative, for as "the They" take over as the primary mode of being-in-the-world, their epistemic authority denotes, rightly or wrongly, what can and cannot be conceived of as knowledge in the name of "normalcy." The power of the social "they" world is so strong that it not only provides epistemic authority to particular non-threatening knowledge claims but also creates "insiders" and "outsiders" in the world. With regard to the philosophical enterprise, "the They" support naturalized ideas that the philosopher is a White male and, based on this assumption, hinder the infiltration of the philosophical kingdom by all that are perceived as different.

In light of the above, as a Black female interested in pursuing philosophy within a Canadian multicultural context, I feel that I am taking part in a continuous battle with mainstream philosophy's conceptions of a philosophical insider, and that, most importantly, my positioning is always from the outside. As Yancy (1998) notes, "the 'aboutness' of philosophy has historically had nothing to do with Black people; rather, philosophy was *about* "othering," silencing, muting, and effectively invisibilizing" (p. 4). Within the academy, there is rarely an opportunity to voice my position or to suggest the importance of talking explicitly about race without attempts by those with epistemic authority to discredit the relevance of such dialogues since philosophy, at least until relatively recently, did not deal with such topics. Why are explicit discussions of race so strongly resisted?

In *The Emperor's New Clothes*, Williams (1997) discusses what she terms "the greatest public secret": race. In her analysis, the facticity of racial difference is hidden by discourses of "colour-blindness," which suggest that no differences exist amongst human beings, and that we are all treated equitably. While these overt opinions are being propagated, we, the public, *know* that we are keeping a secret—that we see, read, understand, and experience the world through a racialized lens (Williams, 1997, p. 12). In a similar fashion, Heidegger (1962) suggests that "the They" tell comparable tall-tales. "Racial differences do not exist," say "the They." "Don't you see? The world is colourless!" While "the They" contend that philosophical circles hold no racial or gender biases, philosophical circles paradoxically hold steadfast to the hierarchies of racial difference, taking note of who belongs inside and outside of their socially constructed boundaries. However, this dispute takes place within hidden spaces, outside of earshot of the "others" who are said not to exist.

Birt (1987) also discusses this issue, noting that the African-American philosophical agenda of bringing claims of colour-blindness into question begins by exposing that,

> the dominant agenda's claim to be race and colour-blind only appears to be true when simplistically looked at in isolation. But if viewed in a larger dynamic of philosophy as a collection of discourses (definitive of what is philosophically significant of what counts as philosophy at all), the dominant agenda is inclined to be supportive of racism in society. (p. 118)

Consequently, the "other" is allowed to dabble in philosophical studies but will never be granted approval if that individual considers trying to infiltrate the inside and lay claim to the label "philosopher."

Often, it seems philosophers are unable to see beyond differences of race, gender and/or sexuality when deciding who is allowed to play within the boundaries of philosophical discourses. The clash between philosophers' naturalized sensibility of who does and does not belong within the boundaries of academic philosophy, and the "other" that stands before them, requesting to share in their philosophical epistemological discourses, is often considered an irrelevant concern. Yet, it is not irrelevant, but an important aspect of philosophical epistemology, for it is these presumed ideas of who belongs and does not belong in the discipline that form the backdrop upon which new epistemologies are created, proliferated and, consequently, more deeply entrenched. Using this understanding of the creation of philosophical insiders as the basis, I will discuss how secondary school philosophy classrooms in Ontario might become possible sites in which to challenge hegemonic notions of Whiteness within the philosophical discipline.

SECONDARY SCHOOL PHILOSOPHY: CHALLENGING WHITENESS

At the university level, undisclosed discourses of Whiteness that frame the discipline itself have forced discussions of race and "other philosophies" to create their own spaces in the margins. Conversely, an examination of the Ontario Ministry of Education's secondary school philosophy curriculum presents a decidedly different scenario. I argue that it is within these classrooms that an opportunity to challenge inherent discourses of Whiteness can be initiated.

During the 1994-1995 academic year, a small number of high school classrooms across Ontario began introducing an optional stand-alone philosophy credit to their students. In this first year, enrollment in the optional philosophy course was recorded at 200 students in some 10 to 15 schools. Student enrollment increased significantly due to informal discussions among teachers and students about the benefits of secondary school philosophy (Jopling, 2001). Jopling (2001) notes that,

> By 1997-1998... word had spread through informal teacher networks and subject associations, and enrolment for the course (according to Ministry statistics) had grown to 5,500, in over 135 secondary schools across the province—a 27-fold increase in enrolment in just four years! In 1998-99, enrolment was over 6000, in some 140 schools (of the province's approximately 800 secondary schools). (p. 39)

The number of students interested in taking this optional credit continues to grow. In the 2003-2004 school year, the Ministry of Education recorded that 28,254 students were enrolled in philosophy courses (grades 11 and 12) in 290 schools across Ontario http://www.arts.yorku.ca/phil/undergrad.html#PHILOSOPHY_ HS. Based on these statistics it seems clear that, with scores of Canadian secondary school students choosing to enroll in philosophy, it has become increasingly important to ensure that the content be socially conscious. Moreover, challenging the normative discourse of Whiteness apparent in traditional philosophy classrooms is necessary.

In *The Ontario Curriculum Grades 11 and 12, Social Sciences and Humanities* document, it is stated clearly that, "Philosophy trains students in critical and logical thinking, writing, and oral communication, and *acquaints them with principles underlying their own values and beliefs as well as those of other people and traditions*" [emphasis added] (Ministry of Education, 2000, p. 111). Hence, the Ministry of Education officially requires that teachers incorporate topics that are relevant to their students. Specifically, the Grade 11 course includes "Philosophy in Everyday Life" as one of the five strands examined in the classroom[2]. Similarly, Ministry documents for the Grade 12 course state explicitly that within Metaphysics, Epistemology, Ethics, and Social and Political Philosophy the student is required to demonstrate the relevance of the particular strand to concrete everyday issues (Ministry of Education, 2000, p. 119-123)[3]. Could the inclusion of everyday issues in philosophy classrooms become the opening through which to introduce critical discussions of Whiteness?

The extent to which teachers choose to transform policy into practice varies and studies focusing on such issues are most valuable. Sadly, this particular paper has left these concerns unaddressed. In spite of this shortfall, I would like to offer two interconnected considerations. Firstly, what would happen if, when discussing issues of everyday importance to students in philosophy classrooms, teachers incorporated issues of race into their discussions? Such an inclusion may signal a change in how the traditional philosophy classroom is perceived. This novel philosophical environment, by moving discussions of race from the marginalized periphery into a central position within philosophical dialogue, may help to breakdown the theoretical wall separating philosophical insiders and outsiders that has plagued the discipline for so many years.

Secondly, if teachers did incorporate issues of race in their classrooms, what would happen if they began with Whiteness? In short, what benefit might there be from attempts to begin a dialogue about race not from the typical perspective of the "other," but rather, beginning from another contentious standpoint—that of Whiteness? Such an overt challenge to traditional sensibilities could help unearth common assumptions about who can play within the boundaries of philosophical dialogues. Taking these considerations seriously could become a catalyst for positive change by broadening the boundaries of the discipline of philosophy and, consequently, challenging normalized notions of "the philosopher" and his discipline.

DISCUSSION

This analysis has revolved around one basic assumption: that philosophy classrooms are opportune sites of self-reflexivity. But is this really the case? In short, what is the overarching goal of a philosophy classroom? Remarkably, the overall aims of secondary school philosophy have remained the same over several years. As early as 1976, some of these goals included enhancing critical thinking in students and recognizing the ideological underpinnings of the world around them in the hopes of increasing the students' understanding of themselves (Link, 1976). Similarly, theorists including Jopling (2001) have forwarded analogous goals for philosophy classrooms.

> Training in philosophy can provide high school students with powerful tools of analysis and critical reasoning, new ways of looking at the world, and new approaches to problem solving. It can also help students to situate their inquiries within the context of a 2,500-year-old discipline, and thereby develop their sense of themselves as part of a shared and ongoing conversation. (Jopling, 2001, p. 37)

I believe these overarching goals to be important tools for students who have to find ways to live in a racialized body. Moreover, I contend that if the secondary school philosophy teacher takes seriously the goal of taking up hegemonic notions of Whiteness that have beleaguered the discipline of philosophy, than students may be provided with the tools to re-think and re-evaluate hegemonic ideologies both within and outside of their school culture. As Tatum (1997) argues, discussions about race and racism must be initiated in order to create a more positive world for all people.

> We need to talk about it at home, at school, in our houses of worship, in our workplaces, in our community groups. But talk does not mean idle chatter. It means meaningful, productive dialogue to raise consciousness and lead to effective action and social change. (Tatum, 1997, p. 193)

I maintain that we need to talk about race. We need to make these discussions explicit in order to counter notions of colour-blindness that pervade Canadian discourses. We need to talk about race because it is time to acknowledge and dispose of one of today's most prominent "public secrets." It is only if we acknowledge that we are not colour-blind, but rather, *far too colour conscious* that we might have a chance to combat racism. Why shouldn't we arm our philosophy students with the necessary intellectual ammunition to participate in this fight?

QUESTIONS FOR REFLECTION

1. Is "applied" or "practical" philosophy genuine philosophy, and would race be an applicable topic for discussion in such a context?
2. Do discussions of race in secondary school philosophy classrooms necessarily include discussions of Whiteness? In short, is it necessary to consider Whiteness in discussions of race?
3. Are discussions of Whiteness better executed as topics on their own, outside of any other discourses of race that may arise in schools?
4. Does Canadian multiculturalism hinder possibilities of discussing Whiteness openly within schools and communities?
5. How can discussions of everyday issues in philosophy classrooms help initiate self-reflective practices on the part of students and teachers regarding the effects of Whiteness on the discipline?

NOTES

[1] It might be argued that the philosopher carries with him three separate prereflexive parenthetical adjectives: (White)(male)(*heterosexual*)philosopher. This is likely the case, especially in light of homosexuality being largely repressed throughout history. In spite of this, I have chosen race and gender as the two prereflexive categories for no reason other than the use of my own personal experiences, which have focused on concerns of gender and race as a springboard for this particular discussion.

[2] The five strands for the Grade 11 course are as follows: Philosophical Questions, Philosophical Theories, Philosophy in Everyday Life, Applications of Philosophy to Other Subjects and Research and Inquiry Skills.

[3] The seven strands for the Grade 12 course are Metaphysics, Logic and the Philosophy of Science, Epistemology, Ethics, Social and Political Philosophy, Aesthetics, Research and Inquiry Skills.

REFERENCES

Birt, R. (1987). Negation of hegemony: The agenda of philosophy born of struggle. *Social Science Information, 26*(1), 115–127.

Braithwaite, K. S., & James, C. E. (1996). *Educating Black Canadians.* Toronto, ON: James Lorimer.

Eze, E. C. (1997). *Postcolonial African philosophy: A critical reader.* New York, NY: Blackwell.

Forsyth, D. (1971). *Let the Niggers Burn!: The Sir George Williams University affair and its Caribbean aftermath.* Montreal, PQ: Our Generation Press.

Gordon, L. (2000). *Existentia Africana: Understanding Africana existential thought.* New York, NY: Routledge.

Heidegger, M. (1962). *Being and time.* New York, NY: Harper & Row.

Jansen, C. (2005). *Canadian multiculturalism.* In C. E. James (Ed.), *Possibilities and limitations: Multicultural policies and programs in Canada.* (pp. 21–33). Halifax, NS: Fernwood.

Jopling, D. (2001). "The coolest subject on the planet": How philosophy made its way in Ontario's high schools. *Analytic Teaching: The Community of Inquiry Journal, 21*(2), 37–42.

Mills, C. (1998). *The racial contract.* Ithaca, NY: Cornell University Press.

Williams, P. (1997). *Seeing a color-blind future: The paradox of race.* New York, NY: Farrar, Strauss & Giroux.

Yancy, G. (Ed.). (1998). *African-American philosophers, 17 Conversations.* New York, NY: Routledge.

Yon, D. (2000). *Elusive culture; Schooling, race and identity in global times.* New York, NY: State University of New York Press.

REFRAMING: LAURA MAE LINDO (2014)

Taken as a whole, it appears that little has changed since the initial publication of my chapter, *Whiteness and Philosophy* in 2007. The philosophical discipline remains as White today as it was in 1998 when a young, Black woman walked down the halls of the university, seeking a letter from the Graduate Program Director who held the key to her future in (or outside of) philosophy.

On May 27, 2011, education correspondent for *The Guardian*, Jessica Shepherd (2011), presented data from the Higher Education Statistics Agency in the UK. Their statistics revealed that of more than 14,000 British professors, only 50 were Black. Noting that similar numbers had been produced in 2003, Black academics in the UK again argued for the need to address this lack of representation in the academy. Thinking through these data, the *Feminist Philosophers* website included these details on their blog, adding that it did not appear that any of the 50 Black professors in Britain specialized in philosophy. Citing Kathryn T. Gines (2011), the *Feminist Philosophers* blog continued: "Still fewer than thirty Black women (including Black women who are not African American) hold a PhD in philosophy and work in a philosophy department in academia" (p. 435). Reader comments about these findings persisted for over a year on the blog, with people citing more research, more statistics and more concrete facts demonstrating that the status quo remained unchanged over the years – more work was needed to shift the hegemonic, race-based norms upon which the discipline of philosophy was based.

Seeking details of Canadian philosophical programs and the plight of Black philosophers here, I was again reminded of the firm grip of Whiteness on the philosophical discipline. Statistics provided by Service Canada (2012) on university professor employment across the country showed a clear discrepancy among male (62 percent) and female (38 percent) university professors, but stated nothing of the race and/or ethnicity of the professors in question or of their area of expertise and/or disciplinary affiliations. Gosine (2007) described the academic experiences of Black Canadians in the Canadian university system, but none of the 16 academic participants interviewed worked or studied in the discipline of philosophy. These silences spoke to me, and with a preliminary search for statistics on Black philosophers working in Canadian institutions, I have readied myself for the emergence on Canadian soil of a story similar to that of the UK.

And yet, I am that young woman who boldly challenged the Whiteness of philosophy with her mere presence in Canadian philosophy classrooms. I have since completed a doctoral degree in education, using that opportunity to expand my own thinking and theorizing on structural Whiteness in academic programs. Most interestingly, I have found a name for the theoretical thinking provided at the end of *Whiteness and Philosophy* under the guise of two interconnected considerations (i.e.,

D. E. Lund & P. R. Carr (Eds.), Revisiting The Great White North?, 239–240.

first, that expanding traditional philosophical spaces to consider the impact of race on these ever evolving philosophical dialogues is crucial and second, that explicit discussions of Whiteness in philosophy classrooms – considering its shape, its form, its assumptions and its limitations – can help initiate these important discussions). It is with a turn to critical race theory (CRT) that I have been able to find more words to describe my encounter with the Whiteness of philosophy. There, CRT has shown me that sharing stories like the one used to introduce my critical examination of the discipline of philosophy provides a wealth of opportunities for re-imagining the Canadian academic landscape.

Sharing these stories allows for the merging of the lived experience of Whiteness with the theoretically understood realities of living in a Black body. Sharing these stories, then, becomes an attempt to think differently about a field I have been so passionate about. It also provides a reminder of the importance of bringing young people back into the centre of educational dialogues. Their lived experiences are in need of deeper reflection and the discipline of philosophy can provide for them the much-needed space to think critically and reflexively on their place in today's world. For marginalized youth in particular – young people whose circumstances and choices have led them to stray from traditional school settings – providing them with the tools of philosophy to deconstruct and re-construct their own understanding of how Whiteness works in their world is indispensible to their growth as citizens of this world. In short, to teach "the system" to youth in crisis *is* to teach Whiteness. And the need for work like this remains as key an aspect of our world today as it was when this article first came out in print some seven years ago.

REFERENCES

Feminist Philosophers. (2011, June 1). How few blacks are there in philosophy? Retrieved from http://feministphilosophers.wordpress.com/2011/06/01/how-few-blacks-are-there-in-philosophy/

Gines, K. T. (2011). Being a black woman philosopher: Reflections on founding the Collegium of Black Women Philosophers. *Hypatia, 26*(2), 429–443.

Gosine, K. (2007). Navigating the Canadian university system: An exploration of the experiences, motivations, and perceptions of a sample of academically accomplished black Canadians. *Journal of Contemporary Issues in Education, 2*(1), 3–21.

Service Canada. (2012). *Analytical text 4121: University professors*. Government of Canada. Retrieved from http://www.servicecanada.gc.ca/eng/qc/job_futures/statistics/4121.shtml

Shepherd, J. (2011, May 11). 14,000 British professors: But only 50 of them are black. *The Guardian*. Retrieved from http://www.theguardian.com/education/2011/may/27/only-50-black-british-professors

DEBBIE DONSKY & MATT CHAMPION

DE-CENTERING NORMAL

*Negotiating Whiteness as White School Administrators in a
Diverse School Community*

INTRODUCTION

Recognizing, reflecting on, and working towards dismantling our own biases, privilege, and Whiteness as elementary school administrators is a challenge we meet each day in the school setting. We work together at an elementary school with approximately eight hundred students from Kindergarten through grade eight in the greater Toronto area. This school[1] has a diversestudent population, including students who are either first- or second-generation Canadians with origins in East Asia, Southeast Asia, the Middle East, and the West Indies. Approximately 85 percent of the families at our school have self-identified as either Cantonese-, Mandarin- or Chinese-speaking when enrolling their children. Less than one percent of our students are White.

How do we, as White[2] administrators, provide leadership in a community that is different from our own? What is the place of a White administrator within the anti-racist discourse to rupture power and privilege, and to transform learning environments to make way for multiple ways of knowing? Anti-racist theorists have different opinions on this issue. Dei (1996) suggests that "the interrogation of Whiteness can, and should be, an entry point for members of dominant groups in society to join the antiracism debate" (p. 28) and that "there needs to be a recognition of how one is helped or hindered by such a system" (p. 4). Suggestions from hooks (2003) and Lee (2003) underscore the use of language as a place to start. A recognition and purposeful transformation of language that perpetuates race and racism within educational settings begins to acknowledge the White supremacist discourse, which disregards systemic racism. Claims of "colour-blindness" (Delpit, 1994; Sleeter, 1993, pp. 161-163) among educators must be problematized and recognized as the denial that racism exists at all. Delpit (1988) also suggests that, "those with power are frequently least aware of—or least willing to acknowledge—its existence [and] those with less power are often most aware of its existence" (p. 282). This is echoed by Solomon, Portelli, Daniel, and Campbell (2005), who found that White educators are perceive their privilege as invisible and that "the failure to examine notions of whiteness facilitates the maintenance of its incorporeal nature thereby reinscribing its dominating power" (p. 148).

D. E. Lund & P. R. Carr (Eds.), Revisiting The Great White North?, 241–249.

This chapter investigates the reflective[3] process we engage in as administrators challenged with issues related to our own privilege and Whiteness working within the reality of systemic racism and bias. To change the school as a place of compliance which acts to support a "mythical White norm" (Lorde, 1990, p. 292)—privileging some and not others while supporting the myth of meritocracy—we must challenge our own perceptions of each situation and understand our own roles[4] in these situations from different perspectives through dialogue with students, parents, staff, and members of the broader community.

THE ADMINISTRATORS

We have identified ourselves based on personal histories, experiences and understandings to frame the stories and struggles. At the same time, we recognize the privilege of telling these stories. Solórzano and Yosso (2002) suggest:

> Whether told by people of color or Whites, majoritarian stories are not often questioned because people do not see them as stories but as "natural" parts of everyday life. Whether we refer to them as monovocals, master narratives, standard stories, or majoritarian stories, it is important to recognize the power of White privilege in constructed stories about race. (p. 28)

Debbie: My grandparents came to Toronto between the two world wars as young children, leaving siblings and other relatives behind. There was a brief window of opportunity for them to escape the pogroms of Eastern Europe and Russia before immigration laws changed and subsequently refused entry of Jews to Canada. Although my great-grandparents endured many hardships prior to their arrival in Canada, by the time the third generation lived in Toronto, we knew nothing of those days. They simply weren't talked about. Assimilation into Canadian culture was all that mattered. I lived out my childhood in a suburban community in a five-bedroom house in an area that was predominantly Jewish and upwardly mobile. I was not aware of my privilege growing up because many of the people I interacted with always seemed to have more than I did. They travelled more, had better clothes, and more expensive cars. I knew that being Jewish made me different. However, when surrounded by those who are the same as you, as a child, it is hard to understand difference.

It wasn't until I attended university in another part of Ontario that I began to understand what it meant to be Jewish, or to be defined as Jewish by someone else, to be named[5]. As a first-year student, I had pennies thrown at me; I had JEW scratched into the doorframe of my residence-apartment; I was not invited to the Christmas party for "fear of offending" me.

My own journey has been one of understanding and reflection as to my role as an ally in anti-racism education[6]. As a Jewish woman, I have had to negotiate my place in this dialogue with colleagues, professors, students, and parents. I have had to struggle with understanding Whiteness and privilege, and how I am implicated in the discourse of power and oppression. Now, as a leader in education, I am always cognizant of this power, and reflect on my practice from this place.

Matt: Ten years ago, the land on which my current school sits and the surrounding community was a farmer's field. My father, who was a farm implement dealer, probably knew the owners well, and very likely attended school with them. I grew up in this small agricultural community, and went to elementary school where there was one Chinese student, and her family owned the local Chinese food restaurant. My classmates were in awe of this student because she drove a car to school. She was 16 in grade 7 while the rest of us were 12. At that time this is how English-as-a-Second-language (ESL) education was handled.

I grew up, bought a home with my wife, and started my family in this community. Over the years I watched urban sprawl turn that community of 4500 into a metropolitan suburb of close to 220,000 where bank machines function in two languages, English and Chinese, in spite of the fact that Canada's two official languages are English and French. After 12 years, my marriage dissolved and I became the custodial parent of my three children aged 4, 6, and 8. It was at this time that I first became aware of my White privilege. I was teaching in a school where many of the parents were new immigrants. I was living in a community where I was well known, my family was close by to offer support, working in a school system that I had known since kindergarten, and ironically, I felt totally alone. How did these parents handle the challenge of raising children in a culture that bore no resemblance to the world they grew up in, working and living in environments where they had to fight for respect, and often taking several jobs in order to support their families? It was clear to me that I had it easy by comparison, and, in my eyes, I was barely surviving.

THE STUDENTS

A young boy in grade two is experiencing difficulty at school and at home. He has severe anxiety provoked by perfectionism and high intelligence, and frustration escalates each day at school. His mother speaks Cantonese and comes into the school tired, crying, frustrated—silenced in words but not in actions. His father speaks both Cantonese and English. He has tried to help both his son and wife but does not know what to do. He comes to the office and requests that his son be taken out of his current classroom because he feels it is the teacher's fault that his son is struggling. The father wants his son to be in the Cantonese-speaking teacher's room instead. He refuses to come to school.

We go to the house to bring him to school because the mother cannot fight with him anymore. We call on the attendance counselor for support. Throughout the year, we engage the special education team, the behaviour team, and the community-liaison to aid the school's ability to communicate with the mother. We invite the mother in to work for the first hour of school in the library hoping this will help her son come to school. This works for a week and then the same patterns ensue.

Matt: As a principal, one of the many roles I fulfill at the school is one of support—for students, teachers and parents. When a child's behaviour or academic success is brought to my attention, it is important to take the time to build a relationship with the parents so they don't feel judged or take the situation personally. Supporting parents in this way when they have very little experience with Canadian schools, and they speak a language other than English, presents new challenges. If we consider that it is our own barrier to communicate with the parents of our students, we have then shifted the deficit onto our own ability to function within the community rather than the community's ability to function in the school.

We decide, with the support of the special education teachers and other resources that the best option is to move the student. At least this way, the mother will be able to communicate with the teacher, and we will be able to work with the family more effectively. The parents continue to work with counseling services and medical support. The move to the new classroom does not change the boy's behaviour; in fact, it is more severe. He becomes violent. What has changed is our ability to support and communicate with the family. We have gained their trust and work together as a team.

The first teacher expresses her frustration with our decision to remove the child. She feels that this is a reflection on her and her ability to "handle" the child. She thinks that the request to move the child in the first place is acquiescing to the wishes of the parents and demonstrates their lack of respect for her, and that by supporting the parents in their request, we have disrespected her rights. She feels that we have given this "badly behaved" child too much power rather than understanding that the move was to empower the family and the relationship between school and home in the best interest of the student.

Matt: I have learned that, generally, when we are faced with a challenging child, the behaviour we experience at school is far less than what the parents face at home. Often, these parents have run out of strategies to cope with their child, and feel they are to blame for the unacceptable behaviour. More than anything they need the support of the school. Our mandate is to support student learning. The resistance from the original teacher was discussed with her but, ultimately, she was unwilling to accept the need for the transfer to enable the family. Student success has to be the driving force behind our decisions.

THE STAFF: THE OCCASIONAL TEACHER AND TRUST

Imagine if every time you walked into a school the secretary or whomever you met looked at you and questioned your intent, found you to be suspicious. This would only serve to heighten insecurities when anticipating this type of reception in the schools.

I (Matt) am going outside to supervise the entry into the school at the beginning of the day. A man is waiting at the front desk before school starts. He has a closely shaved beard, brown hair, and brown skin. He waits patiently behind the students and parents who are awaiting the assistance of our secretary. I went outside to supervise the entry to the school and when I returned the secretary asked me to check on this teacher. I went down to the classroom, and he was standing at the front of the class speaking clearly to the students. He was answering their questions, and had already learned some of their names. He smiled at me, and went over to help the students with his morning assignment. His rapport with the students was natural, as if he had met these children before. I had no concerns. I returned to the office and talked to the secretary about bias, and how we judge people based on their appearance, stereotypes perpetuated in the media.

Debbie: As administrators, we must constantly examine our own prejudices, and challenge others on staff to do the same, which is neither easy nor comfortable. Ryan (2003) suggests that administrators are "limited by their own life histories and ideological frameworks" (p. 129). Our board policy clearly states that "all persons are entitled to work and learn in an environment that promotes human rights and equity of opportunity, free from discrimination and harassment" (York Region District School Board, 2006) and yet, in reality, violations of the policy and people's rights occur regularly.

There is resistance to discuss these incidents openly, as anonymity and fear of being exposed make it difficult within a school group. Pointing fingers and accusing colleagues of racist actions and judgments can immediately sever conversations rather than begin them. Carr (1997) has found that "principals emphasized how multi-faceted, complex and diverse school settings are, arguing that the implementation of policies requires a great deal of finesse, local understanding, coalition-building and 'management'" (p. 45). Within the shadow of political correctness, we silence and condemn our colleagues who do not belong to the dominant group through whispers and judgment, while we continue to benefit from racism on a daily basis through permanent jobs, and representation of their cultures in schools through staffing, curriculum, and communication.

The words "start where they are, not where you want them to be" echo in my head, and yet, Brathwaite (2003) suggests that "we need to be alarmed at the slow pace of change in the curriculum" (p. 11) as well as the equally lethargic response to a change in attitudes and actions in our schools.

THE COMMUNITY: BIAS AND NEGOTIATING IDENTITIES WITH PARENTS

A bullying incident occurred at our school where two boys continuously taunted a girl in class, in the halls, at recess and at lunch. The girl had asked the boys to stop, walked away, asked for help, and yet the boys continued to taunt her. Finally, she retaliated by hitting one of the boys. Each student was spoken to, and each student was asked to write a report about what happened. The reports were sent home to be signed by parents, thereby informing parents about the incident and ongoing bullying. The boys were Muslim, one from Pakistan and the other from Iran. The girl was of Chinese origin.

245

Debbie: The father of the boy who was hit came into the office to speak to the principal, uttering threats of calling the *Toronto Star*, the superintendent, or anyone who would listen. He was irate. He son would not do such a thing. How can we condone the behaviour and violence of the girl who hit his son? His son was, for him, clearly the victim. The father suggested that perhaps the girl was not punished because, as a woman, I had supported her "violence against him." I sat beside this father in Matt's office while he criticized and judged me, just as he felt I had done to his son. While the father addressed Matt as Mr. Champion, he peered at me out of the corner of his eye and referred to me as "she" as he scowled at me.

When parents make threats to escalate issues, we contact our superintendent and inform her that a call may be coming in regard to this event. Following the event, Matt and I discussed the father's reaction. It was clear that he did not agree with the allegations made of his son as a "bully" and yet the letter, written by his son, stated that he was bullying another student. His reaction could be explained as one of an irate parent, frustrated by allegations made of his son, but Matt and I both felt it was deeper, as he also suggested that this issue was made to victimize his innocent son, due to my belief that violence against men was acceptable.

I had a personal reaction to these allegations as I felt that the father judged my choices because I was a woman. I felt conflicted by my reaction to this event. I had to question whether I became defensive because of the father's words or was it because these words were coming from a Muslim man? Did I judge him by stereotypes associated with his cultural group or was he judging me as woman? When I am in a position of leadership, is there room for my own victimization? Do I abdicate my right to be discriminated against because I hold power within the school? Relations of power and privilege are so complex, and I continue to grapple with this incident and my reaction to it, asking myself, was he just protecting his son or was he fighting something more? To utter my thoughts to him when I, myself, felt silenced was not an option. Some situations leave me with more questions than answers.

DISCUSSION

In recounting some of our experiences, we also write the stories of others, and choose which stories to tell. This challenges us to question our own notions of identity within the context of educational leadership and negotiating Whiteness, understanding that "the notion of identity is intertwined with the processes of knowledge production" (Dei, 1996, pp. 31-32). In doing my thesis (Debbie), I was confronted with a situation in a classroom. We were working on a unit for the Ontario Grade Four Social Studies curriculum, Medieval Times. Students had chosen their topics and were researching the various areas linked to the curriculum expectations. There were two Muslim girls who had chosen the topic of celebrations during Medieval Times. They were busily writing about Christmas celebrations and I asked them if they thought there were any holidays for Muslim people to which they responded, "there weren't any Muslim people in the medieval times" (Donsky, 2006, p. 91). If the knowledge we share with the students does not reflect multiple perspectives, then we are compliant in the perpetuation of Whiteness and White history as *the* history. If these pertinent questions are not asked, then students continue to study history as a denial of their own history and identity. How do we move our teachers towards asking these questions rather than remaining complacent and compliant with White supremacist interpretations of history within their classrooms?

There is a responsibility in naming the representations of others. To speak in pseudonyms and pronouns does not offer complete anonymity. We are accountable to the students, their families, and the staff at our school, the District School Board and ultimately the Ministry of Education. To reflect in a public space, such as this text, is to open ourselves, and those we represent, to scrutiny. Dei (2003) asserted that "the question today is not really to ask who can do anti-racist work. Rather, it is for each of us to ask whether we are prepared to face the risks and consequences that come with doing such work" (p. 5).

Each situation described can be seen from different vantage points. As administrators we either work towards inclusion by creating places and spaces where multiple perspectives can be heard or we are compliant with the systemic "othering" of our communities. The assumption and perception that a student struggles to function within a school can also be understood from a critical perspective that it is in fact the school and those within that school who create the struggle while supporting the culture of power within its walls which results in a deficit model rather than a model based in assets. Rather than "students at-risk" we must speak and problematize from the perspective of "students who have historically been underserved" (Lindsey, Robins, & Terrell, 2003, p. xx). Parental involvement can be viewed from the deficit model, which assumes that parents who are not present in the school are also not present in their own children's lives and schooling—an assumption often articulated within schools. From a critical perspective, we try to understand the many ways in which we can engage parents in *our*[7] schools always from the perspective that we are serving "other people's children" (Delpit, 1988). Staff development and open dialogue around our own biases and actions as they intersect and are influenced by our Whiteness is an issue which is met on a day-to-day, informal basis as well as through staff meetings, teachers' leadership in these areas, the community, and board-wide initiatives. Moving from what Banks has called a *Contributions Approach* to *Decision-Making Social-Action* and *Transformative Approaches* (1998) is a goal that should necessarily be presented and addressed in our own school improvement process.

QUESTIONS FOR REFLECTION

1. How can meaningful and transformative dialogue occur with all members of a school community about issues of systemic racism and White privilege?
2. How can we create conditions in a school where multiple perspectives can inform definitions of "normal" in "circles" rather than "hierarchies" (Dei, 2003, p. 4)?

3. How does the assumption of Whiteness impact on all understandings, conversations, and learning in the schools?
4. How can we, as administrators, challenge ourselves and the people in our schools in terms of their own privilege, biases, and actions?
5. How do policies aimed at equity and anti-racism play out in the schools? Are they enough and, if not, how do we continue to move forward in the struggle against oppressive practices and systemic racism in the education system?

NOTES

[1] We worked together in this school until December 2007. Ladson-Billings (1999) suggests that the defining of diversity within education is yet another way to "other," to place blame, and focus on deficits within a particular community (pp. 216-219).

[2] Whiteness is like a moving target. Who is defined as White is dependent on the time in history. As a Jew, at the turn of the century, Whiteness would not have been a label the dominant group would have assigned to my (Debbie) ancestors. Whiteness, although clear to some, is socially constructed, as are all racial identities and labels which Omi and Winant (1993) name as being part of the "racial formation process" (p. 3).

[3] This paper is organized as a dialogue between Matt and Debbie. We feel that what makes our partnership so powerful is our ability to dialogue with each other. This model is based on an article by Heather Sykes and Tara Goldstein (2004).

[4] Dei (2003) suggested that "starting with the self means the white anti-racist education must acknowledge his or her dominance and allow other whites to see their privilege by virtue of a white identity" (p. 4)

[5] Freire (2000) discussed the power in naming. He suggests that when a person or a group is named, it is the colonization of the individual and identity.

[6] We are using Dei's definition of integrative antiracism (2003), which recognizes the intersecting oppressions of race, ethnicity, gender, class, and sexual orientation as being interwoven and impacting each other through the discourse of oppression.

[7] In this case, *our* represents all members of the school community including students, parents, teachers, administration, support staff, community members, caregivers, grandparents, and the list continues. Dei (1996) addresses the concept of schools as "working communities" by co-existing with all community members by "instilling mutual respect, collective work and collective responsibility" (p. 33).

REFERENCES

Banks, J. A. (1998). Approaches to multicultural curriculum reform. In E. Lee, D. Menkart, & M. Okazawa-Rey (Eds.), *Beyond heroes and holidays: A practical guide to K-12 anti-racist, multicultural education and staff development* (pp. 73–74). Washington, DC: Network of Educators on the Americas.

Braithwaite, K. (2003). Making new explorations and regaining lost ground in anti-racism and equity education. *Orbit, 33*(3), 9–11.

Carr, P. R. (1997). Stuck in the middle? A case study of how principals manage equity-related change in education. *Education Canada, 37*(1), 42–49.

Dei, G. J. S. (1996). *Anti-racism education: Theory and practice*. Halifax, NS: Fernwood.

Dei, G. J. S. (2003). Communication across the tracks: Challenges for antiracist education in Ontario today. *Orbit, 33*(3), 2–5.

Delpit, L. (1988). The silenced dialogue: Power and pedagogy in educating other people's children. *Harvard Educational Review, 58*(3), 280–298.

Delpit, L. (1994). Seeing color: A review of 'white teacher'. In B. Bigelow, L. Christensen, S. Karp, B. Miner, & B. Peterson (Eds.), *Rethinking our classrooms: Teaching for equity and justice* (pp. 130–132). Milwaukee, WI: Rethinking Schools.

Donsky, D. (2006). *Critical pathways towards antiracism in an elementary knowledge building classroom* (Unpublished doctoral dissertation). Ontario Institute for Studies in Education, University of Toronto, Toronto, ON.

Freire, P. (2002). *Pedagogy of the oppressed.* New York, NY: Continuum.

hooks, b. (2003). *Teaching community: Pedagogy of hope.* New York, NY: Routledge.

Ladson-Billings, G. J. (1999). Preparing teachers for diverse student populations: A critical race theory perspective. *Review of Research in Education, 24,* 211–247.

Lee, C. D. (2003). Why we need to re-think race and ethnicity in educational research. *Educational Researcher, 32*(5), 3–5.

Lindsey, R. B., Robins, K. N., & Terrell, R. D. (2003). *Cultural proficiency: A manual for school leaders.* Thousand Oaks, CA: Corwin Press.

Lorde, A. (1990). Age, race, class, and sex: Women redefining difference. In R. Ferguson, M. Gever, T. T. Minh-Ha, & C. West (Eds.), *Out there: Marginalization and contemporary cultures* (pp. 281–288). Cambridge, MA: MIT Press.

Omi, M., & Winant, H. (1993). On the theoretical status of the concept of race. In C. McCarthy & W. Crichlow (Eds.), *Race, identity and representation in education* (pp. 3–10). New York, NY: Routledge.

Ryan, J. (2003). *Leading diverse schools.* Norwell, MA: Kluwer.

Sleeter, C. E. (1993). How white teachers construct race. In C. McCarthy & W. Crichlow (Eds.), *'Race,' identity and representation in education* (pp. 157–171). New York, NY: Routledge.

Solomon, P. R., Portelli, J. P., Daniel, B-J., & Campbell. (2005). The discourse of denial: How white teacher candidates construct race, racism and 'white privilege'. *Race, Ethnicity and Education, 8*(2), 147–169.

Solórzano, D. G., & Yosso, T. J. (2002). Critical race methodology: Counter-storytelling as an analytical framework for education research. *Qualitative Inquiry, 8*(1), 23–44.

Sykes, H., & Goldstein, T. (2004). From performed to performing ethnography: Translating life history research into anti-homophobia curriculum for a teacher education program. *Teaching Education Journal,15*(1), 41–61.

York Region District School Board. (2006). *Respectful workplace and learning environment policy* (Board Policy No. 240.0). York, ON: York Region District School Board.

REFRAMING: DEBBIE DONSKY & MATT CHAMPION (2014)

This book has supported the continued work of equitable and inclusive practices in our schools. Using various chapters from the book, we have been able to support learning within a Canadian context for school, system and aspiring leaders. References to concepts such as the "collective white guilt" and our ability to maneuver psychologically through the collective guilt referred to in Caouette and Taylor's (2007) chapter, *"Don't Blame Me For What My Ancestors Did: Understanding the Impact of Collective White Guilt,"* helps to inform the dialogue that is supported through critical discourse within workshops and presentations. For several years we have used this text to support learning for prospective leaders in principal qualifications courses and, invariably, there are those who resist their complicity in a system that serves them as White middle-class educators. Relying on the story of meritocracy supports the myth of achievement and promotes entitlement. In James' (2007) chapter, *"Who Can/Should Do This Work? The Colour of Critique,"* he explains how we participate in achievement with the understanding that it is a product of our own efforts without acknowledging the privilege which has supported us on our paths to success. The dialogue of entitlement, privilege, and normative Whiteness must be taken up and the expectations of boards when hiring candidates for any position must be framed in a critical understanding of power and how it plays out in our schools, communities and offices.

With the implementation of the Ontario Ministry of Education's *Equity and Inclusive Education Strategy* (2009), boards are accountable to the eight focus areas: i) Board policies, programs, guidelines, and practices; ii) Shared and committed leadership; iii) School–community relationships; iv) Inclusive curriculum and assessment practices; v) Religious accommodation; vi) School climate and the prevention of discrimination and harassment; vii) Professional learning; and viii) Accountability and transparency. The strategy challenges boards to collect race-based data along with data that informs inequities within definitions of oppression as outlined in the Ontario Human Rights Code, expanding definitions of discrimination. In collecting these data, we must question our complicity in marginalizing various groups of students and minimizing their ability to experience success due to systemic barriers.

This questioning is done through revision of board policies and practices, opening dialogue and discourse between and within schools and the communities we serve in all areas, including religious accommodation and the continuum of accommodation that is always changing and asking for redefinition. We are accountable to our students, staff and communities through school climate data and the requirement to report out what these surveys tell us about our organizations and the improvements

D. E. Lund & P. R. Carr (Eds.), Revisiting The Great White North?, 251–252.
© *2015 Sense Publishers. All rights reserved.*

necessary to ensure not only student achievement but also wellbeing. Our chapter should address our changing roles aligned to the *Equity and Inclusive Education Strategy* for it is vital to be reflective and transformative in our actions as school leaders while always bringing to the fore our own Whiteness, privilege, and identity, not as a normative piece but as a context through which we examine our bias and the actions we take based on that location.

In Solomon and Daniel's (2007) chapter, *"Discourses on Race and 'White Privilege' in the Next Generation of Teachers,"* they raise the "importance of providing clear, consistent and comprehensive documentation of Canadian history rather than the antiseptic version that is currently presented in textbooks and classrooms" (p. 170) so that educators understand the untold stories rather than being comfortable in the concept of "Canada the good." As Canadians, we have a unique perspective to offer in this discourse about privilege and Whiteness as it impacts the experience of our students, staff, and communities. The interplay of our communities impacts the learning in our classrooms and the way we do business. The normative white discourse we engage in moves us to define our communities as minorities, diverse, and immigrants perpetuating a deficit model and yet these communities are no longer minorities nor are they necessarily newcomers. Within the global context, and immigration patters through global economy, people move in and out of different locations but what remains constant is white privilege. The arguments, issues and stories raised in this text offer an international perspective on how we move forward as our world grows smaller and the need to always question, reflect, and then take action by sharing power and handing to those we serve through equitable policies and practices, transparency, accountability and the openness to change.

REFERENCES

Caouette, J., & Taylor, D. M. (2007). Don't blame me for what my ancestors did: Understanding the impact of collective white guilt. In P. R. Carr & D. E. Lund (Eds.), *The great White north? Exploring Whiteness, privilege, and identity in education* (pp. 77–92). Rotterdam, The Netherlands: Sense.

James, C. E. (2007). Who can/should do this work? The colour of critique. In P. R. Carr & D. E. Lund (Eds.), *The great White north? Exploring Whiteness, privilege, and identity in education* (pp. 119–131). Rotterdam, The Netherlands: Sense.

Solomon, P. R., & Daniel, B -J. M. (2007). Discourses on race and 'white privilege' in the next generation of teachers. In P. R. Carr & D. E. Lund (Eds.), *The great White north? Exploring Whiteness, privilege, and identity in education* (pp. 161–172). Rotterdam, The Netherlands: Sense.

GULZAR R. CHARANIA

"A GROUP THAT PLAYS TOGETHER STAYS TOGETHER"

Tracing a Story of Racial Violence[1]

INTRODUCTION

This chapter explores ongoing incidents between two groups of young women in Grades 7 and 8, as defined and described by school officials[2]. One group consisted of wealthy students and another of working-class students. The exchanges described by school officials between these students included threats, intimidation, harassment, name-calling, put-downs, and inappropriate comments. There had been suspensions of individuals within both groups as well as in-school disciplinary measures. In response to escalating threats in this conflict, the school administration decided to intervene in a more decisive manner, sending both groups of students and an accompanying teacher to a residential outdoor education centre for several days[3]. The school has Kindergarten to Grade 8 students, consisting of primarily White, middle-class students until grade 7, when a number of primarily Black and working-class students enter the school from a nearby feeder-school. It is at this time that the administration and teaching staff begin to report incidents and conflicts, including the one described above.

The example described is loosely based on one school but also generalized to a certain extent, reflecting my experiences in a number of schools, particularly in relation to recurring and troubling issues I have identified in some aspects of my work[4]. I appreciate that the individuals involved in the example in this chapter may attribute quite different meanings, intentions, and interpretations to the incidents described. I acknowledge the risks involved in such an endeavour, as well as my good intentions and those of my colleagues. Quite often, we recognize our interventions and investments in the incidents as partial and problematic in the face of overwhelmingly complicated bureaucracies and relations of power. However, good intentions are inadequate responses when exploring the impact of our analyses, behaviours, and interventions. While I support efforts to name and make visible Whiteness in anti-racism projects, I am also cautious that such efforts must be vigilant and guard against re-installing themselves as dominant. From my perspective, Whiteness studies should not become a self-referential canon, but must constantly be informed by and in dialogue with racialized academics, communities, and political anti-racist and anti-colonial efforts. Such a commitment can support

D. E. Lund & P. R. Carr (Eds.), Revisiting The Great White North?, 253–266.

the efforts of Whiteness studies to displace Whiteness as a source of authority, rather than resulting in enriching pay-offs—professionally and personally—for Whites, despite the ongoing struggles of Aboriginal and racialized communities to be fully represented in the academy. My participation in this project as a non-White scholar is with the hope that it will make a small contribution to challenging racial hierarchies, rather than re-entrenching them.

My intent in assessing this incident is that the analysis be instructive for educators in thinking more critically about the role that Whiteness and White Supremacy[5] play in the day-to-day life of schools. Given the claims of racelessness, race evasion, and celebrations of multiculturalism that are common place in the Canadian educational system, locating this incident within a critical anti-racist framework is an important intervention in re-thinking how such everyday occurrences are in fact informed by racism and other forms of social oppression. I invoke Willinsky's (1998) "call to history" as a challenge to think about the ways in which the "the past remains present in the way we tend to see the world" (p. 244). As Willinsky (1998) demands, "we need to grow curious about what we have made of the world, beginning with a critical geography of our own map-colouring and -labeling days in school that did so much to define our place in the world" (p. 20). I suggest that this project of constant enquiry be guided by the intent to imagine and disrupt the schooling of children into White Supremacy, with devastating and distorting consequences for how they understand themselves and others in relation. Schooling, despite its implication in the imperial project, also contains contradictions and possibilities. Schools are messy places of claims and counterclaims that do not always align themselves in predictable or already determined outcomes. While such contestations are not significantly centred in my analysis, I nonetheless consider them quite critical in understanding how oppression and relations of power are reproduced, challenged and negotiated in schooling contexts. As Jacobs (2003) writes in relation to cities as "sites of 'meetings,' they are also places that are saturated with possibilities for the destabilisation of imperial arrangements" (p. 4).

ISSUES/ANALYSIS

In this chapter, I attempt to address the following key questions: How was the school constructed and racially organized prior to the arrival of Black students from a nearby feeder school and after? In response to escalating incidents between the young women, why did the administration insist on an intervention that required these students to be removed from the school and housed together in an outdoor education facility? How did school officials imagine dialogue across racial differences? What is at stake in the school officials' mapping of the "official" explanation? I use this analysis as an opportunity to understand and explore the logic that I believe is operating in the school officials' intervention as well as the denial of racial violence through a response that was framed in particular readings of class and gender. I also suggest that the pedagogical response proposed by the school operates within a multicultural reading of difference that tolerates and manages racial conflict but demands the appearance of social and spatial cohesion. I draw some tentative connections between the racial logic operating in the school and the making of the nation. I suggest that it is the White students who are considered the original and entitled occupants of the school in ways that later prepare them to assert claims of ownership and belonging in the nation. These claims necessarily involve the disavowal of those made by the Black students. As Sibley (2001) suggests, an examination of exclusionary practices simultaneously reveals the terms of inclusion for dominant groups (p. xv), and it is this relationality that I elaborate on in this chapter. I also propose that the adjudication of this conflict produces citizens in training who are schooled in various forms of conduct, particularly in relation to negotiating race. Throughout this chapter, my focus remains on excavating the dominant story in which I found myself, and in which I participated.

MAPPING THE DOMINANT STORY

The dominant story, according to school officials, is one of two groups of young women, equal actors in the school community, participating in behaviours that are dehumanizing and disrespectful to each other. It is with the arrival of the working-class students in Grade 7 from a nearby feeder school that conflicts between students are heightened and visible to teachers and administrators. I first turn my attention to the construction of the school prior to the arrival of the working-class, Black students. The school is represented as a harmonious and peaceful community. Absent from this depiction are racial conflicts, or at least those conflicts that might require resources and efforts beyond the capacity of the school to respond. It is a place of respectability and productive learning, where racialized others are encountered symbolically through curricular representations or in few enough numbers that their presence does not significantly alter the landscape of the school. With the arrival of Black, working-class students in significant numbers, and the numbers are significant, there is in the dominant mapping the arrival of chaos, disorder and threat (Goldberg, 1993, p. 187; Sibley, 2001, p. 51). In discussions with school officials and through them, related concerns of White parents, there is an all-too familiar ring of moral panic (Sibley, 2001, p. 41) and racist nationalist sentiment, echoed in the claims that the "school is being taken over."[6] There is considerable anxiety articulated about Black bodies out of place, entering and contaminating a place of respectability (Sibley, 2001, p.8; Mohanram, 1999, p. xiii). While Black students might have a formal claim to a place in school in a liberal democracy, it is certainly not at this particular school. The refrain that the "school used to be different," or that "these problems did not exist before," as described by school officials, fix the Black students as the source of degeneracy (Fellows & Razack, 1998, p. 346). As Said (1979, p. 3; 1994, p. xi-xii) is careful to illuminate, these representations are not innocent or symbolic, but bound up with the conferring of rights and identity, authorizing relations of domination.

I argue that this story is one that in some ways echoes White settler mythologies where the school comes to stand in place of the nation as the White children of the nation are schooled into dominance and the Black students into subordination. Here I borrow from Sibley's (2001) notion that exclusionary practices in the home, locality, and nation, while not mappable onto each other directly and, perhaps seemingly distant, are all accompanied by "echoes of otherness [that] travel backwards and forwards, reinforcing neighbourhoods, providing electoral support for restrictive immigration policies and legitimating foreign policy" (p.112). It is these ideas, policies and practices that Sibley argues need to be seen as connected and mutually constituting at multiple sites. I apply these insights to explore how the school establishes belonging and exclusion in ways that reference the nation and national mythologies, with Sibley's qualification that this mapping is partial and more complex than my initial analysis suggests. As citizens in training, these White adolescents are staking a claim to the school and coming to *"know themselves as entitled to it"* (Razack, 2002, p. 129, emphasis in original). It seems to me that the school is one of the central places where White students are instructed to enact these privileges and claims as they begin to see and know themselves as subjects in control, with rights and entitlements that are later connected to claims on the nation. However, this claim and ordering of relations on the part of White students and the relegation of Black students as not entitled or without a place in the school is not without response from the Black students. It is within these claims and counter-claims that I suggest the ongoing incidents and conflicts between the White and Black female students need to be placed.

For the primarily White school officials, as for the White students, the arrival of Black students signals the arrival of noticeable tensions and conflicts in the school. The story of the school officials conveniently locates the origin of conflict in the Black bodies. The conflicts in which the White female students find themselves are also attributed to the presence of the Black students. This leaves unexamined school policies and practices as well as the behaviours of White students as sources of violence and conflict. In the conversations and meetings in which I participated, school administrators called on class differences as a partial explanation, not to draw attention to the systemic and asymmetric production of economic poverty experienced by the Black students, on the one hand, and the accumulation of wealth enjoyed by the White students, on the other. Rather, class was discussed in much more individualistic terms, to talk about the lack of opportunities that the Black students from working-class backgrounds experienced. It is the liberal story of the body that is marked "through race, gender or poverty... as a product of traits internal to the body" (Mohanram, 1999, p. 38) that is told by school officials. The body is the explanation. In my phone conversations with various school officials, what was not easily offered up was the fact that the wealthy students were White and the working-class students were Black. I suspect that race was not easily discussed due to their preoccupation to disavow racism as part of the conflict between the two groups of female students. I speculate that, for the school officials, the myths of individualism, meritocracy, equality, and justice would be profoundly compromised and challenged by the acknowledgment of racism. With the denial of and inability to name racism, what is also at stake is that racism falls outside the purview of possible interventions.

In asking how the spaces and bodies involved in this conflict are constituted and represented, what becomes apparent is the insufficiency of class as an explanation but also the need to understand how it is that a particularly narrow notion of class is invoked along with a simultaneous disavowal of race. I argue that the school officials' foregrounding of class eclipses the insidious ways in which the incidents between the two groups of young women are profoundly shaped by racial violence. This move to focus on class reflects what Jacobs (2003) describes as the ways in which the "complex politics of race is translated into a variant form of class differentiation" (p. 32). This obscures the complicated ways in which poverty is produced and sustained, making it impossible to fully discuss outside an analysis of interlocking oppressions (Fellows & Razack 1998, p. 447)[7]. An analysis of interlocking oppressions provides a framework to understand the complicated ways in which incidents, including the one described here, cannot be isolated or reduced to the familiar mantra of race, class and gender. Building on Collins, Fellows, and Razack (1998) provide an instructive lens for thinking about this complexity in ways that are important, not only theoretically but also for imagining more effective pedagogical interventions. They explicate the operation of interlocking oppression as follows: "this 'interlocking' effect means that the systems of oppression come into existence in and through one another so that class exploitation could not be accomplished without gender and racial hierarchies" (Fellows & Razack, 1998, p. 335). An analysis of interlocking oppression provides a basis for imagining and engaging in broad-based social action that is not limited to one system. As Fellows and Razack (1998) argue, efforts to change only one system through which one is subordinated does nothing to alter the foundations which give rise to and sustain oppression. They provide the following example and theorization:

> When a woman fails to pursue how she is implicated in other women's lives and retreats to the position that the system that oppresses her the most is the only one worth fighting and that the other systems (systems in which she is positioned as dominant) are not of her concern, she will fail to undo her own subordination. Attempts to change one system while leaving the others intact leaves in place the structure of domination that is made up of interlocking hierarchies. (p. 336)

This interlocking analysis is also particularly relevant in this site, given that school officials, both in this school and others, are increasingly concerned about the growing conflicts and violence between girls and young women. While these incidents are narrated in particular gendered and classed terms, they are rarely raced. I speculate that given the way in which the conflict is framed as the arrival of threat with Black students, there is an unspoken concern about protecting White femininity. White female students are conceptualized as requiring protection of the school system,

257

rather than enacting and contributing to racial violence. The respectability of White students was reproduced as the White students were, for the most part, from middle- and upper-class homes and were high academic performers, respectable in all ways. The Black students, on the other hand, were, for the most part, from working-class families and were not considered high academic achievers. As a result of this dominant framing, the unspoken positioning of the Black female students as instigators of violence and the White female students as victims or merely responding to this threat was reproduced and seen as legitimate.

As Batacharya (2004) argues in relation to the murder of Reena Virk[8], it is exceedingly difficult to name the violence of White women as they are constructed, and I would argue, construct themselves, primarily as victims of patriarchal violence (p. 63). When White women draw attention to power, it is often to further their rights and secure their place in racial hierarchies, in relation to men of their class, rather than to situate themselves as benefactors of practices of domination or broaden their efforts beyond the interests of their narrow class and race positions. It seems to me that these White adolescents are being schooled into dominance, which requires claiming for themselves particular forms of oppression and marginalization that in fact mask their complicity in relations of power. Complicating gendered relations between women, in this case young women, draws attention to the fact that while women may be oppressed, this does not preclude them from simultaneously occupying spaces of oppression and domination (Razack, 1998, p. 158). I suspect that what makes relations of power so difficult to name is also the age of the students involved. Because youth are so often positioned as vulnerable and with little power, and in some cases they are, it makes it all the more difficult to draw attention to relations of power or to intervene in such incidents using an interlocking analysis. However, I would argue that the age of the Black students does not secure for themselves a place as primarily vulnerable.

SO HAPPY TOGETHER?

In trying to further uncover the logic of this official story, my next point of inquiry is to interrogate why school officials insisted that any intervention would have to include both groups of young women together. The suggestion of myself and a colleague that it might be productive to work with the two groups of young women separately and have a White woman facilitator work with the White students and a Black woman facilitator work with the Black students was met with overwhelming opposition. Our position was based on the assumption that prior to having the groups come together in any way that *might* be useful, different work was required with each group of students around issues of power, privilege and entitlement[9]. Why were school officials so invested in the position that both groups stay together in the school intervention? I speculate that there are a number of things at stake and I frame them within the imperative and performance of racelessness required by liberalism, and most often articulated as multiculturalism in schools. To separate the students would be to suggest that the conflict between the two groups is raced. In order to avoid the possibility that race would be named, the response of school officials was one of stubborn resistance at the suggestion that the groups be separated and eventually brought together. In fact, by keeping them together, the myth of students from different backgrounds existing together in tolerance at the school, as in the nation, is maintained. Where there are conflicts, they are not named as having racial dimensions.

Goldberg's (1993) analysis of how racial marginalization is reproduced in the absence of more obvious modes of exclusion is particularly instructive here (p.192). His notion of "*periphractic* space," that is a space that does not require absolute removal or displacement of racialized bodies but rather achieves "dislocation, displacement, and division" through "limitation in terms of access—to power, to (the realization of) rights, and to goods and services" (Goldberg, 1993, p. 188) is relevant in the reproduction of racism in the educational system and in this particular instance. Applying Goldberg's insight to this incident, the multicultural school requires the appearance of difference but only on conditions and terms defined by the students and community that are rightly entitled to the space. Racialized students are not excluded from the school officially or denied access all together. However, their success or failure is thought to be about qualities intrinsic to who they are, qualities worn on their bodies as explanation, rather than in the systemic processes of marginalization they experience and the racially ordered opportunities (Goldberg, 1993, p. 173) offered to them. Curiously, the inclusion of these less-desirable students also has the effect of producing the White students and community as gracious, tolerant hosts, making space in their school community at considerable inconvenience and disruption. Gratitude is required of the guests.

The similarities between the narratives of the nation and the school are difficult to miss. Difference is required but carefully managed, and performances of difference are regulated, primarily through cultural displays and celebrations that belie insidious practices of racism and colonialism at work (Dei, 1996, p. 58). Any further demands on the part of racialized others, demands of rights and opportunities that are real and lived, work to produce them as ungrateful and are considered out of order. In fact, I would argue that the separation of students racially threatens to violate the principles of multiculturalism as well as the myth of harmonious existence and regulated mechanisms for adjudicating conflicts. Given that the students are White and Black, the picture is too apartheid-like and what might be read as separate and unequal spaces too threatening and, I suggest, too proximate to reality. It is important to acknowledge that not all Black students would uniformly articulate critical or oppositional analyses and in fact, such an expectation does not capture the complexities of power and divergent meanings made of experiences. However, even the possibility of Black students calling attention to racism and exclusion, in relation to the incidents with the White students, and in relation to their experiences of schooling more broadly, must be contained by the school, to the extent that it is possible. But, of course, this possibility cannot be permanently or fully secured and, consequently, school official anxiously reproduced claims of racelessness.

I further suggest that the separation of students racially, working with a facilitator of the same race and gender, is troubling as there was no Black teacher on staff. As a result, an external resource would be required to work with the Black students[10]. The possibility that school officials would be denied access to Black students created a great deal of anxiety and concern on the part of school officials. The notion of the dominant subject, the subject who can go anywhere and have access to anything, is profoundly destabilized by this restriction on movement, access and knowledge. As Alison Jones (2004) argues:

> A sense of exclusion and outrage marks the refusal of the already privileged to accept that some knowledge and relationships might not be available to them/us. The Enlightenment project of mapping the world, rendering it visible and understood, does more than shape our education system: It is also at the root of the threat we feel when nonwhite peers separate from us... Our education system is based in the western desire for coherence, authorization, and control. (p. 63)

The idea of not knowing what the Black students might be saying, the notion that there might be spaces that escape surveillance and regulation, cannot be permitted. It is not just a fear of regulating the Other but also of knowing the self as dominant, knowledgeable and in control in relation to the other that is at stake (Schick, 2002, p. 102). I suspect that this fear of bodies and spaces beyond the reach and control of this dominant subject is part of this curious mix and preoccupation with racially segregated spaces on the part of school officials.

THE ROLE OF HIKING AND DIALOGUE[11]

As elaborated earlier, the decision of school officials to intervene in the escalating conflicts by placing the young women together supposes that the conflict originates with the arrival of the Black students at the school, and it is the White female students who are drawn into this dynamic. I adopt Fellows and Razack's (1998) term "race to innocence" (p. 335), used to describe the victim posture to which women retreat in their unwillingness to interrogate their own complicity in subordinating other women. I suggest that the removal of the students from the school is a move to innocence on the part of school officials. What it precludes is an examination of school policies and practices as well as the much more pervasive behaviours of White students as sources of violence, racism and conflict, securing their collective innocence. School officials articulated their hope for the intervention as creating dialogue between the students with the expectation that this would ease the escalating conflicts once the students returned to school. According to school officials, the need for dialogue, while crucial, also needed to be located in a context where students, accompanied by a teacher, could participate in activities over a number of days. An outdoor education centre where this intervention took place would provide the context for the young women, accompanied by a teacher and outdoor education staff, to eat, sleep, ski and hike together.

School officials hoped that the students would be able to get to know each other by having positive interactions and this, in turn, would lead to a reduction in conflict at the school. What is made possible in these outdoor adventures (Philips, 1997, p. 55)? Following Jacobs (1997), I suggest that there is the ordinary kind of reconciliation implied here, and that is a "narrative in which parties which were at one time estranged then become friends (Hardimon, 1994, p. 85)" (p. 206). There is a turn to working together in the land, a story of "some form of harmonious – co-habitation" (Jacobs, 1997, p. 208) made possible by being together in nature. As with dialogue, there is the fantasy of togetherness and friendship that dissolves power and history, securing and protecting domination. The focus of my exploration is less on the physical space, although that itself presents its own set of social and spatial arrangements. I turn to explore how it is that dialogue between the students is imagined and what it produces.

Following the official logic of the school interventions, thus far, dialogue between the students is imagined to take place between individual students involved in a conflict. The conflict is framed in terms of mutual dislike, misunderstanding, lack of knowledge about each other, and the solution is to dialogue and cultivate an ability to empathize, focus on similarities, and see things from perspectives other than their own. Relationship-building across differences emerges as the central goal of dialogue. Power imbalances, history, racism, and oppression are taken out of the equation, and are replaced by tolerance, shared human identities, and individual responsibility. What is accomplished through this conceptualization of dialogue? I argue that it is a strategy that further entrenches dominant subject positions, enabling White students and school officials to remain innocent and unaccountable for domination and privilege. I am suspicious of efforts that are directed at producing empathy as the role of the dominant listener is often to offer an emotional response. Recounting painful and traumatic encounters with racial violence can also be voyeuristic when dominant audiences unreflectively consume such experiences. In centering White supremacy, Razack (1998) argues there is an expectation that people of colour will "tell our stories for your (White people's) edification" (p. 48). There is a perpetual postponement of responsibility in educating oneself as this demand is placed on those who have been racialized. Razack (1998) interrogates this call for stories of oppression in which the dominant listener remains intact, unshifted, and in the imaginary space of innocence.

Bannerji's (1995) demand is that people who oppress move from expressions of guilt, empathy, and victimization to become accountable for that oppression. Typically, moves to pre-empt accountability result in a collapsing of self and other, based on false identification with the oppressed without locating self as oppressor in constituting systems of domination. As Bannerji challenges, "why don't they move from the experience of sharing our pain, to narrating the experience of inflicting it on us" (1995, p. 117)? Because my proposed pedagogical effort is framed as an illumination of racism and oppression as well as tracing oneself through them, empathy alone does not lead to shifting power relations and, as Boler (1997) argues, passive empathy satisfies only the most benign multicultural agenda. An exclusive reliance on empathetic responses sustains the de-linking of stories of oppression from those systems authorizing these stories, and in this way "suffering… is not referred beyond the individual to the social" (Boler, 1997, p. 261). Typically, these moves to pre-empt accountability result in a collapsing of self and other, based on false identification with the oppressed without locating self as oppressor in constituting and benefiting from systems of domination.

My own investments in facilitating dialogue, while structured differently to allow processing within and subsequently across the groups, also reflect some troubling assumptions about the role of dialogue in the context of racial violence. So how do I understand my investment in dialogue in this context? If, as Boler (1997) contends, "these 'others' whose lives we imagine don't want empathy, they want justice" (p. 255), what is possible for dialogue to achieve, and how has it become so central in my understanding of approaches to destabilizing racism and oppression? Does it preclude me/us from thinking of other pedagogical interventions? What is possible for dialogue to achieve in this context and would my approach, though rejected by the school, place an unfair burden on the Black students to share their experiences with the hope that they might be heard by the White students? Would these stories necessarily be oppositional? Would the White students accept the responsibility to shift the narratives of their stories and terms of listening? Were any of these expectations achievable in a relatively short amount of time? Would they result in any shift or disinvestment in power and if so, what might that even look like in this context? What meaning might this hold in shifting the experiences of Black students in schools?

Increasingly, I came to feel that I was positioning dialogue as a panacea as well as framing my intervention in terms determined by the school, where there was a relative safety for school officials in locating the intervention on the bodies of a small and select group of students. This became a recurrent theme in my school-based interventions. This is not to suggest that I do not think dialogue has a place, and an important one, only that it is far more complicated. How, for example, might a focus on interpretive structures as well as stories that are carefully and contextually considered, move beyond the production of empathy, guilt, anger, and/or shame to political and personal responsibility? Who is being required to do the work in dialogue, and is dialogue a remedy that will diminish racial violence and injury?

CONCLUSION

The investment in multiculturalism in schools cannot be understood outside of the production and reproduction of White-settler mythologies of the nation. In fact, my speculative reading of this school-based incident suggests that White students are inducted into dominance in schools, where national mythologies are reproduced in troubling ways. In this case, the production of White students who come to see themselves as the entitled and rightful occupants of the school prepares them to install themselves as the rightful occupants of the nation, as the subjects "who have the right to go anywhere and do anything" (Razack, 2002, p. 127). It is precisely this claim of entitlement that gets activated with the arrival of the Black, working-class students in Grade 7 in what had otherwise been a predominately White, middle-class school. The Black students are positioned as an unwelcome and disruptive presence, uninvited guests to be tolerated, managed and where possible, removed. If, in fact, it is through place that rights are secured, the right to the school and the nation are much more than symbolic practices. If, as Goldberg (1993) reminds us, "conquering space is implicated in and implies ruling people" (p. 185), what these practices secure are material privileges and entitlements at multiple sites while at the same time disavowing that these preferential practices are ongoing, and can be traced to a history and present of White-settler violence, colonialism, racism and exploitation.

There are always at least two levels of stories in operation, the dominant story of formal equality told by school officials, and my effort to excavate the foundations of this story to illuminate the underside of Canadian liberalism, or what Bannerji (1997) characterizes as its "colonial heart" (p. 33). Both stories cannot be true so the latter is kept at bay as is threatens to name the violence required to create and maintain the liberal democratic state, in both material and symbolic ways. The effort to understand the exclusion of Black students in the school cannot be understood without an analysis of the terms of inclusion for White students. I argue that these processes cannot be understood outside of structures of racial belonging in the school and nation. This does not require a removal of the racialized body all together but rather what Sibley (2001) terms "more opaque instances of exclusion" (p. iv), including practices that appear to be inclusionary. Multiculturalism provides such practices where difference is variably tolerated, required, sought after, and even celebrated but in ways that erase history, and mask relations of power and the racial conditions on which belonging is established. I suggest that school officials make what is otherwise a story of White exclusion and entitlement into a respectable story through the denial of race, domination and history. Encouraging dialogue and forced interaction between the students becomes the mechanism to overcome "conflict," a convenient euphemism that denies accountability and eclipses the insidious operation of racial domination. Civility between students in the school as with citizens in the nation comes to stand in place of justice. As long as the students appear to be civil, tolerant and perhaps even friendly at times, as long as visible incidents of violence are reduced, the school has, theoretically, intervened successfully. This was the end of the story, as I came to know it, through school officials[12].

QUESTIONS FOR REFLECTION

1. How does explicitly naming Whiteness and White Supremacy (rather than racism and racialized communities), shift notions of responsibility for the incident presented, and for racist incidents in schools, in general?

2. How does the framework of interlocking oppressions reframe issues of girl violence? How does this theoretical lens also challenge the saliency of class to explain the scenario between the groups of young women?
3. To what extent does the emphasis on uncovering the dominant story throughout this paper position the Black students through the lens of White Supremacy, rather than on their own terms?
4. How does the operationalizing of multiculturalism in schools and the wider Canadian context eclipse the naming and analysis of race, racism, and White Supremacy in this incident?
5. What kinds of anti-racist pedagogical interventions might emerge from a more critical reading of the incidents between these groups of young women?

NOTES

[1] This chapter owes much to Sherene Razack, and I am grateful for her valuable insights and assistance. Thanks also to Carmela Murdocca for her critical feedback, encouragement, and engagement. Finally, I am indebted to Amynah Charania and Sabrina Hasham for their time, feedback, and support.

[2] I use the term school officials to refer to the principal, vice-principal, and teachers, both in this school and others with whom I had contact.

[3] Much of the information I received about the school was from the administrative team. My contact with the teachers and students was quite limited. The language used by school officials to describe the incident is relevant, and I will explore it throughout the chapter.

[4] The work-period I refer to is from September 2001 to August 2004 when I worked in the Equity Department at the Toronto District School Board (TDSB). In addition to curriculum development and other equity based work, I was also invited to come into schools, often after a particular "incident" had occurred, and to support staff and students in developing a response. These incidents, broadly speaking, were described as equity or human rights concerns, issues or violations. Quite often, the work I did was with colleagues in the Equity Department as well as other colleagues in the TDSB. However, I use the pronoun "I" to reflect my own thinking about this often collaborative work.

[5] Ann Russo (1991) elaborates on the significance of using the language of White supremacy. Following bell hooks, she argues that the term "White supremacy" rather than racism "correctly places the responsibility on white women and men, rather than focusing on people of colour simply as victims of an amorphous racism. 'White supremacy' as a concept forces us to look power directly in the face, and when we do that there is less room for denial, guilt, and paternalism in trying to change it... part of the problem is that many of us white feminists still do not see racism as our issue" (p. 299). To frame racism as an issue and responsibility for White people, I also use the term White supremacy.

[6] I use quotes here and in other places where sources are not attributed to specific individuals but reflect specific examples relayed to me by school officials.

[7] In explicating an analysis of interlocking oppressions, I rely on the insights and writings collaboratively developed with my colleague, Tabish Surani during our M. A. research and writing (see Charania, 2001; Surani, 2001).

[8] Reena Virk was a 14-year-old South Asian woman who was fatally attacked by seven women and one man in 1997 in Saanich, near Victoria, British Columbia. As Batacharya argues, racism as a factor was dismissed by most media coverage of the murder and subsequent trial. However, she argues that in order to understand Virk's murder, it must be placed in the context of interlocking systems of oppression, complicating the narrative of girl violence that was most readily offered up.

[9] While I do think that my own assumptions about what constitutes a more productive intervention are worth investigating, particularly in terms of thinking about what interventions might be worthwhile, this does not constitute the focus of this chapter.

[10] Given that there was not a Black teacher on staff, an external resource would be required to work with the Black female students. This points to the lack of representation of teachers and administrators that reflect the diverse racial composition of schools.

[11] I rely on ideas and insights about storytelling collaboratively developed and written in my M. A. thesis with Tabish Surani. For a related discussion of the role of storytelling in anti-homophobia education, see Charania (2005).

[12] One of my lingering discomforts with my analysis remains the focus on the subject through the "perception that everybody else has of the subject" rather than also on self- referential terms (Mohanram, 1999, p. 30).

REFERENCES

Bannerji, H. (1995). *Thinking through: Essays on feminism, Marxism and anti-racism.* Toronto, ON: Women's Press.

Bannerji, H. (1997). Geography lessons: On being an insider/outsider to the Canadian nation. In L. Roman & L. Eyre (Eds.), *Dangerous territories: Struggles for difference and equality* (pp. 23–41). New York, NY: Routledge.

Batacharya, S. (2004). Racism, 'girl violence', and the murder of Reena Virk. In C. Alder & A. Worrall (Eds.), *Girls' violence: Myths and realities* (pp. 61–80). New York, NY: State University of New York Press.

Boler, M. (1997). The risk of empathy: Interrogating multiculturalism's gaze. *Cultural Studies, 11*(2), 253–273.

Britzman, D. (1991). *Practice makes practice: A critical study of learning to teach.* New York, NY: State University of New York Press.

Charania, G. R. (2001). *Encounters with northern development workers: Reflections from the 'field'* (Unpublished Master's thesis). Ontario Institute for Studies in Education of the University of Toronto, Toronto, ON.

Charania, G. R. (2005). Regulated narratives in anti-homophobia education: Complications in coming out stories. *Canadian Woman Studies, 24*(2,3), 31–37.

Dei, G. J. S. (1996). *Anti-racism education: Theory and practice.* Halifax, NS: Fernwood.

Fellows, M. L., & Razack, S. (1998). The race to innocence: Confronting hierarchical relations among women. *Journal of Gender, Race and Justice, 1*(2), 335–352.

Gill, S. D. (2002). The unspeakability of racism: Mapping law's complicity in Manitoba's racialized spaces. In S. H. Razack (Ed.), *Race, space, and the law: Unmapping a white settler society* (pp. 157–183). Toronto, ON: Between the Lines.

Goldberg, D. T. (1993). *Racist culture: Philosophy and the politics of meaning.* Malden, MA: Blackwell.

Jones, A. (2004). Talking cure: The desire for dialogue. In M. Boler (Ed.), *Democratic dialogue in education: Troubling speech, disturbing silence* (pp. 57–67). New York, NY: Peter Lang.

Kirby, K. (1998). Re: Mapping subjectivity: Cartographic vision and the limits of politics. In N. Duncan (Ed.), *Body space* (pp. 45–55). New York, NY: Routledge.

Mohanram, R. (1999). *Black body: Women, colonialism, and space.* Minneapolis, MN: University of Minnesota Press.

Mohanty, C. T. (1991). Cartographies of struggle: Third world women and the politics of feminism. In C. T. Mohanty, A. Russo, & L. Torres (Eds.), *Third world women and the politics of feminism* (pp. 1–47). Indianapolis, IN: University of Indiana Press.

Nelson, J. J. (2002). The space of Africville: Creating, regulating, and remembering the urban 'slum'. In S. H. Razack (Ed.), *Race, space, and the law: Unmapping a white settler society* (pp. 211–232). Toronto, ON: Between the Lines.

Phillips, R. (1997). *Mapping men and empire: A geography of adventure.* London, UK: Routledge.

Razack, S. (1998). *Looking white people in the eye: Gender, race, and culture in courtrooms and classrooms.* Toronto, ON: University of Toronto Press.

Razack, S. H. (2002). When place becomes race. In S. H. Razack (Ed.), *Race, space, and the law: Unmapping a white settler society* (pp. 1–20). Toronto, ON: Between the Lines.

Razack, S. H. (2002). Gendered racial violence and spatialized justice: The murder of Pamela George. In S. H. Razack (Ed.), *Race, space, and the law: Unmapping a white settler society* (pp. 121–156). Toronto, ON: Between the Lines.

Russo, A. (1991). We cannot live without our lives: White women, antiracism, and feminism. In C. T. Mohanty, A. Russo, & L. Torres (Eds.), *Third world women and the politics of feminism* (pp. 297–313). Indianapolis, IN: Indiana University Press.

Said, E. W. (1979). *Orientalism*. New York, NY: Vintage Books.

Said, E. W. (1994). *Culture and imperialism*. New York, NY: Vintage Books.

Schick, C. (2002). Keeping the ivory tower white: Discourses of racial domination. In S. H. Razack (Ed.), *Race, space, and the law: Unmapping a white settler society* (pp. 99–119). Toronto, ON: Between the Lines.

Sibley, D. (2001). *Geographies of exclusion: Society and difference in the west*. New York, NY: Routledge.

Smith, L. T. (1999). *Decolonizing methodologies: Research and indigenous peoples*. New York, NY: St. Martin's Press.

Surani, T. (2001). *Shaping the north-south encounter: The training of northern development workers* (Unpublished Master's thesis). Ontario Institute for Studies in Education of the University of Toronto, Toronto, ON.

Willinsky, J. (1998). *Learning to divide the world: Education at empire's end*. Minneapolis, MN: University of Minnesota Press.

REFRAMING: GULZAR R. CHARANIA (2014)

It is not easy to revisit older pieces of writing. So much seems outdated and in need of revision so it is a pleasure to have the opportunity to think back on this particular chapter as well as the educational context in which it is situated.

Schools can be terrifying places, terrifying for the ways that hierarchies get sedimented and all things "normal" get normalized. Maybe they're terrifying because I experienced so much of them through this lens. This undoubtedly shapes my own orientation towards educational research. Schools occupy a large presence in the lives of most children and young people and since they are such big places, a lot is at stake in what "goes down" in schools. When I read this chapter today, I read the anger that animated so much of my time in schools. I also increasingly appreciate that advancing anti-racism requires the skills of sharp analysis alongside the ability to work with people from a variety of entry points and politics in the often-fraught conversations of racism and oppression.

As I write in the chapter, the force of schools is not without response and students make their own demands and interventions in schools, naming their experiences of oppression and the differential opportunities and vulnerabilities it engenders. In a context where discourses of post-feminism and post-racism are ubiquitous, it is pressing to centre the voices and experiences of students who continue to be marginalized in the school system. They have much to teach us about how racism, sexism, and oppression are lived and experienced, and their consequences. Whiteness and its associated privileges have not been invisible for many of these students. But it is not enough to solicit and document student experiences if nothing materially changes in their educational experience. It seems unfair to ask so much from them if we can offer so little in return.

It is also important to trace the mechanisms through which racial oppression works. It often comes wrapped in the language of morality, intelligence, character, and potential. It can be tricky business to make a case for the continued nature of racial oppression and harm in the aftermath of an African American man being elected president of the United States. If we live in a post-racial world, what happens to the experiences of students who continue to live with the powerful legacies of racial taxonomies in their lives and educational experiences? Are they just not working hard enough?

Race and racism have also taken more unexpected turns and configurations. In a disturbing move, some whites now advance claims of White marginalization, most often articulated as "reverse racism." White people, it is argued, are now disproportionately harmed by racism and experiences of racial discrimination while racialized populations receive unfair advantages. Behind such rhetoric lurks the demographic threat and panic of being "taken over" by racialized populations, a

D. E. Lund & P. R. Carr (Eds.), Revisiting The Great White North?, 267–268.

response to unearned privileges, long enjoyed, being challenged and a version of racism devoid of history. Vacillating between vociferously denying of racist realities, and opportunistically appropriating the language of racism, both strategies ensure that White entitlement remains firmly in place.

We need to attend to the multiple and discordant ways that racial hierarchies are being shored up. There is the fight against the perspective that racism is a historic artifact, something relegated to a distasteful past and there is also the contest to determine what constitutes racism, whom it harms and how it works itself out. Much is at stake in these disputes. They are far from academic and far from settled. They speak in powerful ways to neoliberal discourses and the shrinking public language that we have to describe and alter our social realities.

I have also become increasingly concerned with and preoccupied by how racialized people are differentially called into racial hierarchies. Whiteness is a powerful set of ideas and histories in our lives, too, and it is important to make space to look at some of these difficult questions. I say difficult because they open up a broader set of concerns around complicities, of relations between and within racialized communities, and the ways that we live with and respond to racism. Questions of settler colonialism, imperialism, anti-Black racism, and the war on terror, for example, continue to create new and old categories of racial others and mechanisms of racial surveillance and regulation. Oppression does not necessarily generate solidarity across heterogeneous populations or racial classifications. As harmful as racism is, it also seduces us with promises of escape and relief, with invitations to be the "good" people of colour, the "model minorities," the ones who don't make too many demands or create too much discomfort. Of course all of these relationships require careful unpacking because they too can be used as a way to obfuscate Whiteness.

It matters from where we read, the specific places, because race and racism get worked out on the ground in incredibly nuanced ways. Attending to racism and Whiteness contextually and in historically specific ways is important. Discourses of multiculturalism in Canada, and the erasure of ongoing colonial violence, operate to make racism appear and disappear in particular ways that mark both its subtlety and force. How do they work from where you are reading?

PAUL R. CARR

THE WHITENESS OF EDUCATIONAL
POLICYMAKING

INTRODUCTION

How do governments and educational decision-makers consistently avoid being held to account for social justice?[1] Why do reforms routinely ignore or omit dealing with racism? Is this institutional response merely willful neglect, systemic dysfunction, a contrived, intricate web of inequitable power relations, or is it the fomenting of ingrained racist interests? What is the role of White people in sustaining and shaping racism? This chapter focuses on Whiteness within an institutional environment in education by examining the case of the Ontario government and educational policymaking in 1995.

My vantage point in this discussion is not that of a dispassionate on-looker. While I firmly believe that our identities are socially constructed, I also believe that our society both gives status and discriminates on the basis of physical, religious, ideological, and other markers of identity. Therefore, in order to contextualize my identity, notwithstanding the myriad factors that have shaped and continue to form who I am, I am (among other things) a White male of European, middle-class origin, who has strongly felt concerns about social justice.

Two components, in particular, frame my experiential identity, both of which help contextualize and inform my perspective on Whiteness:

a) My doctoral thesis and subsequent research have examined institutional change and anti-racism, starting in the Toronto School Board, in the early 1990s, and extending to other jurisdictions. While undertaking this research I met, befriended and, in some cases, collaborated with a number of activists in the area of equity in education; and

b) For 17 years I was a Senior Policy Advisor in the Ontario Government, principally in the Ministry of Education, where I worked on and led several anti-racism, diversity, and equity-based initiatives. My experience there consisted of undertaking research and policy analysis, providing advice, coordinating and overseeing initiatives, developing policy, and supporting a range of government operations and functions.

In particular, my analysis will focus on two inter-related themes, both of which are critical to social justice in education:

D. E. Lund & P. R. Carr (Eds.), Revisiting The Great White North?, 269–279.

a) *Whiteness*: How is White power and privilege understood, operationalized and experienced by diverse stakeholders? Fine, Weis, Pruitt and Burns (2004) and Feagin and O'Brien (2003) have addressed the issue of White people generally not acknowledging that they are White, and, further, denying that they have any privilege in society based on their racial heritage and legacy. From a moral education vantage point, Applebaum (2005) has unraveled three of the anti-racism myths underpinning Whiteness, namely, the discourses of colour-blindness, meritocracy, and individual choice, demonstrating that due consideration must be given to group identification and inequitable power relations in addition to individual identity.

b) *Accountability*: How does the institutional culture and structure support and measure accountability for equity (Fullan, 2005; Leithwood, 2001)? How does government conceptualize, develop, implement, and evaluate educational policy related to social justice (Dei, Karumanchery, & Karumanchery-Luik, 2004; Levin, 2005)? Hoover and Shook (2003) provide a strong argument against the way "accountability" is used to buttress current reforms in education, and Lipman (2004) has generated a strong critique of how "accountability" is used to further marginalize groups.

POLITICAL CONTEXT IN ONTARIO

The transfer of power in Ontario in 1995, from a left-leaning New Democratic Party (NDP) government to a right-leaning Progressive Conservative Party (PC) one, has been considered a watershed moment in education (McCaskell, 2005). The education agenda for the incoming Conservative government was characterized by a neo-liberal schism in relation to the elimination of equity policies, the realignment of governance structures, and aggravated relations with the educational sector (Corson, 2001; Rezai-Rashti, 2003). This period of change also included a "back to basics" pedagogical approach focused on employability, funding cuts, the push for private and charter schools, school-business partnerships, and the promotion of standardized testing for students (McCaskell, 2005).

The NDP had an articulated rhetorical commitment to the equity agenda, with visible policies, programs and resources dedicated to employment equity legislation, the *Ontario Anti-Racism Secretariat*, a range of specific community initiatives, and anti-racism policies in the educational realm. When a government "stakes out" a particular focus, there can be a number of "trickle-down" effects. For instance, a cabinet-level committee was established on anti-racism, and equity became a mandatory component of cabinet submissions. In other words, before a policy proposal could proceed to the highest decision-making levels, consideration would have to be given to the equity domain. This, in turn, meant that there would be environmental scans, research, studies, consultation, and community input into the policy process. What members of racial minority communities think about a particular issue would then be a key factor in determining the decision-making outcome. However, this is not a guarantee that other economic and political forces will not override social justice concerns, only that there would be room to discuss such matters. If these matters are not considered during the policy development process, what chance is there that there will be a solid social justice foundation in the resultant policy?

Within the space of a few weeks of being elected on June 8, 1995, the government outlined a very clear direction, and equity was not included in the list of priorities. There was a visible "divide and conquer," "we won, you lost" spirit to the time. By controlling the political agenda, the PC government was able to avoid mentioning the word racism publicly for nine years, thus ensuring that there would not be any anti-racism initiatives, all interdisciplinary efforts to address race-based concerns would be dismantled, any hopes of meeting with social justice groups would be unconditionally ruptured and, in general, there would be no emphasis placed on social justice.

When the PC government spoke of their refusal to acquiesce to the pressure of "special interests," meaning anti-racism and social justice groups, it ironically excluded business from this designation. Moreover, the Conservative government kept its promise to cut taxes—although it is arguable what the impact was, given the increased federal taxes, user-fees, lost or reduced public services, and the privatization of other services—but it did not keep its promise to introduce an "anti-discrimination education" program, as stipulated in its *Common Sense Revolution* platform. However, the media labeled the PC government as one that kept its promises, and the NDP government as one that was generally perceived as reckless and unable to faithfully do what it said it would, in large part because of a larger than expected deficit combined with a recession.

OPERATIONAL WHITENESS IN GOVERNMENT

In this section, I provide flesh to the theoretical Whiteness framework in the form of an analysis of experiences from inside government. Public servants are generally a reflection of mainstream society in that their personal ideologies will most likely not be radically different than those of the political trends of the majority. However, a significant minority are probably slightly more left of centre than the population in general. After all, they have chosen, either willingly or by default, to work in government because they did not wish to work in the private sector. Many want to make change and to assist in a cause, whether it be women's rights, minority francophone rights, the rights of racial minorities, or some other advocacy cause. How and why decisions are made is not always rational, coherent and/or justifiable, and many an honourable public servant has left government more than a little discouraged because of this. In general, during my seventeen years in government, the notion of White privilege did not appear to be considered, or was simply rejected without discussion.

In 1995, with the abrupt end to the NDP regime, many in the equity area were left numb at the thought of the new government's mission to eliminate the anti-racism file. This had become more than another policy issue; it was, for those committed to the principle, a cause, a mission, and a virtue worth fighting for. Rezai-Rashti (2003) speaks of the commitment of "equity workers," and McCaskell (2005) has outlined the ideological motivation of a core of activists in the Toronto Board of Education in the 1980s and 1990s to make progressive change from the inside. One of the shortcomings of the Ministry of Education's *Anti-racism and Ethno-cultural Equity Education Branch* was that most of the staff, the majority whom were racial minorities, had been seconded from the school board sector, and they did not have experience in government, which represented a radically different institutional culture. The Branch was not seen to be an integral part of the Ministry but, rather, an outside entity, almost a "special interest group," itself, and this fact disadvantaged it greatly.

The dynamic of White privilege is brought to the fore when considering how these new arrivals to the Ministry were seen to be attempting to disrupt the conventional, accepted educational terrain. Not everyone in the Ministry was as welcoming to the newcomers, and there were a number of complaints from people saying they resented "being treated like a racist" at anti-racism training sessions. One incident sums up the imagery of the informal resistance by Whites: a colleague in the anti-racism area attended a committee meeting of Ministry staff working on a document intended for middle-school children related to values in education, and was told the moment he entered the room that "This is not an anti-racist committee," to which he promptly responded, "Oh, then it must be a racist committee."

Shortly after the Conservatives took power, I recall a late afternoon discussion about the context for, and analysis of, a few proposals we were developing in relation to at-risk students. I made the point that, without including marginalized groups and gathering data to document and develop measures and outcomes for the whole system in an inclusive way, we could be creating and amplifying systemic barriers, effectively achieving the opposite of the intention of the business plan, which was measurement and accountability. The response by a senior official, in a slightly exasperated tone, was clear. While pointing to the door, the official stated: "You know where the door is; if you don't like it you don't have to stay." I inferred that public servants were not to provide strategic advice, to consider the research, to caution government of the implications or, especially, to discuss social justice when it does not intersect with plans originally designed from a business perspective.

Many public servants questioned why and how the business model should be transposed on public education, where the "bottom-line," it could be argued, was never intended to be profit. The most disappointing aspect of the business plans was the fact that there was no visible, credible, follow-up on the goals, targets, measures, and other barometers of success that required untold meetings and resources to generate. As a direct appendage of Whiteness, it became problematic that the social justice domain was not considered a priority-area for measurement, goal-setting and data collection.

Access to government is pivotal to be able to have input into the decision-making process. With the downfall of the NDP, who had entertained a broad range of social justice consultation and stakeholder involvement, the stark reality of the new Conservative era was brought to light at a meeting of the new *Equal Opportunity Office*, the supposed replacement for the *Ontario Anti-racism Secretariat*. The manipulation of the terminology from anti-racism to equal opportunity is illustrative of the politicization of the social justice agenda. The *Equal Opportunity Office* was widely criticized by the equity sector for being redundant, as no equal opportunity policies were made mandatory, but this did not receive any attention in the media, nor at the governmental level. I was alarmed to hear a senior official describe how the social justice groups were no longer an irritant because they simply did not exist on the government radar. The official claimed in a matter-of-fact way, that the social justice groups were "defeated." Clearly, the notions of democracy, accountability, and the need to represent and serve the whole population, are often more theoretical constructs than operating principles.

With the change in government a substantial amount of promising equity work was simply left unfinished and sent to the archives. One example of this was a document produced by Ministry staff on preventing hate-crime activities that was destined for school principals. The document provided direction on what to do to detect, prevent, and deal with hate-crime activities on school grounds, including information on graffiti, music, dress, and other signs that commonplace bullying and violence may actually be connected to insidious organized hate activity. The document, completed under the NDP's reign, was never released by the Conservatives[2], who chose not to distribute it, due to ideological issues and, most likely, because it was produced by the NDP. Several other documents—including a *Teacher's Guide for Anti-racism in the Classroom*, *Equity in Learning Materials*, which sought to assist educators in selecting, developing, evaluating, and using resources in the curriculum, *Afro-Canadian Studies*, and *Aboriginal Anti-racism Education*—were also archived. In the absence of formal guidelines, the system is able to vacillate with the ebb and flow of daily concerns without focusing on the larger picture and, in this regard, social justice was an unfortunate casualty.

My involvement in anti-racism and equity projects included leading the analysis of school board anti-racism policies, coordinating two resource-document committees, and producing a training video for teachers as well as a resource guide with practical activities for educators, primarily within the French-language education side. Minority (White) francophones felt that the main issue was one of linguistic and cultural assimilation in relation to English-language hegemony. In general, there appeared to be less comprehension of the anti-racism problematic there than in the so-called "majority" English-language sector.

Racial minority francophones have spent the last twenty years attempting to have their voices heard. The definition of the term "Franco-Ontarian" became the starting-point for endless conflict when developing anti-racism educational policy. Almost all of the personnel working in French were part of the minority Franco-Ontarian community, and many had been involved in a generations-long struggle seeking to have legitimate control of their schools. The ability to introduce the race issue was, therefore, extremely limited. As an anglophone[3] in a francophone milieu, I was told quite directly by one colleague during a presentation I made: "We are discriminated against, too, based on our accent," thus downplaying the issue of racism in the francophone community. At another presentation to a French-language advisory group to the Minister, I was told that "the problem is not the same in the francophone community." I took note that the three racial minority francophones present at the latter meeting did not concur with this position, and throughout my tenure inside and outside of government I found that racial minorities, based solely on their racial origin and lived experience, believed that racism did exist and, moreover, felt it necessary to do something about it. Some of my research has focused on different perceptions of race between racial minority and White teachers (Carr & Klassen, 1997), illustrating how lived experience can shape reality and racialized ideas. This fact, aligned with the propensity to prioritize individualism over group experience, has led to "White solidarity and White silence" (Sleeter, 2000). Thompson (2003) has highlighted the difference between being a friend of someone of colour, and understanding one's own implication in the power and privilege of being White.

Leading the analysis of French-language school board[4] anti-racism plans toward the end of the NDP mandate was a particularly enjoyable and nerve-wracking task. Only one of the six education officers on the committee was a racial minority. Each board was required to produce a rather extensive report documenting how it would plan for and meet the expectations outlined in the Ministry's anti-racism policy (Ontario Ministry of Education, 1993). We set aside an entire week to pore over the stacks of paper before us, providing ratings, scores, commentaries, and analysis for each report. We all knew one another, and we established a cordial environment, sharing lunches and breaks, and also socializing in the evening. The five White francophones were long-time educators who knew one another well, and were extremely familiar with those from whom the reports had been received. The francophone population in Ontario is relatively small, and those in senior positions would typically share many of the same experiences, networks, and values.

As we systematically examined the policies, some appeared to be well-thought-out, and others were clearly a little more haphazard. However, we were determined to provide as much leeway as possible in order to not discourage those who had put significant effort into these first reports. We ultimately landed on a report that was, in my opinion and, in a less vocal way, the opinion of the one racial minority educators at the table, extremely flawed. It contained racist overtones, a serious marginalization of minorities, and was, according to our established criteria, less than satisfactory. I stated the obvious: "We're going to have to talk to the superintendent in charge. This is not in line with our standards, and the plan they presented could be potentially dangerous." The education officer responsible for the area from which the report was filed recoiled, and then made it clear that nothing could be done: "I know the superintendent personally, and I could never say this to him." The implication was clear, that personal networks combined with representing the interests of one "minority" over that of another were to be considered more significant. The manifestation of the privilege and power accorded to Whiteness coalesces here to achieve the result of sustained marginalization, both for the Franco-Ontarian and the francophone racial minority communities.

Another example of the power of government to shape policy is the way the Ontario curriculum was rewritten under the PC government. This was a massive undertaking, involving tens of millions of dollars, hundreds of teachers and curriculum writers, and an army of communications staff to get the message out. The message from the Premier's Office was clear: The new curriculum should be focused uniquely on high standards. In all of the preparations for this vast remaking of formal school knowledge[5], the word on the exclusion of equity concerns was equally clear. This caused infinite problems for educators who considered it central to learning, especially those in the social sciences (Fielding, 2002). Some colleagues working directly in this area felt a sense of shame that Ontario, the province long considered one of the most progressive, would turn so radically to a business-model approach. What made matters worse was the involvement of business groups in the writing of the curriculum, people whose main interest in this regard was on employability, preparing students for the workplace, and being competitive (Fielding, 2002).

In another highly unusual experience, I accompanied a colleague in the soon-to-be defunct *Anti-racism and Ethno-cultural Equity Branch* in 1995 to an evening meeting with the leaders of the teachers' federations to discuss the impending changes to the employment equity legislation. After a few pleasantries and some conjecturing about the rapidly changing political climate, my colleague laid the issue bare: "As you know, the employment equity legislation is going to be revoked, and under the new Act, you will not be allowed to collect or maintain data based on racial origin." The five union representatives on the other side of the table grinned, chuckled, and collectively shook their heads, then one of them summed up the general feeling with this rhetorical question: "Let me get this right. We spent five years resisting, and trying to be convinced, and fighting the government against the employment equity legislation, and now we're in a position to make some gains, and we understand why we're doing it, and you're now telling us to destroy all of the data?" As a compendium, despite the fact that there are no data to prove it, it seemed as though there was a rather dramatic Whitening of the senior levels in the Ministry of Education once the Conservatives reclaimed power.

DISCUSSION

While undertaking my doctoral thesis I interviewed a senior education official of racial minority origin who made me reflect about White privilege with the following comment: "How would you like it if you were the only White with 11 Black people around the boardroom-table, and every time you spoke the others would smile and whisper to each other that this is the White perspective?" The ability to intervene freely within an institutional context can be largely shaped by the privilege accorded to Whiteness, which is rendered more salient when considering that many White educators are unaware of their racial identities and connection to the perpetuation of racism (Thompson, 2003):

> To pursue social justice, we have to decenter whiteness from programs for social change. Among other things, this means relinquishing our cherished notions of morality: how we understand fairness, how we understand what it means to be a good person, how we understand what it means to be generous or sympathetic or tolerant or a good listener. When we are challenged for our whiteness, our tendency is to fall back on our goodness, fairness, intelligence, rationality, sensitivity, and democratic inclusiveness, all of which are caught up with our whiteness. "How can you call me (me, of all people!) a racist?" (pp. 16-17)

I was somewhat surprised and frustrated by the reaction of some educators with whom I was working, many of whom openly refused to entertain anti-racism training, curricula, resources, or policies because "all of our kids are White." This was said as if it somehow precluded the White students from understanding the human condition, how they interacted with and benefited from racism, the reality that there were probably First Nations people in their schools who would go unnoticed. Moreover, they were ignoring that rampant diversity already existed in their midst at the cultural, socio-economic, religious, and family levels, not to mention that they would eventually need to interact with a diverse world. If there is no anti-racist organizational strategy, program, or curriculum, how could there be progressive, critical engagement in the area of social justice?

A critical realization from this review of how government functions in support of Whiteness resides in the infinite number of subtleties and nuances framing the discourse. Despite the numerous efforts, resources, and pronouncements in support of social justice at the formal, institutional level, the results appear to be extremely mitigated and the impact rarely sustained. Aldous Bergeron (2003), in her research on critical race theory, questions the legitimacy of arguments hinged on neutrality, merit, and colour-blindness, notions that are consistently used to dilute social justice initiatives and, importantly, to avoid any discussion of Whiteness.

The power to manipulate and omit language has been used to convince broad sectors of society of the high level of "democracy" and "accountability" in education (Hoover & Shook, 2003). Henry and Tator (2005) have skillfully argued that there is a *de facto* democratic racism at play since all of the key forces, including the courts, the legislature, big business, the media, and others, have agreed with one another that racism is not what people of "colour" say it is.

Within the context of the institutional analysis of the Ontario case, it is noteworthy that the rationale for eliminating employment equity and anti-racism in 1995 was that these policies did not respect the merit principle. The question raised by many activists was: "Merit by whose standards?" It is telling that the elite White sector never questioned discrimination in employment and education against racial minorities when there was clearly a quota or outright exclusive bias for Whites in positions of authority for centuries. Marx and Pennington (2003) raise an issue that troubles and confounds many Whites, concerning the perceived paradoxical relationship between goodness and anti-racism:

> Thus, naming racism within themselves [White pre-service teachers] was at first cause for great concern. This is the point where guilt, fear, and even trauma came into the picture. Because they viewed goodness and racism as a dichotomy, their first glimpse of their racism led them to the conclusion that they must be horrible people. It seemed that, in coming to terms with their own racism, our students/participants necessarily had to make the connection that they could still be good be people and still be racist.... Moreover, despite their altruistic hearts and their efforts to "hide" their racism, it is still possible for their racism to hurt the children they teach. (p. 105)

Referring back to the general theme of investigation for this chapter, in relation to educational policymaking, particular concerning Whiteness and accountability, it is clear that some form of a social justice framework at the institutional level would be advantageous in order to create a space for discussing and dealing with the issue of inequity. Understanding how identity shapes the process and outcome of decision-making is critical for there to be responsive policies in place. These policies could then more effectively take into consideration the manifestation of inequitable power relations. Democracy needs to consider difference, diversity, and lived experience and, therefore, educational systems would benefit from a continual analysis of how Whiteness influences the normative values of the educators, schools, and decision-makers.

QUESTIONS FOR REFLECTION

1. How should Whiteness be broached within an institutional context by those who may not be in positions of power?
2. How should Whites be made aware of, and become engaged in, the conceptualization and application of race and anti-racism?
3. What types of research can best be used to support social justice work?
4. What strategies and research could be formulated to address disenfranchisement in the policy process?
5. What do members of minoritized racial groups need to be aware of as they become part of the decision-making process?

NOTES

[1] Social justice, for the purposes of this article, is considered to include a focus on the human condition, discrimination, equity, racism, and other forms of oppression and difference, and, within the educational policy context, is concerned with inclusion, representation, processes, content and outcomes from a critical perspective, seeking to contextualize, frame and promote debate and action

around these issues. The term "equity," although there are some nuanced interpretations, is used as a complement to social justice herein. Vincent (2003) focuses on identity in her definition of social justice, and this is also to be considered pivotal in this paper. Although I examine primarily the issue of race in my analysis on Whiteness, it is implicit that race is socially constructed, and, therefore, that we must consider the intersectionality of identity, including gender, class, sexual orientation, and other markers of identity.

2   Although I did not hear this directly, I was told that one of the problems with the document, according to staff in the Minister's Office, was that it was unfair to point to White supremacist groups but not Black supremacist groups.

3   I use this terminology here since identity is socially constructed, and for minority francophones I am considered an "anglophone." Perhaps this is part of the power and privilege of a majority-person to be able to critique the socio-linguistics of identity, but I feel that the notion of an "anglophone" is laded with cultural connotations that do not necessarily relate to the vast majority of those considered anglophones, including racial minority, non-Christian, non-English-speaking immigrants.

4   There are now twelve French-language school boards, but at the time of the review mentioned above, there were some 73 French-language sections, essentially parts of English-language boards, and two French-language boards.

5   Here, I make a distinction between formal and informal curricula.

REFERENCES

Applebaum, B. (2005). In the name of morality: Moral responsibility, whiteness and social justice education. *Journal of Moral Education, 34*(3), 277–290.

Bergeron, A. (2003). Critical race theory and white racism: Is there room for white scholars in fighting racism in education? *Qualitative Studies in Education, 16*(1), 51–63.

Carr, P. R., & Klassen, T. (1997). Different perceptions of race in education: Racial minority and white teachers. *Canadian Journal of Education, 1,* 68–81.

Corson, D. (2001). Ontario students as a means to the government's end. *Our Schools/Our Selves, 10*(4), 57–80.

Dei, G. J. S., Karumanchery, L., & Karumanchery-Luik, N. (2004). *Playing the race card: Exposing white power and privilege.* New York, NY: Peter Lang.

Feagin, J., & O'Brien, E. (2003). *White men on race: Power, privilege, and the shaping of cultural consciousness.* Boston, MA: Beacon Press.

Fielding, J. (2002). Tales from the crypt, or writing the Ontario Canadian studies and world studies curriculum. *Our Schools/Our Selves.* Retrieved from http://www.policyalternatives.ca/index.cfm?act =news&call=789&do=article&pA=BB736455

Fine, M., Weis, L., Powell Pruitt, L., & Burns, A. (2004). *Off white: Readings on power, privilege, and resistance.* New York, NY: Routledge.

Fullan, M. (2005). *Leadership and sustainability: System thinkers in action.* Thousand Oaks, CA: Corwin Press.

Henry, F., & Tator, C. (2005). *The colour of democracy: Racism in Canadian schools.* Toronto, ON: Thompson Nelson.

Hoover, R., & Shook, K. (2003). School reform and accountability: Some implications and issues for democracy and fair play. *Democracy and Education, 14*(4), 81–86.

Leithwood, K. (2001). Five reasons why most accountability policies don't work (and what you can do about it). *Orbit, 32*(1), 1–5.

Lipman, P. (2004). Education accountability and repression of democracy post-9/11. *Journal of Critical Education Policy Studies, 2*(1). Retrieved from http://jceps.com/?pageID =article&articleID=23

Marx, S., & Pennington, J. (2003). Pedagogies of critical race theory: Experimentations with White preservice teachers, *Qualitative Studies in Education, 16*(1), 91–110.

McCaskell, T. (2005). *Race to equity: Disrupting educational inequality.* Toronto, ON: Between the Lines.

Ontario Ministry of Education and Training. (2003). *Antiracism and ethnocultural equity in school boards.* Toronto, ON: Ministry of Education and Training.

Rezai-Rashti, G. (2003). Educational policy reform and its impact on equity work in Ontario: Global challenges and local possibilities. *Education Policy Analysis Archives, 11*(51), 1–15.

Sleeter, C. (2000). Multicultural education, social positionality, and whiteness. In E. Manual Duarte & S. Smith (Eds.), *Foundational perspectives in multicultural education* (pp. 118–134). Reading, MA: Longman.

Thompson, A. (2003). Tiffany, friend of people of color: White investments in antiracism. *Qualitative Studies in Education, 16*(1), 7–29.

Vincent, C. (2003). *Social justice, education and identity.* New York, NY: RoutledgeFalmer.

REFRAMING: PAUL R. CARR (2014)

MOVING FORWARD, BEYOND POLITICS, POLICY, AND PARTISANSHIP: SEEKING THE TRUTH IN SPITE OF THE ANSWERS

Since writing this chapter, and being involved in this evolving project with Darren Lund over the past seven years, I have come to realize that Whiteness is within us all, in a more deeply embedded way than I had originally thought. I can see how race, then and now, is pivotal to our daily experiences and larger social questions but I also understand more clearly now how it is inextricably linked to the broader macro-level. Globalization, hegemony, international affairs, the political economy, war and peace, and other subjects of considerable importance are not far away; they are right in front of us, even if we dispute that they have any direct relevance to what we are doing here and now. I do not say this as though I have found the answer. On the contrary, I have come to accept more fully how epistemology and philosophical orientations underpin what we see, here and now, and what we wish to see, here and now.

When I wrote the chapter in our first edition of *The Great White North?* I was trying to make sense of these seemingly disparate educational policy realities that coalesced to make me believe that racism within anti-racist work was not a coincidental affair. I look back at the examples I provided, and I can remember living through real social interactions that were hurtful, painful, forbidding, unnecessary, and senseless. At the same time, not everyone felt that way. Rather, many people felt the contrary, that the real problem is that some people were insisting that there was a problem in the first place. The heart of the matter is power – who has it, how it is used, how it is understood, how it is obeyed, and how it affects people disproportionately.

There are many ways to understand power and, here, I believe that my own thinking has evolved somewhat. As Foucault and others have noted, it is diffuse, not held in one person's hands, and, importantly, it is manifested throughout cultural interplay. Therefore, cultural capital is pivotal. It is wonderful to hope for change, and to preach for it, as the almost iconic first Black President of the United States is well known for, but this is where I believe that we have hit another layer of the Whiteness onion. It might be called Whiteness 2.0, a hazy terrain where even Barack Obama knows that he should not really touch these most fundamental and pivotal issues that define us.

Not only have race, racism, and racialization in the United States not disappeared under a Black President, some would even argue that the absence of critical debate and acknowledgement, as Cornel West has argued, is dangerous to the mainstream

D. E. Lund & P. R. Carr (Eds.), Revisiting The Great White North?, 281–282.

psyche. Race does not have to be brought under a lens for every single gesture, act, and movement, but it should not be so mainstreamed that we are led to believe that it is only through capitalism and normative hegemonic relations that we can succeed.

This leads me to my field of research over the past many years: democracy, political literacy and the quest for transformative education. I now more fully embrace the macro-context, and how it impacts our most innate micro interactions. How I experience relationships, cultures, economics, politics, and other vital aspects of life cannot be detached from the macro power structures. Am I to believe that the US invading Iraq was an innocent gesture, and what can be made of the notion that the US President who initiated the act of war has been sought as a war criminal for crimes against humanity by many around the world? How should I understand that his predecessor has not critically interrogated the place of US empire, including the war industry? How can I understand poverty in Africa? How can I understand social inequalities here at home? What am I to make of the overwhelming internalization of untold quantities of superfluous reality-shows within our society?

So where is Canada in all of this? Are we improving? Is our only or main measure of progress solely economic growth and wealth accumulation? Why are so many stories and realities absent from the mainstream? How can Aboriginal peoples, in 2014, still be fighting for what most would consider the most basic of concerns?

I remain firmly committed to the notion that change will come but only if our educational framework is radically infused with critical, meaningful curriculum, pedagogy, institutional culture, experiential knowledge/action, and, significantly, educational policy that seeks to go beyond the common strictures of maintaining and constraining power. The goal cannot be simply an economic one, employability, and the endless reproduction of social relations. There has to be a commitment to what Paulo Freire called *conscientization*, and also radical love, which Freire invoked to move us beyond the individual, selfish, power-driven sense of sustaining inequitable relations.

Whiteness has not gone away. It has morphed into the venomous stew of supposedly normalized capitalist relations that are considered, in our society, as the only alternative and option. There are many voices, thoughts, and concerns speckled throughout all lands, and a more transformative, decentred, counter-hegemonic education would be a very good start to altering the balance of power. We should celebrate what has been achieved, the solidarity and networks that exist, and the beauty of all children, regardless of the origin of their parents. And we should also seek to problematize why injustice has been so thoroughly infused in what we do, on a daily basis, and within the broad, less comprehensible big-picture sphere.

If I could sum up my analysis over the past many years, I would simply say that a great deal of humility is required to engage in these most important discussions, and then the real work of addressing the reality that these problems actually exist can begin.

GINA THÉSÉE

A CHRONIC IDENTITY INTOXICATION SYNDROME: WHITENESS AS SEEN BY AN AFRICAN-CANADIAN FRANCOPHONE WOMAN (2014)

INTRODUCTION

> My work requires me to think about how free I can be as an African-American woman writer in my genderized, sexualized, wholly racialised world. To think about (and wrestle with) the full implications of my situation. (Morrison, 1992, p. 4)

Who am I? Who am I within the gaze of the Other? Who am I within my own reflection? I've been looking for the answers to these identity questions in a deforming mirror that constantly sends me the same message, a negative one that hurts. I can try to clean, polish, and soften this image but the unforgiving mirror always returns a merciless verdict: Ugly! Undesirable phenotype, outside of the well-established Western canon of beauty. I am a Black woman…. Who am I cognitively? Who am I cognitively in the minds of the *other*? I have been seeking answers in the expectations of my peers, my teachers, the media and society, in general, who often present me with a disqualified report card: Loser! Low intellectual quotient (IQ)! I am a Black woman… Who am I professionally? Who am I professionally according to the standards and criteria established by the Other?

I have been seeking answers to my great professional aspirations, frustrated by the relentless social representations that have encircled me even despite my own accomplishments: Incompetent in everything! Competent to undertake domestic work in White people's homes! I have been looking for answers in my relations with women, men, Black, White and other, who have accompanied me throughout my studies, my work, my leisure activities, my travels, and my daily life. Within the discreet, suspicious surveillance of the cashier, the doorman, the security-guard or the immigration officer, I understand that their verdict has already been made: I am suspected of being incapable of paying the rent, of theft, or illegal entry into my country because: I am a Black woman…

What is the nature of this deforming mirror of my image? Who oversees my educational exclusion? Who benefits from my professional exclusion? Why is my body marked with the slashing swaths of metal chains rooted in poverty? Especially, what are the mechanisms of this quadruple social negation enterprise of my person,

D. E. Lund & P. R. Carr (Eds.), Revisiting The Great White North?, 283–292.

and how can I undo all of this? These are some of the many existential questions that the generic "I" has formulated, an unidentifiable Black woman, who feels guilty, quite simply, for existing. The complexity of the social negation mechanism and self-negation suggests a chronic identity intoxication syndrome that contains insidious toxicity, which is present at all times within the social, professional, family, conjugal and intimate spheres. This toxicity is particularly of an epistemological nature because the "particles" at work in the intoxication process are forms of knowledge, validated and largely diffused by artistic, cultural, educational, media, political, religious, and other institutions. These forms of knowing also take multiple forms: representations, stereotypes, opinions, dogma, principles, beliefs, theories, laws, rules, norms, research results, and the like.

Whiteness is an epistemological poison that intoxicates in a chronic way the Black woman in the most common facets of life. I address the concept of Whiteness, from the perspective of a Black female, as a chronic intoxication process that manifests itself in a complex and multi-faceted syndrome. In this chapter, I have chosen to explore three identity dimensions that seem to me to be fundamental: the esthetic dimension, the cognitive dimension, and the socio-professional dimension. The generic "I," as narrator of the text, takes into consideration my own personal experiences but is not limited only to them; rather, it is hoped that my own voice will be able to speak, however modestly, for other voices facing the chronic intoxications that I have outlined above. In the following pages, I analyse the chronic intoxication known as Whiteness through the gaze of a Black, francophone female of Haitian origin in Quebec, who came to this society in 1970. I attempt to link Whiteness with what I consider to be one of the principal effects: the learned or acquired impotence and the identity erosion mechanisms within the spheres of esthetics cognition and socio-professional realities. I end with some reflections on the beginning of a detoxification epistemology.

I. WHITENESS: CHRONIC IDENTITY INTOXICATION, AND A LEARNED/ ACQUIRED IMPOTENCE

Although the Anglophone/English-language term Whiteness has been widely studied in the English-language academic literature (Carr & Lund, 2007; Frankenberg, 1993; Henry & Tator, 2009; Morrison, 1992), it does not have a French-language equivalent. In the French-language translation of Morrison (1993), there is reference to *blancheur*, whereas Carr (2010) has proposed the French-language term *blanchitude*. Blanchitude echoes the French-language term *Négritude* developed by Aimé Césaire in 1939, which laid bare the raw and bloody reality for Blacks within a White colonial empire, and also spoke to the struggle through art, ontology, philosophy and emotion to unite those in conditions that were imbued in exploitation and domination (Senghor, 1967).

The concept of Whiteness is defined as a posture of structural privilege, an advantaged social position, considered as the universal norm, neutral, objective and normative, and is framed with the notion that Whites are naturally superior over Others, exhibiting knowledge, traits and traditions that naturally marginalize and exclude those not in the dominant group (Frankenberg, as cited in Henry & Tator, 2009). Therefore, Whiteness is inextricably linked to epistemological racism because of the broad range of knowledge of diverse realities (epistemology), values (axiology), and the ways of accessing knowledge (methodology) that are intertwined around social interactions.

The relationship that one has to Whiteness is a constitutive component to one's multiple identities and social positions, hinged on particular geographic, cultural, family and other contexts (Henry & Tator, 2009). This is how I personally relate to whiteness, as a chronic intoxication process with powerful pathogens and toxic knowledge, which give rise to an autoimmune pathology: learned/acquired impotence. My objective is not to essentialize Whiteness and to develop it as a monolithic, homogeneous, stable phenomenon, but rather, to illustrate the lived experiences that are inscribed in the epistemological contours of the specific context of a Black Canadian woman of Haitian origin within the French-language academy. According to Monture (2009), since Whiteness deals with a form of *de facto* privilege for the dominant social group, it is, therefore, found at the intersection of critical sociological concepts, including race, class and gender. However, the migratory, ethical, linguistic, religious and academic trajectory as well as the fundamental facets of one's professional life are all characteristics that serve to further influence and exacerbate Whiteness.

From my perspective, the principal effect of Whiteness on the Black woman is one of learned/acquired impotence. The learned impotence or acquired resignation can be linked to the concept of *learned helplessness*, from the work of the French scholar, Martin Seligman and his colleagues in developmental psychology in the 1960s and 1970s (Nolen-Hoeksema, 1986; Overmier, 2002). At the theoretical and experimental levels, the acquired resignation is associated with the causal attribution theory elaborated by Weiner (Lafortune & Saint-Pierre, 1996; Thésée, 2003). This theory has four dimensions: the place of power (internal or external); the breadth (specific or general); the duration (stable or instable); and the level of control (controllable or incontrollable).

The learned/acquired helplessness is defined as a state of mind that results from unpleasant, painful and abrasive situations that are uncontrolled and repeated, and which have the following outcomes: 1) the difficulty for someone to establish a link between his/her actions and tangible results; 2) the feeling of having no control over the results of one's actions, and, therefore, are considered independent from the person at the origin of these actions; 3) a progressive diminution of one's self-esteem and motivation; and 4) behaviours associated with passivity, inaction and resignation, even within situations characterized by great adversity (Nolen, 2009). According to Pervin and John (2005), the perception of independence between actions and the subsequent results may have motivational, cognitive and affective consequences that could undermine future actions. Further, these authors argue that learned/acquired impotence can lead to highly destructive social conditions, including low educational attainment, poverty, drug abuse, domestic violence, child abuse, alcoholism, depression and other forms of discrimination.

Thus, I am seeking to develop here a direct relationship or correlation between Whiteness, as experienced by Black women within the chronic identity intoxication and the learned/acquired impotence, which is a major effect of such intoxication. In the next few sections, I attempt to outline the process of Whiteness intoxication in three dimensions of identity: the physical-aesthetic dimension (the body); the cognitive dimension (the intellect); and the socio-professional dimension (competencies within the work content).

II. WHITENESS AS AN INTOXICATION PROCESS IN THREE DIMENSIONS OF IDENTITY

1. WHITENESS INTOXICATION WITHIN THE PHYSICAL-AESTHETIC DIMENSION

The body is of central importance in how we understand and identify ourselves, and I believe that this is the first salient dimension in the intoxication process. What relation do I, as a Black woman, have to my body within the dual context that I must negotiate daily in which the White body is held as the standard of beauty? How am I to understand my body within the guise of diverse forms of educational, acculturated and socialized alienation? How am I to love my body, knowing that it is not the object of admiration and desire of the Other? I am shunted from side to side trying to understand the place of the Black woman, never as desirable as the White woman, not considered as virile and erotized as the Black male, or as complete as the quintessential power and knowledge of the White male, seeking some social acceptance of the Black female body that has been stereotyped, vilified, and portrayed as hired help, domestic worker and an outsider of drastic proportion?

It is important to question how the White male has portrayed the Black female through dominant discourse, images, representations, knowledge, art, expositions, sculptures, cinema, videos, and a host of other media. I perceive the present context as a sophisticated extension, almost unchanged, of the colonizer-slaver dynamic that has characterized European colonialism these past few centuries (Henry & Tator, 2009). Here, we might highlight that the White colonizer systematically misunderstood African nudity, believing it to be a symbol of hyper-sexualisation as compared to the concomitant hiding of the White European female body (Jeurissen, 2003). Within this ethnocultural production, the "exotic" body is exhibited and objectified as a cultural artifact alongside jungle landscapes and tropical animals. The Black female body has been conquered through race and gender, violated and abused, and it has been transformed by the White colonizer into the domesticated care-giver for children, the elderly, the disabled, and others who dominate power structures. The unfavourable and painful images of the Black women, sometimes obese, sometimes subjected to female excision, sometimes molested, elicits, at the same time, compassion and revulsion (Jeurissen, 2003). Thus, the relationship between the White man and the Black female has always been clouded with insipid notions of whether or not she is a prostitute, a subjugated and unequal partner, the nanny or the real mother of their children, etc., which is compounded by the cultural issue of many Black men wanting and desiring White or lighter-skinned Black women.

The contemporary beauty of the Black women, which is celebrated on fashion runways, movie-sets and music-videos usually involves those qualities most resembling the desired attributes of the normatively sought-after White woman: light skin, straight hair, aquiline nose, slender body, and the like (Jeurissen, 2003). "Colourism" is in vogue, and the preference is definitively for lighter shades of dark than darker ones. The difference here from racism is that racism generally concerns people from different racial groups whereas colourism concerns people within the same racial group, as is the case in Haiti, and throughout Latin America, Africa and Asia. One just has to look at the power structures in any of these racialized regions to determine the salience of racial identity, and women are always further placed lower on the power hierarchy. We can debate the degree to which colourism was a dominant feature to all societies before colonialism and slavery, but it is undeniable that it has taken on greater proportions as a result.

The learned/acquired impotence of Whiteness has the cruel effect of imprisoning the Black female body, with the potential of labelling it ascetically unappealing, condemning it to an awkward and unacceptable phenotype and genealogy that can lead to low self-esteem and the potential for emancipation.

2. THE COGNITIVE DIMENSION

"All babies are born White; it's only afterward that some become Black." This phrase was pronounced in a relaxed and knowledgeable way by a catechism teacher I had in a French-language school in Montreal in the second year of secondary school, which equates to roughly Grade 8 in English-language schools in North America, at the beginning of the 1970s. As the only Black student in the class, I slowly experienced the mysterious and somewhat compassionate gaze of all of the other students on me. Bothered and embarrassed, this lonely Black student tries to understand why. Have the other students just found their lost sister, or has this lonely girl been contaminated by the Black mark that has permanently scarred her? I can think of characters in books who have been so maligned, and I also look around at all of the iconography of White men and women, White children, White leaders, White prophets, and White religious and spiritual symbols of the most fundamental importance. The saintly always have blue eyes. Later in science class she discovers the basis of genetic configurations that determine innate and acquired genes and physical characteristics.

However, the interest in science will soon reveal to this girl the underside, or hidden face, of the discipline, notably in favour of neo-racism in alliance with social derivatives of the genetic, unearthing the theory of the natural inequality of the races, the inherent superiority of some populations over others, eugenics, deleterious IQ tests, and the like. The epistemology of Whiteness is marinated within the supposed obvious sentiment that Blacks are not as bright, engaged, intelligent and successful. By way of example, and there are so many that it boggles the mind when one is actually looking for them as opposed to being a passive recipient, I refer to the December 8, 2004, edition of the newspaper, *Le Devoir*, which profiled the under-performance of Québécois students on international education (PISA) tests. Under the article, there was a large photo of a Black student, not normally considered the mainstream of Quebec society, and then there was a second photo of a classroom full of Black students.

The francophone literature and research contain myriad keywords, concepts, and theories that disable the function-key leading to an insightful epistemological deconstruction of toxic knowledge for Black men and women. The concepts of race, racism, Blacks, Whiteness, *negritude, Africanicity, Afro-descendants,* and *Creole* are all taboo, at one level or another, within the French-language educational research canon. Presenting on Whiteness, as I have done, within the French-language context often leads to the pointed and accusatory question of relevance, foundation and legitimacy: the accepted position is that such a thing simply does not exist.

The learned/acquired helplessness effect of Whiteness can be illustrated by the metaphor of the "Oreo" cookie, which is well known to have a white cream centre covered by two chocolate biscuits. In one of my classes, a Black student gave a presentation, to which a White student congratulated him by saying: "In reality, you are like an Oreo cookie, black on the outside but white on the inside." Obviously, for the White student, the White part related to high academic achievement. The Black student can be seen through the causal attribution of his academic success through external factors (to be like Whites), notions of intelligence (normative IQ), uncontrollable issues (being judged by Others), and questions related to stability (there will always be astonishment that he is "smart," like Whites). This framework and context can only have a negative effect on those who are continually observed as being negatively different. Supposed intrinsic values within a particular group are magnified, thus affecting, labelling and marginalizing individuals within a specific group. This can almost be considered as identity theft. This feeds into the hegemonic, relativistic value-set that blankets young Blacks, particularly in the United States, where they are told to work hard, study more, be disciplined, and conform, what some have labelled as "acting White," which can then lead to a mocking estrangement from others within their own community (Ogbu, 2004).

3. THE SOCIOPROFESSIONAL DIMENSION

"When I first saw you in front of a group of students, I thought you were a supply teacher." This phrase, seemingly innocuous, was said to a new teacher at a secondary school in Montreal, a Black woman who was newly qualified to teach. Why did he think that she must have been a supply teacher? The sub-text must be that his perception is that a Black teacher must be unqualified, incompetent, or unprofessional. In Montreal, probably like elsewhere, supply teaching is associated with instability, no or limited qualifications, difficult working conditions, and a non-professional status. This is not an isolated situation: How many times has a Black mother of a mixed-race child been considered the child's nanny? Or the Black female professor who was viewed as a graduate student? Or the Black female doctor assumed to be a nurse? All of these situations have a common point: there is a natural belief that the Black woman does not have a high socio-professional status. Her credibility is attacked, and she must justify how she made it to where she did. She must prove that she has the qualities and competencies to lead, which is not necessarily the case for other people and groups. The questioning of what is excellence in the academy, for example, has long been a concern related to Black women candidates (Kobayashi, 2009). How do we understand hegemony in such a context, and do Black women face different and debilitating barriers to which others may not be subjected?

The norm in universities is the knowledge produced by White men, and the Black woman faces a triple aesthetic threat related to her gender, race and power (Jeurissien, 2003). The Black woman academician must content with direct (intentional acts) and indirect discrimination (negative impact related to supposedly "neutral" rules and laws). The invalidation of knowledge, through a form of epistemological racism, leads to the accusation of being an imposter against those whose knowledge is considered inacceptable or irrelevant.

The learned/acquired impotence of Whiteness can be understand here as a mechanism to silence the Black woman, to seek her assimilation, cooptation and/ or conformity. In seeking to legitimize her presence within the White academy, that which has created formal knowledge, the Black woman must carefully navigate the halls of power, seeking tenure while also wishing to contribute in ways that honour her very being, all of which can lead to an internal questioning of her place: does she belong? She may question her internal qualities or she may question the external factors, which are not controllable, which can the lead to a professional epistemology of learned/acquired impotence.

In comparison to Canadian anglophone universities, there seems to be less diversity with the francophone academic milieu. Black women are rare and isolated, which presents the problem of solidarity and collaboration needed to be able to confront and reconcile Whiteness at the professional level. If others are imbued within the grasp of Whiteness, how is the Black woman to attempt to address what she sees as practices, realities, and contexts that adversely affect her and others?

III. DETOXIFICATION OF WHITENESS?

Whiteness identity intoxication is chronic (continual), systemic (everywhere), and systematic (in everything), and manifests itself so thoroughly and completely that the physical-aesthetic, cognitive and socioprofessional dimensions for the Black woman appear to be blanketed by the learned/acquired impotence that makes engaging in a detoxification process almost unimaginable. There have been many movements that have sought to re-imagine Blackness, and to render it on to its own plain, outside of or in spite of Whiteness. The world has seen the success, achievements and accomplishments of Black women in music and dance (i.e., jazz, blues, African dance, hip hop, contemporary music), verbal expression (i.e., Ebonics, Slam, Rap), literature (i.e., Toni Morrison, Nobel Prize winner for literature, and Maya Angelou), sports (i.e., the Williams sisters in tennis), culture and philosophy (i.e., negritude), and so on. Other important models have also emerged, including within the realms of sociopolitical activism (Angela Davis), academics (bell hooks), media (Oprah Winfrey), and within the political field (Michaëlle Jean), Canada's first Black Governor-General. How have these women helped to unveil the veneer of Whiteness that filters society? How have they contributed to the Whiteness detoxification process?

As I write this I am struck by the enormous celebrity, success and important of these women. Yet, apart from Michaëlle Jean, a fellow Haitian, all are African-American women, Black women from the English-speaking United States. This striking realization makes me wonder about the role of Black women within the francophone world. Is American culture so important that we have difficulty relating to anything without relating to the hegemonic grasp of our neighbours to the South? I will not delve into the importance of having a Black president of the United States, and what that might mean for Black women, given the focus of this chapter and the space available but wonder how Whiteness might be perpetuated, quite successfully, even with Blacks in very prominent leadership positions. The sociological intersection of race, class and gender would appear to be critical in how any detoxification might take place.

CONCLUSION

I have sought to highlight in this chapter that the Whiteness within the Black female body, mind and being is complex, relentless and imbued with painful situations that make addressing it extremely challenging. Is this paranoia, or is there a *bone fide* foundation to the lived experiences of Black females? Can Black feminism be part of the answer? How can alliances with Whites enable a Whiteness detoxification?

I would like to end by suggesting that Whiteness exists in French, and in all languages, even if we don't have words for it, or we don't openly present it as a dominant feature in our identities. Thus, education is key to chipping away at what Whiteness means, how it manifests itself, and what we can do about it. The sociocultural context cannot be ignored, and we need to collaborate more closely across boundaries, religions, ideologies and languages. Being a Black woman in a predominantly White French society presents infinite nuances, complexities, and problems, and it has also led to many positive, uplifting and wonderful things, such as human relations, children, grandchildren, and solidarity with others. Whiteness cannot leave us indifferent, and the detoxification process is a necessary cleansing that all of us need, at one level or another.

QUESTIONS FOR REFLECTION

1. How can the Black woman resist the intoxication process and liberate herself from the cultural values, images and words of the Other?
2. Are Black women able to consider new alliances and solidarity with other women of colour and all other sectors of society, and begin the process of self-love and emancipation?
3. What is the responsibility of Black men, White women and White men in the Whiteness experienced by Black women?
4. How does (mis)education intersect with Whiteness to alienate Black women? How can education help to deconstruct and dismantle the connectivity of Whiteness and gendering?
5. Why do you think the francophone spheres of education, research, and literature are so reluctant to consider Critical Race Theory and the concept of Whiteness?

NOTE

[1]   I would like to thank Paul R. Carr for translating this chapter as well as his comments that helped enrich the arguments contained therein.

REFERENCES

Abramson, L., Seligman, M., & Teasdale, J. D. (1978). Learned helplessness in humans: Critique and reformulation. *Journal of Abnormal Psychology, 87*, 49–74.
Carr, P. R. (2010). L'interculturel et la race blanche: La face cachée des relations de pouvoir inéquitables. Dans G. Thésée, N. Carignan, & P. R. Carr (éds.), *Les faces cachées de l'interculturel: De la rencontre des porteurs de cultures* (pp. 201–222). Paris, France: L'Harmattan.
Carr, P. R., & Lund, D. E. (Eds.). (2007). *The great White north? Exploring Whiteness, privilege and identity in education.* Rotterdam, The Netherlands: Sense.
Césaire, A. (1956). *Cahier d'un retour au pays natal.* Paris, France: Présence africaine.
Chouinard, M.-A. (2004, December 8). Éducation: Le Canada perd des points au classement mondial. *Le Devoir.* Retrieved from http://www.ledevoir.com/societe/education/70306/education-le-canada-perd-des-points-au-classement-mondial
Cottereau, D. (2012). Habiter par corps. Éducation relative à l'environnement. Regards – Recherches Réflexions, *10*, 17–34.
Frost, P. (2010). *Femmes claires, hommes foncés. Les racines oubliées du colorisme.* Québec, PQ: Presses de l'Université Laval.
Jeurissen, L. (2003). *Colonisation au masculin et mise en corps de la féminité noire : le cas de l'ancien Congo Belge.* Retrieved from http://www.congoforum.be/upldocs/Jeurissen.pdf
Kobayashi, A. (2009). Now you see them, how you see them: Women of colour in Canadian academia. In F. Henry & C. Tator (Eds.), *Racism in the Canadian university: Demanding social justice, inclusion, and equity* (pp. 60–75). Toronto, ON: University of Toronto Press.

G. THÉSÉE

Lafortune, L., & Saint-Pierre, L. (1996). L'affectivité et la métacognition dans la classe. Montréal, PQ: Les Éditions LOGIQUES.
Monture, P. (2009). Doing academia differently: Confronting 'whiteness' in the university. In F. Henry & C. Tator (Eds.), *Racism in the Canadian university: Demanding social justice, inclusion, and equity* (pp. 76–105). Toronto, ON: University of Toronto Press.
Morrison, T. (1992). *Playing in the dark: Whiteness and the literary imagination.* Cambridge, MA: Harvard University Press.
Morrison, T. (1992). *Playing in the dark. Blancheur et imagination littéraire.* Paris, France: Christian Bourgeois Éditeur.
Nolen, J. L. (2009). Learned helplessness. *Encyclopaedia Britannica.* Retrieved from http://www.britannica.com/EBchecked/topic/1380861/learned-helplessness
Nolen-Hoeksema, S., Seligman, E. P., & Girgus, J. S. (1986). Learned helplessness in children: A longitudinal study of depression, achievement, and explanatory style. *Journal of Personality and Social Psychology, 51*(2), 435–442.
Ogbu, J. (2004). Collective identity and the burden of 'acting white' in Black history, community, and education. *The Urban Review, 36*(1), 1–35.
Overmier, J. B. (2002). On learned helpnessness. *Integrative Physiological Behavioral Science, 37*(1), 4–8.
Pervin, L. P., & John, O. P. (2005). *La personnalité : De la théorie à la recherche.* Montréal, PQ: Éditions du Renouveau pédagogique.
Senghor, L. S. (1967). Qu'est-ce que la négritude? *Études françaises, 3*(1), 3–20. Retrieved from http://www.erudit.org/revue/etudfr/1967/v3/n1/036251ar.pdf
Thésée, G. (2003). *Le rapport au savoir scientifique en contexte d'acculturation: Application à l'étude de l'expérience scolaire en sciences d'élèves du secondaire d'origine haïtienne* (Thèse de doctorat nonpublié). Université du Québec à Montréal, Montréal, PQ.

292

ADDITIONAL WHITENESS RESOURCES (2014)

ARTICLES

Adair, J. (2008). White pre-service teachers and 'de-privileged spaces.' *Teacher Education Quarterly, 35*(4), 189–206.

Aveling, N. (2006). Hacking at our very roots: Rearticulating white racial identity within the context of teacher education. *Race, Ethnicity and Education, 9*(3), 261–274.

Crozier, G., Reay, D., & James, D. (2011). Making it work for their children: White middle-class parents and working-class schools. *International Studies in Sociology of Education, 21*(3), 199–216.

DiAngelo, R. (2012). Nothing to add: A challenge to white silence in racial discussions. *Journal of Understanding and Dismantling Privilege, 2*(1), 1–17.

Goyette, K. A. (2008). Race, social background, and school choice options. *Equity and Excellence in Education, 41*(1), 114–129.

Lawrence, B., & Dua, E. (2005). Decolonizing antiracism. *Social Justice, 32*(4), 120–143.

McCarthy, C. (2005). Contradictions of power and identity: Whiteness studies and the call of teacher education. *International Journal of Qualitative studies in Education, 16*(1), 127–133.

McIntyre, A. (2002). Exploring whiteness and multicultural education with potential teachers. *Curriculum Inquiry, 31*(1), 31–49.

Picower, B. (2009). The unexamined whiteness of teaching: How white teachers maintain and enact dominant racial ideologies. *Race, Ethnicity and Education, 12*(2), 197–215.

Schoenfeld, S. (1983). The transmission of Jewish identity among families in a non-Jewish neighborhood. *Contemporary Jewry, 6*(2), 34–42.

Terwilliger, C. (2010). Mapping stories: Taking detours to challenge whiteness. *Making Connections, 11*(2), 14–25.

Yoon, E.-S., & Gulson, K. N. (2010). School choice in the 'stratilingual' city of Vancouver. *British Journal of Sociology of Education, 31*(6), 703–718.

BOOK CHAPTERS

Lund, D. E., & Carr, P. R. (2012). Disrupting denial and white privilege in teacher education. In P. C. Gorski, K. Zenkov, N. Osei-Kofi, & J. Sapp (Eds.), *Cultivating social justice teachers: How teacher educators have helped students overcome cognitive bottlenecks and learn critical social justice concepts* (pp. 108–125). Sterling, VA: Stylus.

Smith, A. (2006). Heteropatriarchy and the three pillars of white supremacy. In Women of Color Against Violence (Eds.), *Color of violence: The incite! anthology* (pp. 66–73). Cambridge, MA: South End Press.

BOOKS

Biale, D., Galchinsky, M., & Heschel, S. (Eds.). (1998). *Insider/outsider: American Jews and multiculturalism.* Berkeley, CA: University of California Press.

DiAngelo, R. (2012). *What does it mean to be white? Developing white racial literacy.* New York, NY: Peter Lang.

Hughey, M. W. (2012). *White bound: Nationalists, antiracists, and the shared meanings of race.* Stanford, CA: Stanford University Press.

Kendall, F. E. (2013). *Understanding white privilege: Creating pathways to authentic relationships across race*. New York, NY: Routledge.

Kenny, L. D. (2000). Daughters of suburbia: Growing up white, middle class, and female. New Brunswick, NJ: Rutgers University Press.

Lee, S. J. (2005). *Up against whiteness: Race, school, and immigrant youth*. New York, NY: Teachers College Press.

Leonardo, Z. (2009). *Race, whiteness, and education*. New York, NY: Routledge.

Levine-Rasky, C. (2013). *Whiteness fractured*. Farnham, UK: Ashgate.

Orelus, P. W. (2013). *Whitecentrism and linguoracism exposed: Towards the de-centering of whiteness and decolonization of schools*. New York, NY: Peter Lang.

Painter, N. I. (2011). *The history of white people*. New York, NY: W. W. Norton.

Reay, D., Crozier, G., & James, D. (2011). *White middle-class identities and urban schooling*. New York, NY: Palgrave Macmillan.

Stanley, T. (2011). *Contesting white supremacy: School segregation, anti-racism, and the making of Chinese Canadians*. Vancouver, BC: UBC Press.

Thobani, S. (2007). *Exalted subjects: Studies in the making of race and nation*. Toronto, ON: University of Toronto Press.

Weis, L., & Dolby, N. (2012). *Social class and education: Global perspectives*. New York, NY: Routledge.

White, E. (2012). *Whiteness and teacher education*. New York, NY: Routledge.

ONLINE AND MEDIA RESOURCES

Australian Critical Race and Whiteness Studies Association. (2014). *ACRWSA* [website]. Retreived from http://www.acrawsa.org.au/

Butler, S., & Butler, R., Directors. (2006). *Mirrors of privilege: Making whiteness visible* [video recording]. Oakland, CA: World Trust Educational Services.

White Privilege Conference. (2014). *White privilege conference* [website]. Retrieved from http://www.whiteprivilegeconference.com/

Wise, T. (2008). *Tim Wise: On white privilege* [video]. YouTube. Retrieved from http://www.youtube.com/watch?v=J3Xe1kX7Wsc

BIOGRAPHIES (2014)

Kathleen S. Berry is a retired professor of education in critical studies, literacies, and drama, formerly at the University of New Brunswick, Canada. She has published chapters on critical media studies, critical pedagogy, and counter-memory, and co-authored a book, with Joe Kincheloe, on bricolage as a post-empiricist rethinking of doing educational research. She has written a book on literacy studies and critical pedagogy, hoping that someday the discourses of critical studies will enter the multiple locations of education, including schooling, and contribute to social justice policies and practices.

Julie Caouette is an adjunct research professor at Carleton University, and an instructor at John Abbott College. Her research focuses on the social psychology of intergroup relations, especially the attitudes of mainstream society towards minority groups, such as Aboriginal peoples. Beyond the general role of prejudice, her research delves into the specific role of social emotions, such as collective guilt, in understanding the nature of conflict between such groups. In parallel, she has also been involved in fieldwork exploring bilingualism and its role in the maintenance of Aboriginal heritage languages and cultures.

Paul R. Carr is professor in the Department of Education at the Université du Québec en Outaouais, a French-language university in Gatineau, Québec, which is part of the national capital region with Ottawa. His research interests include political sociology, interculturalism, democracy, transformative education, media literacy, and peace studies. He is the Principal Investigator of a Social Sciences and Humanities Research Council of Canada (SSHRC) research project entitled *Democracy, Political Literacy and Transformative Education* (www.education4democracy.net). He has 10 edited books and one sole-author book, *Does Your Vote Count? Critical Pedagogy and Democracy*, in addition to about 100 articles and book chapters. He collaborates with a range of colleagues internationally through the *Global Doing Democracy Research Project* (GDDRP), for which he is a co-founder and co-director. His website is www.paulrcarr.net

Matt Champion began his career in education with the York Region Board of Education in 1983. He has taught all regular grades from three to eight and self-contained special education classes at both primary and junior levels. He has served as vice-principal and principal in York Region since 1999, where he has worked to develop further critical and reflective practices among staff working towards community engagement to increase student achievement and success. He is now retired and teaching ESL in a private high school in China.

Gulzar R. Charania is a doctoral candidate at the Ontario Institute for Studies in Education of the University of Toronto. Her research interests include critical race and queer theories, transnational and anti-colonial feminisms, processes of political formation, the affective legacies of oppression, and the politics of activism and educational practices. She has taught high school and university students and was a former employee of the Toronto District School Board, where she worked in the Equity Department. Some of her published work can be found in *ACME: An International E-Journal for Critical Geographies,* and *Canadian Woman Studies.*

Lisa Comeau completed her PhD at the Faculty of Education, University of Regina in 2005. While there, she worked at the Centre for Social Justice and Anti-Oppressive Education, and taught undergraduate and graduate courses in anti-racism education for the University of Regina and the Saskatchewan Urban Native Teacher Education Program (SUNTEP). Since 2008, Lisa has been working as a research analyst with the Canadian federal government in Ottawa.

Beverly-Jean M. Daniel is professor at Humber College in Toronto in the School of Social and Community Services where she also coordinates a Community Justice Program that focuses on constructs and practices of anti-oppression and social justice in a Canadian context. Her graduate and undergraduate teaching interests include preparing teachers for working within urban school settings, structuring anti-racist pedagogy within teacher education curriculum, and a focus on women and gender studies in education. Her research interests include an analysis of constructs of leadership within ethno-racial communities; highlighting the impact of cohort and community on learning to teach; the identification of effective strategies for learning and teaching about race; and constructs of whiteness in teacher education. She is involved in a number of research projects that examine the experiences of students of colour in the college system; the relationship between experiences of schooling and the incarceration of black males and females; and the educational experiences of children of incarcerated parents.

Debbie Donsky completed her doctoral studies at the Ontario Institute for Studies in Education at the University of Toronto, focused on critical literacy in knowledge building classrooms as it relates to power in pedagogy. Currently, Dr. Donsky is a principal in the York Region District School Board and has been an elementary educator for eighteen years. She is a member of system equity teams in the York Region District School Board focused on religious accommodations, staff and leadership training, and the system equity symposiums working towards equity goals in school improvement planning, as well as supporting LGBTQ Positive Spaces. She was a member of a provincial team through the *Ontario Principals' Council*, creating support documents for district school boards throughout Ontario in writing policies aligning to the Ontario Ministry of Education's *Equity and Inclusive Education Strategy* (2009). In the schools, Debbie works towards sharing knowledge and power to create inclusive and critical learning communities that value and support student voice, social justice, and the gift of diversity working with, for, and on behalf of students, staff, and the communities she serves.

James Frideres is professor of sociology and director of the *International Indigenous Studies Program* at the University of Calgary. He has worked in the area of ethnic relations, immigration, and integration for nearly thirty years. He also has been an active member in the community, supporting the efforts of local community organizations and non-government agencies. Dr. Frideres migrated to Canada from the United States in 1971 and has shared his knowledge and expertise with scholars and students around the world. He has worked on major educational projects in India, Australia, Malaysia, Philippines, and Viet Nam. He currently holds the *Chair of Ethnic Studies* in addition to his other duties. He has published extensively in his field of study and is the author or co-author of 12 books. His book on *Aboriginal People in Canada* is in the seventh edition and is considered a standard text for classes in the area. He is currently the editor of *Canadian Ethnic Studies/etudes ethniques au Canada,* and has been a guest editor for many journals in his discipline. Dr. Frideres also has supported the publication of Canadian materials as the chair of the *Aid to Scholarly Publication Program.*

Carl E. James is the Director of the York Centre for Education and Community (YCEC) in the Faculty of Education, York University. He teaches in Faculty of Education and in the Graduate Program in Sociology. A Fellow of the Royal Society of Canada, his research interests include examination of issues of equity, particularly in relation to access and inclusivity in the educational and occupational experiences of racialized people, particularly youth, and of the limitation of multiculturalism as a state policy to address racism and discrimination. His most recent publication is the book, *Life at the Intersection: Community, Class and Schooling* (2012).

Cynthia Levine-Rasky is associate professor in the Department of Sociology at Queen's University. She teaches courses on racialization and on research methodology. Her book entitled *Whiteness Fractured* (2013, Ashgate Publishing) explores the intersections between Whiteness, class, and ethnicity, and Whiteness as a psychosocial phenomenon. Cynthia has published her work in journals such as *Race Ethnicity and Education, Journal of Modern Jewish Studies, Canadian Ethnic Studies,* and *Social Identities*. Recently, her research interests have turned to the Roma people. An ethnographic study of the Roma's integration experiences and settlement needs is underway, and a SSHRC-funded project initiated in 2011 culminated with the website, *AmaroGlaso.com* ("Our Voice" in Romanes). In her field research on the Roma community, Cynthia has had the privilege of working closely with key individuals associated with the Roma Community Centre including its Executive Director, Gina Csanyi, and international authority on the Roma, Ronald Lee, as well as numerous activists, volunteers, legal professionals, and refugee claimants.

Tracey Lindberg is one of the As'in'i'wa'chi Ni'yaw Nation Rocky Mountain Cree and citizen of the Kelly Lake Cree Nation. She holds a Canada Research Chair in Indigenous Traditional Knowledge, Legal Orders and Laws, and is associate professor in the Centre for World Indigenous Knowledge and Research at Athabasca University. She writes fiction, academic work on Indigenous laws and legal orders, sings in a band, and spends a great deal of time thinking.

Laura Mae Lindo is assistant professor at the University of Prince Edward Island. Her unique approach to anti-racism education in pre-service classrooms as well her use of traditional curriculum to challenge structural oppression in varied educational settings has resulted in her continued work to re-envision teacher education classrooms. Her research interests also include co-creating methods for supporting marginalized youth by providing alternative experiences to pre-service teachers in university, public, and private school settings, integrating technology and technology-based curriculum in schools, and re-envisioning teacher education as a site for social activism and change.

Darren E. Lund is professor in the Werklund School of Education at the University of Calgary, where his research examines social justice activism in schools, communities, and professional education programs. Darren was a high school teacher for 16 years, and formed the award-winning *Students and Teachers Opposing Prejudice* (STOP) program. Darren has published over 300 articles, books, and book chapters, and is creator of the popular on-line *Diversity Toolkit* project. Darren has been recognized with a number of awards and honours, including the inaugural *2013 Alberta Hate Crimes Awareness Award*, the *2012 Scholar-Activist Award* from the American Educational Research Association (*Critical Educators for Social Justice*), being named a *Reader's Digest National Leader in Education*, and one of Red Deer's *Top Educators of the Century*.

Tim McCaskell is a long-time activist and educator in Toronto. After working in immigrant services and community organizing, he joined the Toronto Board of Education to do anti-racist work with students in 1983. That work soon expanded to include anti-homophobia initiatives, support for students facing sexual harassment, and projects on disability rights, and social class and poverty issues. He is author of *Race to equity: Disrupting educational inequality* (2005).

Herbert C. Northcott was born White in 1947 in Brandon, Manitoba, Canada, and grew up in the then very white Winnipeg suburb of St. James. In the 1950s, WASPs (White Anglo-Saxon Protestants) dominated St. James such that even the Ukrainian neighbours across the street were thought to be "different." Aboriginal, Black, Latino/a, and Asian people were virtually unknown in St. James in the 1950s, and were perceived at that time as exotic, distant "others." Herb completed his undergraduate university education in 1970 at United College (now the University of Winnipeg) and the University of Manitoba, majoring in sociology. He did his Master's in sociology at Brigham Young University in Utah in 1971, and completed his doctorate in sociology at the University of Minnesota in Minneapolis-St. Paul in 1976. He has taught sociology at the University of Alberta since 1976 where he has specialized in the sociology of health and illness, aging, and dying, death, and bereavement. Herb has taught sociology courses to Aboriginal students for the University of Alberta's extension program, traveling to Slave Lake, Alberta, in 1987 and 1988, Maskwachees Cultural College in Hobbema, Alberta, from 1994 to 2004, and Blue Quills First Nations College in St. Paul, Alberta, in 2003.

Brad J. Porfilio is the Director of Doctorate in Educational Leadership for Social Justice at California State University, East Bay. His research interests and expertise include urban education, gender and technology, cultural studies, neoliberalism and schooling, and transformative education.

Kelly D. Powick has completed her Master's degree in education. In her graduate work she explored White racial identity, Whiteness, and the influence of teachers' identities on their pedagogical practices. Her research drew on her experiences living and working internationally. She is currently teaching at Niagara College.

George J. Sefa Dei is professor and chair, Department of Sociology and Equity Studies, Ontario Institute for Studies in Education at the University of Toronto. He has published numerous books and journal articles in the areas of anti-racism, minority schooling, international development and anti-colonial thought. He has won many prestigious awards for his research and for his community work in Toronto, including the *2002 Race, Gender, and Class Project Academic Award, 2003 Community Builder Award* from the Continuing Education Department of the Toronto Catholic District School Board, and the *2003 African-Canadian Outstanding Achievement in Education* from the *Pride Magazine* in Toronto. He has two co-authored books set for upcoming release: *Schooling and difference in Africa: Democratic challenges in contemporary context* and *Anti-colonialism and education: The politics of resistance*.

R. Patrick Solomon taught in the Faculty of Education, York University. His professional career as an educator included teaching in elementary and secondary schools, being a school administrator in special education settings, and teaching at the university level in the pre-service, field development, and graduate education programs. In 2003, he was presented the first annual *Exemplary Multicultural Educator's Award* by the Canadian Council of Multicultural and Intercultural Education (CCMIE) for his multicultural and antiracist research and practice. His research projects have included the impact of educational reform on teacher preparation for equity and diversity work in schools and communities, and community involvement with a service learning approach to teacher education in Jamaica.

His book publications include *Urban teacher education and teaching: Innovative practices for diversity and social justice* (2007) (with D. Sekayi); *Teaching for equity and diversity: Research to practice* (2003) (with C. Levine-Rasky); *The erosion of democracy in education: Critique to possibilities* (2001) (with J. Portelli); and *Black resistance in high school: Forging a separatist culture* (1992).

Donald M. Taylor is professor of Psychology at McGill University. His field is intergroup conflict, and he has authored over 100 scientific articles as well as several books on issues related to the experience of disadvantaged group members in society. He has worked extensively with minority groups around the world including in the US, Indonesia, South Africa, and the Philippines, and particularly with disadvantaged groups in Canada. His most recent book, published by Praeger, is entitled *The Quest for Identity* and focuses on his experience with First Nations and Inuit groups in Canada.

Gina Thésée is associate professor in the Department of Education and Pedagogy at University of Quebec à Montreal (UQAM) in Montreal, Canada. She is the past Director of the Bachelor in Secondary Education program at UQAM, and is currently a member of the Teacher-Education Committee (CAPFE), an advisory committee to the Quebec Ministry of Education in Quebec, which reviews all teacher-education programs in the province. In 2006, she was a laureate for the Montreal Black History Month, which honoured her for her work in the Black community in general, and the Haitian community in particular. Her research focuses on interculturalism, epistemology, social justice, and science education.

Susan A. Tilley is professor in the Faculty of Education at Brock University and currently Director of the interdisciplinary MA in Social Justice and Equity Studies Program. Her research areas include critical pedagogy and anti-racist practices, critical white studies, teacher identity, curriculum theory, qualitative methodology, research ethics, and international research collaborations. She teaches courses related to social, cultural, and political contexts of education, curriculum theory, teaching pedagogies, and qualitative methodologies.

Christine Wihak is the Director, Prior Learning Assessment & Recognition (PLAR), at Thompson Rivers University – Open Learning, and Director of the Prior Learning International Research Centre (PLIRC). Before this she was an Assistant Professor in Workplace and Adult Learning at the University of Calgary, where she taught in the on-line graduate programs in the Faculty of Education. She carried out research in the area of White racial identity development, work-related informal learning, and PLAR. Previously, she lived in Nunavut for over a decade, as an administrator and instructor with Nunavut Arctic College, where her Inuit students and colleagues began to teach her what it means to be White in Canada. Dr. Wihak holds a PhD in Educational Psychology from the University of Alberta, a Master's of Psychology and a Graduate Diploma in Public Administration from Carleton University, and an Honours BA in Psychology from Queen's University. She was also a registered psychologist (Alberta), specializing in Occupational and Organizational Psychology. She has conducted social policy research projects for Cabinet Commissions in British Columbia and Ontario, as well as for departments in the Alberta, Ontario and Federal governments, and non-profit organizations such as the Canadian Mental Health Association.

INDEX

A

Aboriginal, xxvi, xxx, 3, 25, 28, 29, 35, 39n1, 45–47, 52n3, 55, 59–68, 69, 89, 90, 92, 94, 95, 98, 99, 105–107, 112, 117, 118, 148, 151n2, 152n2, 152n6, 181, 184, 185, 187n1, 189, 223, 254, 273, 282,

African–American, 21, 89, 92, 112, 231, 234, 239, 267, 283, 290

Alberta, 42, 59, 70, 84

anti-homophobia, 265n11

anti-Semitism, 162, 171n2

auto-ethnography, 13–25, 27

B

barriers, 4, 7, 46–47, 50, 89, 97, 99, 100, 135, 164, 209, 213–216, 231, 244, 251, 272, 289

Black, xxvi, xxix, xxx, 2, 4, 16, 17, 32–36, 41, 42, 47, 48, 59, 72, 114, 115, 119, 123, 128, 131, 135n1, 142, 144, 149, 152n4, 155, 161, 166, 167, 198, 207, 230, 231, 233, 239, 240, 253–260, 262, 263, 264n3, 265n10, 275, 278n2, 281, 283–290, 291n1–4bodies, xix, xx, xxi, xxii, xxvi, xxvii, xxviii, xxix, xxx, 16, 21, 23, 72, 75, 77, 126, 131, 134, 142, 144, 196, 230, 231, 236, 240, 255–257, 259, 260, 262, 263, 283, 286, 287, 290

British, 19, 20, 44, 167, 239

British Columbia, 123, 264n8, 301

C

Canada, xxv, 2–8, 13, 15, 17, 19, 20, 24, 25, 27, 31, 33–35, 37, 38, 39n2, 41, 44, 45, 47, 52, 52n3, 55, 59, 69, 70, 84, 90–95, 97, 105–107, 111, 115, 117–119, 123–125, 135n1, 138, 143, 146, 155, 156, 163, 167, 175, 179, 181, 186, 190, 195, 197–200, 202, 203, 205, 213, 218, 223, 230, 239, 242, 243, 252, 268, 282, 290

Canadian

government, 69, 94, 105, 106, 115, 117, 190, 223

schools, xxv, 111, 218, 244

society, 5, 13, 14, 16, 24, 25, 45, 94, 98–100, 111, 193, 198, 199, 201–203

Catholic, 4, 17–19, 23, 31, 36

church, 16–19, 28, 31, 32, 64

civil rights, 3, 5, 37, 197, 208

classroom, 20, 43, 46–50, 55, 56, 60, 61, 63–68, 79, 81, 87, 125–128, 131, 132, 134, 137, 138, 141, 147, 165, 181, 196, 200, 202, 205, 206, 209, 215, 217, 218, 224, 230, 231, 234–237, 239, 240, 243, 244–247, 252, 273, 288

conservative, xxix, 28, 36, 39n3, 270–273, 275

critical theory, 28, 111, 163

D

denial, xxii, xxv, xxvii, 3, 5, 17, 18, 27, 62, 91, 114, 146, 151, 183, 189, 195, 201, 202, 230, 241, 247, 254, 257, 263, 264n5

discourse, xxvi, xxvii, xxviii, xxx, 13–18, 22–25, 28, 29, 45, 69, 96, 132, 133, 138, 141, 142, 144, 145, 155, 163, 179, 181–183, 186, 187,

193–203, 205, 208, 218, 230–232,
234, 235, 237, 241, 243, 248n6, 251,
252, 267, 268, 270, 276, 286

E
education
schools, 159, 170, 210, 230, 241, 243
 elementary, 24, 127, 131, 137, 159,
  163, 170, 210, 212, 230, 241, 243
 secondary, 35, 47, 55, 230, 231,
  234–237, 287
equality, 61–63, 65, 71, 90, 96–98, 100,
 101, 125, 161, 170, 180, 205, 216,
 257, 263
equity, xx, xxvi, 5, 7, 8, 24, 35–36, 56,
 78, 84, 125, 141, 145, 146, 150, 151,
 151n1, 156, 161, 189, 195, 196, 217,
 245, 248, 251, 252, 264n4, 269–273,
 275–277, 277n1

F
female, 35, 43, 48, 126, 135n2, 144,
 193, 197–201, 207–218, 223, 230,
 233, 239, 256–258, 260, 265n10,
 284, 286, 287, 289, 290
francophone, 4, 7, 271, 273–275,
 278n3, 283–291
French, 19, 20, 31, 33, 36, 47, 180, 243,
 273, 274, 278n4, 284, 285, 287, 288,
 290

G
gay, 18, 31, 34, 37, 42, 152n4, 155
gender, xxv, xxvii, xxviii, 5, 6, 16, 18,
 19, 23, 27, 38, 62, 72, 101, 125, 143,
 152n4, 156, 161, 162, 170, 175, 176,
 179, 197–201, 213–216, 218n3, 223,
 232, 234, 237n1, 248n6, 254, 256,
 257, 260, 278n1, 285, 286, 289, 290
government, 5, 15, 21, 36, 55, 69, 79, 84,
 94, 98, 105, 106, 115, 117, 185, 189,
 190, 190n3, 207, 214, 223, 269–276

guilt, 7, 17, 24, 35, 37, 38, 67, 89–101,
 105-107, 114, 116, 117, 120, 129,
 130, 147, 150, 151, 167, 199, 200,
 205, 251, 261, 262, 264n5, 277, 284

H
hegemony, 2, 13, 17, 150, 202, 212,
 273, 281, 289
homophobia, 34, 35, 37, 42, 208, 217

I
inequality, 60-65, 89-101, 159, 175,
 179–182, 185–187, 194, 288

L
language, xxviii, 20, 28, 41, 43, 64,
 65, 79, 91, 116, 117, 125, 128, 129,
 152n3, 160, 161, 163, 164, 167–169,
 181, 183, 185, 186, 194, 199, 230,
 241, 243, 244, 264n3, 5, 267, 268,
 273, 274, 276, 278n4, 284, 285, 287,
 288, 290
lesbian, 18, 34, 152n4
liberalism, 170, 194, 258, 263
linguistic, xxii, 3, 7, 22, 47, 62, 135n1,
 170, 273, 278n3, 285
love, xxxi, xxxiii, 28, 65, 74, 84–86,
 144, 166, 208, 216, 230, 282, 286,
 291

M
Manitoba, 59
Mexico, 69, 115

N
Native, 59–68, 77, 117, 144, 147, 182
neo-liberalism, xx, 2, 163
North America, 2, 4, 29, 44, 96, 112,
 129, 130, 171, 180, 183, 207,
 209–211, 213, 214, 217, 223,
 287
Nunavut, 111, 115–119

O

Ontario, xix, xxxiii, 20, 31, 39n1, 3, 135n4, 200, 214, 230, 234, 235, 242, 246, 251, 269–271, 273–276

P

post-colonial, 84, 147, 203
post-secondary, 47, 48, 50, 55, 56, 76, 83, 134, 230
poverty, 41, 65, 132, 166, 170, 181–185, 207, 211, 219n6, 256, 257, 282, 283, 286, 298
power, xx, xxi, xxii, xxv, xxvi, xxviii, xxix, xxx, 2–8, 13–17, 20–22, 25, 29, 34, 39, 41, 42, 44, 45, 47, 55, 65, 78, 91, 94, 97, 117, 131, 141, 147, 149, 150, 159, 161–163, 170, 175, 176, 184, 186, 189, 195, 197, 199–202, 205–208, 211–213, 215, 217, 223, 224, 232, 233, 241–244, 246–248, 251–254, 258, 259, 261–263, 269, 270, 272, 274–278, 281, 282, 285–287, 289
protest, 73, 224
Protestant, 4, 17–19, 31, 59, 73, 224

Q

Quebec, 6, 20, 31, 190, 284, 288

R

racial identity, xxvii, 3, 5–8, 17, 35, 36, 47, 50, 55, 111, 113–120, 123–135, 137, 138, 196, 287
refugee, 41, 196

S

Saskatchewan, 84, 179, 181, 186, 187n1, 189
social justice, xxv, xxvi, xxx, xxxi, xxxiii, 1, 3, 7, 8, 24, 75, 91, 98, 100, 116, 119, 120, 125, 131, 132, 150, 165, 195, 201, 209, 217, 269–273, 276, 277, 278n1

strangers, 149, 152n6, 167
students, xxi, xxii, xxv, xxvi, xxix, xxxi, xxxiii, 2, 6, 7, 17, 20, 21, 24, 25, 28, 33–35, 37, 43–52, 55, 56, 59–68, 70, 71, 78, 81, 82, 87, 93–95, 98, 105, 111–113, 115, 119, 120, 123–135, 137–139, 142–152, 159, 162, 171, 181–185, 187, 194, 202, 205, 207, 208, 212, 217, 223, 224, 229, 230, 235–237, 241–248, 251–265, 267, 270, 272, 275–277, 287–289
superiority, xxviii, 2, 15, 20, 22, 49, 51, 61, 143, 164, 180, 182, 190, 197, 203, 288
systemic barriers, 93, 94, 97, 100, 214–216, 251, 272

T

teacher education, 19, 20, 47, 126, 181, 193–196, 198, 201–203, 205, 208, 209, 217, 218n3, 223
textbooks, 19, 20, 28, 59, 60, 63–66, 69, 85, 89, 202, 252
tolerance, 133, 179, 186, 190, 230, 259, 261
Toronto, xix, 3, 5, 31, 34, 36–38, 39n1–3, 120, 143, 151n1, 241, 242, 246, 264n4, 269, 272

U

United States, 3, 41, 48, 111, 113, 155, 197, 198, 207, 208, 213, 267, 281, 288, 290
universities, xix, xxxiii, 4, 6, 7, 19, 20, 23, 33, 46, 47, 59, 67, 69–71, 77, 80, 82, 84, 93, 95, 123, 126, 133, 135n2, 137, 138, 143, 145, 146, 148, 151, 152n1, 159, 165, 166, 195, 196, 215, 216, 223, 229, 230, 235, 239, 242, 289

W

White
    identity, xxvi, xxvii, xxviii, xxix, 6, 7, 36, 38, 46, 93, 111–120, 123, 129, 248n4

privilege, xxi, xxii, xxvii, xxviii, 1, 7,
17, 22, 25, 35, 36, 38, 43–47, 50,
52n4, 69, 90–93, 114, 125–135,
137, 138, 145–148, 151, 152n3,
4, 165, 189, 193–203, 208, 217,
218, 242, 243, 247, 252, 271,
272, 275

Whiteness
women, xxviii, 4, 16, 18, 32, 35, 62, 71,
72, 74, 75, 77, 79, 82, 118, 125, 126,
138, 145, 152n4, 5, 155, 181, 189,
199–201, 209, 211, 213–216, 231,
239, 253–255, 257, 258, 260, 264,
264n5, 8, 271, 283, 286–291

CPSIA information can be obtained
at www.ICGtesting.com
Printed in the USA
LVOW04s0200021216
515427LV00001B/1/P

9 789462 098671